"Absolute poverty," says Robert S. McNamara, President of the World Bank, "is a condition of life so limited as to prevent realization of the potential of the genes . . . , a condition of life so degrading as to insult human dignity—and yet a condition of life so common as to be the lot of forty per cent, some 800 million, of the people of the developing countries."

The Assault on World Poverty, as he explains in his Preface, is a part of the Bank's effort to analyze the nature and causes of such poverty, to examine ways of alleviating the problem through action in five related fields, and to outline specific programs for bringing the benefits of development to the poorest of the poor by increasing their productivity.

The book's main focus is established in the first paper, on rural development, since by far the largest numbers of the very poor in developing countries live in rural areas. This and companion papers, on agricultural credit

(continued on back flap)

from front flap)

:form, offer proposals to im-
litions among smallholders,
ners and the landless.

papers, on education and
stion the direction in which
l systems and health policies
ed in the past and suggest
an be made more responsive
ds of developing countries.
rs examine the educational
problems of the urban as
well as the rural poor, since nearly a fifth of the developing world's poorest live in the squalor of city slums.

The Assault on World Poverty will be important to those involved in research into the causes of poverty in developing countries, to those who are working actively to overcome them, and to all concerned about the world's future.

Published for the World Bank by The Johns Hopkins University Press.

The
ASSAULT
on
WORLD
POVERTY

The ASSAULT on WORLD POVERTY

Problems of Rural Development, Education and Health

With a preface by Robert S. McNamara

Published for THE WORLD BANK
by THE JOHNS HOPKINS UNIVERSITY PRESS
Baltimore and London

Library of Congress Catalog Card Number 75-7912
ISBN 0-8018-1745-5 (clothbound edition)
ISBN 0-8018-1746-3 (paperbound edition)

PREFACE

Among our century's most urgent problems is the wholly unacceptable poverty that blights the lives of some 2,000 million people in the more than 100 countries of the developing world. Of these 2,000 million, nearly 800 million are caught up in what can only be termed absolute poverty—a condition of life so limited as to prevent realization of the potential of the genes with which they were born; a condition of life so degrading as to be an insult to human dignity.

The collection of papers in this volume, while dealing with five related subjects, share a common theme. They seek to analyze the causes of that poverty, to examine ways in which it can be alleviated, and to outline programs in which the World Bank plans to help.

These sector policy papers reflect a sobering fact: that although there has been encouraging economic growth in most of the developing countries over the past three decades, a very large proportion of their people have not shared in its benefits. On average, the poorest 40% of their societies is not much better off than it was.

As I pointed out in my address at the Bank's Annual Meeting in Nairobi, the basic problem of poverty and growth in the developing world can be stated very simply. The growth is not equitably reaching the poor. And the poor are not significantly contributing to growth. Development strategies, therefore, need to be reshaped in order to help the poor to become more productive.

By far the largest number of the poor live in the rural areas of the developing world. The centerpiece of this volume is, therefore, the paper on *Rural Development*. As it points out, the objectives of rural development extend beyond any one particular sector. Rural poverty is reflected in poor nutrition, inadequate shelter and low health standards. These, in turn, affect the productivity of the rural poor and their quality of life. What are required are production improvements, and mutually reinforcing programs of better nutrition, preventive health, improved water supply, basic sanitation and practical education.

The papers on *Agricultural Credit* and *Land Reform* examine certain aspects of the productivity problem in greater detail. Agricultural credit is a key element in helping the poor become more productive. But traditionally the flow of credit to small farmers has been inadequate, both because they lack sufficient collateral and because of the high administrative costs of small loans. The World Bank is experimenting with new methods to help governments overcome these obstacles.

Similarly, realistic land reform is consistent with the development objectives of increased agricultural production, more equitable distri-

v

403014

bution of income and expanded employment. Such programs are, however, difficult to carry out, for they affect the power base of the traditional elite groups in the developing society. The Bank will support such programs when they are designed to increase agricultural output and to improve the lives of the rural poor.

The final papers on *Education* and *Health* are also concerned with rural poverty, though not exclusively so. They provide insights, as well, into the problems of poverty in the urban areas whose slums entrap nearly 150 million of the developing world's people. Educational systems in developing countries are all too often inequitable, favoring city dwellers and the relatively rich, and in many countries, they have served educational objectives that were irrelevant to economic and social development. What is required is that the systems should be reshaped to ensure that all members of society get at least a minimum basic education. More equal educational opportunities would enable the poor to become more productive, and to participate more fully in the development process. The same can be said of most health programs in developing countries. They too need to be redesigned so that they can reach the poor more effectively.

In the long run, virtually nothing going on in our time is likely to affect the future of mankind more than the drive towards development. These papers are offered as a modest contribution to the understanding of that task. While they do not pretend to provide final answers for the questions they raise, they will, I hope, encourage a more intensive search among governments for feasible solutions to the massive problem of absolute poverty. If, in the end, governments fail in that effort, then I fear it will matter a great deal less what their other successes may be.

President, World Bank Group

CONTENTS

Page

Preface   v
The World Bank Group.   xi

Rural Development   1
   Summary and Recommendations.   3
   Chapter 1: The Nature and Extent of the Problem   16
      Toward an Operational Strategy   16
      The Measurement of Rural Poverty.   19
      The Dynamics of Rural Poverty   24
   Chapter 2: Policies and Programs for Rural Development   28
      The Policy Framework.   29
      Organization and Planning   33
      Implementing Rural Development   40
   Chapter 3: The World Bank's Program   58
      Past Trends.   58
      The Way Ahead.   62
      Deployment of Bank Resources   70
   Annexes   77

Agricultural Credit   99
   Introduction   103
   Summary and Guidelines   105
   Chapter 1: Agricultural Credit Practices and Problems   121
      Evolution of Current Approach   121
      Problems of Agricultural Credit Markets.   126
      Constraints on the Role of Credit in Development   131
   Chapter 2: Agricultural Credit Programs and Policies   135
      Designing Credit Programs   136
      Financial Viability of Credit Institutions.   140
   Chapter 3: Systems for Delivering Agricultural Credit.   151
      Policy Making and Administrative Issues.   151
      Channels of Agricultural Finance   153
      Agricultural Credit Agencies.   154
      Guidelines on Delivery Systems.   161
      Principles.   162
   Annexes   165

	Page
Land Reform	187
Introduction	191
Summary	193
Chapter 1: Characteristics of Land Reform	203
Man and Land	203
Context of Land Reform	204
Dimensions of Land Reform	208
Chapter 2: Land Reform and Economic Development	213
Implications for Productivity	215
Land Reform and Employment	217
Land Reform and Equity	218
Effects on Marketed Surplus and Savings	219
Tenancy Reform	222
Implementation Issues	223
Chapter 3: The World Bank and Land Reform	226
Changing Concerns	226
Technical Assistance	226
Lending Operations	228
Major Policy Options	234
Annexes	235
Education	263
Foreword	265
Summary	269
Chapter 1: Trends in Education and Development to 1970	276
Chapter 2: Education Development Strategy for the 1970's and Beyond	280
Poverty-oriented Development Strategy	280
Major Issues Facing Education Systems	281
Formation of Skills Corresponding to the Needs of Developing Countries	286
Development of Skills for Rural Areas	289
Ensuring Mass Participation in Education and Development	293
Education and Equity	299
Increasing Efficiency in Education	302
Improving Management and Planning Capacity	308
Chapter 3: The World Bank's Education Lending Policy and Program	313
Bank Policy and Activities: 1963-74	315
Objectives of Bank Lending for Education	318
Bank Lending Programs and Possibilities	323
Conclusion	327
Annexes	329

	Page
Health	341
Introduction	345
Chapter 1: Health Conditions in Developing Countries	348
General Measures of Health	348
Differences between and within Countries	350
The Disease Pattern	351
Chapter 2: Causes of Poor Health	356
Demographic Factors	357
Malnutrition	359
Unsanitary Conditions and Housing	360
Causes of Improved Health	364
Chapter 3: Approaches to Health Policy	366
A Social Goal	366
A Productive Investment	367
Better Health for Socioeconomic Development	369
Role of Government	371
Chapter 4: Present Policies of Developing Countries	374
Expenditures on Health	374
Resources for Medical Care	375
Coverage of Official Health Services	377
Effectiveness of Official Health Services	380
Chapter 5: A Health Policy for the Future	382
Financing Extended Coverage	383
The Reformed Health Service	384
Increasing Effectiveness of Official Health Services	388
Chapter 6: World Bank Lending for Health-related Projects	389
Chapter 7: Policy Alternatives for the Bank	398
Conclusions	403
Annexes	407

THE WORLD BANK GROUP

The World Bank Group comprises the Bank itself, officially named the International Bank for Reconstruction and Development, and its two affiliates, the International Development Association and the International Finance Corporation. Each of the three institutions was established to fulfill a distinct function, but all are devoted to the same general objective — the provision of financial and other assistance for the economic development of member countries.

The World Bank was founded at the Bretton Woods Monetary and Financial Conference in 1944 and began operations in 1946. It is a Specialized Agency of the United Nations, as are its two affiliates. The Bank's principal role is the provision of loans to developing countries for a wide variety of productive projects. At present, the Bank is the largest multilateral source of development financing in the world. By the end of December 1974, the Bank Group had committed more than $33,000 million in over 110 countries.

The International Development Association (IDA) was established in September 1960. IDA performs the same function as the Bank and has the same staff, but its loans (known as credits) are on much easier terms and are made to the poorest member nations.

The International Finance Corporation (IFC), established in 1956, is the member of the World Bank Group that encourages the growth of productive private enterprise in developing countries. In partnership with other investors, local and foreign, it finances most types of commercial enterprises through investments in equity, loans without governmental guarantees, and underwriting commitments.

THE METROPOLITAN FRONTIER

RURAL
DEVELOPMENT

RURAL DEVELOPMENT
CONTENTS

Page

Summary and Recommendations.   3
Chapter 1: The Nature and Extent of the Problem   16
    Toward an Operational Strategy   16
    The Measurement of Rural Poverty.   19
    The Dynamics of Rural Poverty   24
Chapter 2: Policies and Programs for Rural Development   28
    The Policy Framework.   29
    Organization and Planning   33
    Implementing Rural Development   40
Chapter 3: The World Bank's Program   58
    Past Trends.   58
    The Way Ahead.   62
    Deployment of Bank Resources   70

Annexes
   1. Estimates of Total Population and Rural Population in Poverty in
      Developing Countries, 1969.   79
   2. Estimates of Relative Poverty in Developing Countries, 1969   79
   3. Rural Population and Rural Poverty in Developing Countries.   80
   4. Landless Farm Workers in Selected Countries   81
   5. Nutrition Levels by Income Class.   82
   6. Population per Medical Doctor in Urban and Rural Areas   83
   7. Availability of Primary Schools in Urban and Rural Areas.   84
   8. World Bank/IDA Lending for Agriculture: Number of Projects and
      Amount Lent, FY1948-74   84
   9. World Bank/IDA Lending for Agriculture, by Subsector, FY1948-74   85
  10. World Bank/IDA Lending for Agriculture, by Per Capita GNP of
      Borrowing Countries   85
  11. World Bank/IDA Lending for Agriculture and Rural Development,
      FY1968-74   86
  12. Share of Agriculture and Rural Development in Total World Bank/
      IDA Lending, FY1968-74.   88
  13. Estimated Rural Population in Poverty, by Region and Income Level
      of Country, 1974.   89

14. Comparison of the Distribution, by Region, of the Rural Poor and of Prospective World Bank/IDA Lending for Agriculture and Rural Development 89

15. The Nairobi Speech 90

SUMMARY AND RECOMMENDATIONS

Rural development is a strategy designed to improve the economic and social life of a specific group of people—the rural poor. It involves extending the benefits of development to the poorest among those who seek a livelihood in the rural areas. The group includes small-scale farmers, tenants and the landless.[1]

A strategy for rural development must recognize three points. Firstly, the rate of transfer of people out of low productivity agriculture and related activities into more rewarding pursuits has been slow; and, given the relative size of the modern sector in most developing countries, it will remain slow. Secondly, the mass of the people in the rural areas of developing countries face varying degrees of poverty; their position is likely to get worse if population expands at unprecedented rates while limitations continue to be imposed by available resources, technology, and institutions and organizations. Thirdly, rural areas have labor, land and at least some capital which, if mobilized, could reduce poverty and improve the quality of life. This implies fuller development of existing resources, including the construction of infrastructure such as roads and irrigation works, the introduction of new production technology, and the creation of new types of institutions and organizations.

Since rural development is intended to reduce poverty, it must be clearly designed to increase production and raise productivity. Rural development recognizes, however, that improved food supplies and nutrition, together with basic services such as health and education, can not only directly improve the physical well-being and quality of life of the rural poor, but can also indirectly enhance their productivity and their ability to contribute to the national economy. It is concerned with the modernization and monetization of rural society, and with its transition from traditional isolation to integration with the national economy.

The objectives of rural development, therefore, extend beyond any particular sector. They encompass improved productivity, increased employment and thus higher incomes for target groups, as well as minimum acceptable levels of food, shelter, education and health. A national program of rural development should include a mix of activities, including projects to raise agricultural output, create new

---

[1] All references to the World Bank in this paper are to be deemed to refer also to the International Development Association (IDA), unless the context requires otherwise. The fiscal year (FY) of the two institutions runs from July 1 to June 30.

employment, improve health and education, expand communications and improve housing. Such a program might be made up of single-sector or multisectoral projects, with components implemented concurrently or in sequence. The components and phasing must be formulated both to remove constraints and to support those forces prevailing in the target area which are favorable to development.

The nature and content of any rural development program or project will reflect the political, social and economic circumstances of the particular country or region. Where the scope and need for rural development are not accepted by government leaders, or where the shortage of resources is acute (especially the supply of skilled manpower), initial projects may be experimental in nature or restricted in extent. Where particular needs are pressing, such as in cases of famine or disease, narrowly focused projects may be appropriate.

Target Population

Approximately 85% of the 750 million poor in the developing world[2] are considered to be in absolute poverty—based on the arbitrary criterion of an annual per capita income equivalent to $50 or less. The remaining 15% are judged to be in relative poverty—having incomes above the equivalent of $50, but below one-third of the national average per capita income.

Three-fourths of those in absolute poverty are in the developing countries of Asia, reflecting both the low levels of national per capita income and the large size of the rural sector there. As for those in relative poverty, most of them are found in developing countries that are less poor, a large fraction being in Latin America.

Of the population in developing countries considered to be in either absolute or relative poverty, more than 80% are estimated to live in rural areas. Agriculture is the principal occupation for four-fifths of the rural poor. These people are found in roughly equal proportions in densely populated zones (over 300 persons per square kilometer) and sparsely populated zones (less than 150 persons per square kilometer). Thus, poverty is found in the highly productive irrigated areas of Asia, as well as in the adverse conditions of the Sahel, northeast Brazil, the Andean Altiplano and the dry zones of India.

The rural poor include small-scale farmers, tenants, sharecroppers, landless workers and their families. There are over 80 million small-

---

[2] *The poor are defined as those with per capita incomes of $50 or less, plus others with per capita incomes that are less than one-third of the national average.*

4

holdings of less than two hectares, many of them comprising several small fragments of land, most of which generate incomes below the absolute poverty level. The tenants, sharecroppers and squatters, who represent another 30 million or more families, are often less well-off. While the largest proportion of workers in agriculture is self-employed, the number of landless or near-landless workers is growing—especially in Asian countries. They depend on seasonal work and are among the poorest of the rural community.

Despite high rates of migration from rural to urban areas, the rural population is growing by approximately 2% a year. The consequent worsening of the man-land ratio means that increases in output and income must come primarily from better yields per acre and cultivation of higher value crops. This will require both access to new technology and the capital to utilize it. That, in turn, implies the need for new or improved service systems to support a modern system of agriculture. The new seed-fertilizer-water technology for wheat, rice and maize provides the first major opportunity for extending science-based agriculture to low-income, small-scale producers of traditional crops. Further adaptive research and extension are required to ensure an adequate rate of technological change. Special programs are necessary to help the rural poor to contribute more fully to an increase in output. The programs must include the provision of infrastructure and on-farm improvements.

The need for special intervention to raise rural production and incomes applies also to the provision of social and other services, such as health and education. Poverty is reflected in poor nutrition, inadequate shelter and low health standards. These affect not only the quality of life but also the productivity of rural people. In particular, there is a need for nutrition and preventive health programs, including improved water supplies and sanitation. Better education is an important element, and may also provide an opportunity for the rural young to escape from poverty. In order to remedy both quantitative and qualitative educational deficiencies, increased use of "basic education" is considered imperative.

Compared with urban areas, rural areas have a smaller share of economic infrastructure services, such as domestic water, electricity and waste disposal. Even where the services exist, the poor often do not have access to them because organization is inadequate and the cost is high. A special effort is needed to provide appropriate social and economic infrastructure for the rural poor, and it is important to integrate these components into rural development projects. Without a concerted effort, rural poverty will remain pervasive.

Policy Framework

Experience indicates that a strong commitment to rural development at the national policy level is necessary if the impact is to be effective and broad-based. In many countries, the commitment is lacking. However, most governments are prepared to experiment at the project level and to examine the results. This should provide the basis for a dialogue between these countries and the Bank from which a broader approach may eventually develop.

Often, macroeconomic policies are inconsistent with agricultural and rural development. Price policies that favor manufacturing and processing industries, and those which aim to keep food prices low in urban areas, work against rural development. In such cases, subsidies on farm inputs may be justified. Fiscal policies also often militate against the rural poor, who are less well organized and less vociferous than other groups. Thus, public sector spending is heavily skewed in favor of urban dwellers, and in rural areas the rich get favored treatment. Yet the poor often pay considerably more taxes in proportion to income because indirect commodity taxes may be high, while direct taxes are low. In addition, there is often a reluctance to charge those benefiting from publicly financed investments, thus widening the gap between the few who have access to such investments and those who do not. Land policy has obvious implications for the rural poor, given that their incomes depend on the extent to which they control land and its output. In many instances, therefore, land reform is a necessary part of a rural development program.

Policies aimed at ensuring a flow of new, field-tested technical knowledge relevant to smallholder production are essential for the success of rural development. Often the poorest areas are overlooked by such policies, or the subsistence farm is not treated as a system. Where technology is available, it is frequently not applied because extension services, support services, finance and marketing facilities are lacking. Research and demonstration on a local basis to facilitate adoption is required in all these areas.

Organization and Planning

Ideally, the planning and implementation of rural development programs involve adequate regional planning, strong central coordination, effective local level organization and the participation of the rural people in the planning and implementation processes. Few countries have been able to come close to this ideal. Regional planning is desirable both because rural development cuts across all sectors and because rural programs need to be framed to meet regional conditions. Such planning necessitates the collection of statistics on a regional rather than a sectoral basis, and the use of regional surveys and resource inventories. Interregional allocations of technical and financial resources must be decided in relation to resource endowments, the domestic and foreign funds available, a balance of equity and growth considerations, and mutually acceptable arrangements for sharing responsibilities between the central and local authorities. All these elements should be brought together into an internally balanced rural development plan. However, the lack of a comprehensive rural development plan should not prevent the evolution of programs on a local level.

Strong coordination at the center is increasingly regarded as essential to the successful implementation of a rural development program. This is a reflection both of the political nature of many of the decisions that must be made and of the need to coordinate the activities of ministries or departments organized along sectoral lines. A special office or unit is favored, having responsibility for definition of target groups, coordination of national and regional efforts, and integration of the activities of national sector agencies. It has also to ensure that all sector policies are commensurate with rural development objectives.

Coordination at the local level is emphasized because of the growing evidence that multisectoral programs can be implemented most effectively through a substantial increase in decentralization. Local control provides the flexibility needed for the proper integration and timing of activities, and for modification of programs in response to changing conditions. Community involvement, which is essential to a sustained development process, is greatly facilitated by local rather than centralized control. One particular advantage is that the problems of the community, as perceived by its residents and those imputed by local officials, tend to be more easily reconciled.

Group arrangements such as cooperatives provide an organized basis for handling many of the problems of providing access to services for large numbers of rural people. They allow a measure of involvement through participation, but also provide a vehicle for collective negotiation of credit, input supplies and delivery of marketable surpluses. Even land management can be organized on a cooperative basis, as in Egypt. Group approaches enjoy widespread support among governments, even though the results have been mixed. They provide an impetus to rural development that is difficult to secure in any other way. In many cases, they build on an established base of mutual aid within the rural population. A major requirement for the successful operation of cooperative groups and for regional and local government is the provision of trained manpower. Thus, training facilities are needed to prepare full-time staff, and to improve the effectiveness of community leaders, school teachers, religious leaders and other agents of change.

Program Design and Implementation

Existing rural development projects can be classified for purposes of discussion into three approaches:

1. The minimum package approach, as exemplified by the Bank-supported projects in Ethiopia and the Republic of Korea (seeds).

2. The comprehensive approach, which can be either (a) nationally integrated programs or (b) area development and settlement schemes. Examples of nationally integrated programs are the Joint Commission for Rural Reconstruction in the Republic of China and PIDER in Mexico. Area-specific projects can be either single-product projects such as tea in Kenya, tobacco in Tanzania, cotton in Mali and oil palm in Malaysia; or comprehensive area projects which have more diversified crop and integrated farming systems, such as Comilla in Bangladesh, Lilongwe in Malawi and Caqueta in Colombia.

3. Sector and other special programs, including rural public works, education and training and credit schemes.

A review of these projects points to the many difficult issues in rural development planning, and in project formulation and implementation. Time and again, problems arise from lack of knowledge, incomplete understanding and limited institutional, technical and financial capabilities. It is possible, however, to make a few simple affirmative propositions:

1. Given sound preparatory planning, leadership and the involvement of local people, the small farmer can become an instrument of change to the advantage of the nation as well as of himself.

2. The material resources required for rural development need not be disproportionately large. In many successful schemes, the capital cost per beneficiary has been quite low. Although low capital cost per beneficiary is not by itself a criterion for a good project, it is an important element in designing projects to reach large numbers in the target groups.

3. Rural development schemes benefiting large numbers of people can be as productive and economically attractive as schemes of a conventional kind directly benefiting far fewer people.

4. With well-designed programs, offering proper incentives to small farmers, development can be much more rapid than is sometimes

believed, and the impact on levels of living following the expansion of cash incomes from a subsistence baseline can be dramatic.

5. Finally, while much remains to be done, conviction of the need for a change in strategy, and commitment to specific actions and programs for rural development, have probably never been greater in developing countries than at the present time. This is an important bridgehead on which new understanding can be built and from which new programs can be launched.

Country Guidelines

The following are desirable characteristics of a framework within which to design and implement rural development programs.

1. *Central leadership and coordination:* Effective rural development planning should be given high priority. Steps to improve planning capacity might include establishing a small but expert unit charged with the development of a national program of action. Such a body should provide leadership and should have a coordinating role in project identification and preparation and in monitoring ongoing programs. Where nationally integrated rural development programs are desired, the central unit should also be actively involved in project identification and preparation.

2. *Decentralization and participation at the local level:* Provision of an institutional framework at the regional or local level and of good center-local communications and coordination, with appropriate devolution of responsibility to local bodies, are critical. There is no single model for dealing with these problems, but the importance of evolving planning and programming units in both regional-local government institutions and sectoral departments cannot be stressed too strongly. Also important is the need to involve local people in planning, in making decisions and in implementation.

3. *Research:* Expanded technical and economic research into small farm systems, and into crops and techniques generally appropriate for use by the small farmer, should have high priority. A second type of research which is important but neglected relates to the dynamics of traditional rural societies as they begin to enter the modern sector.

4. *Training:* The shortage of trained manpower is perhaps the most serious obstacle to large-scale rural development efforts. An intensified training effort, particularly directed toward the needs of local level institutions, and calling for greater efforts focused on training in the local environments where people work, must also be pursued.

5. *Intermediaries:* The establishment of effective group organizations, such as farmers' associations and cooperatives, should have high

9

priority. They provide the best means of lowering the cost of delivering services and marketing output, so that larger numbers can be reached.

Activities related to rural development planning include the following:

1. *Identification of target groups:* Identification should be in terms of category, number, location and other attributes, with detailed specification of the relationships between these categories and the proposed project actions.

2. *Project design:* Several different kinds of projects may be appropriate:

(a) Some projects may emphasize specific functional services, such as minimum packages of inputs like fertilizers and seeds, and phasing, so that moderate benefits can be introduced progressively, at low cost per beneficiary, in order to cover a wide cross-section of the rural poor.

(b) Other more comprehensive projects may involve the integration of related economic and social services in order that full advantage is taken of opportunities to build better balanced and more focused efforts.

(c) In some cases, sectoral and other special programs may be needed to remove a binding constraint (such as an endemic disease problem) or to meet a special need (such as public works to employ the landless).

In any event, each project must contain the blend of inputs and services necessary to ensure a sustained increase in productivity for the beneficiaries. Particular attention should be given to the appropriate balance between the directly productive and indirectly productive elements in a project. The balance should reflect the levels of services proposed for the sector on a national basis, the most economical means of providing such services, and restrictions on resources that can be used for this purpose.

3. *Implementation:* Items requiring specific attention include:

(a) Local level training schemes and use of locally available human resources in order to minimize demands on the rest of the economy.

(b) Adherence to sectoral and regional planning considerations so as to ensure that proper attention is paid to linkages between sectors and regions.

(c) Establishment of user charges, graduated according to ability to pay, and provision for adequate savings to be drawn from local communities so that funds are available to extend programs on a broader scale.

(d) Local agricultural research to provide a basis for continuing productivity gains from small-scale agriculture.

(e) Full use of existing local governmental structures, and assistance in strengthening them for greater subsequent use.

(f) Promotion of institutional structures which enable the beneficiaries to participate in the running of projects.

(g) Use of simple monitoring and evaluation systems, both as integral parts of the project management system and as a method of benefiting from experience in designing future projects.

Changes in World Bank Activities

The World Bank's activities in rural areas have related mainly to lending for agriculture. The Bank is now the largest single external source of funds for direct investment in agriculture in developing countries. This has resulted from a deliberate shift in the Bank's policy over the past five years that has been reflected in changes in the lending program. The changes include a shift in the sectoral pattern, a widening and deepening of the purposes of lending, and the emergence of "new style" projects. The share of agriculture has increased from 6% of total Bank lending in fiscal 1948-60 to 16% in fiscal 1971-72 and 24% in fiscal 1973-74. The share of agriculture, furthermore, has increased over a period when total lending has expanded several times.

The Bank's lending for agriculture has widened over this period to include financing of storage, marketing, processing, farm credit, fisheries and forestry projects, in addition to the more traditional irrigation and infrastructure projects. The deepening of lending is reflected in the fact that lending to countries with per capita Gross National Product (GNP) below $150 has increased from 22.5% of the total up to fiscal 1968 to 38.2% of the total in fiscal 1969-74. The number of projects providing benefits to the rural poor has increased. The increase has been facilitated by "new style" projects which: (1) are designed to benefit directly large numbers of rural poor; (2) take a comprehensive approach to small-scale agriculture and may include components that are indirectly as well as directly productive; and (3) have a sufficiently low cost per beneficiary so that they may be extended or replicated over broader areas.

In short, the Bank's changing philosophy on agricultural development has resulted in: (1) a larger proportion of total lending being devoted to agriculture, within which poverty-oriented projects are getting an increasing share; (2) an increased share of lending going to the poorest countries; (3) a larger number of people benefiting from

Bank-supported projects; and (4) projected net output increases well above the 5% target suggested by the President, Mr. Robert S. McNamara, in his Nairobi speech.[3]

The Way Ahead

It might be asked whether an emphasis on rural development is inconsistent with the urgent need to increase food production, since: (1) it implies a heavy investment in the small farmer group (two hectares or less) which controls only 16% of the land; (2) it is sometimes more costly to provide services to large numbers of small farmers than to a smaller number of large farmers; and (3) it may conflict with a concentration of resources in areas of high potential which are not always among the poorest.

Rural development does not necessarily mean diverting resources away from increased food production since: (1) most of the rural poor are engaged in agriculture; (2) employment of the landless and near-landless on rural public works can provide them with the income to purchase food while creating productive facilities for agriculture; and (3) small farmers are often more efficient in the use of on-farm resources. Recognizing the high priority of food production, the Bank looks upon the need to reduce poverty in rural areas and to increase food production as twin goals. Its emphasis on rural lending, therefore, includes lending not only for those in the poverty target groups but also for the larger-scale farmers when it is necessary to raise their production in order to increase domestic food supplies and/or contribute to exports.

Assessing the measures required to achieve an annual growth of output of 5% from small-scale farmers is a complex task. It involves not only estimating the financial resources needed, but also assessing the problems of transferring technologies and the many manpower and institutional constraints. Many of these parameters are difficult to quantify and the available data do not allow detailed analyses. Experience indicates that finance alone is seldom the limiting factor: frequently technological, institutional, procedural and manpower factors are more critical. Nonetheless, approximate indications of the investment needed to achieve the goal of a 5% output increase by small farmers have been calculated by use of a simple model and by reference to recent Bank experience. These rough estimates range from $70,000 million to over $100,000 million—the highest figure being based on an analysis of Bank experience with 25 "new style" rural

---

[3] *References to "the Nairobi speech" in this paper relate to the address delivered by Mr. Robert S. McNamara, President of the World Bank Group, at the Annual Meeting in Nairobi on September 24, 1973. (See Annex 15.)*

development projects in which, on the average, 50% of the direct project beneficiaries were poor rural families with annual incomes of less than $50 per capita. However, this estimate is subject to a substantial margin of error because the 25 "new style" projects analyzed do not constitute a very secure base from which to make such projections.

Even the figure of $100,000 million, or $10,000 million a year when taken over a ten year period, may appear relatively modest when viewed in the light of the projected $170,000 million total investment in developing countries in 1974 alone. However, for low-income countries, where the poor are concentrated, investment in 1974 will be nearer $25,000 million, so that proportionately the investment required for rural development is extremely large.

The Bank's Program

The Bank's projected lending for agriculture and rural development during fiscal 1975-79 is approximately $7,000 million for projects with total costs estimated at $15,000 million. Assuming a lending program of this size, half would be for agriculture and half for rural development. The total investment in Bank-supported projects would be one-fifth of the investment needed to expand the productivity of the rural poor by at least 5% per year during 1975-79. The agriculture and rural development program of the Bank would reach a total rural population of 100 million, of whom 60 million would be in the poverty target group. The numbers of rural poor are expected to increase by 70 million in the same period.

Deployment of Bank Resources

In order to meet the goals of rural development, the Bank is giving attention to: (1) monitoring progress of economic, sector and project work; (2) adjusting the project cycle, especially in the case of project preparation work; and (3) modifying the technical assistance program, including training and research.

The increased emphasis given to project identification in rural development suggests the need for greater attention to identification in country economic and sector work. Special reconnaissance missions may be useful for this purpose.

Project preparation acquires greater importance because of the number and variety of components and the special implementation needs. The lead time is generally longer. Possible measures for providing assistance in preparation include expanded use of reconnaissance missions; creation of project planning units in developing countries;

and special preparation projects. In recognition of the importance of "implementation" in realizing goals, particular attention should be given to planning, monitoring and evaluation systems within project organizations.

No significant changes are required in project appraisal procedures, but specific guidelines are necessary for assessing those components for which benefits cannot be reliably estimated. In such cases, attention should be given to sectoral policy standards, minimum cost alternatives, appropriate pricing of services, replicability and the availability of fiscal resources to maintain and carry on programs on a broader basis.

The kind of technical assistance required to support the Bank's proposed lending program for rural development includes training to overcome manpower constraints, attention to public sector organizations, and research and information gathering to provide more adequate understanding and guidelines.

The Bank will encourage and, where requested, provide technical and financial assistance to governments that wish to devise comprehensive rural development plans. Where governments do not appear interested in developing a strategy for reducing poverty in rural areas, the Bank will seek to identify and prepare rural development projects, while engaging in a dialogue on possible changes in development strategies and policies. Where governments are interested in experimental rural development programs or projects, the Bank will support them.

The Bank's economic, sector and regional planning missions will try to identify the target groups in the rural areas and the key technical, policy, organizational, management and manpower constraints. Their reports will be used as the basis for a dialogue with governments with a view to removing constraints through such actions as:

1. Special missions to identify the institutional causes of low absorptive capacity in the public sector, paying particular attention to civil service procedures and conditions of service which militate against efficiency in the planning and implementation of suitable projects and programs.

2. Projects to provide greater training facilities for indigenous personnel, such as "corps of development managers," regional and project planners, cooperative managers and accountants.

3. Provision for training specialists in larger projects.

Within the lending program, an increasing effort will be made to develop projects which:

1. Reach large numbers in the low-income groups of the rural population.

2. Are low in cost per person reached relative to benefits.

3. Provide a rate of economic return at least equal to the opportunity cost of capital.

4. Provide a balance between productive and welfare components, consistent with minimum cost standards and fiscal resources.

5. Involve local participation in decision making.

6. Incorporate rural works for the landless as part of an integrated rural development effort.

There will be continued experimentation with:

1. The design of projects and the development of economical delivery systems for all facets of rural development (such experimentation will include the evaluation of low-cost minimum packages, area development projects and public works and other special programs).

2. Multisectoral projects designed within sectoral and regional contexts rather than within a purely project context. Putting projects in these contexts provides guidelines for minimum national standards.

There will be greater emphasis on the ongoing evaluation of projects as part of internal management control systems; the scope of supervision missions will accordingly be broadened to include fuller evaluation of the impact of the project.

In designing rural development projects, account will also be taken of the possibility of including family planning elements, where desirable.

Chapter 1: THE NATURE AND EXTENT OF THE PROBLEM

Toward an Operational Strategy

The objectives of development include sustained increases in per capita output and incomes, expansion of productive employment and greater equity in the distribution of the benefits of growth. This implies reducing poverty and human misery by increasing the productivity of the poor and providing them greater access to goods and services. A large proportion of the poor live in rural areas. Rural development must constitute a major part of a development strategy if a large segment of those in greatest need are to benefit.

Past strategies in most developing countries have tended to emphasize economic growth without specifically considering the manner in which the benefits of growth are to be distributed. The assumption has been that increased growth *per se* would lead to a reduction in poverty as the benefits of an expanding economy spread among the people. Accordingly, the emphasis has been on increasing the rate of growth, with a corresponding concentration of effort on the "high growth," modern sectors of the economy—to the virtual exclusion of the traditional sector, where the smallholders, tenants and landless make up the bulk of the rural poor. Although, in the long run, economic development for the growing rural population will depend on expansion of the modern sector and on nonagricultural pursuits, too strong an emphasis on the modern sector is apt to neglect the growth potential of the rural areas. Failure to recognize this has been a major reason why rural growth has been slow and rural poverty has been increasing. At the other extreme, a few governments preoccupied with promoting social equity in the rural areas may have discouraged investment in growth to the point where economic stagnation has resulted. With rapidly growing populations, per capita incomes in the rural areas have declined, even though the range of differences in incomes is much narrower than it was.

A strategy for rural development aimed at raising growth rates and distributing the fruits of growth more fairly implies greater interaction between the modern and traditional sectors, especially in the form of increased trade in farm produce and in technical inputs and services. While the main concern of this paper is with direct ways of tackling problems of rural poverty—because such problems have been relatively neglected in the past—other methods are also required to deal with rural poverty in all its forms. For this reason, modern sector and

16

macroeconomic policies are important; the World Bank needs to continue to devote part of its resources to helping the rural poor, indirectly, through projects designed to increase output, exports and growth generally.

The central concept of rural development presented here is of a process through which rural poverty is alleviated by sustained increases in the productivity and incomes of low-income rural workers and households. The emphasis is on raising output and incomes rather than simply redistributing current income and existing assets, although the latter may be desirable or even essential in an overall rural development strategy which links production with distributive or equity objectives. Operationally, this concept of rural development requires that target groups be specified among the rural poor, for whom specific measures to raise production and income can be designed, and in whose case the resulting flow of benefits—direct and indirect—is both identifiable and potentially measurable. The notion of target groups lies at the root of the definition of rural development as a separable and distinct component of general development strategy. It provides that necessary focus on groups of the rural population in terms of whose well-being policy actions and programs can be designed and evaluated. Target groups are best defined in the context of the individual country. However, a basic standard for identifying target groups would be the income necessary to cover minimum nutritional requirements and essential nonfood expenses. In addition, an income equal to or less than one-third the national average would be an appropriate additional criterion to allow for extreme relative poverty—in developing countries. Target groups identified by low incomes, absolute or relative, include smallholders, tenants and the landless; each separate group may need a special program of its own to handle the specific problems it faces.

The operational goals of rural development extend beyond any particular sector: they include improved productivity, and thus higher incomes for the target groups, as well as minimum acceptable levels of food, shelter, education and health services. Fulfillment of these objectives calls for an expansion of goods and services available to the rural poor, and institutions and policies that will enable them to benefit fully from the whole range of economic and social services. In order that the development be self-sustaining, it is of special importance that the members of the target group participate in the organization of the program.

A program of rural development must embrace a wide range and mix of activities, including projects to raise agricultural output, to improve health and education, to expand communications and to improve

17

housing. The mix of activities will vary with the requirements of a region and the priorities assigned to components within a program at particular times and at particular stages of development. The program may be based on a series of sequential projects—first health, then education, then agricultural development. Or it may attempt a broad-based, multisectoral approach whereby a series of activities are to be undertaken almost simultaneously. In all cases, the constituent elements should be complementary and reinforcing.

Most of the low-income groups in the rural areas depend heavily on agriculture for their livelihood. It follows that many of the programs intended to raise rural incomes must center on agricultural development. For the landless, who are among the lowest-income groups, public works programs that generate employment can be an important element in rural development programs. The same applies to health and education when these services focus on the rural poor. In these instances, however, the effect of the programs may be to increase the capacity of the poor to become more productive rather than to increase output and incomes directly.

Approaches to rural development are also influenced by a country's circumstances. Countries with surplus revenues—including many that are rich in petroleum and minerals—may be in a position to invest heavily in social overheads as well as in directly productive activities. Where economic dualism prevails, a rural development program may be an effective way of both redistributing income and expanding output by increasing the share of the budget allocated for services to low-income groups. Elsewhere, economic circumstances may dictate that the primary emphasis be on increasing short-run output to generate increased income—which can then be the basis for increased savings and further investment in development. The nature and content or mix of activities in any rural development program will vary, depending on the political, social and economic circumstances that prevail in a given country or region. There is no universal formula that prescribes the right mix, or the most effective sequence, of activities to raise the incomes of the rural poor.

In sum, rural development programs or projects are intended to provide a sustained increase in the output and level of living of a significant proportion of the rural poor in a given area. In some instances, this may require emphasis on indirectly productive operations. But, in the main, the focus is on activities which either raise incomes directly, or at least provide the potential to be more productive. The implementation of such a strategy requires trained manpower and efficient institutions. The rural poor must participate in designing and operating a program which involves so many of them.

The Measurement of Rural Poverty

The Extent of Rural Poverty

There is no uniquely correct way of measuring the extent of poverty, or of rural poverty. In Mr. McNamara's Nairobi speech, emphasis was given to programs for increasing the productivity of "that approximately 40% of the population of our developing member countries who have neither been able to contribute significantly to national economic growth, nor to share equitably in economic progress." Some illustrative calculations have been built from this baseline. They take into account absolute poverty (defined by income levels below which even minimum standards of nutrition, shelter and personal amenities cannot be maintained) and relative poverty (reflecting extreme differences in levels of living between the top and bottom strata of society). Relative poverty is often more of a problem in the better-off developing countries than in the poorer ones.

The extent and regional concentration of absolute poverty can be illustrated by adopting an arbitrary standard—that a person is in a state of absolute poverty when he or she has an annual income equivalent to $50 or less.[1] On this basis, an analysis of all developing countries with populations of more than one million reveals that:

1. Approximately 85% of all absolute poverty is in the rural areas.

2. In all, about 550 million people are suffering from absolute poverty in the rural areas of the developing world in the mid-1970s.

3. About three-fourths of this total are in the developing countries of Asia, with almost two-thirds of the number found in only four countries—India, Indonesia, Bangladesh and Pakistan.

4. In contrast, the developing countries of Latin America and the Caribbean account for only about 4% of the population in absolute poverty.

5. Fifty-three countries with per capita incomes above $150, taken together, account for only 8% of the absolute poverty in rural areas.

Thus, much of the rural poverty is a direct reflection of low levels of national per capita income and the size of the rural sector in these economies.[2]

To provide a quantitative illustration of relative poverty, calculations were made of the total number of people with per capita incomes

[1] In 1969 prices—the year to which the original data used in these calculations refer. It would be preferable to use "household" or "family" income levels in place of the per capita measure used in this analysis, but data are lacking on the distribution of household or family incomes.

[2] See Annexes 1 and 3; the figures quoted in the text are rough projections from the 1969 estimates shown in the tables.

below one-third of the average per capita income of their own country.[3] (See Annex 2.) By this standard of relative poverty:

1. The relatively poor make up 18% of the total population of developing countries (in contrast to 34% under the $50 absolute standard).

2. But a much larger fraction of the relatively poor (27% of the total) belongs to countries in Latin America and the Caribbean; by this criterion, over 30% of the people of that region are poor.

If the estimates of the number of the poor, measured by the absolute standard given, are added to the number of those whose per capita incomes exceed $50 but fall below one-third of the national average for the countries in which they live, then approximately 750 million or 40% of the total population of developing countries must be considered to be living in absolute or relative poverty. Of this total, almost 70% are accounted for by the developing countries of Asia; 19% by Africa; and 13% by Latin America and the Caribbean. The fraction of the rural population counted as absolutely poor varies from over 40% in rural Asia to under 20% in Latin America and the Caribbean. Allowing for both relative and absolute poverty, however, these proportions fall between 37% and 47% of the rural populations of the various regions.

The data presented above indicate the geographic spread and magnitude of poverty. An estimated 600 million of the poor—or more than 80% of all the poor—live in the rural areas. These 600 million constitute 40% of all the people in the rural areas. Nearly 550 million people living in the rural areas have incomes that are the equivalent of $50 or less.

The estimates also suggest that rural poverty is more severe and intractable in some countries than in others. The most difficult circumstances are those in which extensive rural poverty is combined with low levels of mobilizable resources. Countries in this situation include all the South Asian nations, many of the larger African countries such as Ethiopia, Sudan and Tanzania, and a few Latin American and Caribbean countries like Bolivia and Haiti. Rural development is the major development problem facing these nations.

At the other end of the scale are countries with pockets of rural poverty, varying in extent and intensity, but with resources adequate to deal with the problem, provided the political commitment is made. In this group are Iran, Argentina, Malaysia and Yugoslavia. In an intermediate category are countries with relatively extensive rural poverty but not inconsiderable resources to deal with it. This group includes petroleum exporters such as Indonesia, Nigeria and Algeria, middle-income countries such as Brazil, Colombia and Mexico, and moder-

---

[3] A ratio which corresponds very roughly to the "poverty line" at which incomes begin to be supplemented through welfare payments in many developed countries.

ately poor countries such as Thailand, the Republic of Korea and the Philippines.

Characteristics of the Rural Poor

There is little detailed information on the levels and distribution of income within rural areas and little analysis of the anatomy of rural poverty. In most cases, however, the poor are found living alongside the prosperous. They sometimes suffer from limited access to natural resources. But more frequently they suffer because they have little access to technology and services, and because the institutions which would sustain a higher level of productivity are lacking. In many cases, vested interests operate to ensure not only that the benefits of productive activity are distributed inequitably, but that the poor are denied access to the inputs, services and organization which would allow them to increase their productivity. Thus, the socioeconomic system operating in the rural areas is often hostile to the objectives of rural development, serving to reinforce rural poverty and to frustrate the efforts of the poor to move up. Clearly this is not always the case, for example, there are isolated communities where all the people suffer from poverty and ignorance, where there is no dominance by privileged groups and where the ultimate rights to land are exercised by a tribal or clan council of elders. The important point is that devising effective programs calls first for a clear understanding of the system which perpetuates poverty.

Dependence on Agriculture for a Livelihood

Labor surveys in Africa and Asia show that agricultural employment is the principal occupation for 75% to 85% of the rural population; with the partial exception of some relatively advanced countries, and areas close to cities, almost everyone has some connection with agriculture. There is a correspondingly thin scatter of jobs in rural industry, commerce, transport and services (including educational and administrative services). Data concerning the activities of the rural poor are scarce. Such data as there are serve to show that agriculture is even more important as a source of income for this group than for the rural population in general. A detailed evaluation of the relatively commercialized and developed areas of rural Malaysia, for example, confirms that agriculture is more significant for the poor than for others: it is the principal source of livelihood for 82% of the poor householders, compared with only 50% of rural households not classified as poor. In the remoter regions of most developing countries, almost every family either rears animals or raises crops as a main activity.

21

Importance of Nonagricultural Sources of Income

Though agriculture provides most of the work and incomes in rural areas, nonagricultural activities are important supplementary sources of incomes for rural households. A shortage of remunerative work opportunities off the farm during the slack season may greatly increase the poverty of those whose holdings are too small or too unproductive to provide an adequate livelihood. The poorest income groups in rural areas—the landless and near-landless—often depend on activities which may contribute only indirectly to higher agricultural output. This is one of the fundamental reasons why rural development efforts cannot be confined simply to measures to increase productivity, without explicit regard for their effects on poverty target groups.

Variety of Climatic and Ecological Conditions

Most of the rural poor living in absolute poverty are concentrated in the fertile areas and the relatively favorable climates of South and East Asia where the density of population is great and where many holdings are less than one-third hectare in size. But poverty persists also in sparsely populated areas where the land is infertile and the climate adverse; such areas include parts of the Sahel zones of Africa, the Andean Altiplano or the dry zones of India and Pakistan. A calculation based on a country-by-country breakdown shows that about 40% of the population is in absolute or relative poverty in the more densely populated zones (300 or more persons per square kilometer); the proportion is also about 40% in the less populated zones (150 or less persons per square kilometer). Rural development efforts obviously have to be shaped according to the widely differing ecological circumstances in which rural poverty occurs.

Compounding Effects of National Calamities

There are times—typically after floods or drought have ruined the harvest—when virtually the entire population of a large area is seriously affected. An important region where such a situation is common is represented by the so-called "drought prone areas" of India, which cover about 600,000 square kilometers and have a population of approximately 66 million. The bulk of this population is engaged in a perennial struggle to meet subsistence needs in a generally harsh environment. Within this broad zone, drought has occurred in three or four years out of every ten — with good and bad years tending to cluster together. The succession of drought years has severely affected the harvest, and has resulted in absolute poverty for more than 50 million people, or three-fourths of the total population of the zone. A similarly extreme situation exists in the drought prone areas of northeast

Brazil, affecting more than 20 million people. Elsewhere, severe floods (partly occasioned by typhoons) contribute to perennial poverty. Such floods occur every two or three years in Bangladesh and in parts of the Philippines; they tend to diminish the already low incomes in those areas.

Small and Fragmented Holdings

Incomes at the farm level are determined by a host of factors that include the quantity and quality of inputs such as land, labor and water, the technology used, the prices received for outputs, and the prices paid for inputs. Thus, an irrigated farm of one hectare using high-yielding varieties of rice and fertilizer can generate double the income of the same area farmed by traditional methods. One hectare devoted to tea can yield an income seven times as great as when it is used for maize. The acreage required to generate the same level of income will also vary with ecological conditions. Thus, a recent Agricultural Sector Survey conducted in Kenya indicated that, for rainfed agriculture, the farm size needed to produce approximately $40 per capita per year increased progressively from 2.6 hectares to 6.4 hectares, and then to 16.4 hectares, according to the ecological zone. Between 90 and 135 hectares were needed to generate the same level of income in range areas bordering the Sahel. But while the use of inputs varies widely, land remains the most important of the factors of production that determine levels of output and income. Studies indicate that most of the smallholdings in Asia, Africa and Latin America are used for traditional low-yielding subsistence production. These studies also indicate that very few farms of less than two hectares of arable land, producing traditional crops, generate incomes above the poverty line. According to the 1960 World Census of Agriculture, there are 80 million smallholdings with less than two hectares of land.[4]

Tenants and Sharecroppers

There are instances—especially in the more developed regions—where large holdings are leased under fixed rentals and where those who operate the farm have relatively high incomes. However, most tenants and sharecroppers in the poorer countries share their output with landowners and often operate under insecure tenancies. Other things being equal, tenants' incomes will be even lower than those of the small operator-owners, and the amount of land required for an income above the poverty line is correspondingly larger. The greatest

---

[4] See the World Bank's paper on Land Reform, Annex 1, Table 1:6, included in this book.

numbers of low-income persons in these categories are in Asia (26 million, or 89% of the total).[5]

Landless and Other Rural Workers

Most workers in rural areas are classified as self-employed or family workers, but the poorest farm households also derive a significant proportion of their income from wage employment in agricultural and nonagricultural activities. There is a large and growing group of landless and near-landless workers—heavily concentrated in those Asian countries with the largest concentrations of the poor . (See Annex 4.) Most of the landless work irregularly, often on a seasonal basis; many work only when labor requirements are at a peak. Wage rates are extremely low, often less than the equivalent of 50 cents a day. Not all farm workers are so badly off; some workers in plantations and in enclave enterprises have incomes that place them above the poverty level. In the main, however, agricultural workers and the landless whose employment is seasonal are among the poorest members of the community.

The Dynamics of Rural Poverty

Rural Population and Agricultural Production

Despite high rates of rural-urban migration, the rural population is growing by approximately 2% per year.[6] In the past, in most countries, the increase in rural population could be accommodated by expanding the acreage under cultivation. This may continue to be the case in countries which have an ample supply of land that can be brought into production at relatively low cost, but in most places the opportunities for such low-cost expansion have diminished substantially. With a worsening man-land ratio, increases in output and farm income must come from a widespread increase in yields per acre and from the cultivation of higher value crops.

The need to raise yields per acre places the poor farmer at a disadvantage under present programs, and encourages the view that poverty will increase unless the development strategy in many countries is reoriented. To raise the output and incomes of the bulk of the rural poor means that they should have access to suitable technology and to the capital required to utilize that technology. At present—for reasons discussed at length in the Bank's papers on *Agricultural Credit* and *Land Reform*—the public and private institutions that can promote

---

[5] *Ibid, Annex 1, Table 1:10.*
[6] *Except in some countries of Latin America where population growth rates are low.*

technological change tend to bypass the poor farmer typically operating a holding of two hectares or less, and to ignore the needs of the landless laborer.

The new seed-fertilizer technology for wheat, rice and maize has provided the first major opportunity to increase yields among small-scale, low-income producers of traditional crops. Although considerable adaptive research and breeding is required, the technology can lead to substantial increases in output in many areas, even where the density of population is very high and where there are large numbers of small-scale, low-income producers, such as in Bangladesh and Java. However, as long as the institutions that provide the inputs for technological change continue to be biased against the small producers, the latter will become more and more impoverished as they have to share their output among increased numbers. A special effort must be made to help the rural poor to contribute more to an increase in output. This can be done only by special programs which include the provision of infrastructure and on-farm improvements.

There are opportunities for considerably expanding employment in agriculture for both farmers and landless labor, particularly by increasing cropping intensities on irrigated lands. But agriculture cannot absorb at ever increasing levels of productivity all of the prospective additions to the working age population in rural areas. Consequently, rural development programs have to include provision for promoting nonagricultural activities in rural areas and for the linkages with agricultural sectors on the one hand, and the urban, industrialized sector on the other.

Health and Education

The logic regarding special intervention to raise the agricultural incomes of the poor also extends to the provision of minimum standards of food, clothing, shelter, health and education. These not only improve the quality of life, but also indirectly affect human productivity. An income of less than $50 per capita implies inadequacies of nutrition, shelter, health standards and other components of a basic level of living. As a consequence, rural areas are notable for high levels of morbidity and mortality, especially infant mortality; physical and mental lethargy and inability to sustain hard work on a regular basis; limited ability to recognize or to respond to problems and challenges; lack of awareness; inactive and poor motivation toward improvement and learning; and, often, hostility toward outside sources of change (and sometimes toward potential achievers inside who threaten the cohesion of the group). Some of these reactions, particularly those that are more psychological than physiological, are associated as much with the deprivations of relative poverty as with those of absolute poverty. A link between rural poverty and food intake has been established for a number of countries. (See Annex 5.) Nutritional deficiencies affect all age groups, but the toll is greatest among the very young. In most low-income countries, children under five years of age, although they generally constitute less than 20% of the population, account for more than 60% of all deaths. Malnutrition is the largest single contributor to child mortality in these countries.

One of the important elements reinforcing rural poverty is that those most needing medical or health care are precisely those who are too poor or too remote from any facility to obtain it. (See Annex 6.) Since almost everywhere[7] the medical doctor remains the lynchpin in the system of public health care, the shortage of doctors generally means that medical facilities are inadequate. It is estimated that more than 80% of the rural population is completely out of touch with the official health services.

Another factor that exacerbates the health problems of the rural poor is that preventive services are neglected. Approximately 70% to 80% of public health expenditures are usually allocated to curative services, even though it is generally recognized that preventive health programs, primarily environment-oriented, are essential to check the diseases which have contributed to the prevailing high rates of morbidity and mortality. Through improved water supply and sanitation, the incidence of a whole range of diseases can be diminished.

Although it may take time, access to education can well provide some chance for the rural young to escape from poverty. There are, however, two important considerations which militate against the rural poor receiving satisfactory education. The first is the relative shortage of facilities and the poor quality of education in the rural areas. The second is the relatively high cost of education to the poor in terms of fees, books and other materials.

There has been a significant increase in educational opportunities in rural areas. But this has been unevenly distributed and has generally lagged behind educational expansion in urban areas, particularly at levels of education above the elementary. A comparison of the statistics of the United Nations Educational, Scientific and Cultural Organization (Unesco) for the primary level shows that the ratio of "complete" schools to the total number of schools by area is significantly less in rural than in urban areas. (See Annex 7.) On the basis of an intensive survey of the general situation, the judgment of one expert was

---

[7] *The People's Republic of China is the most noteworthy exception. Tanzania is also developing its rural health services with strong emphasis on the use of medical auxiliaries rather than doctors.*

that, "in a country with an overall primary school participation rate of, say, 50%, the chances are that in some of the poorer rural areas as many as 90% or more of all young people (especially girls) are reaching maturity without knowing how to read or write."[8] It is probable that unless the situation changes greatly, millions of children in rural areas will remain illiterate. One reason is that, despite what may be substantial public expenditures on educational facilities, charges for education, though nominal, are often well beyond the means of the rural poor. In many countries, education for large numbers of rural poor children ends after two years of primary school, even where a school is available for use.

Not only are the rural areas discriminated against in the provision of educational services, but the type of education often is not appropriate to the needs of rural dwellers. It is increasingly recognized that to remedy both the quantitative and qualitative deficiencies of education in rural areas more widespread use of systems of "basic education" will be required.[9]

Other Services

Compared with urban areas, rural areas tend also to be provided with a lower proportion of such services as domestic water supply, electricity, waste disposal and other economic infrastructure. The relative scarcity of these services means that they are not available in the areas where most of the poor live; the poor simply do not have access to them. Even where such services are available, the poor tend to benefit less from them than do other groups. When the services are subsidized, at least some payment has often to be made for them; so, despite the subsidy, the personal contribution may serve as an effective barrier to use by the poverty stricken.

The analysis indicates that special efforts to provide appropriate social and economic services for the rural poor should focus on meeting the needs of the lowest-income groups—smallholders, tenants and the landless—in the rural areas. To this end, not only must the services be geared to rural requirements, but special pricing arrangements must be maintained so that the poor will have access to services which can help them to break out of the cycle of poverty. The analysis also indicates the importance of integrating economic with social services in rural development projects, since poor health and lack of educa-

---

[8] *Coombs, P. H., with Prosser, R. C., and Ahmed, M.* New Paths to Learning for Rural Children and Youth. *Prepared for UNICEF by International Council for Educational Development, October 1973.*

[9] *See the World Bank's paper on* Education, *included in this book.*

27

tion are important reasons for low productivity and resistance to change.[10]

The reduction of rural poverty will require an enormous effort both within and outside the rural sector. The emphasis here is on a direct attack against poverty in the rural areas, although the expansion of nonrural sectors is essential if employment opportunities for the rural poor are to increase. This is especially the case in the more populous countries of Asia where man-land ratios are already unfavorable. Furthermore, other indirect measures may well be essential. For instance, with the growth in population, the increase in the number of the rural poor could be greater than the number of those likely to benefit from the proposed program of lending by the World Bank for rural development. (See Chapter 3.) Thus, the need for population control is obvious.[11] Family planning, in turn, has a better chance of success if rural development programs raise living standards.

Chapter 2: POLICIES AND PROGRAMS FOR RURAL DEVELOPMENT

The national commitment to policies and programs for rural development is a recent phenomenon in many countries. In only a few has such a commitment long been reflected in national policies (for example, Japan and the Republic of China). In addition, numerous pilot projects have been launched in different parts of the world—such as Comilla in Bangladesh, Puebla in Mexico and the special rural development projects in Kenya. The Bank's support for activities in this area is relatively new, and sufficient time has not yet elapsed for proper evaluation of the more recent efforts. Also, due to the diversity of rural conditions, a country's experience often provides insights relevant only to the circumstances of that particular country. At this stage, therefore, it is important to emphasize that much remains to be

---

[10] *One specific study, recently undertaken for the Bank, of low-income workers in Indonesia stressed the mutually reinforcing impact of poverty and a deficient diet on production. It stated:*
"Once infestation of anemia occurs, the environmental, economic and nutritional factors are likely to enhance the debilitating effects of the disease resulting in a vicious circle. An anemic individual will tend to work less, and thus earn less income if he is on a piece-work or an incentive basis. This in turn predisposes him to a poorer nutritional status (less food), aggravating further the anemia, and increasing susceptibility to infection. Increased absenteeism and lowered productivity will therefore result, and he is trapped in a series of events in which he can neither improve his income, his nutrition nor his health."

[11] *See "Population Planning: Sector Working Paper", in* World Bank Operations, *pp. 291-369. Baltimore and London: The Johns Hopkins University Press, 1972. See also* Population Policies and Economic Development. A World Bank Staff Report. *Baltimore and London: The Johns Hopkins University Press, 1974.*

learned about the nature, complexity and scale of the problems to be tackled. Consequently, any conclusions derived remain tentative and preliminary; they are likely to be modified considerably with a fuller understanding of the process of change in rural areas.

The Policy Framework

The Role of Government

A strong commitment to rural development policies at the national level is required if the impact on the problems of rural poverty is to be effective and broad-based. In some developing countries, present policies and institutional structures are so far from favorable to rural development that a policy shift could only follow a major political change. This is a key problem in situations demanding extensive land reform; it applies even more where the government itself is dominated by special interests unsympathetic to the objectives of rural development. In most other countries, governments are prepared to experiment at the project level. But some hold the view that rural development is technically difficult or economically unsound as it may lead to slower growth in output and exports. Whatever the reasons, unless more governments commit themselves firmly to devising strategies and policies to raise the standards of living of the rural poor, the lot of millions of people will not improve significantly.

Rural development objectives can be sought in various ways once there is firm commitment. The choice of methods, and the sequence in which they are used, will reflect social, cultural and political factors, as well as narrower technical considerations. So far, however, while numerous rural development projects and activities have been launched, the great majority of countries still operate without fully articulated policies, programs or plans for rural development. Similarly, national policies are often inconsistent with agricultural and rural development.

Price Policy

Price policy is one example. It is important for rural development that the overall relationship between input and output prices within agriculture, and the terms of trade between agriculture and other sectors of the economy, should be such as to stimulate growth in the rural areas. The Bank's analyses indicate that all too often government policies discriminate against development, particularly agricultural production, in the rural areas. They are designed to provide assistance to manufacturing and processing industries, or to raise government revenues. As such, they tend to raise the cost of agricultural inputs relative to output prices, making innovation unrewarding and highly risky for the farmer.

Many governments defend low prices for food on the ground that it is necessary to keep down the cost of living in urban areas. In some cases, governments seek to compensate the farmer through subsidies on inputs or credit. Frequently, however, such subsidies lead to undesirable distortions in the economy, are costly to implement, and are available only to those in contact with and enjoying the confidence of the organization through which they are provided. The small farmer, typically, is excluded from the advantages. In general, therefore, it is more beneficial or less costly to provide incentives by guaranteeing minimum prices than to subsidize inputs; it is also better to subsidize specific inputs in order to transfer specific technologies rather than to have general subsidies such as subsidized interest rates.[1]

Fiscal Policy

Fiscal policies in many countries have been inconsistent in their approach. They have tended to develop piecemeal in response both to particularly urgent revenue needs and to powerful pressure groups. As such, they militate against the rural poor, who are either unrepresented or inadequately represented in the councils of government. For instance, in most developing countries, the distribution of public sector expenditure is heavily skewed in favor of urban dwellers; and in rural areas the relatively rich receive favored treatment. These inequalities are apparent across a broad spectrum of services.

Through high levels of indirect commodity taxation and low effective rates of income or property taxes, the poor often pay a considerably larger share of their income than the rich. In the rural areas, the failure to extract a reasonable contribution from the richer members of the community is most obvious in the case of taxes based on property ownership—especially landownership. A properly constructed tax on agricultural land is probably most desirable to mobilize resources for public purposes, since it can function without destroying incentives related to agricultural output. Yet few countries appear to have effective land taxes of any sort. Where they do, there is—more often than not—widespread evasion through nominal transfers of parcels of land to relatives and through false classification of land potential.

A related and highly significant aspect of fiscal policy concerns cost recovery. Most countries are unable or unwilling to impose charges on those benefiting from publicly financed investment or current services—on the ground that the poor cannot afford to pay. Seldom, how-

---

[1] *The World Bank's paper on* Agricultural Credit *, included in this book, provides an analysis of interest rates.*

30

ever, is any attempt made to impose progressive charges which subsidize the poor by recovering proportionately more from the rich. Failure to impose adequate charges, in turn, severely limits the rate at which investments can be undertaken or services provided in the rural areas, even though the social and economic returns may be high.

Land Policy

Land reform has obvious implications for the rural poor, since their subsistence depends for the most part on the extent to which they control land and the output from that land. The recent Bank paper on *Land Reform* stresses the necessity of viewing land reform in the context of the multiple objectives of rural development. But smallholders can increase their incomes considerably without land reform (1) in densely populated areas where the tenancy ratio is low, the distribution of land is not excessively skewed and the private marketing system effectively reaches the small as well as the big farmers; and (2) by participating in settlement schemes in areas where there are large tracts of land which can be exploited productively. Land reform, however, must precede any massive input of resources into small farms or rural works where the incidence of onerous tenancy is high, the distribution of land is extremely skewed, or the rural oligarchy controls credit and marketing institutions, appropriating for itself the bulk of the input and even the income generated by rural works.

Regional Policy

When rural development programs and projects incorporating a variety of objectives and activities are contemplated, including not only private agricultural and industrial activity but also governmental infrastructure and social services, the locational aspects of the units of nonfarm activities require careful consideration. Whereas agricultural activity is soil-bound, many alternative locations may be feasible for nonfarm activities. Economies of scale and external economies due to the interdependence of different activities can be very significant. Problems obviously arise in determining the optimal areas and populations to be served by a local market center, an electricity transmission station, a water supply system, a school, an extension office, a research station, a medical clinic, a feeder road, a bank or a credit cooperative.

Many of these service units are best located in towns serving the surrounding rural area rather than in every village rural settlement. Alternatively, service units with a small capacity may be located in the villages and larger units in towns and cities. As regional planning of rural areas spreads, it will have to be coordinated with urban regional planning. Increasing migration and changes in the geographical distribu-

31

tion of the poor and the unemployed add urgency to the need for a coordinated provision of public services in contiguous rural and urban settlements.

Regional development policies require a careful appraisal of the growth potential of different areas. Resources to finance minimum standards of public services and infrastructure facilities should be available to all regions, particularly those that are most poorly endowed. Of particular importance is expenditure to identify the natural resources and growth potential of every area. It is a disturbing fact that, in vast areas of the developing world, comprehensive scientific surveys of natural resources have not yet been completed. Many regions remain poor because their resource endowments and potential for growth have not been properly established as a basis for investment.

Technology Policy

A constant flow of new, field-tested technical knowledge relevant to smallholder production is a precondition for the continuing success of most rural development programs. Many of the poor live in a harsh environment where investments would produce little extra income until technological discoveries create reliable new opportunities. Major improvements in production technologies and product mixes must be evolved for arid lands, some mountain regions, areas of low-quality soils where shifting cultivation is practiced, and rain forest areas. Failing this, migration may be the only solution.

Inappropriate research programs and the inadequacies of adaptive research and extension have in many cases been major factors limiting the benefits reaching poor farmers. One common problem that is emerging is the failure to treat the subsistence farm as a system of cultivation, requiring a comprehensive approach to on-farm technological improvement. Another problem is the lack of attention to factors that are especially important to the small farmer. These include risk-reducing innovations, such as better pest- and weather-resistant crops; more intensive research into the so-called poor man's crops, including sorghum, millet, cassava, pulses and upland rice; and better advice on simple improvements in crop husbandry and soil and fertility conservation. Although more research has been done on small farm equipment than is generally supposed, the efforts have not been coordinated nor the results subjected to simple production engineering for manufacture. One approach to this problem being pioneered by the International Rice Research Institute in the Philippines and other groups involves dissemination of research results and prototype specifications for local manufacture.

Commitment, Planning and Resource Requirements

The commitment of resources to rural development and the extent to which promotion of rural development programs is reflected in national economic policy depends both on the nature and severity of the problem and on the resources which the nation can allocate to it. As noted in Chapter 1, where rural poverty is restricted to small pockets and resources are available, individual countries may follow very different policies with regard to rural development. For instance, the fifth Five-Year Plan of Iran, covering the period 1972-73 through 1977-78 and drawn up before the recent increase in petroleum prices, projected investment outlays for the agricultural sector equivalent to some $900 million per year. The rural population of Iran is approximately 18 million. Of these, some 8 million could be counted among the target group of rural poor, as defined in Chapter 1. It follows that if half of the total investment outlay projected for agriculture were to be directed toward Iran's rural poor, annual per capita investment among that group could be over $50 per year.

By contrast, in Bangladesh over 90% of the population lives in rural areas and at least 40 million of these rural people must be counted among the poor. A feasible investment outlay for agriculture was assessed by a recent Bank economic mission at the equivalent of approximately $300 million per year during the mid-1970s. Applying the same arithmetic, in Bangladesh less than $4 per capita is available annually to help improve the productivity of the rural poor—about one-fifteenth of the amount available in Iran. While rural poverty is far from negligible in Iran, it clearly is not the dominant development concern that it must be for Bangladesh. At the same time, the resources available to Iran allow much greater latitude in its approach to rural poverty and permit a much faster pace of implementation. It is obvious that planning, program formulation and implementation will vary considerably from one case to the other.

Organization and Planning

There is a growing consensus that the effective planning and implementation of rural development programs require the following elements:

1. A national plan or program of action for rural development, together with supporting national and regional policies and adequate center-local financing arrangements.

2. A strong organization at the national level to coordinate vertically organized, central government sectoral departments.

3. Greater decentralization with effective machinery at the regional and local level to coordinate the sectoral activities of national departments operating in the region and regional and local departments.

4. Participation by the rural poor in the planning and implementation processes through local government, project advisory committees, cooperatives and other forms of group organization.

National Rural Development Programs and Plans

Few countries have designed an overall plan for rural development. The task is not an easy one, for several reasons: (1) by definition rural development cuts across all sectors; (2) rural programs, more than most other kinds of programs, ideally should flow from national and regional planning; (3) the kinds of supportive policies discussed earlier involve fundamental political considerations; and (4) the information base is poor.

Yet the advantages of a coordinated effort, focused on a national plan or program for rural development, are almost self-evident. Basic questions such as the financial, technical and administrative efforts to be allocated to the program, the areas for major concentration, the phasing and sequencing of activities, the linkages among sector programs and the developmental impact aimed for, can seldom be addressed effectively in a piecemeal fashion. At the present time, the effort tends to be fragmented and dispersed because there is no clear idea of the overall size of the problem; the location, density and economic characteristics of specific target groups; or the developmental potential in the areas where rural poverty is concentrated. To obtain the benefits of planning, however, calls for great determination in the face of very real difficulties.

At the level of the central government, the concerns of rural development tend to cut across the conventional boundaries of department organization and responsibility. At the other extreme, regional and local planning involves the delegation of some central authority for program design and implementation to staff who are in touch with local requirements and are able to assess the local potential. Finally, it is increasingly recognized that to create a basis for self-sustaining development in rural areas requires that local resources—financial and human—be mobilized within a planning framework involving the active participation and assistance of local people. Local self-reliance implies involvement, as distinct from simply reaching the low-income rural population through development programs. This, too, calls for major new efforts in the many countries where the administrative system has been highly centralized. In view of the difficulties, partial planning, for particular areas or regions, may be more realistic and effective in some circumstances.

Coordination at the Center

Some experience—although not a consensus—is emerging on approaches to the organizational problems of rural development planning. There appear, for instance, to be advantages in creating a special unit or office, located directly under the president or prime minister, to coordinate national planning and program development for rural development. The experience is that such units are most useful when they coordinate efforts rather than if they themselves undertake the specialized work of other agencies. Coordination is particularly important in: (1) national-regional efforts to overcome the current lack of data and improve the information base generally; and (2) the activities of the major sector agencies. The success of a rural program or project initiated by one department or agency often depends on complementary actions taken by another department. Experience in many countries suggests that inadequate preparation, including attention to those linkages, is an important cause of failure or disappointment. Finally, (3) there is the very important and difficult task of ensuring that national and sector policies are in line with the overall objectives of rural development.

Decentralization and Coordination at the Local Level

Experience indicates that the planning and implementation of rural development calls for a substantial measure of decentralization, involving the strengthening of local government and other development institutions. The adjustments needed vary significantly from country to country. Unless the functional aspects of rural development projects are completely delegated to some level of regional and/or local government—an unrealistic and probably undesirable situation—problems typically arise with regard to overlapping functions of central and local government departments. An institutional arrangement—perhaps in the form of regional planning units or coordinating committees—must be found to resolve issues and, in the last resort, to provide adjudication machinery. Where national investment priorities are concerned, provision has to be made to ensure that the central planning authority is brought into the picture.

The many meanings of decentralization should be clearly distinguished. Decentralization may mean decentralization of authority: (1) to formulate projects; (2) to administer projects and run enterprises; (3) to allocate expenditure; and (4) to raise revenue. If three major levels of government are considered—the central or federal, the state or provincial, and the district[2]—it will be seen that in large countries the responsibility for planning, budgeting and executing rural development schemes usually rests at the provincial level, and in small countries at the central level. But, almost everywhere, central planning agencies and ministries are playing an increasingly dominant role in directing and providing funds for rural development. In some countries, special ministerial or presidential units have been established to plan, coordinate and accelerate the rural development activities of central as well as regional agencies.

Opinion is now almost unanimous on the need for strong planning and executive machinery for rural development at the district or subdistrict levels. The advantages in planning and administering development from local levels are particularly great where there is a complex, multisectoral mix of activities that need to be properly integrated and scheduled. At the same time, local level management provides the flexibility needed to modify programs as conditions become better understood or as circumstances change. More generally, the combination of authority, responsibility and accountability focused at the local level leads to much more active promotional efforts than otherwise. This is particularly true in the more backward and isolated regions which tend to be neglected under a highly centralized system. In the People's Republic of China, reliance on decentralized local-level management is a cornerstone of the economic system. There is a clear trend in the same direction in a number of other countries—Algeria, Tanzania, Kenya and India, for example. However, apart from use of the special project authority—often separate from the existing local authority—progress toward decentralization is generally still modest.

At the present time, the proportion of expenditure on development which is allocated as a result of local decisions is fairly small—perhaps in the range of 10% to 20%. Budget authority continues to rest with the central authority, with a major part of the funds allocated on a departmental basis. Funds which provincial authorities can allocate out of their own revenues for rural development are generally hopelessly inadequate or insignificant. Even where there is a considerable measure of local autonomy in spending, reliance on central transfers is very great. Central governments usually curtail local powers to raise additional revenue directly from local sources, although there are some arguments favoring such local resource mobilization to supplement central government allocations. For one thing, total resources for investment may be increased. For another, local contributions would

---

[2] The exact terminology and hierarchy, of course, differ as between countries. But in all countries at least three levels are clearly distinguishable. The word "district" is used here to cover all levels below the provincial.

strengthen the basis for local participation in program conception and design and, more generally, would increase fiscal responsibility at the local level. Some countries, Indonesia for example, are experimenting successfully with schemes to increase local-level contributions, in this case using a matching grant system as an inducement.

Importance of Local Participation

Community involvement in the selection, design, construction and implementation of rural development programs has often been the first step in the acceptance of change leading to the adoption of new techniques of production. The manner in which early participation is to be achieved, and balanced with the need for overall guidance and control from the center, is a problem which can only be resolved within each country. There is some evidence, however, such as at Comilla in Bangladesh, that a strengthened local authority is better able to secure effective participation than are officials answerable to faraway central governments. It appears that Tanzania has gone further in its attempts to deal with these problems than most other countries. For example, preparation of regional development budgets now begins with proposals from a system of local committees, composed of villagers and low-level officials. The proposals are then filtered through higher-level district and regional committees, again composed of a mixed group of officials and party members, before being presented to the central government. Agreement must be reached at each level before the proposals are passed on to the next higher level. A somewhat similar system of decentralized planning and decision making is practiced in Malaysia, and one is being developed in Indonesia. Several countries have found that rural people have perceptions of needs and possibilities which are generally different from those of "rational" officials. The "right" balance in this relationship is hard to strike. At one extreme, local politicians may completely dominate local officials, with the possibility of perverse results. At the other extreme, also common, officials may make the final decisions and recommendations.

Local institutions, such as farmers' associations and cooperatives, have obvious potential advantages for coping with administrative difficulties in reaching the rural poor. On the one side, they provide some measure of participation through the involvement of their members. On the other, they perform intermediary functions which make it possible to provide credit to larger numbers than can be done through official agencies. Group members can be held jointly responsible for repayment of credit, for acceptance of input supplies or other produce purchased from outside, and for delivery of the marketed surplus to the appropriate agencies (public or private). In some systems, cultivation is arranged on a cooperative basis, possibly with the application of more or less uniform cultivation practices to land and crops that remain the responsibility and property of the individual cultivators. Local groups and associations can thus, in principle, reduce the need for government servants or personnel of government-supported agencies to deal with the individuals and families that comprise the target groups.

Almost all governments support cooperative development for the rural areas in one form or another. Experience indicates that the performance of cooperatives has been mixed. In some, the skills—particularly entrepreneurial and trading skills—required of the managers have been underestimated. With inefficiency and losses, the cooperative becomes a high-cost purveyor of services for its members. In some places, these difficulties have been accentuated by active and effective opposition to the cooperative from private traders, landlords and others to whom organization among low-income families is not advantageous. At times, such groups capture much of the benefit by working from within: for example, when membership of a cooperative is a condition for access to subsidized credit. Dishonesty among the officials has also been a major problem.

But experience with cooperatives is not all bad, and such organizations provide the participation and impetus in rural development programs that is hard to secure in any other way. Moreover, in most societies, there is a well-established informal system of mutual aid upon which to build. The work of nongovernmental agencies furnishes some of the more successful examples in fostering cooperation, usually working outside the framework of officialdom, and often in quite modest circumstances. The Bank expects to explore ways of working more closely with nongovernmental agencies, especially where they have gained useful local experience and have experimented with pilot projects.

Manpower and Institutional Constraints

The shortage of skilled staff to implement rural development programs should be a major consideration in their design. In many countries, particularly in Africa, the scarcity of skills is found at all levels: experienced and junior staff, technical and administrative. Even when the supply of trained manpower is more adequate, the number of personnel serving the rural areas is often small in comparison with urban areas. This may be because rural development has been assigned low priority or because the shortage of financial resources is acute. Typically, however, the salary scales, allowances and status of people working at the bottom of the development hierarchy in the rural areas are low. Their promotion prospects are uncertain. The lack of amenities in rural locations deters well-trained persons from staying there. Moreover, in many countries civil service practice does not respect and reward specialization. Therefore, the turnover of rural staff is very high; and officers appointed to supervise rural development are frequently generalists in the very early or the very last stages of their careers.

The remedies for this situation are obvious but seldom instituted. Staff working in the rural areas should be given better pay and allowances. Distinguished rural service should be given special recognition. Promotion prospects for specialized field staff should be improved. But competitive pay and career prospects must be regarded as complementary to the development of the motivation and commitment to service that accompany true professionalism. Manpower can often be used more effectively than it is at present. In particular, where good managers and higher-level staff are scarce, lower-level staff must be utilized much more effectively. The need for formally trained manpower is determined largely by the way in which the delivery of services is organized. Thus, many agricultural credit programs, following conventional forms of credit administration based on complex criteria of creditworthiness of the applicant, involve the processing of complicated forms and thus require large amounts of highly-trained manpower. Modification of such procedures could free this manpower for other tasks.

If decentralization is to be effective, regional and local government, development authorities and cooperative-type organizations must be provided with the trained manpower to fulfill their obligations. The evidence indicates that present systems of training are weak, especially in the handling of relationships with the local population. Recruitment must be localized to strengthen the links between development services and the community. Training exercises for agricultural extension agents, health workers and cooperative staff must be relevant to the actual needs and priorities of particular local situations. More consideration also should be given to the possibility of training community opinion leaders, such as primary school teachers, religious leaders and village cooperative secretaries as agents of change. The number of people who need to be trained is so large that the only practical way is to adopt a multiplier approach by training the trainers. This could be done by establishing internationally financed regional training institutes. The institutes would prepare experienced staff to return to their countries and set up courses to train development managers, regional and project planners, cooperative staff, agricultural extension agents and other specialists.

Implementing Rural Development

Because experience with rural development projects is limited, and conditions vary widely from one area to another, generalization about project design is fraught with the danger of being either too specific or too trite. Nevertheless, an attempt has been made to distill some lessons of experience by examining a cross-section of projects in which the alleviation of poverty in the rural areas was a major objective. In this respect, it is notable that rural development schemes usually do not aim to provide benefits exclusively to the rural poor. The reasons are several. Often, the rural development objective is subordinate to the objective of increasing agricultural output (or marketed output). Even where this is not the case, a program aimed at providing advice or extension to the small farmer will rarely exclude the medium-sized farmer, if by including him sizable increases in output can be achieved.

Moreover, it may frequently be desirable to design a program so that all sections of a rural community benefit from it to some degree. Often, in this way, the program can benefit the main target groups more effectively. Involving the community implies providing some element of general interest. In many countries, avoiding opposition from powerful and influential sections of the rural community is essential if the program is not to be subverted from within. Program design must take into consideration the existing social system if lasting benefits for the poor are to be achieved. Thus, in cases where economic and social inequality is initially great, it is normally optimistic to expect that more than 50% of the project benefits can be directed toward the target groups; often, the percentage will be considerably less. But, in all cases, project design should reflect the particular needs and conditions of the developing country in question.

At one extreme, some countries are seeking to provide a package of minimum requirements to as large a group as resources permit. This may be described as the minimum package approach to rural development. At the other extreme are the more comprehensive programs which include social as well as directly productive elements. Partly because of the heavy financial and human resources required for such programs, however, experience with them relates mainly to specific area or regional schemes (e.g., settlement schemes) rather than to nationwide programs. This is referred to as the comprehensive approach. Finally, there are a variety of supporting programs which provide benefits to the rural poor. They usually need to be integrated with a

40

broader effort if their full potential is to be realized. A rural works program intended to help the landless laborer is one example of such an approach. A national credit scheme for smallholders would be another. Most sector-specific programs fit into this category, including those related to education, health, transport, power and water supplies for the rural poor. Such programs are described as sector or special programs in the detailed discussion. It is worth emphasizing, however, that most of the experience with rural development stems from various *ad hoc* or piecemeal approaches, and not from the application of an overall rural development plan. Thus, the classification of project activities serves mainly as a basis for organized discussion of issues, and the examples used do not necessarily reflect intention or conscious design on the part of those who originated the programs.

The Minimum Package Approach

Minimum package programs aim to provide generally modest but broad-based improvements in levels of living through increased agricultural output. Special attention is given to the sequencing of operations in the light of the development needs and requirements of the target groups on the one side, and financial and staffing constraints on the other. The great advantages of minimum package approaches are the promise of low-cost, extensive coverage with comparatively simple objectives and operating procedures. The importance of sequencing is also worth attention. An initial emphasis on a broad-based increase in productivity, through a minimum level of institutional development, may be the most effective way of ensuring mass participation in a subsequent more complex type of program.

An illustration of the approach in operation is the Minimum Package Program (MPP) established in Ethiopia in 1971, which is supported by IDA. Designed eventually to reach all the small farmers in Ethiopia, MPP provides extension, production credit, cooperative development and feeder roads in 10,000 farm family units or blocks. These blocks typically extend five kilometers on each side of a 75-kilometer stretch of all-weather road. Services are organized through specialized credit agencies and the Ministry of Agriculture, with no regional or local government participation. The experience of those working with the project suggests some important conditions for the success of this approach:

1. A first-class technical package (under the soil and rainfall conditions of Ethiopia's highlands, the application of fertilizers has produced such yield increases as to convince farmers of their usefulness without much persuasion by extension staff).

41

2. An intact social structure in the rural areas, with certain people commanding general respect being prepared to act as model farmers without remuneration.

3. A land tenure system which does not discourage production above subsistence level.

4. A loose system of credit supervision, with satisfactory repayment rates enforced through firm and visible discipline in the case of government credit.

It follows that a different approach will be necessary where the technical package itself is not markedly superior to existing practice and where the initial requirements for raising productivity are more complex—for example, where the rural poor are stratified by access to land, farm type, level of skill and occupation. This partly explains why there are few examples of this type of national program, despite its considerable advantage for countries with limited resources and massive rural poverty. Social and economic stratification in many South Asian countries, for example, would seem to preclude widespread application of the minimum package approach.

One Asian example of the minimum package approach, however, is furnished by a recent seeds improvement project which the Bank is supporting in the Republic of Korea. Under it, 500,000 farmers are to be offered improved varieties of paddy, barley, wheat, soybeans and potato so that they can raise their incomes by a modest but significant 10% over a five-year period. The program includes provision for research to improve the quality of seeds and a system of seed distribution through the national cooperative organization to individual farmers. Credit and extension services, provided mainly through cooperative societies (to which 90% of Korean farmers belong), are already adequate. The cost of the project, at 1973 prices, works out to less than $50 per family.

Under adverse conditions, provision of minimum package facilities tends to result in relatively few direct beneficiaries among the rural poor. There may, however, be favorable indirect effects stemming from minimum package programs addressed to small farmers who are not themselves sufficiently poor to be classified among the target groups on the basis of low income. For example, as small farmers become more prosperous, they tend to make more extensive use of hired labor—drawn from the poorest groups. The expanding demand for trading and transport services also tend to improve the market for hired labor. Clearly, projects for which such indirect effects on the rural poor are a major consideration merit special attention, particularly in otherwise unfavorable situations such as those where the poor themselves have little or no direct access to land.

The Comprehensive Approach

Coordinated National Programs

While most schemes under this category are specifically designed for a particular area, some countries have pursued concerted programs of rural development directed at a wide spectrum of the rural population. The programs have been characterized by careful definition of the needs and resources of the target population; detailed planning of preparation and implementation; phasing of multisectoral components; and extensive adjustments or complete restructuring of related institutions. Some of these programs, for example those in Japan, and in the Republics of China and Korea, have met with notable success. In other countries, such as Pakistan and Mexico, the programs are still at an early stage.

The success of the experience in the Republic of China is reflected by the fact that during the period 1950-70, output in the agricultural sector grew by 5% per year. In addition, the greatest increases were registered on the 890,000 farms with less than one hectare of cultivated land. These represent two-thirds of all farms and one-third of the cultivated area. The farm income of this group exceeded $300 per capita in 1970. The Taiwanese experience is characterized by the rapid adoption of new technology by a large number of small farmers; most of the increase came from improved yields, derived from the use of better inputs and the expansion of irrigation.

It is generally agreed that the success would not have been achieved without the organization of farmers into associations. Farmers are organized into a federated three-tiered system of multipurpose organizations. At the base are the small agricultural units made up of several families, who are collectively represented in the 328 township farmers' associations. Above them are 20 county associations and the apex organization. Although multipurpose, the farmers' associations have become an important source of institutional credit, and this appears to have been one of the major factors responsible for the acceleration of agricultural development. The organization of the farmers was accomplished under the aegis of an autonomous central development agency known as the Joint Commission on Rural Reconstruction (JCRR).

In contrast to the Taiwanese experience, the Mexican integrated rural development program, PIDER, is very new and thus has no spectacular achievements to report. It is of particular interest, however, because of the detailed planning and institutional adjustments that have been made. The primary objective of the program is to provide resources and services in selected rural areas in order to increase permanent and temporary employment; raise rural living standards by introducing directly productive activities; and improve basic social infrastructure and production services. The criteria for selecting regions for the programs are that each must be economically depressed, with potential for expanding agricultural, mining or industrial production; it must have at least one growth point for development; and it must have fairly high levels of unemployment and underemployment. The program reflects Mexican endeavors to improve the planning and implementation of systems for the distribution of investment and services. It also is indicative of efforts to decentralize budgeting and resource distribution at the state level, and to encourage local and state participation in the decision-making process.

Finally, there is one other example of a national approach which on grounds of general importance merits separate and detailed discussion—that of the People's Republic of China. Although application to other countries and regions is a subject for debate, the Chinese achievement itself is no longer in question. It appears to have been based on broad acceptance of communal and national goals over individualist or personal goals.

Area Development Schemes

An emphasis on area development is common in many countries, for agricultural as well as rural development projects. Basically, arguments in its favor stem from the often complex nature of the target groups; the complexity calls for specific programs locally prepared and tailored to local conditions. Technical considerations related to specific requirements for agricultural improvement also tend to favor placing development schemes in the framework of an area. Even when the focus is on promoting a single product, the very nature of modern agriculture may require a large number of inputs to be put together by private or public effort: improved varieties of seeds, or animal breeds, irrigation facilities, fertilizers and chemicals, energy and equipment, credit, extension, storage, marketing and transport services, and price incentives. One type of area approach is illustrated by a variety of "single product projects," such as the promotion of tea in Kenya, groundnuts or tobacco in Tanzania, cotton in Mali and Tanzania, and coffee in Papua New Guinea.

The special advantage of comprehensive area development projects, however, is the opportunity to focus directly on the needs of the rural poor through diversified crop and integrated farming systems. The development of these activities can then be linked with training and social services, and possibly with rural works programs. A close examination of some successful examples suggests that area or regional rural development programs can encompass a great variety of objectives, organizational forms and possible responses. At one extreme, the primary objective of some of the most successful schemes is not so much to help the poor farmer or settler as to generate additional output for disposal in the marketplace. Thus, some schemes put heavy emphasis on one or two major crops. They also provide services to growers in the form of a good technical package and credit and marketing arrangements, associated with relatively close control of farm operations and supervision of credit.

Typically, such schemes operate through a well-funded and well-staffed special authority outside the existing local civil service structure, often with little community or other direct local participation. Under such schemes, arrangements may be made to mobilize resources for schools or medical facilities, and settlement may include provision of basic amenities, like water supplies. While the impact on productivity may be an important influence, these services are typically supplied in an *ad hoc* way, without much consideration for wider programs of development. The Gezira settlement scheme in Sudan had many of these features. Begun in the 1920s, it extended over nearly 2 million acres of irrigated land by 1970, and directly benefited 75,000 farm families.

Settlement schemes have a number of special advantages. They provide an opportunity to break through modes of thought and action that are often a handicap in traditional, closely integrated and inward-looking rural communities. They also afford an escape from communities where power is concentrated in the hands of a few large landowners who are opposed to measures that are designed to reduce their special status and are likely to raise the cost of labor. The opportunity may also arise to select well-motivated settlers; and, especially where new crops are involved, the package of technical advice and services made available is likely to be accepted more readily.

An example to be contrasted with Gezira, in terms of concern with community involvement and application in the very different circumstances of long-established settlement, is provided by the Comilla projects in Bangladesh. This series of pilot schemes, designed by the Pakistan Academy of Rural Development during the period 1958-71, demonstrated a potential for substantially raising the incomes of small farmers in a limited but fairly large area within ten years. It also provided models for improved local organization and administration (at modest cost and with a limited number of professional staff), including training systems. Large numbers of people, many of them at village level, were trained in cooperative organization, pump irrigation, taxation, conciliation court procedures, Muslim family law and literacy.

45

A rural public works program, growing out of Comilla, achieved an impressive record of road building and repair, canal excavation and construction of flood embankments, serving over 4.6 million acres of farmland. An irrigation program, adopted throughout the province in 1968, had by 1972-73 placed 32,900 low-lift pumps and tubewells to irrigate an estimated 1.3 million acres. The Academy was also responsible for establishing a village cooperative credit system, with emphasis on self-help through thrift among workers. Associated in part with the credit system and farmer extension services, fertilizer use quadrupled in the area that was mostly affected, while the incomes of village farmers more than doubled. Another important innovation was a system for coordinating the activities of the various government departments in a local development center (the Thana center).

The Comilla project was fortunate in enjoying exceptionally innovative and imaginative local leadership. The success achieved was particularly impressive, given the limited resources available and an environment with many unfavorable factors. A distinctive feature was the careful phasing of program development, based both on pretesting and use of experience gained under pilot or trial schemes and on the flexible evolution of program design as further knowledge and experience were gained. While such schemes can be successful, the Comilla experience illustrates the critical importance of leadership and commitment to program goals.

A model of another type is provided by the Puebla project, developed for a relatively homogeneous area with about 50,000 small farmers in Mexico. The project, begun in 1967, is more voluntary in inspiration than Gezira and more technically agricultural in orientation than Comilla. The Puebla approach has stressed the provision of new technical packages for smallholder farmers based on local adaptive research, mostly for maize. Much of the initial work is on identifying problems concerning soil, seed, disease and cultivation practices, and on training technicians to work in small farm development. The scheme also includes credit and marketing facilities. For participating farmers, the increase in maize yields (net of climatic effect) averaged 9.5% per year over the 1968-72 period, raising farm family incomes by approximately $110. The total cost of the project over the six-year period to 1974 was approximately $1 million, or $135 per farmer receiving credit. The Puebla project has not, however, been very successful in integrating its activities into the fabric of regular governmental services, and banks must still be prodded to lend to small farmers. The Puebla research and extension functions are largely outside regular government channels. Organizations which articulate local farmers' opinions and concerns have not emerged, and are therefore not tied into the higher levels of the service system. Significantly, while the achievement is considerable, only 25% of those in the maize-growing area have responded to the project so far.

A final example, which combines some of the features already discussed, is the Lilongwe Land Development Program (LLDP) begun in 1967 in Malawi. It is the focal point in a large-scale area development approach to rural transformation. At present, the program covers an area of 1.15 million acres with a population of 550,000, most of whom are small farmers. It was organized as a special department of the Ministry of Agriculture. Access to the services and staff of other departments, including staff specially seconded to the program, has been a feature of LLDP. As a consequence, the program benefits from the close cooperation and coordination among departments that should (but often does not) flow from the integration of activities in a national policy framework.

The program has concerned itself with a wide variety of activities and functions, most notably with physical planning of subregional centers for markets and services; provision of regional infrastructure (roads, bridges, water supplies, health clinics and service buildings); consolidation of landholdings; community organizations and village committees for local participation in decision making and planning; and credit schemes—initially, unsecured loans to individuals, but with progressive adaptation to group credit systems based on shared responsibility for repayments. Considerable importance is given to agricultural extension and to the training of extension workers. (The program has trained all its field staff.) Program targets were set in relation to a 13-year development period, and a full assessment is difficult to make at this stage. It is expected that by 1980 net income per farm family in the project areas will increase 75%, accompanied by roughly doubled yields of maize, smaller increases for other crops, and improvements in animal husbandry.

There are perhaps three major potential dangers with such area development schemes:

1. As already mentioned, the schemes may concentrate a disproportionate share of the resources on providing benefits to a group that is relatively small in relation to the overall size of the national target group.

2. The schemes tend to suffer from a program design that is too ambitious and complex, calling for exceptional leadership that cannot always be made available on a sustained basis.

3. They may distort priorities in the allocation of resources among sectors.

The need for quality staff and management in such schemes is often met by providing foreign technical and financial assistance. Donor agencies have tended to favor providing large numbers of highly qualified experts (local or foreign), and often new institutional arrangements, as a condition for launching such projects. But high-powered management, with and often without foreign backing, sometimes means that too large a part of the available resources is taken for "showpiece" or "enclave" projects. Technical feasibility and economic viability, together with weak central planning and control over resource allocation, may lead to the adoption of project objectives that are unnecessarily ambitious. Sometimes a doubling or tripling of income may be feasible and economically viable but not, in the light of the overall circumstances of the country, an appropriate target. It is necessary to look closely at schemes during the design stage to see whether a modest objective—perhaps an increase in incomes by 50% over a ten-year period—might not enable significant economies to be made, particularly in the use of high-level staff.

In some cases, however, particularly in irrigation and land improvement projects, the problem lies less with the objectives than with the failure to reform the structure of landholdings. Thus, a project that doubles the carrying capacity of the land may be utilized to increase the density of settlement—so providing modest benefits to a wider group of participants. The combination of land reform and land improvement—potentially an attractive approach to rural development in conditions of land scarcity—needs to be more vigorously pursued.

The comparative affluence in terms of management and finance enjoyed under many of these projects during the implementation period often does not survive the transfer of functions to the local administrative system. Firstly, the indigenous regional administrations may not have the capability to carry out the necessary policy and coordinating functions at the regional headquarters. This capability is critical in administering complex integrated programs when they involve the activities of a number of departments and local governmental agencies, for instance, agriculture, transportation and health. Secondly, institutions to handle the commercial aspects of the programs, such as agricultural credit and input and output marketing, either do not exist—since the programs have handled these functions— or do not yet have the administrative capability to manage the activities on a large enough scale. Thirdly, the local organizations and local administrative units developed under the programs may not correspond to the existing local governmental institutions, raising difficult questions related to the maintenance and expansion of the various local services.

These problems cannot be resolved quickly and so cannot be entirely avoided if more rapid progress is to be made. The experiment with decentralization and with the working of new administrative structures and procedures must begin somewhere. If the improvement of the system is to await its functioning everywhere, it may not improve anywhere within an acceptable period of time. In fact, demonstrating the efficiency of new structures and procedures in a few pilot areas is often the only way to convince traditionalists of the feasibility, as well as the necessity, of improving the general system. This being said, however, greater efforts must be made to design area development schemes on the basis of a realistic assessment of the quality and number of the officials and technicians likely to be made available in the long term. This approach to area development should help to foster greater concern for training activities, which are a particular weakness of programs that rely heavily on expatriate manpower.

Balancing Economic and Social Components: A special aspect of the resource allocation problem in multisectoral activities concerns the balance of outlays between sectors. Projects aimed at the rural poor are likely to contain a mix of elements—directly productive components, as well as social services and amenities such as health, water supplies, basic education and village electrification. In principle, the different sectoral elements need to be consistent with individual sector objectives and should conform to a logic that is internal to the project or program as a whole so that the components are mutually reinforcing. This need to conform to a well-considered and carefully structured rural development program may result in the better design of such services than would be the case under a nonintegrated or sector program. Sector programs often reflect inappropriate standards and result in elaborate and costly services, poorly structured in terms of the overall priority needs of rural communities.

The principles involved in balancing social and economic components are, however, more easily stated than observed, and in practice a good deal of judgment regarding the inclusion of items is called for. If good sector programs do not exist, they cannot be improvised and made to work within the context of an individual rural development project. Moreover, the indirectly productive impact of such services as better health care and environmental sanitation is inherently difficult to measure, and the base of good research studies is lacking. Such difficulties add to the importance of making sure that the social service components of a rural development project are the "least costly" among alternative methods, that they are potentially replicable over broader areas, and that the recurrent costs involved can be sustained within the limits of the fiscal resources available.

Two other points are worth making about the inclusion of social services and amenities in rural development programs. Firstly, there is evidence that rural people rate selected social or amenity services— particularly health and access to water—very highly indeed, sometimes above productive benefits, as a quick means of improving the quality of life. Participation fostered through community involvement in the design, construction and use of such facilities may be the first step toward the acceptance of proposals for change relating to production techniques and methods. Secondly, it is worth recalling that the allocation of resources among sectors (as among regions) is likely to reflect a balance of considerations, and economic criteria may not necessarily be the most important. Concentration of resources in more productive areas may increase interregional inequality, particularly where migration from the less favored regions is not feasible. A relatively strong emphasis on interregional balance and equity may be justified where the poorer regions contain a heavy concentration of the rural poor (for example, in northeast Brazil) or for countries with access to an unusually generous flow of resources (like Algeria).

Sector and Special Programs

The types of activity described under this heading are usually organized on a nationwide basis. They may or may not be tailored to meet the specific needs of the rural poor. In practical terms, it is usually impossible to confine the benefits to a particular class of beneficiaries, even if that were desirable. Thus, roads built under a works program are available for the benefit of all. Schools and health facilities in rural areas can hardly turn away potential users on the ground that they are too rich to qualify. The most important feature of these programs, however, is that they generally do not, by themselves, constitute a basis for self-sustaining increases in productivity and income. Rather, they are complementary to or components of programs with this objective.

Rural Public Works: Rural public works programs have been receiving increasing attention. In the off-peak seasons, large numbers of landless laborers and very small farmers are idle or severely underemployed. Their poverty is worsened by the fact that they earn little or no income during these seasons. Rural works programs can provide direct and timely income to those needing it most, while creating productive infrastructure at low social opportunity costs. However, in practice, such programs have rarely developed their full potential. Opportunities for improvement exist in the primary benefits, and also in the secondary benefits flowing from the infrastructure created within the program. A review of past and ongoing rural works programs identifies these recurring weaknesses in the design and implementation of the primary programs:

1. The portion of total program expenditures going to unskilled workers is frequently less than it might be because unnecessarily equipment-intensive construction methods are used.

2. Projects may be poorly selected and designed, resulting in high-cost investment and low efficiency in terms of income supplements to the needy.

3. Inadequate management and supervision may produce a "make-work" character and consequent high-cost structures and low morale.

4. Some programs have tended to extend into the peak demand periods for agricultural labor.

5. When "self-help" elements are included, the poor usually are required to contribute their labor with very small or no wage payments.

6. Payment in kind is administratively cumbersome and frequently very inefficient for the workers as they resell inappropriate commodities at a large discount.

7. The appropriate blend of local initiative and decision making with central control is difficult to achieve.

8. Influential groups may alter programs so as to increase their own benefits at the cost of the poor.

Even in the best designed and managed programs, the wages of unskilled labor will not be much above one-half of total expenditures. Secondary income distribution effects flowing from the created assets may be substantially greater than the primary effects. Without careful integration into a progressive rural development program and without complementary public policies, the secondary effects may be very small for the poorest rural groups. The secondary benefits reach these groups mainly through the induced demand for labor in productive activities which arises from the infrastructure that is created. Most of the opportunities for such growth in employment is in more intensive land cultivation; this is also consistent with increased agricultural output which is a necessary condition for continuing benefits to the poor. The sustained expansion and intensification of productive activity will require complementary inputs and supportive policies and programs. The rate of induced employment generation may be quite sensitive to public policies, such as those relating to farm mechanization and intensive cropping patterns.

While the target groups among the rural poor gain from secondary employment, the owners of assets, especially land, typically obtain large benefits from the infrastructure created. The benefits constitute one motivation for the political support of public works programs by

51

nontarget groups, which is a necessary condition for the success of these programs in most countries. However, if landownership is highly inequitable, the incidence of the secondary benefits will be similarly inequitable, and the public recovery of part of the landowner's benefits should have high priority. The services of some created assets can be priced, but in many cases land and income taxes would be necessary. Some governments may be tempted to introduce public works programs as a substitute for more fundamental reforms and policies which promote a sustained growth in income for the rural poor. Such a course of action should be resisted because the scope for immediately reducing underemployment and poverty—necessarily limited by budgetary constraints and a shortage of suitable projects—would be offset by the inequitable distribution of the secondary benefits of the program.

The most important general conclusion is that public works need to be part of a larger employment and development strategy. They have to be used in coordination with other programs and activities if their potential is to be developed fully. Basic decisions on such issues as target groups, wage levels, location and type of projects, taxes or other measures to recoup secondary benefits, and program administration would then be made in conjunction with national or regional development planning. In particular, such planning must ensure that the output of wage goods increases to match the higher demand for such goods created by any large-scale works program. Public works activities should also be coordinated with specific local development schemes. Public works, particularly because they are decentralized in implementation, provide an excellent opportunity to begin local-level planning but this potential generally remains unrealized.

Education and Training: A major share of public sector outlays for which the impact on the rural poor is an important justification relates to education. Here attention is focused on minimum learning needs for all members of rural society. Such "basic education"[3] includes functional literacy and numeracy, and knowledge and skills required for earning a living, operating a household (including family health, child care, nutrition and sanitation) and civic participation. Thus defined, basic education is the minimum of education necessary for an acceptable rate of development, and for the wider distribution of its benefits.

In many countries, basic education can be offered partly through the primary school system, but major constraints in providing it to the

---

[3] *This has been defined as the threshold level of learning required for effective participation in productive life as well as in social and political processes.*

rural poor have been time and cost. Considerable interest has, therefore, been shown in schemes for providing nonformal and more cost-effective education and training to adults and adolescents. Many of the schemes surveyed as part of a recent Bank-sponsored study indicated typically small-scale operations promoted by a wide variety of different agencies and often not integrated into a national education system or development plan.[4] The study drew particular attention to:

1. The need for the horizontal integration of rural education programs, both with other education activities and with other development activities in the same geographic area, and vertical integration with organizations and services at higher levels to provide support and backstopping services.

2. The need for the decentralization of planning and management so that education activities can be effectively adapted to local needs and conditions.

3. The need for greater equity to avoid widening the socioeconomic gaps in rural areas. Worthy of particular note is the neglect of training for women, although the importance of their roles in making decisions and doing farm work is acknowledged.

To meet the needs of rural development, primary education has to be improved, particularly to reduce wastage, lower costs and raise quality. Other possibilities invite further experimentation, including adjustments with regard to age of entry in school, length of cycle, size of class, simplification of curricula, use of mass media, and adaptation of indigenous learning systems. A number of other actions might also be taken to spread basic education more effectively to the rural poor:

1. Schooling should be integrated with employment and development. This may be done through skill training of those who have left the schools, or through a program, such as that of Botswana, where practical skill training directly related to the creation of new opportunities for self-employment is given in the schools.

2. Rural education should be functional in serving specific target groups and in meeting identified needs.

3. Rural education programs should be designed as part of a total education delivery system. They can themselves become the focus of coordinated action through the use of multipurpose centers to serve other activities, such as cooperatives and health services. This is being done in Tanzania at both district and village levels through the establishment of Rural Training Centers and Community Education Centers.

---

[4] *Coombs, P.H., with Ahmed, M. Attacking Rural Poverty: How Nonformal Education Can Help. Prepared for the World Bank by the International Council on Educational Development. Baltimore and London: The Johns Hopkins University Press, 1974.*

4. Rural education projects should be integrated with other development activities, and linked wherever possible to the provision of other appropriate inputs and services. This has been effectively demonstrated in a number of integrated rural development projects, such as the Comilla project in Bangladesh and the PACCA program (Program on Agricultural Credit and Cooperation in Afghanistan). It may also be achieved through the design of functional literacy programs.

5. The provision of basic education and training should be designed flexibly to make use of existing facilities and resources, and to use mobile units in order to remain replicable in terms of costs and management requirements.

Credit: Credit schemes illustrate some of the difficulties encountered in sectoral programs. The Bank's paper on *Agricultural Credit* draws attention to a number of common deficiencies and problems in lending to small farmers. In particular, large farmers have been the main beneficiaries of institutional credit. Commonly, 60% to 80% of the small farmers in a given country have limited or no access to institutional credit. Moreover, the available supply of credit is heavily skewed in favor of short-term credit, particularly in the case of small farmers. Although not always essential, the conditions under which credit is needed and can be used effectively are characterized by:

1. Clear opportunities for economic gain from adoption of new production technology or other improvements.

2. Widespread recognition and acceptance of such opportunities on the part of the farmer, along with access to training in the necessary skills.

3. Delivery systems which provide ready and timely availability of the inputs required, and market outlets for farm production.

For small farmers, it is essential to provide a comprehensive package if the potential for increased productivity is to be translated into a commercial reality. There appears to be scope for using institutional credit to replace or augment credit from traditional sources in order to check monopoly situations which cause excessively high interest rates; to overcome inelasticities in the supply of credit which become apparent when new opportunities emerge; to ease the seasonal financial problems of rural households; and, most importantly, to encourage small subsistence farmers to raise their output and enter the commercial sector. Furthermore, land reform, if pursued widely, could sharply increase the credit needs of the former tenants who were previously supplied by landlords. In this general context, several recent experiments warrant further examination, including the "passbook" scheme in Pakistan, the Cooperative Production Credit Scheme in Kenya, and the Masagana 99 program in the Philippines.

Other Sector Programs: Other specific sector programs—for example those concerned with the provision of feeder roads, village electrification, water supplies, health facilities and the promotion of rural industry—may be important means of conveying benefits to the rural poor. The major issues involved have been covered earlier—namely, the need to integrate such programs with programs of rural development and with particular projects, and choosing appropriate design standards suited to rural conditions. The latter is a serious problem for a number of these services, and in some cases, pending further technical development, extension of facilities to villages will remain prohibitively expensive. One reason for the neglect of the small-scale system suitable for the rural areas is the convenience and lower unit cost of preparing and appraising projects for larger undertakings that are better suited to the urban environment or, in the case of transport, for interurban connections. Here too, however, recent research indicates some promising new approaches calculated to reduce difficulties in the future.

The promotion of rural industry in the context of rural development merits special attention. In many countries, existing village crafts are disappearing rapidly, while modernization of agriculture creates a demand for new inputs and consumer goods which could often be produced locally. If these two trends can be combined through relevant planning and support measures, the outcome might be modernized local industrial structures, geared to serving the rural areas and with linkages to national industry as well. Such rural industry could provide employment, increase incomes, slow rural-urban migration, increase the supply of goods and services to farmers at lower cost and generally stimulate further rural and regional development.

Expansion of rural industry at an early stage of agricultural development may, in the long run, permit a more rational spatial distribution of industrial and economic activity than might otherwise occur. Much of rural industry is likely to be located in market towns. That would generally be a more desirable form of urbanization than the expansion of already large urban centers. Modernization of agriculture creates a demand which has great potential for pulling certain categories of industries into rural towns. These industries are, in general, small; and their interaction with medium and large enterprises is, in the long run, essential. Consequently, some urban-based industry can be decentralized, with little or no economic sacrifice, in order to achieve better interaction and more balanced distribution of industrial activity. At the same time, with an industrial base to provide for continuing expansion and development, such regional centers can serve to attract and retain professional and technical skills that otherwise tend to concentrate in the major cities.

Apart from the linkages with agriculture itself, there are other important cross-sectoral requirements for rural industry. Thus, at some stage, the villages must have access to electricity for productive purposes. It is equally essential to develop the capacity to design and manufacture simple producer goods appropriate for small-scale village industry. The reservoir of potential skills—technical and entrepreneurial—in the rural areas is often large. Without special efforts, however, to upgrade the skills, to improve tools, to diversify production, to open up markets and to change the outlook of the artisans, this important asset threatens to disappear. In many circumstances, the mechanization of agriculture requires small pumps and motors (up to 20 or 25 horsepower), as well as the services of tractor drivers, tubewell operators, tractor and small-motor mechanics, and people skilled in maintaining and repairing mechanical equipment. Rural homes need basic furniture and improved kitchen utensils. Such requirements are either not fulfilled or are met from the cities. It would seem natural to upgrade the skills and organization of village blacksmiths, carpenters, shoemakers, weavers and potters, so that they could assume new manufacturing and service roles in modernizing rural communities. This kind of support should be part of an integrated plan to modernize and develop rural communities.

Thus, in the same way that agricultural extension services are considered essential for introduction of new technology and development of agriculture, industrial extension should also be seen as a necessary element in developing rural industry. Essential characteristics of such an extension service are mobility and relevance to rural industries in meeting local demands. An important aspect of any such program must be the development and support of the existing industrial structure in order to capitalize on the base of technical and entrepreneurial skills which today exist in villages, market towns and urban centers. Development of rural industries requires a nationally supported program to provide inputs like credit, raw materials and equipment, electricity, training for technical and managerial skills, and efforts for research, development and engineering. Provision of such a package is, in principle, facilitated by linking efforts with a rural development program. Indeed, the general lack of rural development planning cannot be more clearly illustrated than by the weakness of current efforts to promote rural industry.

The variety of programs and approaches that have been examined confirms that no single package or formula is likely to be either necessary or sufficient for effective rural development. On the contrary, the activity mix most likely to work is the one that is tailored to fit a particular, and probably unique, set of conditions and country circumstances. A number of other general conclusions are listed below in summary form.

The experience of rural development programs and projects appears to confirm that:

1. It is possible to reach large numbers of the rural poor at moderate cost, with reasonable expectations of acceptable economic returns.

2. If this is to be done, it involves political commitment to a strategy for rural development and to the general policies necessary to support such a strategy.

3. Low-cost delivery systems for supplying inputs on credit terms, for providing extension and marketing services, and for organizing communal activities are of crucial importance in reaching large numbers of the rural poor. Greater use of special financial intermediaries, cooperatives, community groups and farmers' associations should be explored.

4. It is important to balance overall central control with decentralized regional and project planning. Rural development projects require a degree of flexibility in design and in responding to the lessons of experience, but flexibility must be within the limits of minimum national or regional standards and financial resources.

5. Greater efforts should be made to integrate project management into existing and, if necessary, reformed central and local government organizations and procedures.

6. It is important to involve the rural poor in the planning and implementation of rural development programs.

7. Increased training is necessary at the local level, particularly for development managers, regional and project planners, cooperative staff and extension agents.

8. Equitable and adequate provision should be made for the recovery of costs in order to provide funds for additional rural development projects in other areas.

9. Technical packages have to be devised, appropriate to the requirements of small farmers and based on adaptive national research.

10. It is necessary to improve knowledge of national resources and provide an improved flow of disaggregated information as a basis for realistic national, regional and rural project planning.

11. Although increases in output can be achieved with existing technology, increases in productivity will require new technology suitable for use by small farmers.

57

Chapter 3: THE WORLD BANK'S PROGRAM

Past Trends

The major thrust of the World Bank's activities in rural areas has been in lending for agricultural development. The Bank is now the largest single external source of funds for direct investment for agricultural development in developing countries. This is the result of a purposeful shift of emphasis in the Bank's policy over the past five years. It reflects, firstly, a change in the Bank's perception of development and its underlying processes; and, secondly, an awareness of the growing pressures on the agricultural and rural sectors in developing countries. These shifts have been characterized by changes in the pattern of lending, including changes in its sectoral distribution, by a widening and deepening of the lending program, and by the emergence of "new style" projects.

Change in Lending Patterns

Sectoral Changes: In the early years of the Bank's operations, the lending for agricultural development was relatively small. Between fiscal 1948 and fiscal 1960, 17% of all Bank projects and 6% of total Bank investments were for agriculture. Subsequently, it became apparent that greater agricultural output was not only necessary for the expansion of most economies, but was perhaps the only way to achieve growth in many areas. There was a corresponding increase in the share of lending for agriculture. (See Figure.) As a result, lending for agriculture rose from 12% of the total in fiscal 1961-65 to 24% of a much bigger total in fiscal 1973-74. (See Annex 8.)

Widening of Lending: In the early years of the Bank's operations, the emphasis was on the transfer of capital and the development of capital-intensive projects, notably in irrigation. From fiscal 1947 to fiscal 1970, 48% of all Bank investment in agriculture was in irrigation. Between fiscal 1961 and fiscal 1965, the proportion for irrigation was 79%. Since then, although investment in irrigation has increased in absolute terms, the proportion has fallen—to about 30% in the years since fiscal 1970. (See Annex 9.) The Bank will continue to invest in irrigation. But the growing realization that agricultural development involves a whole complex of interdependent components has led to a substantial widening of the patterns of lending for agriculture—including investments in tertiary canals and land leveling to ensure that irrigation water is used effectively at the farm level.

By the mid-1960s the Bank was financing a wider range of activities—agricultural and livestock credit, storage, marketing, processing, fish-

**World Bank/IDA Lending for All Sectors, and for
Agriculture and Rural Development, FY1950—74**

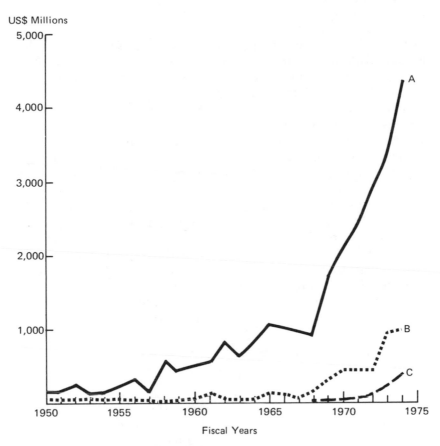

A: Lending for all sectors
B: Lending for agriculture
C: Lending for rural development

eries and forestry development. Much more emphasis was given to promoting technological change at the farm level through programs to enable farmers to acquire improved seed, fertilizers and equipment. The Bank has also recognized the importance of agricultural research by supporting both individual projects and international research institutions. In addition, individual projects are becoming more comprehensive. They now include not only a greater variety of agricultural elements, but also nonagricultural components such as rural roads, health, training and water supply.

Deepening of Lending: In recent years, there has been an increasing awareness that agricultural growth does not necessarily diminish rural poverty. As a result the Bank has been attempting to "deepen" its lending in the rural sector as part of a program intended to help lower-income producers to become more productive. This is indicated, firstly, by the fact that the poorer countries have been receiving a greater proportion of Bank funds, and a deliberate effort has been made to reach more of the lower-income groups through projects. In fiscal 1954-68, $138.8 million, or 22.5%, of the lending for agriculture was for countries with per capita GNP lower than $150. During fiscal 1969-74, the figure rose to $1,356 million, or 38.2%, of the total lending for agriculture. (See Annex 10.) Secondly, between fiscal 1968-72, the percentage of Bank-assisted agricultural projects where the participating farmers owned less than five hectares rose from 17% to 67%. Since there is some correlation between size of holding and income, this indicates that Bank lending has been increasingly directed toward lower-income groups. Finally, there has been an increase in lending for projects that are directly focused in some way on providing benefits to the rural poor. (See Annexes 11 and 12.) The number of such projects increased from five in fiscal 1968 to 28 in fiscal 1974, involving an increase in lending from over $29 million to almost $474 million. The projects accounted for 17% of all lending for agriculture in fiscal 1968, but 47% of a much larger total in fiscal 1974.[1]

Emergence of "New Style" Projects

The changes in emphasis that have taken place over time, and the focus on reduction of poverty, have necessitated the introduction of what might be termed "new style" projects. These have been designed to encompass some, though not all, of the characteristics desired for rural development, as described in Chapter 2. The main elements of the projects are:

1. They are designed to benefit large numbers of the rural poor, while earning an economic rate of return, that is, at least equal to the opportunity cost of capital.

2. They are comprehensive in their approach to small-scale agriculture and provide for a balance between directly productive and other components (where inclusion of the latter is appropriate).

---

[1] *A word of caution is in order regarding these figures. Until recently, a large number of projects did not describe the beneficiary group in any detail, and it is not easy to determine the intentions of a project precisely several years after it was prepared. The large increase in fiscal 1974 compared with earlier years owes something to the better definition of project objectives, but the underlying change remains a considerable one.*

3. They have a low enough cost per beneficiary, so that they could be extended to other areas, given the availability of additional resources.

The "new style" projects have included a variety of approaches. They are intended to reach large numbers of people through area development, settlement, irrigation and land improvement schemes. Most of the projects have an agricultural base and involve technological change—frequently the introduction of water, credit, improved seed and fertilizer. Many of the projects also include some diversification of agricultural production. The area projects often have some social components—health services, basic education and water supplies. Whenever possible, costs have been held down by evolving low-cost delivery systems and working through intermediaries that can absorb some of the overhead costs—notably farmers' associations, cooperatives and other groups. Much remains to be done in this regard.

The expansion of "new style" projects has led to a substantial change in the nature of lending for agriculture. An analysis of the appraisal reports for 56 agricultural loans approved in fiscal 1974 shows that:

1. In 38 projects for which information is available, the number of beneficiaries is expected to total 11.8 million. The total does not include beneficiaries who are not farm operators, such as farm laborers and others whose incomes might have risen because of a project.

2. The average income per beneficiary before the projects were started was $69 per year; but the range of beneficiaries' incomes was from $22 to $1,460 per year.

3. The projects, taken as a whole, involve a total investment of $2,000 million, and are expected to lead to an average increase in income of 7.3% per year over the development period (an average of eight years).

4. The average cost per beneficiary is $160; however, five projects accounted for 8 million of the 12 million beneficiaries at a cost per beneficiary of only $17 and the increase in income expected from these five projects is also much less than the average increase for the projects taken as a group.

The change in the Bank's philosophy on agricultural development over the years, as reflected in the pattern of lending for agriculture, can be summarized as follows:

1. The share of agriculture in total lending has increased considerably; and, within agriculture, poverty-oriented projects now have a larger share.

2. The share of the poorest countries in lending for both agriculture and poverty-oriented projects has increased significantly.

3. The number of people benefiting directly from the Bank's operations in agriculture is increasing.

4. Based on information from the Bank's appraisal reports, the production of the beneficiaries, including many of the rural poor, are expected to increase at a rate higher than the 5% target suggested in Mr. McNamara's Nairobi speech. But it must be remembered that this increase is for Bank-assisted projects only; the share of such projects in total investment in agriculture and rural development in developing countries is relatively small.

The Way Ahead

The extent to which direct programs to improve the lot of the rural poor can be launched and "new style" projects pursued will be determined by: (1) the extent to which the goals of equity and growth can be reconciled; and (2) the size of the resources available in relation to the magnitude of the problem.

Reconciling Goals

An important question for the Bank and member governments is whether, or to what extent, greater emphasis on rural development implies a diversion of resources away from meeting the urgent need for increasing food production. The possibility of such diversion arises for various reasons. Among these are:

1. Heavy investment in projects for those with the lowest incomes could lead to a concentration of effort on a group which commands a small proportion of the basic resource required for food production land. Based on a sample of 52 developing countries, if the poor smallholders are considered to control less than two hectares of land per family, collectively they would control only about 16% of the arable land.

2. It is sometimes more difficult and takes more time to provide services to large numbers of small farmers than to a smaller number of large farmers. The Bank's experience indicates that the cost of providing credit to small farmers can run 14 percentage points or more above that for large farmers. Similarly, large numbers of small farmers need more extension workers, so there may be a diversion of scarce resources away from larger producers in addition to the higher costs of expanding these services.

3. The urgency of the need to expand food supplies over the next few years may mean that investment resources will have to be concentrated in areas where the potential is greatest for substantially increasing food production within a short period of time. Farmers in these

areas might well be better off in terms of resource endowment and infrastructure; they may not be among the rural poverty target groups.

However, rural development does not necessarily conflict with the objectives of higher food production. Small farmers are often more efficient in the use of resources on the farm than are large farmers. Most of the rural poor are engaged in agricultural production, so that any steps taken to help them to become more productive will add to agricultural output. The food problem is most severe in the South Asian and African countries which have the greatest concentration of absolute rural poverty; in many of these countries, the distribution of land and income is such that raising the agricultural output of the low-income groups in rural areas is the only means by which both production and consumption of food can be increased. This applies also to the landless workers for whom rural public works can lead to the creation of productive facilities as well as generating income to purchase food. Finally, at a more general level, the poorest rural families who do not themselves produce sufficient food for their own needs stand to suffer most from shortages and high prices of food.

The Bank recognizes the interdependence of the two objectives of increasing food production and alleviating poverty in rural areas. Its policy is to aid all agricultural producers, but to put the emphasis on deepening the lending to help small-scale farmers—those with holdings of up to five hectares (including those within the low-income target groups)—who account for 40% of the land cultivated in developing countries. A policy of assisting agricultural development, with emphasis on smaller farms and rural development to help the rural poor, will contribute both to raising food output and alleviating rural poverty.

Resource Requirements

The Nairobi speech set the ambitious target of raising the annual rate of growth of output of small farmers to 5% by 1985.[2] Achieving such a target requires that demand, for domestic consumption and for export, increase sufficiently to maintain producer prices; that institutional and organizational constraints be eased; and that resources be mobilized to assist small farmers. The experience of countries and of the Bank itself in implementing projects confirms that, in many instances, finance alone is not the limiting factor in bringing about a sustained increase in output among small-scale producers; frequently technological, organizational, procedural and manpower difficulties

---

[2] As explained in Chapter I, the target poverty group has been changed from the acreage basis in the Nairobi speech to an absolute and relative income basis. Nevertheless, the 5% target rate of growth refers to all small-scale farmers and not just those in the lowest-income groups.

limit the effective use of additional investment. Nevertheless, it is possible to give some rough estimates of investment needs.

Although the estimates were obtained through two different approaches they yielded broadly similar results. The first approach was based on a simple model so that some analysis might be made of how sensitive the results were to crucial assumptions and policies. The second approach drew directly on the Bank's experience.

The parameters of the model include the capital-output ratio, the rate of depreciation of capital, the population growth rate of small farm households, the time-lag before investment becomes productive, and the share of the benefits from investment which accrue to small farmers. Calculations based on this model yielded an estimate of $70,000 million as the total cumulative capital cost of achieving by 1985 an annual growth rate of 5% in small farmers' production. To maintain this rate of growth beyond 1985, annual investment expenditures of approximately $20,000 million would be needed. Moreover, the estimate of total cost derived from such calculations is sensitive both to variations in the share of benefits assumed to accrue to the target group and to different assumptions about rates of population growth. For example, an overall production growth rate of 5% might be achieved with either a population growth rate of 1% per year and a per capita production increase of 4% or a population growth of 3% with a per capita production increase of 2%. Calculations based on the model indicate that cumulative investment costs by 1985 would be $5,000 million lower in the first of these cases, that is, with a lower rate of growth of population.

Calculations based on the Bank's own experience also show that the share of project benefits accruing to the target population has an important influence on estimates of the total cost of reaching the objectives outlined in the Nairobi speech. As indicated in Annex 11, there was a subset of 25 agricultural projects (single and multisector) approved in fiscal 1974 where at least 50% of the direct beneficiaries are likely to be farm families with annual incomes below $50 per capita. Including those outside this poverty group (a substantial number of whom would nevertheless be small farmers with holdings of less than five hectares), these projects are expected to benefit some 11 million people. As a result of the projects, net output per farm family is projected to increase by more than 5% per year over an eight year development period, beginning from a level of annual income that averages approximately $60 per capita. With total project costs of almost $900 million, the average project cost is under $80 per capita. If sufficient projects at this average per capita cost of $80 could be implemented solely for the rural poor (expected to number 700 million by the end of the 1970s), the implied global cost would be $56,000 million. But if it is not feasible to reduce the per capita cost significantly, nor desirable to increase the percentage of direct beneficiaries among the rural poor (as distinct from other small farmers) above the 50% level that is representative of recent Bank experience, the overall cost of projects and programs with direct benefits for the rural poor and small farmers could amount to over $100,000 million.

These estimates are, however, subject to a substantial margin of error because:

1. The mix of investment opportunities during the next decade could vary significantly from that in fiscal 1974 (though a provisional analysis of Bank-assisted projects in fiscal 1975 indicates a pattern similar to that of fiscal 1974).

2. Indirect beneficiaries, such as landless laborers, are not included in the project appraisal estimates.

3. It is uncertain how far projects can be designed differently in order to reduce the costs and increase the benefits.

4. Greater government commitment, more appropriate government policies, and better rural, regional and project planning could also result in significant economies and greater benefits.

5. The cost estimates do not necessarily include all those costs which are external to the projects but essential for broader programs of rural development.

6. Because output may increase faster in the future than consumer demand, farm-gate prices may decline and hence the net benefits may be less.

On some counts, even the higher estimate of $100,000 million would seem a remarkably modest amount for providing the impetus for sustainable increases in productivity and real income for the rural poor. Estimates of income, savings and investments in the developing countries, including the petroleum and mineral exporters, indicate that total investments in developing countries in 1974 would be approximately $170,000 million. Allowing for phasing over, say, a 10-year period, $10,000 million per year for rural development would account for only 6% of this total. But for the low-income developing countries (those with per capita incomes below $200 at 1967-69 prices), the picture is very different. Their total investment in 1974 would be of the order of $25,000 million. In their case the investment required for rural development would be large relative to the availability of resources, since these countries account for more than 60% of the rural poor. The regional breakdown is shown in Annex 13.

The Lending Program

There are many constraints in lending for agriculture and rural development. Nonetheless, the compelling financial and human needs of the rural sector justify an ambitious five-year target. Under the Bank's lending program for fiscal 1969-73, $3,400 million was allocated to agricultural development, or about 20% of total lending over this period. The preliminary fiscal 1974-78 program allocated 26% of total lending to agricultural development, i.e., $6,500 million (at constant fiscal 1974 prices). Omitting the amount for fiscal 1974 and adding that for fiscal 1979 would increase this figure to approximately $7,200 million for the five-year period, fiscal 1975-79. Based on past experience of cost-sharing, this would involve a total investment of approximately $15,000 million in the rural sectors of developing countries.

Assuming a program of $7,200 million for agriculture and rural development, the question arises of how the resources are to be allocated within the rural sector. Past trends in lending, and particularly the experience in fiscal 1975, indicate that it is possible to design "new style" projects that can fulfill many of the objectives of Bank policy. Close to half of the loans approved in fiscal 1974 were for "new style" projects; and the indications are that this will be true of a large proportion of those approved in fiscal 1975 also. While information is limited about the projects in the latter part of the five-year period, there is every reason to expect that a high proportion of "new style" projects can be maintained during fiscal 1976-79.

The Bank, therefore, plans to double the fiscal 1974 or fiscal 1975 level of lending for rural development by fiscal 1979. This implies a total Bank/IDA investment rising from $500 million in fiscal 1975 to $1,000 million in fiscal 1979 (at 1974 prices). Over the five-year period, this would represent one-half of the total projected Bank/IDA lending for agriculture and rural development. Allowing for local contributions and other funds, the proposed lending program would support a total annual investment program of approximately $2,000 million by fiscal 1979. This is 20% to 30% of the annual requirement for financing the target of a production increase of 5% per year, i.e., $70,000-$100,000 million spread over 10 years would average $7,000-$10,000 million a year.

The proposed lending program would test the absorptive capacity of many developing countries, especially the poorest countries most in need of external resources. Substantial new efforts to mobilize local resources would be needed, together with organizational changes to utilize existing resources more effectively. The role of the Bank in supporting such changes is discussed later. In some countries, the changes will call for a greater degree of political and social commitment to the general objectives of rural development than has been evident so far.

An analysis of the projected lending program for agriculture (based on the aggregate of the country lending program projections) shows some differences between the regional distribution of lending and the regional distribution of the rural poor. In particular, the concentration of the rural poor in South Asia considerably exceeds the share of this region in total projected Bank lending for agriculture. If the proposed program of lending for agriculture and rural development were distributed among regions according to regional concentrations of rural poverty, the projected lending for South Asia in these sectors would need to be more than double the present prospective regional total. The calculation reflects the fact that South Asia accounts for 75% of the 360 million rural poor in the low-income, resource-poor group of countries. Annexes 13 and 14 provide the details.

The South Asian problem is numerically by far the most severe and, in view of the poverty of the countries involved, probably the most intractable. It is likely that rural development projects will play a considerably greater role in South Asia than in the past. For one thing, the previous emphasis on agricultural credit operations (which accounted for more than 50% of all agricultural lending for South Asia in the fiscal 1969-73 period, and were not primarily oriented toward specifically identified target groups of rural poor) was greatly reduced in the fiscal 1975 program. This change in emphasis is confirmed by estimated totals of agricultural lending Bank-wide by type of project, as planned for the fiscal 1975-79 period. Compared with fiscal 1969-73, the fiscal 1975-79 share of area development projects (which include area-based rural development projects) will increase from 6% to 30%, the increase being matched by declines in the relative importance of credit operations, irrigation projects and livestock projects.

Should additional resources become available, the claims of agriculture and rural development, particularly in South Asia, seem persuasive. Questions concerning the technical and other assistance which the Bank can supply for this purpose are taken up later in this Chapter.

The proposed program is unlikely to be achieved unless the Bank maintains a major effort to support and further develop innovative approaches to project design and implementation. It is difficult to foresee the forms these innovations might take, but some of the kinds of changes that will be needed are already embodied in recent projects. Many of them might be suitable for application on a wider scale. For example, a recent IDA-supported project in Upper Volta has established a Rural Development Fund. Its purpose is, in part, to deal with the uncertainties of government finance, particularly after the project implementation period has ended, and to mobilize additional local resources. A model for capitalizing effectively on the benefits of new agricultural research is provided by a seeds project in the Republic of Korea. The project is to help establish a modern seeds industry in that country, including the capacity to undertake continuing research into a range of crops. It is expected to increase the incomes of a large group of farmers at very low cost. This is an example of a national minimum package program.

Another project in Asia—the Keratong land settlement project in Malaysia—includes the financing of project towns in the settlement area. It provides an example of a linked or integrated approach to rural development that includes recognition of the impact on regional urban settlement. In this project, there is a positive attempt to provide for the conditions and facilities calculated to be necessary to attract skilled persons away from the largest cities and to reduce the migration of the unskilled, partly educated rural youth to these cities. In Eastern Africa, the Kigoma project in western Tanzania is an example of the use of a regional government authority for project management. The broad range of skills and expertise thus available enables a variety of services to be financed under the title of a regional development plan, of which the project itself is the core. The project is also providing finance for the preparation of other rural development programs in the context of improved regional and rural planning.

Another feature of growing significance is the support for ongoing programs of rural development where there is sufficient experience or commitment on the part of the government, and where scope exists for improving the design and increasing the effectiveness of the program. One example is the Mauritius rural development project, which supports the rural works program there. Others include a project in India which supports the Government's programs for drought-prone areas; another in Mexico which supports the Government's PIDER program of rural development; and a third in Indonesia which will provide services and facilities for improved training of local officials in program formulation and implementation relating to the INPRES program of rural works.

Many of these are nationwide programs, or have the potential to become nationwide programs. Increasing importance will be attached to supporting a range of project activities under the umbrella of an overall strategy or rural development plan. A series of projects in Nigeria provides one example of this approach. The size of the Mexican PIDER program referred to above implies that it is, in effect, a series of projects that can be packaged as one because of the common philosophy and set of objectives to which they relate.

68

It is likely that the proposed program will also require greater efforts to prepare multisectoral, integrated programs, involving not only a mix of directly productive and social elements, but also a greater range of productive components than is now the case. In particular, it is highly desirable in some areas to prepare integrated rural industry projects, involving as possible components rural electrification, training and credit as well as agricultural elements. Such efforts might fit particularly well into the later phases of the multistage type of project activity that will be called for in the more sophisticated environment. There will also have to be a greater emphasis on helping the landless through industrial and training types of projects, as well as single or multisector efforts focused on training and education more specifically designed for rural people. Multisectoral approaches are especially suitable for providing rural health, family planning and other social services. For example, the Bank will help to introduce selected elements of reformed health services into rural development projects, and to link control operations for specific diseases (such as river blindness and sleeping sickness) with rural development programs.

In addition to innovation and experiments with new approaches, however, it is necessary that the Bank's experience in more conventional types of activities be used in dealing with concentrations of rural poverty—through schemes of general land improvement, irrigation, clearance for settlement or drainage, credit programs, and programs for more specialized groups such as fishermen and herdsmen. Support for such activities will be further extended into the most challenging and difficult agro-ecological areas, such as those of the Sahel and the mountainous regions of Latin America. This will involve more national research and pilot testing of technology and special institutional arrangements in particular areas. According to the needs and circumstances of each country, therefore, there will continue to be a mix of minimum package, area development, national comprehensive and public works programs in the rural areas.

Two other points can be made. Firstly, the innovation and experimentation in rural development will inevitably yield some failures. But the risks can be reduced by providing facilities for monitoring and evaluation, so that the lessons of experience are learnt. Secondly, the Bank's program—ambitious as it is—will scarcely keep pace over the five-year period with the increase in the numbers of the rural poor resulting from population growth. The increase could amount to 70 million, while the number of the rural poor benefiting from these programs will probably not exceed 60 million. (The total number of beneficiaries, including those outside the target groups, can be estimated at 100 million.)

Deployment of Bank Resources

What other steps are necessary to ensure that the manner in which the Bank processes projects is conducive to meeting specific targets and the broader policy objectives? Recent actions have included providing guidelines for rural sector work and for elements of the Bank's policies and procedures which might be considered constraints on designing, processing and implementing rural development projects; assisting governments with in-depth research; increasing resources for agriculture and rural development; and improving control and monitoring procedures.

It is important to spell out at an early stage in project identification the basic project rationale together with a broad project profile. This should indicate the number of farmers and other target groups; their income classes; the projected impact on productivity; the cost of the project and its replicability; and a breakdown showing how much of the investment is directly productive and how much is not. This would help to point up the institutional constraints at the local and national levels, define the scope of the project, and indicate the nature and extent of components which should or should not be included.

The Project Cycle

Project Identification

Internal monitoring of the progress of economic, sector and project work is very useful for reviewing progress in meeting the objectives. But if the system is to provide a more positive stimulus, other action is required.

Firstly, an intensive effort is needed at the level of country economic and sector work in order both to provide guidance and support for project planning strategies and tactics, and to facilitate more systematic consideration of rural development criteria in the selection and design of projects. Agriculture and rural development sector work is essentially of two kinds: that which is needed to support country economic work, and that which facilitates project identification. The concern here is with the latter; it has to be given higher priority.

Rural sector studies need to be oriented toward: (1) identifying and focusing on target zones and populations; (2) assessing technological constraints and the potential for small farms; (3) examining infrastructure requirements; (4) evaluating the capacity of existing service systems and their potential; (5) reviewing the administrative arrangements and capability for the rural sector; and (6) examining national policies relating to rural development. Preliminary guidelines to encourage such an approach have been issued and will be reviewed from time to time in the light of experience.

It is not feasible to present a statistically complete picture of sector work because some sector work is done on other kinds of missions—reconnaissance, appraisal and supervision. Thus, it is difficult to find a standard to measure the output of varied sector work activities. But the work program for the next four years is being developed. In addition to the Bank's program, the U.N. Food and Agriculture Organization (FAO) plans to have "Country Perspective Studies" in Malaysia, Burma and the Sahelian countries of Western Africa. Work is just ending on Iraq, Iran, Pakistan and Bangladesh. The International Labour Office (ILO) is also planning rural development country studies under its World Employment Program. The Bank and FAO are now actively coordinating their sector work and have established informal cooperative arrangements with ILO in order to avoid duplication.

Experience so far suggests the usefulness of a new type of activity known as rural reconnaissance missions, to supplement agricultural sector studies, especially in the integration of agriculture and other sector work, and the evaluation of governments' rural development programs. Such reconnaissance missions may be restricted to one region or one area of a country, as opposed to studying the rural sector as a whole, but they have a broader purview than a project mission. They are particularly useful in assessing new government proposals for rural development which are larger than a project but provide the administrative context within which rural development may be organized. Their function thus falls between that of a typical Bank project mission and a sector mission.

A clear program for project identification needs to be developed. It would include both sector and subsector review missions and rural reconnaissance missions. The development of such a program is likely to mean that more resources will have to be devoted to identifying and preparing a pipeline of projects.

Project Preparation

Because the number and variety of components in rural development projects make their design a complex task, a relatively long lead time is required for project preparation. Since constraints on increasing the Bank's manpower resources (including consultants) are likely to continue, it is necessary to examine the feasibility of rearranging the time spent on the various phases of the project cycle.

The identification and preparation of rural development projects is not well organized in many developing countries. Consequently, additional assistance is required and could take one or more of the following forms:

1. Technical assistance to establish or strengthen planning and programming units.

2. Expanding the project preparation capacity of the Cooperative Programs with FAO, the World Health Organization (WHO) and the United Nations Industrial Development Organization (UNIDO).

3. Introducing a special type of project, which might be termed rural preparation, the purpose of which would be to design rural development projects in detail prior to the appraisal of the actual projects themselves. This activity would be analogous to the "engineering credits" used in the first phase of some transportation projects.

4. Making more use of pilot projects, but on a scale sufficient to test the scope for expansion.

The extent to which the Bank needs to shift and/or increase its resources for rural development work will depend in part on the degree to which member governments develop project planning and programming units. Experience confirms the great importance of establishing decentralized planning units with project preparation sections. In the case of rural development programs, such units are best located in the planning organizations of regional or local governments, where these exist. Such an approach is in keeping with the tenet that rural development should build on local initiative. It has the advantage of not only strengthening local planning capacity, but also having a direct bearing on the implementation of projects. Where there is no regional or local government, and where nationally integrated programs are desired, preparation should be undertaken by a central office for coordinating rural development or in a ministry of planning and development.

Project Appraisal Methods

Rural development projects, with their particular emphasis on distributional as well as productivity aspects, tend to be more complicated than agricultural projects generally are. This is particularly true of those multisectoral projects which yield benefits that cannot easily be quantified in monetary terms. However, the experience has been that all the rural development projects approved so far have shown adequate rates of return when the quantifiable benefits and costs are assessed in the usual manner. In some projects, the rates of return have also been satisfactory when the costs of those project elements for which the benefits cannot be quantified have been included along with other costs. It does not follow, however, that this will always be the case in

72

the future. It is important, therefore, to consider more closely the non-quantifiable benefits and income distribution aspects of rural development projects, bearing in mind the need to maintain the Bank's high standards of project appraisal.

The benefits of some project elements can be quantified (usually the directly productive components) while the benefits of others cannot (usually social service ones). There may be some project elements where all the benefits cannot be quantified, but they may nevertheless be necessary for achieving production targets; in such cases, the costs of these elements should be included in total costs. On the other hand, there may be project components for which the benefits cannot be quantified and which are not necessary for achieving production targets directly, but which nevertheless are important for increasing production indirectly and for improving the quality of life of the rural poor; in such cases, the costs should not be included in total costs for rate of return calculations.

In either case, how does one assess whether the levels of services proposed are justified? In the first place, reference must be made to sector or national policies, which should preferably establish minimum standards criteria (e.g., so many health clinics of a certain standard per head of population, possibly stratified by population density). Secondly, one should make certain that, within the national or regional minimum standards, the discounted total cost is the lowest among alternative ways of providing the services; the process of selecting the least-cost alternative should be made explicit so as to ensure that realistic alternatives have been considered. Such an approach is accepted practice in public utilities and other projects where "administered" prices are charged or benefits cannot be quantified.

Thirdly, care should be taken that the social profitability of one component is not obscuring the negative social profitability of another component. This implies separate evaluation of project components. Fourthly, where charges are made for services but the prices are "administered" ones, the marginal social costs should be estimated. Should it appear that the services are to be provided at less than their social cost, the implied subsidy must be justified in terms of the government's social objectives (including special pricing arrangements for the rural poor) and public savings. For example, are the subsidies going only to those who need them, and are costs being recovered sufficiently to provide funds for projects in other areas? Fifthly, the recurrent costs of such investment must be estimated and the implications for the government's budgetary position justified.

73

Project Implementation

Because the Bank's knowledge and experience of how best to help the rural poor raise their productivity and improve the quality of their lives is limited, it is necessary to:

1. Build a degree of flexibility into projects so that modifications can be made as experience is gained.

2. Devise evaluation systems in order to (a) control and monitor the extent of deviations from expectations, and (b) learn the lessons of experience. But such systems can be expensive and governments are naturally reluctant to tie up scarce human and financial resources in what might be regarded as sophisticated and esoteric monitoring systems. Such systems are necessary, not because aid agencies want them, but because they ought to be an integral part of the internal management control structure. If they are introduced for this purpose, they can facilitate supervision by governments and assistance agencies, and help in learning the lessons of experience.

Technical Assistance

Training

Because the shortage of indigenous supervisory and managerial staff is chronic in most developing countries, the training of "development managers" is a matter of top priority. Much of this must be done "on the job," but it usually has to be supplemented by more formal training. The traditional way of arranging on-the-job training is to provide technical assistance and insist on counterparts being supplied. Some technical assistance experts are better than others in training counterparts, but in general the record has been disappointing. There are many reasons, including a shortage of qualified counterparts and the fact that the experts are often fully and wrongly engaged in executive functions. Consequently, it is important—at least in the larger projects—to make provision for proper training courses for counterpart personnel. This is increasingly being done under Bank-assisted projects. Any increase in the supply of local expertise would help to free scarce technical assistance for new projects.

Public Sector Organization

Much more attention needs to be paid to public sector organization, procedures and personnel management, and to the manner in which project organizations should be fitted into improved public sector systems. The Bank and other donors have shown an understandable tendency to establish project entities outside the cumbersome civil service structures in many developing countries. In this way, highly

74

privileged enclaves have been created to the detriment of longer-run improvement in public sector efficiency. Multisectoral rural development projects, in particular, depend critically on inter-agency cooperation and coordination. Hence those responsible for preparing such projects must identify the real institutional constraints in the public sector and seek practical solutions. The institutional constraints may be so pervasive, however, that general reforms may be required before particular projects can be implemented.

The importance of strengthening local capacity for project planning has been mentioned earlier. Experience so far seems to indicate that there are few links between the preparation and implementation phases, and that "project managers" are appointed too late. Despite the difficulties, it would help if "project managers" were appointed fairly early in the preparation stage, so that they could be involved in designing the projects they are to manage. Not only would this help to reduce delays between approval of projects and commencement of implementation; it might also improve the design of projects and the quality of management.

Research and Information

A recurring point in this paper has been the inadequacy of information concerning the circumstances of the rural poor and the ways in which rural development can be accelerated. High priority needs to be given to conducting research and gathering information. The Bank's work in this area can never amount to more than a fraction of the national and international effort required. Therefore, in addition to doing research itself, the Bank plans to assist member countries in undertaking research and analysis to provide firmer foundations for rural development programs and projects.

The first need is for greater insight into the characteristics of target groups and the dynamics of traditional societies as they begin to modernize. In some cases, this is simply a need for information on how many people there are, where they are, and perhaps who they are. But once a program has begun to be designed, it is also necessary to know more about their skills, resource ownership, incomes, nutrition, health, family structure and general socioeconomic environment. Such information has to be collected through surveys. To be adequate for project planning, it must be current. Some information is available on a global basis in the FAO *World Census of Agriculture* and, on a country basis, from national censuses and surveys. The Bank is currently working with FAO to speed up analysis of the 1970 World Agricultural Census in relation to the small farm sector.

Secondly, the Bank needs to undertake research in order to learn better what motivates people in rural areas, and how they might react to broad policy decisions. The Bank is currently working with several external agencies on a study of "The Analytics of Change in Rural Communities." The aims of the study are to help in: (1) designing and evaluating key features of integrated rural development projects; (2) analyzing the effects on rural communities of different development policy instruments; (3) identifying those features of successful projects which can be replicated in other rural areas; and (4) more generally, providing an efficient feedback system so that project experience may improve knowledge and understanding.

Thirdly, it is important to have more information about the resources available for exploitation by the rural poor and others. To this end, the Bank will encourage others, and join with them, to finance resource inventory and evaluation work based on various kinds of field surveys; the use of ERTS imagery and aerial photography; national income, production and employment statistics disaggregated to the regional and local levels; and sectoral and regional studies to discover additional growth centers and rural/urban linkages. Indonesia provides examples of these kinds of studies.[3]

Fourthly, it is important to step up technical agricultural research in order to adapt known technologies to national and local situations. Such adaptive research includes varietal trials and plant breeding, experiments with fertilizer and water requirements for high-yielding varieties, development of improved cultural practices (especially for food crops), and designing farming systems for smallholdings. Research also needs to be undertaken to collate and synthesize all the work which has been done on "appropriate technologies" and to make recommendations for the production engineering of such machinery and equipment for local manufacture. The Bank is, therefore, supporting projects for strengthening existing and establishing new national research institutions, working in harmony with the international research activities financed by the Consultative Group for International Agricultural Research.

---

[3] Examples of regional planning studies are those of the southern half of Sumatra, Eastern Indonesia, and Sulawesi being carried out with the assistance of the Bank, the Federal Republic of Germany and the Canadian International Development Agency (CIDA). The Bank and CIDA have also been looking into a "national resource inventory and evaluation project" in Indonesia.

RURAL
DEVELOPMENT
ANNEXES

Estimates of Total Population and Rural Population in Poverty in Developing Countries, 1969

Region	Population 1969	Total population in poverty		Rural population in poverty	
		Below $50 per capita[1]	Below $75 per capita[1]	Below $50 per capita[1]	Below $75 per capita[1]
		(millions)			
Developing countries in:					
Africa	360	115	165	105	140
America	260	30	50	20	30
Asia	1,080	415	620	355	525
Developing countries total	1,700	560	835	480	695
Four Asian countries[2]	765	350	510	295	435
Other countries	935	210	325	185	260
		(percentages)			
Share of developing countries in:					
Africa	21	21	20	22	20
America	15	5	6	4	4
Asia	64	74	74	74	76
Combined share, relative to total population	100	33	49	28	41
Share of four Asian countries[2]	45	63	61	62	63

[1] 1969 prices.

[2] Bangladesh, India, Indonesia and Pakistan.

Notes:

1. A calculation of poverty for a majority of developing countries, as defined in Annex 1, was made for the study by the World Bank and the Institute of Development Studies at the University of Sussex entitled, *Redistribution with Growth*, Hollis B. Chenery, Montek S. Ahluwalia, C.L.G. Bell, John H. Duloy, Richard Jolly. London: Oxford University Press, 1974. To these data were added rough estimates for countries not included in that study, using the same data sources with respect to population and per capita income in 1969 prices but with national income distribution based on experience in countries for which data were available.

2. To calculate rural poverty, data for the share of urban population in total population were obtained from *World Urbanization 1950-70*, Kingsley Davis. Population Monograph No. 9. Berkeley, California: University of California, 1972. An assumed ratio of urban to rural income was applied, together with rough estimates for urban income distribution. With these assumptions, data for rural poverty were obtained after deducting estimates for urban poverty from total poverty.

Estimates of Relative Poverty in Developing Countries, 1969

Region	Population 1969	Population in poverty	
		Population with incomes below one-third of national average per capita income	Population with incomes below $50 per capita plus population with incomes below one-third of national average per capita income
		(millions)	
Developing countries in:			
Africa	360	75	125
America	260	80	80
Asia	1,080	145	440
Developing countries total	1,700	300	645
		(percentages)	
Share of developing countries in:			
Africa	21	25	19
America	15	27	12
Asia	64	48	68
Combined share, relative to total population	100	18	38

Source: See notes to Annex 1.

Rural Population and Rural Poverty in Developing Countries

Region	Rural population 1969	Rural population in poverty			Percentage of rural poor in rural population		
		Population with incomes below $50 per capita	Population with incomes below $75 per capita	Population with incomes below one-third of national average per capita income, or below $50 per capita	Population with incomes below $50 per capita	Population with incomes below $75 per capita	Population with incomes below one-third of national average per capita income, or below $50 per capita
		(millions)			(percentages)		
Developing countries in:							
Africa	280	105	140	115	38	50	41
America	120	20	30	45	17	25	38
Asia	855	355	525	370	42	61	43
Developing countries total	1,255	480	695	530	38	55	42
Four Asian countries[1]	625	295	435	295	47	70	47
Other countries	630	185	260	235	29	41	37
		(percentages)					
Share of developing countries in:							
Africa	22	22	20	22			
America	10	4	4	8			
Asia	68	74	76	70			
Total share of four Asian countries[1]	50	62	63	56			

[1]Bangladesh, India, Indonesia and Pakistan.

Source: See notes to Annex 1.

Landless Farm Workers in Selected Countries[1]

	Number of land-less workers (thousands)	Landless workers as a percentage of active population in agriculture	Active agricultural population as a percentage of total active population
Asia			
India[2]	47,300	32	68
Indonesia	5,673	20	70
Pakistan[3]	8,013	29	70
Total	60,986	30	68
Middle East and North Africa			
Algeria	1,099	60	56
Egypt, Arab Republic of	1,865	38	55
Iran	903	25	46
Morocco	484	19	61
Tunisia	210	20	46
Total	4,561	33	58
Latin America and Caribbean			
Costa Rica	122	53	45
Dominican Republic	179	25	61
Honduras	138	27	67
Jamaica	72	41	27
Mexico (1970)	2,499	49	39
Nicaragua (1971)	101	43	47
Argentina	694	51	15
Chile (1971)	378	66	28
Colombia	1,158	42	45
Ecuador	391	39	54
Peru	557	30	46
Uruguay	99	55	17
Brazil	3,237	26	44
Venezuela	287	33	26
Total	9,912	35	39
Grand total	75,459		

[1] Except for India, data presented here are estimated from ILO, *Year Book of Labour Statistics 1971*, pp. 43-294, and *1972*, pp. 44-301. Unless otherwise indicated, data refer to latest year available in 1960s and, thus, do not reflect recent reform actions on the one hand and changes in the work force, on the other.

[2] Agricultural laborers as shown in India: Ministry of Agriculture, Directorate of Economics and Statistics. *Indian Agriculture in Brief* (11th ed., 1971), p. 14.

[3] Includes population now belonging to Bangladesh.

Nutrition Levels by Income Class

	Percentage of families	Daily caloric intake per capita	Daily protein intake (grams per capita)	
Latin America				
Brazil (1960-61)				
Annual family income in rural areas			Total Protein	Animal Protein
(in new cruzeiros per year)				
Under 100	7.94	1,755	50.0	13.2
100-249	27.30	2,267	64.9	21.7
250-499	29.68	2,577	75.9	—
500-1,199	24.56	3,144	95.4	39.1
1,200 and over	10.52	3,674	116.6	32.5
Total average		2,683	80.6	21.3
Colombia (1956-62)				
"Very poor" rural		1,535	30	9
"Middle class" rural		1,538	34	15
"Middle class" urban		3,138	52	22
		2,133	60	31
Mexico (1958-59)				
"Very poor" rural		1,788	45	
"Middle class" rural		1,803	51	
"Middle class" urban		2,275	57	
		2,331	64	
Peru (1951-58)				
Mountain areas		1,794	47	
Coastal areas		2,205	64	
Asia				
Sri Lanka				
Rural (1961-66)		1,864	44	8.3
Upper class in Colombo (1957)		3,271	84	
Iran				
Peasants		1,842	60	
Urban wage earners		2,132	65	
Landowners		2,658	74	
India (1958)				
Maharashtra State				
Expenditure per capita (in rupees)				
Urban and rural areas:				
0-11	21.3	1,340	37.9	1.4
11-18	18.9	2,020	56.6	2.6
18-34	20.7	2,485	69.0	6.6
34 and over	39.1	3,340	85.7	11.9
Total average		2,100	59.7	4.5

(continued)

Nutrition Levels by Income Class (continued)

	Percentage of families	Daily caloric intake per capita	Daily protein intake (grams per capita)	
Africa				
Malagasy Republic (1962)				
Income per family per year (in francs)				
1-20	54.7	2,154	47.3	5.5
20-40	27.7	2,292	54.1	6.5
40-80	11.0	2,256	53.6	9.4
80-130	3.8	2,359	61.2	15.2
130-190	1.5	2,350	59.1	15.2
190-390	0.8	2,342	64.6	21.8
390-590	0.3	2,456	65.4	23.6
Other classes	0.2			
Egypt, Arab Republic of (1965)				
"Low income" class		2,204	71	15.0
"Middle income" class		2,818	84	18.0
"Higher income" class		3,130	98	37.0
Tunisia (1965-67)				
Income per person in rural areas (in dinars)				
Less than 20	8.2	1,782		
20-32	16.2	2,157		
32-53	30.8	2,525		
53-102	32.4	2,825		
102-200	10.9	3,215		
200 and over	1.5	3,150		

Source: Turnham, David. *The Employment Problem in Less Developed Countries: A review of Evidence* . Development Centre Studies, Employment Series No. 1. Paris: OECD, 1971.

Population per Medical Doctor in Urban and Rural Areas

		Population per medical doctor		Urban superiority in medical doctors per unit
Country	Year	Urban	Rural	of population
Honduras	1968	1,190	7,140	6:1
Jamaica[1]	1968	840	5,510	7:1
Philippines	1971	1,500	10,000	7:1
Senegal[1]	1968	4,270	44,300	10:1
Panama	1969	930	3,000	3:1
Colombia	1970	1,000	6,400	6:1
Ghana[1]	1968	4,340	41,360	10:1
Iran	1969/70	2,275	9,940	4:1
Haiti[1]	1968	1,350	33,300	25:1
Kenya	1969	880	50,000	57:1
Tunisia[1]	1968	2,912	10,056	4:1
Pakistan	1970	3,700	24,200	7:1
Thailand[1]	1968	800	25,000	31:1

[1]Urban=capital city only.
Rural=all other rural and urban areas.

Availability of Primary Schools in
Urban and Rural Areas

Percentage of the total number of primary schools in each category (urban and rural)
which offer a complete number of grades

	Number of countries	Complete urban schools as a percentage of total urban schools	Complete rural schools as a percentage of total rural schools
Countries by GNP per capita			
Up to $120 (excluding India)	9	53	36
India	1	57	49
$121-250	7	72	32
$251-750	16	77	62
$751-1,500	2	89	56
Over $1,500	6	100	99
By major regions			
Africa	16	79	54
Asia (excluding India)	9	94	66
India	1	57	49
Latin America	10	88	34
Europe	5	98	99

Source: Based on data in *Unesco Statistical Yearbook, 1972.*

World Bank/IDA Lending for Agriculture: Number of Projects
and Amount Lent, FY1948-74

	(1) Number of agricultural projects	(2) Amount lent for agriculture	(3) Amount lent per project (2)/(1)	(4) Average amount lent per year	Agricultural projects as a percentage of total Bank/IDA projects	Lending for agriculture as a percentage of total lending
			($ millions)			
FY1948-60	33	175.9	5.3	13.5	17	6
FY1961-65	33	484.4	14.7	96.9	16	12
FY1966-70	93	1,207.6	13.0	241.5	23	17
FY1971-72	72	855.4	11.9	427.7	26	16
FY1973-74	98	1,893.6	19.3	946.8	30	24

World Bank/IDA Lending for Agriculture, by Subsector, FY1948-74

	FY1948-60	FY1961-65	FY1966-70	FY1971-72	FY1973-74	FY1948-60	FY1961-65	FY1966-70	FY1971-72	FY1973-74
	($ millions)					(Percentages)				
General agriculture	43.9	–	15.0	13.5	24.0	25	–	1	1	1
Agricultural credit	20.2	45.0	183.2	255.8	240.3	11	9	15	30	13
Area development	10.0	9.7	100.4	51.6	272.6	6	2	8	6	14
Irrigation	85.1	383.8	513.2	201.3	621.9	48	79	43	24	33
Livestock	7.0	35.3	252.4	176.7	314.9	4	7	21	21	17
Agricultural industries	4.7	–	19.2	39.6	204.0	3	–	2	5	11
Non-food crops	–	2.8	86.8	95.4	167.3	–	1	7	11	9
Research	–	–	–	12.7	–	–	–	–	1	–
Fisheries	–	7.8	21.0	8.9	28.6	–	2	2	1	1
Forestry	5.0	–	16.4	–	20.0	3	–	1	–	1
Total	175.9	484.4	1,207.6	855.5	1,893.6	100	100	100	100	100

World Bank/IDA Lending for Agriculture, by per capita GNP of Borrowing Countries

	FY1964-68				FY1969-74			
	Agricultural lending		As percentage of total		Agricultural lending		As percentage of total	
Per capita GNP of borrowing countries	Number of projects	Amount ($ millions)	Number of projects	Amount	Number of projects	Amount ($ millions)	Number of projects	Amount
Less than $150	9	138.8	20.5	22.5	101	1,356.0	43.7	38.2
$151-375	18	173.8	40.9	28.2	78	1,069.7	33.8	30.1
$376-700	13	251.2	29.6	40.8	30	782.1	13.0	22.1
Over $700	4	52.0	9.0	8.5	22	341.8	9.5	9.6
Total	44	615.8	100.0	100.0	231	3,549.6	100.0	100.0

World Bank/IDA Lending for Agriculture and Rural Development, FY1968-74[1]

	FY1968	FY1969	FY1970	FY1971	FY1972	FY1973	FY1974	Total
Rural development[2]								
Agriculture								
Number of projects	5	3	6	10	12	17	25	78
Loans ($ millions)	29.1	51.8	53.1	66.6	121.4	246.8	449.8	1,018.6
Multisector[3]								
Number of projects	1	–	–	1	1	1	6	10
Loans ($ millions)	14.0	–	–	8.1	2.2	21.0	59.5	104.8
Single sector								
Number of projects	4	3	6	9	11	16	19	68
Loans ($ millions)	15.1	51.8	53.1	58.5	119.2	225.8	390.3	913.8
Education								
Number of projects	–	–	1	1	–	2	3	7
Loans ($ millions)	–	–	1.5	3.3	–	9.0	23.8	37.6
Roads								
Number of projects	–	–	2	–	2	–	–	4
Loans ($ millions)	–	–	25.6	–	23.5	–	–	49.1

Total for rural development							
Number of projects							
5	3	9	11	14	19	28	89
Loans ($ millions)							
29.1	51.8	80.2	69.9	144.9	255.8	473.6	1,105.3
Other agriculture (excluding predominantly agricultural rural development lending)							
Number or projects							
8	24	25	26	24	29	31	167
Loans ($ millions)							
143.4	315.5	359.8	352.5	314.9	690.9	506.1	2,683.1
Total for agriculture							
Number of projects							
13	27	31	36	36	46	51	240
Loans ($ millions)							
172.5	367.3	412.9	419.1	436.3	937.7	955.9	3,701.7
Total for agriculture and rural development							
Number of projects							
13	27	34	37	38	48	59	256
Loans ($ millions)							
172.5	367.3	440.0	422.4	459.8	946.7	979.7	3,788.4
Other Bank/IDA							
Loans ($ millions)							
781.0	1,417,.0	1,846.0	2,058.0	2,506.1	2,461.0	3,333.9	14,403.0
Total Bank/IDA							
Loans ($ millions)							
953.5	1,784.3	2,286.0	2,480.4	2,965.9	3,407.7	4,313.6	18,191.4

(1)Data refer to original commitments; no cancellations and refundings are taken into account. Information used for the classification of rural development projects is based on project appraisal reports. However, many appraisal reports are deficient in information for this classification, e.g., they are lacking in income distribution data on project beneficiaries.

(2)Projects where it is expected that 50% or more of the primary (direct) benefits will accrue to the rural poor.

(3)Projects involving two or more sectoral components with the dominant sectoral component constituting less than 75% of the net project cost (i.e., cost excluding contingencies and components which are not integral parts of the project). In all multisectoral projects designated as rural development projects, agriculture is the predominant sector, so they are classified under agriculture. Basically they benefit small farmers.

Share of Agriculture and Rural Development in Total World Bank/IDA Lending, FY1968-74

(Percentages)

	FY1968	FY1969	FY1970	FY1971	FY1972	FY1973	FY1974	Total
As percentage of total lending for agriculture								
Rural development								
Number of projects	38.5	11.1	19.4	27.8	33.4	37.0	49.0	32.5
Amount of lending	17.0	14.1	12.9	15.9	27.8	26.3	47.0	27.5
Of which: Multisector								
Number of projects	7.7	—	—	2.8	2.8	2.2	11.8	4.2
Amount of lending	8.1	—	—	1.9	0.5	2.2	6.2	2.8
Single-sector								
Number of projects	30.8	11.1	19.4	25.0	30.6	34.8	37.3	28.3
Amount of lending	8.9	14.1	12.9	14.0	27.3	24.1	40.8	24.7
As percentage of total Bank/IDA lending								
Total rural development lending (both agriculture and nonagriculture)	3.0	2.9	3.5	2.8	4.9	7.5	11.0	6.1
Total agriculture lending	18.1	20.6	18.1	16.9	14.7	27.5	22.2	20.3
Total agriculture and rural development lending	18.1	20.6	19.2	17.0	15.5	27.8	22.7	20.8

Estimated Rural Population in Poverty, by Region and Income Level of Country, 1974[1]

Region	Rural population in poverty in countries with incomes up to $200 per capita[2]	Rural population in poverty in other developing countries	Total rural population in poverty
	(Millions of persons)		
Eastern Africa	60	—	60
Western Africa	15	35	50
East Asia and Pacific	10	105	115
South Asia	270	—	270
Europe, Middle East and North Africa	5	30	35
Latin America and Caribbean	—	50	50
Total	360	220	580

[1]Estimates made by applying assumed population growth rates by region to figures for 1969. The regional breakdown in this table corresponds to the geographical divisions of the Regional Offices of the World Bank and is not precisely comparable to the area breakdown of Annex 1.

[2]Excludes some countries with low per capita income, but with large external receipts from petroleum (e.g., Indonesia and Nigeria).

Comparison of the Distribution, by Region, of the Rural Poor and of Prospective World Bank/IDA Lending for Agriculture and Rural Development

	(1) Distribution of rural poor 1974	(2) Distribution of projected lending for agriculture and rural development FY1975-79	(3) Allocation of agriculture and rural development lending implied by (2) FY1975-79	(4) Allocation of agriculture and rural development lending implied by (1) FY1975-79
	(%)	(%)	($ millions at 1974 prices)	($ millions at 1974 prices)
Eastern Africa	10.3	11.1	800	750
Western Africa	8.6	10.2	750	600
East Asia and Pacific	19.8	18.3	1,300	1,450
South Asia	46.6	19.3	1,400	3,350
Europe, Middle East and North Africa	6.0	18.2	1,300	450
Latin America and Caribbean	8.6	22.9	1,650	600
Total	91.9	100.0	7,200	7,200

THE NAIROBI SPEECH

The following are excerpts from the Address to the Board of Governors delivered by Mr. Robert S. McNamara, President of the World Bank Group, at the Annual Meeting in Nairobi, Kenya, on September 24, 1973:

"In presenting a strategy for rural development I should like: first, to analyze the scope of the problem; second, to set a feasible goal in order to deal with it; and third, to identify the measures required to meet that goal.

"Let me begin by outlining the scope of the problem in the developing countries which are members of the Bank. It is immense:

- There are well over 100 million families involved—more than 700 million individuals.
- The size of the average holding is small and often fragmented: more than 100 million farms are less than 5 hectares; of these, more than 50 million are less than 1 hectare.
- The possession of land, and hence of political and economic power in the rural areas, is concentrated in the hands of a small minority. According to a recent FAO survey, the wealthiest 20% of the landowners in most developing countries own between 50% and 60% of the cropland. In Venezuela they own 82%; in Colombia 56%; in Brazil 53%; in the Philippines, India and Pakistan about 50%. Conversely, the 100 million holdings of less than 5 hectares are concentrated on only 20% of the cropland.
- Even the use of the land which the small farmer does have is uncertain. Tenancy arrangements are generally insecure and often extortionate. In many countries tenants have to hand over to the landlord 50-60% of their crop as rent, and yet in spite of this are faced with the constant threat of eviction. The result is that their incentive to become more productive is severely eroded.

"It has often been suggested that the productivity of small-scale holdings is inherently low. But that is simply not true. Not only do we have the overwhelming evidence of Japan to disprove that proposition, but a number of recent studies on developing countries also demonstrate that, given the proper conditions, small farms can be as productive as large farms. For example, output per hectare in Guatemala, the Republic of China, India and Brazil was substantially greater on smaller farms than on larger ones. And it is, of course, output per hectare which is the relevant measure of agricultural productivity in land-scarce, labor-surplus economies; not output per worker.

"There is ample evidence that modern agricultural technology is divisible, and that small-scale operations need be no barrier to raising agricultural yields.

"The question, then, is what can the developing countries do to increase the productivity of the small farmer. How can they duplicate the conditions which have led to very rapid agricultural growth in a few experimental areas and in a few countries so as to stimulate agricultural growth and combat rural poverty on a broad scale?

"The first step is to set a goal. A goal is necessary both so that we can better estimate the amount of financial resources required, and so that we can have a firm basis for measuring progress.

Setting the Goal

"I suggest that the goal be to increase production on small farms so that by 1985 their output will be growing at the rate of 5% per year. If the goal is met, and smallholders maintain that momentum, they can double their annual output between 1985 and the end of the century.

"Clearly this is an ambitious objective. A 5% rate of growth has never been achieved on a sustained basis among smallholders in any extensive areas of the developing world. Smallholder production has risen on average only about 2.5% per year in the past decade.

"But if Japan in 1970 could produce 6,720 kilograms of grain per hectare on very small farms, then Africa with its 1,270 kilograms per hectare, Asia with 1,750 kilograms and Latin America with 2,060 kilograms have an enormous potential for expanding productivity.

"Thus, I believe the goal is feasible. It recognizes that progress will be slow during the next five to ten years while new institutions evolve, new policies take hold and new investments are implemented. But after this initial period, the average pace of growth in smallholder agricultural productivity can be more than double today's rate and thereby benefit the lives of hundreds of millions of people.

"Now, what are the means necessary to accomplish this goal?

"Neither we at the Bank, nor anyone else, have very clear answers on how to bring the improved technology and other inputs to over 100 million small farmers—especially to those in dry-land areas. Nor can we be fully precise about the costs. But we do understand enough to get started. Admittedly, we will have to take some risks. We will have to improvise and experiment. And if some of the experiments fail, we will have to learn from them and start anew.

"What, then, can we begin to do now?

Measures Necessary to Meet the Goal

"Though the strategy for increasing the productivity of smallholder agriculture is necessarily tentative, the following are essential elements of any comprehensive program:
- Acceleration in the rate of land and tenancy reform.
- Better access to credit.
- Assured availability of water.
- Expanded extension facilities backed by intensified agricultural research.
- Greater access to public services.
- And most critical of all: new forms of rural institutions and organizations that will give as much attention to promoting the inherent potential and productivity of the poor as is generally given to protecting the power of the privileged.

"These elements are not new. The need for them has been recognized before. But they will continue to remain little more than pious hopes unless we develop a framework of implementation, and agree to a commitment of resources commensurate with their necessity. That is what I propose.

Organizational Changes

"The organizational structure for supporting smallholder agriculture is without doubt the most difficult problem. Let me examine this subject first and then turn to the others in sequence.

"Obviously, it is not possible for governments to deal directly with over 100 million small farm families. What is required is the organization of local farm groups, which will service millions of farmers at low cost, and the creation of intermediate institutions through which governments and commercial institutions can provide the necessary technical assistance and financial resources for them.

"Such institutions and organizations can take any number of forms: smallholder associations, county or district level cooperatives, various types of communes. There are, of course, many experiments already

92

going on in different parts of the world. What is imperative is that at each organizational level financial discipline be rigorously required, and that the entire structure be oriented toward initiative and self-reliance. Experience shows that there is a greater chance of success if the institutions provide for popular participation, local leadership and decentralization of authority.

"The reorganization of government services and institutions is equally important. No program will help small farmers if it is designed by those who have no knowledge of their problems and operated by those who have no interest in their future.

"The sad truth is that in most countries, the centralized administration of scarce resources—both money and skills—has usually resulted in most of them being allocated to a small group of the rich and powerful. This is not surprising since economic rationalizing, political pressure and selfish interest often conspire to the detriment of the poor. It will clearly require courageous political leadership to make the bureaucracy more responsive to the needs of the subsistence farmers.

"The ablest administrators, for example, should no longer be reserved exclusively for the urban sectors. Top engineering talent must be devoted to designing low-cost solutions to the problems of small-farm irrigation. Young graduates can be motivated to take on the problems of the rural poor, and be adequately rewarded for solving them. Educational institutions should recognize that the training in practical skills is as important as the accumulation of theoretical knowledge. In short, national managerial and intellectual resources must be redirected to serve the many instead of the few, the deprived instead of the privileged.

Acceleration of Land and Tenancy Reform

"But there are other structural changes necessary as well. And the most urgent among these is land and tenancy reform. Legislation dealing with such reform has been passed—or at least been promised —in virtually every developing country. But the rhetoric of these laws has far outdistanced their results. They have produced little redistribution of land, little improvement in the security of the tenant, and little consolidation of small holdings.

"That is extremely regrettable. No one can pretend that genuine land and tenancy reform is easy. It is hardly surprising that members of the political power structure, who own large holdings, should resist reform. But the real issue is not whether land reform is politically easy. The real issue is whether indefinite procrastination is politically prudent. An increasingly inequitable situation will pose a growing threat to political stability.

"But land and tenancy reform programs—involving reasonable land ceilings, just compensation, sensible tenancy security and adequate incentives for land consolidation—are possible. What they require are sound policies, translated into strong laws which are neither enervated by exceptions nor riddled by loopholes. And most important of all, the laws have to incorporate effective sanctions, and be vigorously and impartially enforced.

"What we must recognize is that land reform is not exclusively about land. It is about the uses—and abuses—of power, and the social structure through which it is exercised.

Better Access to Credit

"But realistic land and tenancy reform—as essential as it is—is not enough. It is one thing to own land; it is another to make it productive. For the smallholder, operating with virtually no capital, access to credit is crucial. No matter how knowledgeable or well motivated he may be, without such credit he cannot buy improved seeds, apply the necessary fertilizer and pesticides, rent equipment or develop his water resources. Small farmers, generally, spend less than 20% of what is required on such inputs because they simply do not have the resources.

"In Asia, for example, the cost of fertilizer and pesticides required to make optimum use of the new high-yielding varieties of wheat and rice ranges from $20 to $80 per hectare. But the small farmer there is spending only $6 per hectare because that is all he can finance. And most of that $6 does not come from government or institutional sources, but from local landlords or village moneylenders at usurious rates of interest.

"The present institutions in the rural areas are simply not geared to meeting the needs of smallholder agriculture. In countries as disparate as Bangladesh and Iran, less than 10% of institutional credit is available to rural areas; in Thailand, the Philippines and Mexico less than 15%; in India less than 25%. And only a fraction of this is available to the small farmer. Even then it is accompanied by stringent tests of creditworthiness, complicated application procedures and lengthy waiting periods.

94

"Existing commercial institutions are reluctant to make credit available to the small farmers because the administrative and supervisory costs of small loans are high. Further, the subsistence farmer is operating so close to the margin of survival that he is simply not as credit-worthy as his more wealthy neighbors.

"Nor do governmental credit policies always help the small farmer, even though the intention may have been to shape them for that purpose. The fact is that concern over the usurious rates the farmer pays the moneylender has led to unrealistically low rates for institutional credit. The smallholder does not need credit subsidized at an annual interest rate of 6% for projects which will yield 20% or more per year. He would be much better off if he had to pay a realistic rate of interest but could actually get the money.

"In reviewing their financial policies for agriculture, governments should take care that good intentions do not have self-defeating consequences. In many of our member countries, radical restructuring of interest rates is long overdue.

Assured Availability of Water

"No less essential than credit—indeed even more so—is an assured supply of water for the smallholder. Without it, seeds, fertilizer, and pesticides are useless. This means continued research into the most productive uses of water, as well as substantial investment in irrigation and increased attention to on-farm irrigation methods.

"It is estimated that the presently irrigated area in the developing world of 85 million hectares can be expanded by another 90 million hectares, but the additional cost would be high: over $130,000 million. And not only is expansion of irrigated land expensive, it is a slow process. No major irrigation dam which is not already in the active design stage is likely to yield significant on-farm benefits before the mid-1980s. Although investments in major irrigation projects will continue to be an important part of national investment plans, and of Bank financing, they must be supplemented by more quick-yielding programs designed to benefit the small farmer.

"This calls for much greater emphasis in on-farm investment which can take advantage of existing large irrigation projects. There are too many cases—in our experience and that of others—in which it has taken ten years or more after the dam was completed for the water actually to reach the farmers. Major irrigation schemes often preempt necessary resources for on-farm improvement. The drama of harnessing a major river may be more exciting than the prosaic task of getting a steady trickle of water to a parched hectare, but to millions of smallholders that is what is going to make the difference between success and failure. The allocation of scarce budgetary resources should reflect this reality.

"Thus, development of major irrigation works, though necessary, is not enough. Too many small farmers would be left unaffected. These programs need to be supplemented by others which can bring water to farms outside major irrigation projects—and do so cheaply. Tubewells, low-lift pumps and small dams can make major contributions to productivity. Moreover, these investments—while not always within the reach of individual poor farmers—can often be afforded by organized smallholders.

Expansion of Extension Services and Applied Research

"The small farmer needs credit and water, but he needs technical information as well. And he is not getting nearly enough of it. The projected number of trained personnel who will graduate annually from existing agricultural educational institutions can at best satisfy less than half the total needs of the developing world. In the developed countries, the ratio of government agricultural agents to farm families is about 1 to 400. In developing countries, it is on average 1 to 8,000. And only a small fraction of even these limited services is available to the small farmer.

"It is not primarily the deficiency of funds that is delaying the necessary expansion of extension services. It is the deficiency of resolve to do more for the small farmer who desperately requires them. There is scarcely a single developing country which does not produce too many lawyers, but there is no developing country which produces enough extension agents. Governments cannot control personal career objectives, but they can offer appropriate incentives, and promote vocational choices which will contribute more directly to economic development and social modernization.

"Thus the annual cost of training the required extension personnel would be modest as a percentage of GNP or budgetary resources. The net cost—after deducting savings from changed allocations—would be even less. As long as the supply of extension workers is grossly inadequate, only the large farmers will benefit and the needs of the poor will be ignored.

"Behind extension services, of course, lies applied research. In a sample of five major developed countries, the governments are allocating annually from $20 to $50 per farm family for such research. The comparable figures for five major developing countries are only 50 cents to $2 per farm family.

"The international network of agricultural research has grown impressively. The Bank, for example, chairs the Consultative Group on International Agricultural Research, and contributes to the financing of the research institutes including the financing of the new institute for the semi-arid tropics. But very much more needs to be done at the national level to explore the special-equipment needs of the small operator, to develop new technologies for the noncereal crops and to help the farmer in nonirrigated areas.

"General expenditures on research and development in the developing countries are notoriously low and must be increased substantially. In doing this, governments should give very high priority to strengthening that type of research which will benefit the small farmer —research to produce low-risk, inexpensive technology that he can put to immediate use.

Greater Access to Public Services

"In other areas too, public services are grossly inadequate. The income of the small farmer could be substantially increased if he were supported by better physical infrastructure. Because of the costs involved, it is not within the power of the developing countries to provide all of this infrastructure quickly to the millions who need it. But governments can provide much of it by organizing rural works programs to construct small feeder roads, small-scale irrigation and drainage systems, storage and market facilities, community schools and health centers, and other facilities which make extensive use of local labor and relatively simple skills.

"There is no mystery about designing these programs. They have worked successfully at various times in experimental projects in Bangladesh, Tunisia, Indonesia and other countries. The major handicap has been their limited scale and inadequate management. The task for governments is gradually to extend these projects to a national scale.

"Basic changes are also necessary in the distribution of other public services. In the rural areas these services are not only deplorably deficient; they are often not geared to the needs of the people they are supposed to serve.

"Educational systems should stress practical information in agriculture, nutrition and family planning for those both within and outside of the formal school program. Health services should be developed which can assist in eradicating the common enervating diseases that afflict the rural poor. Electricity for rural areas should not be considered a luxury, nor should its purpose be merely to place a lightbulb in every dwelling. One of its most important uses is to supply power for production appliances, such as water pumps. Power is admittedly almost always in short supply, but urban lighting and air conditioning should no longer be given such a disproportionate priority in the national systems.

"Every country must examine why it can afford to invest in higher education, but fails to offer incentives to attract teachers to rural areas; why it can staff urban medical centers and export its doctors abroad, but fails to provide doctors for the countryside; why it can build urban roads for the private automobile, but cannot build feeder roads to bring produce to market.

"Resources are scarce in the developing countries, and their redistribution cannot provide enough for everyone's needs. But a major redistribution of public services is required if the small farmer is to have at least the necessary minimum of economic and social infrastructure.

"The programs I have discussed above can all be initiated quickly by governments, and will make a major contribution to the goal of a 5% growth rate in the output of small-scale agriculture by 1985. And all of these programs deserve, and will have, the full support of the Bank Group.

"But the fact remains that the measures I have outlined are primarily the responsibility of the developing countries. It would be a great disservice if the aid agencies were to try to convince either these countries or themselves that policies for alleviating rural poverty can be fashioned and delivered from abroad. The problem must be perceived and dealt with by the countries themselves."

AGRICULTURAL CREDIT

AGRICULTURAL CREDIT
CONTENTS

	Page
Introduction	103
Summary and Guidelines	105
Chapter 1: Agricultural Credit Practices and Problems	121
Evolution of Current Approach	121
Problems of Agricultural Credit Markets	126
Constraints on the Role of Credit in Development	131
Chapter 2: Agricultural Credit Programs and Policies	135
Designing Credit Programs	136
Financial Viability of Credit Institutions	140
Chapter 3: Systems for Delivering Agricultural Credit	151
Policy Making and Administrative Issues	151
Channels of Agricultural Finance	153
Agricultural Credit Agencies	154
Guidelines on Delivery Systems	161
Principles	162

Annexes

Abbreviations for Institutions	167
1. Institutional Lending for Agriculture, in Selected Countries	169
2. Distribution of Agricultural Loans by Type of Lender, in Selected Countries	170
3. Farmers Receiving Credit from Institutional Sources, in Selected Countries	171
4. World Bank Agricultural Credit and Total World Bank Commitments for Agriculture, by Per Capita Gross National Product Group, FY1948-73	172
5. World Bank Agricultural Credit Operations, by Funding Agency and Per Capita Gross National Product Group, FY1948-73	173
6. On-lending to Farmers and Number of Beneficiaries in World Bank Agricultural Credit Operations, by Size of Farm, FY1969-73	174
7. World Bank Agricultural Credit Operations, by Country and Per Capita Gross National Product Group, in Selected Countries, FY1948-73	175
8. Contribution to Project Costs by World Bank Agricultural Credit Operations, by Per Capita Gross National Product Group, FY1948-73	178
9. Interest Rates to Farmers, by Source of Loans	179
10. World Bank Agricultural Credit Operations, by Major End Use and by Region, FY1948-73	180

Page

11. Duration of Loans Made, by Selected Institutions 182

12. Measures of Loan Delinquency of Selected Institutions 183

13. Administrative Costs for Selected Institutions 184

14. World Bank Agricultural Credit Operations, by Lending Channel to Ultimate Borrower, FY1948-73 185

INTRODUCTION

The World Bank's[1] lending for agricultural credit has expanded considerably in recent years. Credit is now the largest component in the Bank's agricultural lending. In the course of this expansion, a number of problems have arisen. They are likely to be compounded as increasing emphasis is placed on lending to small farmers. Accordingly, this paper examines: (1) the issues and problems associated with the use of credit on the farm and with institutional lending; and (2) the guidelines to be followed by the World Bank, including those that will help provide credit to large numbers of small farmers.

Small farmers, for the purposes of this paper, include families farming less than five hectares or, in countries where all farms are small in absolute size, farmers comprising the poorer half of the country's rural population. Since small farmers suffer most from poverty in the developing world, improving their productivity and income is a matter of high priority. But credit also has to be provided to medium- and large-scale farmers in order to help increase the world's food production. The evidence suggests that larger holdings of up to 50 hectares are also short of credit for productive purposes.

The World Bank's credit projects in the agriculture sector are concerned with more than finance for on-lending to farmers. Funds are provided for processing and marketing farm produce, forestry development and fishing enterprises. Provision is likewise made for the support of technical services and training, feasibility studies, project preparation and other institutional assistance. While these are significant elements in Bank lending, the main attention here is on lending for on-farm development.

Data used in this paper were drawn from the Bank's reports as well as from many studies of farm credit. Both sources of information have their deficiencies. The data from studies are generally incomplete and often of poor quality. In particular, little is known of the extent of farmers' needs for institutional credit, of the uses to which borrowed funds are put, or perhaps most significantly, of the impact of credit on output and productivity. In many countries, noninstitutional sources of funds lend more than do formal institutions; but there is little information on lending terms and conditions in the informal market. What is known is based on observations by knowledgeable persons rather than on hard evidence.

Most of the World Bank's data are available in its own project appraisal reports. Sometimes, the data reflect expectations which

---

[1]All references to the World Bank in this paper are to be deemed to refer also to the International Development Association (IDA), unless the context requires otherwise. The fiscal year (FY) of the two institutions runs from July 1 to June 30.

may not be fulfilled. For example, the reports give the average number of people expected to benefit from each project, but not enough experience has as yet been accumulated to compare achievements with projections.

Despite various shortcomings, it is believed that the statistics presented reliably reflect the overall magnitudes on the size of programs, the extent of the coverage and the interest rates charged. The data on institutional arrears and defaults and the costs of administration contain a greater margin of error. Information on the impact of credit on output and on the sources and charges for noninstitutional credit is even less reliable. There is a clear need for better information on all aspects of rural credit and its impact on production and incomes.

SUMMARY AND GUIDELINES

Credit is often a key element in the modernization of agriculture. Not only can credit remove a financial constraint, but it may accelerate the adoption of new technologies. Credit facilities are also an integral part of the process of commercialization of the rural economy. However, no amount of credit, even at the most reasonable rates, can guarantee higher productivity or incomes among the rural poor. Success in this respect depends on many factors, including the availability of complementary inputs and services, sound credit policies, well-managed institutions and appropriate delivery channels.

Dimensions of Credit Problems

Outstanding institutional loans for agriculture in the developing countries are estimated to amount to approximately $15,000 million. Total agricultural credit outstanding in these countries is unknown. The bulk of it originates in the informal sector and probably is not less than five times the estimated outstanding institutional credit.

The percentage of farmers receiving institutional credit varies widely in different parts of the developing world. In certain African countries, around 1% of the total number of farmers used institutional credit, while in the Republic of China (Taiwan) nearly all farmers have access to it. About 5% of farmers in Africa obtain institutional credit, while the proportion in Latin America and Asia (excluding the Republic of China) is about 15%. Large farmers have been the main beneficiaries of institutional credit. It is common to find 70% or 80% of small farmers in a given country with virtually no access to such credit.

Most of the credit that is available to farmers in developing countries is for short-term loans for one season or for up to one or two years. The loans are used for purchasing current inputs, such as seed, fertilizer and pesticides. Some loans are available for two to five years for purchasing livestock, and some longer-term credits for acquiring such items as tractors or irrigation pumps. The supply of credit to all farmers, however, is heavily skewed in favor of short-term credit, particularly in the case of credit for small farmers. Even though most of the limited credit available for small farmers is short-term, the supply is inadequate. The need for credit of this kind is particularly great among small farmers if they are to produce a marketable surplus and thereby contribute to the development process.

The World Bank's Operations

Total World Bank commitments to agriculture rose from $468 million in the 16-year period fiscal 1948-63 to $621 million in fiscal 1964-68 and to $2,589 million in fiscal 1968-73. The credit component rose from 20% of total lending for agriculture in the first period to 56% in fiscal 1968-73. A significant shift has also occurred in the share of credit funds going to countries with lower per capita incomes. In the most recent period, agricultural lending to the poorest countries exceeded $1,000 million, of which more than half was for farm credit. Approximately one-fourth of all credit financed by the Bank was intended for small-scale producers.

The World Bank's initial objectives—to increase agricultural production through the economical use of resources and to develop agricultural credit institutions—resulted, at the outset, in a concentration on commercially viable farms and related enterprises. Recently, however, the emphasis in the allocation of World Bank resources has increasingly shifted in favor of small farmers. Project appraisals during fiscal 1969-73 envisaged that long- and short-term agricultural credit operations would benefit more than 900,000 small farmers with holdings of five hectares or less, located mainly in India (long-term credit for 300,000 small farmers) and in Ethiopia (seasonal credit for 400,000 small farmers). Despite the increase in recent years, World Bank operations probably have reached only a small percentage of the 100 million small farmers in the developing world.

Latin America was the main region for the Bank's farm credit operations, with an input of $507 million in fiscal 1969-73. Asia was next with $442 million, followed by Europe, the Middle East and North Africa region (EMENA) with $258 million, Eastern Africa with $140 million and Western Africa with $61 million. Two countries, India and Mexico, together received nearly two-fifths of all farm credit lending during fiscal 1969-73.

Impact on Output and Incomes

Available evidence demonstrates that credit stands little chance of being used for productive purposes unless it is accompanied by certain other elements, including the following:

1. Clear opportunities for economic gain from the adoption of new production technology or other improvements.

2. Widespread recognition and acceptance of such opportunities on the part of the farmer, along with access to training in the necessary skills.

106

3. Delivery systems which make the required inputs readily available at the time they are needed, and market outlets for farm production.

Conditions like these do not often prevail in developing countries. To be successful in expanding production, the constraints, whether financial or nonfinancial, have to be relaxed. This may involve the development of new breeds of plants and animals, improved water control, basic infrastructure such as access roads, a reliable supply of inputs, or an effective marketing system for farm produce. Price policies, such as unrealistic exchange rates, export duties or artificially low prices designed to favor urban consumers, may reduce the profitability of increased output. Farmers may not know about the economic opportunities that are available, or how to take advantage of them. The lack of extension services may be a limiting factor. If farmers are reluctant to take risks, support prices and possibly crop insurance could contribute to the adoption of a new technology. It is essential to provide a comprehensive package, especially for small farmers, if the potential for increased productivity is to be translated into a commercial reality.

Scope of Institutional Credit

Different types of innovations may have different financial requirements, regardless of the size of the borrower's holdings. Some innovations, such as a switch from one variety of seed to another, may require little additional capital. Other changes, such as the introduction of irrigation pumps, may demand far larger financial outlays than traditional sources can provide. Farm credit is usually a necessary, though not sufficient, condition for an increase in agricultural productivity and incomes. This applies especially to small farmers who have neither savings nor ready access to institutional sources. There appears to be considerable scope for the use of institutional credit to replace or augment credit from traditional sources in order to: (1) alleviate monopoly situations which force interest rates to excessively high levels; (2) overcome inelasticities in the supply of credit which become apparent when new opportunities emerge; (3) ease the seasonal financial problems of rural households; and (4) most importantly, encourage small subsistence farmers to raise their output and become commercial producers. Furthermore, land reform, if pursued widely, could sharply increase the credit needs of former tenants who were supplied by their landlords.

The best manner in which to meet this demand is still the subject of experimentation. Little experience has been built up on which to base firm views on the most effective credit policies and appropriate lending channels and institutions. The need is, therefore, apparent for trying different approaches and for gathering more data, in order to permit flexibility in the implementation and management of World Bank projects.

Credit Policies

Credit policy discussions center on four main issues: (1) eligibility criteria and security requirements; (2) the level of interest rates and the merits of interest subsidies; (3) repayment performance; and (4) credit channels.

Eligibility and Security

Traditionally, credit agencies have required that both large and small borrowers pledge some collateral, usually land, as loan security. This practice, and the low valuation frequently placed on land, excludes tenants as well as small farmers who often lack certified titles to their land. Obtaining and processing documents substantially increases the cost of loans, delays their disbursement and discourages borrowing by small farmers. Lenders, in turn, are discouraged because foreclosure is extremely difficult to implement and often politically unacceptable.

The World Bank has consistently emphasized that the repayment capacity of a borrower should be determined by appraising the productive capacity of his holding and that this should substitute as the essential criterion for security in loan decisions. For long-term credit and large farmers, insistence on land as collateral is quite in order. For those who have the resources but do not repay, there is no real substitute for court action, at least on a selective basis as an example to others. For short- and medium-term credit, chattel mortgages and liens or mortgages on crop production are appropriate. They cost less to document and can be applied more readily than land mortgages. Chattel mortgages and crop liens are not yet used widely because legal procedures are cumbersome, and the security they offer is generally considered to be poorer than with land mortgages.

One way to make crop liens more acceptable as an alternative to land as collateral is to coordinate repayment with crop marketing. This approach is likely to be particularly important in dealing with the security problems of small farmers. It is being used successfully with crops which are subject to monopoly situations and are centrally processed, e.g., tobacco, cotton, cocoa, tea, coffee and sugar cane. A variation would be to employ contracts whereby the credit agency is paid a percentage of the farmer's output rather than a fixed amount.

108

Another approach is to couple crop insurance with credit in order to protect both the borrower and the credit agency against the uncertainties of nature. Some success has also been achieved by lending to such groups as informal cooperatives under which members are held separately and severally responsible for the loan. Solutions to the problem of collateral are important if smaller and tenant farmers are to benefit from credit programs. The best prospects, in the future, will lie in some form of group responsibility for individual borrowings —an approach which has yet to be developed on a large scale.

Small farmers and tenants are usually penalized by the cumbersome and time-consuming procedures involved in applying for loans. Many lending agencies have rigid procedures for processing loans, whether large or small. These include the completion of complex forms and a preaudit of the borrower who, if he is a small farmer, is often illiterate. Before the loan is issued, an official has to visit the farmer's holding, and when the loan is eventually made, the funds and documents have to be collected at the lending institution (which may be far from the holding). The repayment terms will often lack the flexibility needed to accommodate the natural hazards of farming.

There is, therefore, great scope for innovation and modification of the rules and regulations that govern the requirements for collateral and the procedures involved for borrowing by small farmers. The need is for simplification and flexibility to facilitate ready access to credit. This may only be accomplished by modifying the laws governing credit and by relying more on self-management and policing of individual subloans by groups of farmers who assume responsibility for all their members. Whatever the solutions, it is important that every effort be made to minimize the burden imposed on small farmers.

Farmers should generally be required to contribute to the costs of the investment for which they are borrowing. This would emphasize their responsibility for making it a success, increase the lender's security and spread institutional funds further. While significant downpayments should be required from borrowers who can afford them, great flexibility is necessary with regard to small farmers, such as acceptance of a contribution in labor. Strict repayment requirements compatible with cash flows are also justified because they can help in the conservation and generation of resources.

Interest Rates

Capital and credit markets in developing countries are imperfect in varying degrees. As a consequence, interest rates may not allocate resources among competing uses as effectively as they should. Also, pricing or exchange rate policies may nullify the impact of changes in interest rates. Much more information is needed about the effect of differential interest rates on resource allocation between various sectors of the economy—and within agriculture.

In strictly economic terms, it could be argued that interest rates in agriculture and elsewhere should cover the costs of capital and the costs of associated services. In that event, the interest rate would represent the cost of making capital available, thus facilitating the allocation of capital in line with its most effective use. An interest rate to cover the cost of capital would include:

1. The opportunity cost of capital. This represents the forgone opportunity costs of using funds for agricultural credit rather than for other programs. Estimates of opportunity costs for capital are seldom less than 8% in real terms, or approximately the level required to mobilize savings effectively.

2. The costs of administering credit. These costs are directly attributable to processing, delivery and administering loans. An efficient institution making medium- and long-term loans to large farmers can operate at an administrative cost of around 3% of its total portfolio. (The median administrative cost for the lending institutions discussed in Annex 13 is 5%.) Costs of administration rise as the size of loans falls, as the duration of loans shortens, and as accounting services have to be expanded to cope with large numbers of small-scale borrowers. An efficient small-farm credit institution can operate with administrative costs of between 7% and 10% of its total portfolio. These costs would be for providing a mix of short-term and long-term loans, and for services associated with processing and delivering loans. Costs would not include providing extension and other public advisory functions normally made available as a nonprofit public service.

3. The costs of risks and defaults. Costs of lending have to incorporate an element to cover losses through defaults. The limited evidence available indicates that, over time, the level of defaults is no greater among small than among large farmers. The more carefully loans are scrutinized and supervised and delinquents pursued, the lower the default rate (but the higher the administrative costs). The limited evidence suggests that "normal" defaults can be expected to add 4% to the costs of lending.

In sum, total real costs for an efficient institution could be between 15% and 22%, depending on the nature of the operation and the size of the loans. Costs of lending to small farmers would be at the upper end of the range and may well be higher.

These rates contrast with interest rates for institutional credit to agriculture as a whole, which are typically low. Although there is considerable variation among countries and institutions, most nominal interest rates for agriculture range from 6% to 30%, averaging about 10%. After adjustment for price changes, these translate into real interest rates of between -16% and $+16\%$, with a mean of about 3%. Frequently, the real rate for agriculture, even if positive, barely covers administrative costs, let alone providing a profit after allowing for inevitable defaults. The return seldom permits payment of an interest rate on deposits that would attract savings.

The figures in Annex 9 show that commercial lenders charge much higher interest rates than institutional lenders. Petty traders, moneylenders, landlords and some commercial bankers charge anywhere from three to 20 times as much as institutional lenders. Payment of such high interest rates seems to indicate that borrowers would be prepared to accept an institutional interest rate of 15% to 22%— which would be much lower than the commercial rate, but still high enough to reflect the real cost of lending to small farmers.

A number of major factors, however, have to be considered before advocating higher interest rates for loans to agriculture in general and to small farmers in particular:

1. An effective interest rate policy has to take account of comparative intersectoral rates. In practice, real rates throughout most economies are likely to be well below the real economic costs of lending. Forcing up interest rates for agriculture alone can lead to an uneconomic diversion of resources and, not infrequently, may be negated by subsequent leakages between sectors. Correcting the problem for agriculture, therefore, rests on restructuring lending conditions as a whole.

2. Interest rates that are below real costs may be used as a compensation or offset against the adverse terms of trade between agriculture and industry, or agriculture and the rest of the economy. Although this argument has some merit, the use of interest rates for this purpose always carries the danger of proliferating the distortions already existing in an economy. A preferred approach, where possible, would be to eliminate the discrimination or to find better ways to offset the discrimination. This may be achieved through a change in price policy, or a modification of those trade or fiscal policies that encourage high-cost industry while penalizing agricultural exports.

3. Introducing high interest rates for agriculture may discourage farmers from accepting credit. Where agricultural credit rates are very low to begin with—as is often the case—large and abrupt increases in the interest rates may have an adverse psychological effect. The size and frequency of changes in interest rates have to be carefully

considered, especially for their impact on small-scale farmers moving into the money economy.

A common argument against raising interest rates is that agricultural credit is so basic to the needs of small farmers that it should be subsidized. This argument rests largely on the social ground that subsidized interest rates are an instrument for transferring income to the lowest-income groups, and thus help redistribute income. In view of the widespread poverty of small-scale farmers, there is undoubted merit in transferring income to the rural poor. It may well be that the interest rate is a convenient mechanism for this purpose. Against this argument, however, the following points can be made:

1. Subsidized credit *can distort* the use of resources and can lead to excessive capitalization of farm investment, including the use of labor-displacing machinery. There is evidence that farmers—even small farmers—can bear the real costs of credit if it is used productively.

2. Subsidizing credit for small farmers often results in leakages. Experience indicates that larger farmers tend to gain the greater proportion of whatever subsidized credit is available for use in agriculture.

3. Providing subsidized credit to small farmers is open to corruption and political abuse. Subsidized credit intended for small farmers has often been used for financing nonagricultural ventures. Frequently, local politicians use their influence to acquire the low-cost credit; political pressure is used to avoid repayments or write off debts.

4. Subsidized or low-cost credit means that rates charged by lenders do not cover their costs, so that they incur a "loss." Consequently, even with a high repayment rate, the flow of funds into institutional credit may be reduced and the resources of lending institutions depleted. The financial viability of lending institutions could be weakened and the level of lending reduced unless losses incurred from low interest rates are subsidized from other sources such as the national budget. Income distribution is not really improved by subsidizing small farmers who already have access to institutional credit when this reduces the resources which otherwise might be available to those who do not. Additionally, interest subsidies would not help the often large, and even poorer, group of landless laborers.

5. Subsidized interest rates have been advocated to help make small farmers more productive. Subsidies tend to be most effective when they are linked to the introduction of a particular technological change. Thus, where it is deemed desirable to use subsidies to encourage change, it is preferable to subsidize particular inputs related to that change rather than a general item such as the cost of credit. Subsidizing particular inputs, such as fertilizer, has the advantage that

112

the cost of the input to the farmer can be varied over time, and the variation can be made to depend on the acceptability of that input. Subsidized interest rates, on the other hand, have a pervasive effect that spreads beyond any particular technological change.

6. A subsidy that might avoid some of the problems noted above would be one that covers the administrative costs of lending to small farmers. Such a subsidy could equalize interest rates for all loans of equal duration and help foster the most satisfactory allocation of resources. At the same time, unified interest rates would reduce leakages and opportunities for corruption.

Thus, there is no simple or unique answer to the question of what is an appropriate interest rate for agriculture, especially for small-scale farmers. Insofar as the World Bank is concerned, it expects to work toward a long-run objective of positive interest rates which reflect the costs of lending. An intermediate objective might be to cover at least the opportunity costs of capital. Subsidies should, in general, be confined to cases where they can be clearly justified and are likely to be effective in the context of local patterns of financing.

There are obvious difficulties if any single organization—such as the World Bank—seeks interest rates on particular projects that would be different from those charged by the same or by a competing borrowing institution on other similar projects. The difficulties are compounded if many external lenders have accepted the principle that borrowing institutions should on-lend at subsidized interest rates. In these circumstances, the Bank's role would seem to be one of persuading external lending agencies and governments to follow an interest rate policy consistent with the needs of the agricultural economy.

It has already been stressed that credit is only one element in the package of inputs and services needed to raise the productivity of small farmers. In many instances, credit in itself may not be the most significant element. The World Bank will, therefore, tend to view the question of an appropriate interest rate in the perspective of the project as a whole. The Bank's attitude will be influenced by a project's overall potential for raising the productivity of large numbers of small farmers and for achieving a satisfactory economic return.

Repayment Performance

Repayment performance by large and small borrowers on farm loans is typically poor. Nevertheless, while many large arrears are reported, in the long run most loans are eventually paid and the default rate is much lower than the arrears rate. Credit institutions faced with a chronically poor repayment performance face a loss of liquidity, and suffer the additional costs involved in collection activities. The reasons for the large arrears are not related to the size of borrowers and include vagaries of production, such as price, weather and sociological factors. An important factor also is poor organization and management of credit institutions. Given the likely fluctuations in farm income from year to year, a strong case can be made for flexibility in scheduling repayments, provided it does not encourage tardiness or put less pressure on farmers to make repayments when they are able to do so. It requires firmness on the part of institutions, which has seldom been forthcoming, often because of political pressure. Closer supervision provides the most obvious means of minimizing defaults. There appear to be good opportunities for offsetting a higher supervision cost against a lower delinquency rate in many institutions. Supervision has the advantage of encouraging better behavior patterns which may eventually allow a reduction in supervisory activities, whereas unchecked delinquencies only help a situation to worsen. The costs of supervising small farmers, however, will be high, unless the supervision can be done on a group basis, with some collective responsibility for debt collection.

Credit Channels

In considering appropriate and effective credit delivery systems we must come to grips with two major issues:

1. Should institutions specialize in providing credit or, alternatively, should they be multipurpose organizations providing input and other supplies as well as marketing and complementary services along with credit?

2. What is the best way of dealing with large numbers of small farmers?

Whether farm credit institutions should be specialized or multipurpose is a point for discussion, but experience tends to favor the latter approach. Both kinds have had their successes and difficulties. Multipurpose cooperatives sometimes have found it difficult to exercise credit discipline among their members and, accordingly, to some observers, the administration of credit should be kept separate from other functions. On the other hand, specialized institutions have a tendency to remain aloof from the everyday problems that affect the financial needs and repayment capabilities of their clients.

Since credit is often only a component of a package, multipurpose institutional arrangements are generally to be preferred at the primary level in dealing with farmers. Such institutions help provide credit in kind (and on time) and collect repayments by deductions from the proceeds of marketed produce. They are also in a better position to pursue the supervision of credit provisions, ensure good use and assist in credit recovery. They facilitate credit being tied in more effectively with government extension services as a vital catalyst in the process of technological innovation. While, in practice, there is probably a need for both specialized and multipurpose credit institutions, the advantages of delivering credit through the multipurpose type justify the considerable effort required to solve the credit management problems that frequently come up.

The best way of reaching large numbers of small farmers is still not clear. Most World Bank lending for farm credit has been passed through commercial banks, via the central bank. This has proved satisfactory from a management and control standpoint, and has been effective in reaching the clientele of large borrowers. In general, however, such institutions are less likely to deal directly with small farmers, because of high administrative costs, lack of borrower collateral and locational limitations which restrict access. Government efforts to prescribe quotas for lending to agriculture or partially guarantee loans to small farmers, have not substantially persuaded commercial banks to adopt new procedures—despite serious attempts by some. Agricultural banks and development banks are bound by the same kind of limitations, although they lend almost as much to agriculture as do commercial banks.

One way of lending to small farmers is through special crop and project authorities. They have provided a satisfactory channel for reaching relatively large numbers of smallholders. Since crop authorities can provide a guaranteed market (perhaps with quotas) and are usually in a position to ensure a profitable return, they have been able to conduct successful credit operations. These institutions facilitate the delivery of credit in kind because distribution can coincide with field operations. This approach combines support and supervision by technical field staff with collection of repayments by deductions from returns. Clearly, this is an effective means of delivering seasonal credit to smallholders, which should be utilized wherever possible.

An important qualification might be that such credit should not only relate to the needs of producing the cash crop, but also to the subsistence crops grown for the farmer's own use. Repayments for both would be deducted from the cash crop proceeds. Credit administered by project authorities as a component of integrated development schemes has also been a useful means of reaching substantial numbers of small farmers in limited areas—though the overall record has varied. In the Chilalo Agricultural Development Unit (CADU) project in Ethiopia, production of maize rose two or three times over three years. At Lilongwe in Malawi, on the other hand, production declined, but the cause may have been unrelated to the project. This type of approach, although limited in scale, is probably more appropriate in the context of Africa where suitable institutions and basic infrastructure are lacking.

Cooperatives are an important element for reaching small farmers. Almost 20% of the World Bank's farm credit is disbursed through this kind of organization. Cooperatives usually have an apex structure, layered to the local or primary level. India has channeled a large part of its agricultural credit through the land development bank cooperative system, which has performed fairly well. Success has also been recorded in the Republic of China (Taiwan), the Republic of Korea and a number of other countries. But experience elsewhere has often been discouraging in terms of high administrative costs, delinquencies, and inadequate and untimely services. Local cooperatives are often captured by the well-to-do, and smaller farmers have difficulty in obtaining funds. A highly centralized system does not necessarily ensure better performance than a flexible village society structure where the operating decisions are made at the local level. In general, the proficiency and equity with which cooperatives operate reflect the conditions prevailing in the country as a whole. Where there is a strong private sector, cooperatives are difficult to sustain. They also encounter serious problems in countries which have an acute shortage of skilled manpower. Nevertheless, cooperatives probably provide one of the most promising vehicles for reaching large numbers of smallholders and rural producers.

There are other means of reaching small farmers. These include farmers' associations and groupings, frequently informal, which have obtained credit from financial institutions under conditions of group liability. Groups have been organized in several countries, sometimes within a formal cooperative system, to obtain credit for small farmers. These groups are highly diverse and include village societies in Turkey, tribal people in Africa and peasants in Mexico. A difficulty arising from the need to reduce administrative costs, is that institutions representing borrowers as a group must function as a channel to its members and must assume responsibility for administering, supervising and collecting loans at the local level.

In areas where credit institutions are inadequate, it is possible, as an interim measure, to increase the supply of credit for small farmers by using noninstitutional channels. In such cases, traders or merchants can serve as conduits for public credit. These have yet to be proved effective mechanisms. The risk of misuse of funds and the difficulty of integrating credit functions with other elements indicate that the use of noninstitutional channels should be approached very cautiously, usually only as a last resort.

There is a need to learn much more about the most appropriate channels for providing credit at low cost to enable large numbers of small farmers to become more productive. It is clear that any system intended to reach large numbers of low-income producers will have to be based on principles different from those designed to reach a relatively few large producers. In the case of groupings or cooperative institutions, their needs and their importance in the community should be properly identified and their specific nature, to be most effective, should vary according to the different societies and cultures among which they have to function.

Because of the special problems of dealing with small farmers, a case could be made for separate credit institutions for this purpose. Small farmers require much more service, including closer supervision, than the more commercialized large farmers, and more flexible policies relating to credit collateral, downpayment and repayment schedules. But the lack of institutions and manpower is such that few countries are in a position to establish parallel organizations. A practical solution is to separate out the programs and accounts for small farmers. This would make it possible to evaluate performance and costs of providing credit to small farmers by various methods, and to take corrective steps. For the same reasons, a multipurpose cooperative should maintain the credit account separately from its other activities.

To sum up, in order to develop effective credit institutions for dealing with small farmers, it is important that:

1. The institution must encourage acceptance of its role in assisting small farmers and make itself readily accessible at the village level.

2. It must view credit as part of a package to improve small farmer productivity, have specific proven technology to do so and ensure that the inputs required are available.

3. The institution should take into account the advantages of providing credit in kind for purchased inputs. This would relieve the smallholder of further transactions with which he may be unfamiliar and provide the institution with some assurances that the credit is used for the purposes intended.

4. Credit, especially credit in kind, must be timely. If provided too early or too late, it leads to diversion and loss.

5. The basis for selecting smallholder borrowers should be creditworthiness but the criteria need not be as restrictive as for larger borrowers. The important elements should be the reputation of the

individual within the community, the technical feasibility of the proposed enterprise in his own farm situation and the expected cash flow generated.

6. The prospects for repayment of loans are greatly enhanced by group responsibility for individual liabilities. Given the cohesiveness of most rural communities, when the village cooperative society or farmers' association has a stake in an individual's performance, it is difficult for him to withstand the pressure of his peers and avoid his obligations.

7. Institutions should understand that, for small farmers especially, loans and repayments need to be carefully scheduled to meet periods of liquidity shortage and surplus as they arise. This will make supervision much more effective and orderly.

8. Institutions will need to exercise considerable flexibility in rescheduling repayments when unexpected circumstances, such as drought or other disasters, occur. Under such conditions, it may also be necessary to be flexible in regard to lending criteria.

9. The institution must commit itself to continuity of operations, recognizing that performance, in the initial stages, may be inadequate. It will take time and discipline to develop effective credit programs for small farmers.

10. Finally, the authorities should recognize that much remains to be learned about small farmer credit. A process of trial and error on a limited basis may be quite in order, in many circumstances, to provide guidelines for wider application. Ultimately, the program should be conceived as one providing continuing and increasing financial support to the farmer for the evolving process of modernization.

Guidelines for the World Bank

1. The World Bank will continue to expand its efforts to help meet the credit needs of small farmers. Increased attention to small farmers should not, however, obscure the need for additional significant increases in aid to other groups, especially medium-scale farmers. To reach large numbers of small farmers in low-income countries with credit at the farm level, will require a substantial volume of Bank and IDA lending. During the next five years, the Bank proposes to allocate $1,300 million for rural credit, almost half of this sum being for small farmers.

2. The expansion of rural credit will be on a selective basis, related to conditions which will lead to an increase in rural productivity. Credit is not normally the appropriate instrument for transferring income to low-income producers or the rural poor. An expansion of

rural credit programs may reach large numbers of small, potentially productive farmers. But a great number of low-income persons in rural areas, such as the landless and those with holdings too small to be viable, will seldom benefit from them. They will have to be aided by other means.

3. In the initial stages of the transition to a more productive agriculture, access to short-term credit for purchasing fertilizer, improved seeds, pesticides, etc., is often of greater importance for small farmers than long-term credit. Accordingly, in the credit programs for small farmers, emphasis will be placed on short-term seasonal credit in the context of overall on-farm development planning. World Bank lending could provide a permanent working capital fund for this purpose which is rolled over and reused from year to year. As the Bank loan or IDA credit is repaid, domestic sources of credit and capital can gradually replace external funds.

4. In loan decisions, the emphasis will be on the productive capacity of small farmers rather than on collateral. For long-term credit to large farmers, land mortgages are in order. In addition, more use will be made of chattel mortgages or liens on crops as security for short- and medium-term loans. In general, further experimentation with simplified arrangements and procedures to secure credit will be encouraged.

5. Preference usually will be given to a single institution handling all types of credit needed by farmers: short-term credit for production and for living expenses in the lean period, as well as medium- and long-term credit for on-farm development. This would benefit the recipient and enable the institution to oversee his performance and protect its loan. Credit to farmers should be viewed as an integral part of a continuing process to help farmers adopt changing technologies.

6. With regard to small farmers, preference will be given to projects in which credit is designed as an element of a reasonably low-cost package that provides the necessary additional services—as in integrated area or crop development projects.

7. The World Bank will encourage appropriate adjustments to the general structure and level of interest rates so that rates in the agriculture sector are in harmony with those in other sectors of the economy. In general, there is no simple answer to the question of what is an appropriate interest rate on a Bank-assisted agricultural credit project. The Bank will work toward the long-run objective of an interest rate that reflects the costs of capital and of providing the capital. An intermediate objective might be to cover at least the opportunity cost of capital. Subsidies should, in general, be limited to cases where they can be justified and are likely to be effective in

view of the pattern of farming in the project areas. The issue of interest rates, however, should always be seen as one component in a project. The extent to which a project is likely to achieve the overall objectives of World Bank policy should influence the attitude toward interest rates.

8. The World Bank will encourage governments to develop systems of lending through cooperatives and/or groups of small farmers. This approach seems to be the most promising for reaching large numbers at low cost. The nature of the groups will vary according to the culture of different societies. At the same time, it should be recognized that cooperatives perform poorly in most developing countries and ways need to be found to strengthen them.

9. The Bank will continue to support special project authorities, such as those created in limited areas of Africa, as instruments to draw farmers from subsistence to commercial agriculture. At the same time, the Bank will encourage the development of apex institutions which can promote, oversee and service such enclaves within national programs.

10. The Bank will give increasing attention to building and strengthening financial institutions as agricultural credit channels, particularly to orient their efforts toward the small farmer.

The World Bank needs to know a great deal more about the performance of credit programs for small farmers (including nongovernmental programs) in improving productivity and incomes, and about the costs involved in providing such credit. Accordingly, the Bank should, in future, insist that a reporting system be incorporated, at least in major projects, to provide information, from the farm level, on the situation before the project was initiated, and the progress made and the problems that emerged thereafter. In the meantime, the Bank has initiated a study of the administrative and other costs inherent in credit programs for small farmers. This study includes considerations relating to the effectiveness of cooperatives and other group activities as a means of providing low-cost credit.

Chapter 1: AGRICULTURAL CREDIT PRACTICES AND PROBLEMS

Evolution of Current Approach

The goals of government-sponsored agricultural credit programs have changed significantly over the last two decades. Historically, their main objective was to reduce the dependence of farmers, especially small farmers, on the village moneylender, who, it was thought, exploited them through usurious interest rates. In addition, refinancing was often needed, especially in Asia, because of excessive indebtedness at high cost. However, with increasing emphasis on economic growth in the 1950s and the development of new and more productive agricultural technologies in the 1960s, governments have shifted to the use of credit programs to achieve greater output. In a few of the more prosperous developing countries, there has been a further evolution: credit institutions are now used to mobilize rural savings in order to reduce the dependence of agriculture on external funds. The programs receiving support from the World Bank and other international agencies have an increase in production as their primary goal. Many combine this with a concern for the welfare of the small farmer, primarily through raising his output as well as reducing his dependence on the moneylender.

In idealized form, a modern, production-oriented credit program is organized by the government lending its own funds, together with those obtained from other sources (e.g., an international agency), to an agricultural bank. The bank, in turn, re-lends the funds to farmers either directly or indirectly through cooperatives. The farmers use the funds to purchase productive inputs—fertilizer, seeds, pesticides, livestock, tubewells, machinery—which are combined with family labor to produce more output. The additional output is sold, the proceeds being sufficient to repay the loan and still leaving the farmer better off. The payments received from the farmers by the agricultural bank are adequate to cover administrative costs, to pay the interest on the government loan and to regenerate lending capacity.

This sequence suggests several criteria by which to judge credit programs: their success in increasing production and farmers' incomes; their success in generating sufficient interest and repayments to meet institutional costs; and, in the case of programs oriented toward small farmers, their success in channeling credit to large numbers of that group. It is difficult to provide precise evidence of the impact of these programs on production but it appears that few credit programs can pass all three tests. In a number of countries, the availability of institutional credit has undoubtedly helped to increase out-

121

put, but the impact has not been measured. Regarding financial viability, the record is generally poor. Interest receipts seldom cover costs and many programs have high overdues. Without substantial subsidization, few programs could survive. As for the distribution of credit, most of the institutional loans have gone to larger farmers. In addition, a few credit programs may have undermined the position of the smaller farmers. For example, in Colombia, Ethiopia and Pakistan, the new technology financed by loans contributed to the displacement of tenants. This was due to the lack of supporting changes in the institutional structure, especially land tenure.

Credit is an important tool in fostering development. But unless the recipient groups have profitable opportunities for investment, unless the programs are designed and administered well, and unless a great effort is made to hold down the rate of delinquency, credit programs will fail to meet one or more of the criteria of success. This paper attempts to outline the issues associated with agricultural credit— particularly with lending programs for small farmers—and suggests policies for alleviating the problems.

Volume and Nature of Institutional Credit

Outstanding institutional loans for agricultural credit in developing countries are estimated to be in excess of $15,000 million. International support for these programs is of considerable importance. The World Bank is now committing approximately $400 million each year for agricultural credit, of which more than $300 million is on-lent to farmers. The US Agency for International Development (USAID) and the Inter-American Development Bank (IADB) each supply another $50 million per year. Other agencies provide further millions.

Institutional lending to the agricultural sector by representative countries is detailed in Annex 1, which shows total loans outstanding and new loans made, and their ratio per capita of the rural population in the most recent year for which data are available. There is substantial variation: In nine of the 39 countries listed, loans from institutions are less than $5 per rural person, while in five countries the amount is in excess of $100 per capita. On a continental basis, in most countries of Africa and Asia, institutional lending is less than $20 per rural inhabitant, while in a number of Latin American countries the amounts are in excess of $50 per capita. The greater importance of institutional lending in Latin America is confirmed in Annex 2, which reflects the distribution of loans by type of lender for somewhat different sets of countries. Again, the figures vary widely by country, but on a continental basis, the percentage of loans made by institutions in Latin America is high, while in Africa and Asia noninstitutional lending predominates. Within the institutional sector, public institutions are of much greater importance in Asia and Africa, while in Latin America a substantial fraction of loans passes through commercial banks.

The percentage of farmers receiving institutional loans is shown in Annex 3. Again, there is a great difference between certain African countries where little more than 1% of all farmers use credit, and the Republic of China where nearly all farmers have access to institutional credit. On a continental basis, about 5% of farmers in Africa get institutional credit, while coverage in Latin Amercia and Asia (excluding the Republic of China) is about 15%.

In sum, only a relatively small fraction of farmers receive institutional credit today. The majority either do not borrow or depend on moneylenders or friends and relatives for loans. Although institutional credit is growing rapidly, noninstitutional sources are still the major suppliers of credit to farmers in most developing countries outside Latin America.

In the case of small farmers, coverage by institutions is even more limited. In almost all countries, institutions have channeled their funds to the larger farmers. In Pakistan, almost 60% of the farmers received 3% of the institutional credit. In Bangladesh, few farmers hold more than three acres; yet, the larger farmers received more than 80% of the loans from the Agricultural Development Bank and the cooperative banking system. In the Philippines, 27% of the larger farmers working 61% of the land received 98% of the institutional credit. In Thailand, persons receiving institutional credit held an average of 60% more land than the average farmer. In Tunisia, 90% of the farmers could not qualify for institutional credit. In Bolivia, only 3.5% of the institutional credit went to the campesinos. In Brazil, 3% of the farmers received 34% of the loans. Studies of Chile, Colombia, Ethiopia and Honduras indicated that, at the time of the survey, the larger farmers were the main beneficiaries of institutional credit. These figures show that there is scope for expanding institutional credit to small farmers.

Development of World Bank Participation

The World Bank lending for agricultural credit has expanded rapidly, and now constitutes the major part of its lending to agriculture.[1] Total Bank commitments to agriculture rose from $468 million in the 16-year period fiscal 1948-63 to $621 million during the five-year

---

[1]The data discussed here refer to all projects in which a minimum of 10% of the Bank loan was used for agricultural credit purposes. While this creates some inconsistencies with some earlier Bank documents, such as Agriculture: Sector Working Paper, published in June 1972, the broader coverage provides a more accurate measure of the Bank's involvement in agricultural credit activities.

period fiscal 1964-68, and increased more than four-fold—to $2,589 million—in fiscal 1969-73 (see Annex 4). The credit component grew even more rapidly, rising from less than 20% of total lending to agriculture in the first period to 56% of the total in the last five-year period.

An increasingly significant share of credit funds has been funneled to countries with low per capita incomes (as may be seen from Annex 4). In the earliest period of Bank lending for agriculture to countries with a per capita GNP of under $150, less than 4% was for credit projects. In the most recent period, when agricultural lending to the poorest countries exceeded $1,000 million, more than half went to credit projects. Clearly, credit has become an important element in the Bank's agricultural programs for low-income countries.

The World Bank's initial agricultural credit activities were guided largely by three concerns: (1) the funds loaned should lead to increased agricultural production and productivity; (2) the investments financed should constitute an economic use of resources for both the farmers and the nation; and (3) the support provided should help develop agricultural credit institutions. In practice, this has meant a concentration on commercially viable farms and agriculture-related enterprises. Credit was not regarded as a practical means for dealing with the problems of subsistence farmers and agricultural laborers. However, the technological improvements of recent years have changed the economics of small-scale farming, making it possible for once marginal farms to become viable and creditworthy enterprises. The World Bank has been increasingly concerned with this group. Although the Bank continues to assist in programs for medium- and large-scale farmers, there has been a significant shift in the allocation of its resources to the small farmers (see Annex 6). Approximately one-fourth of the credit financed by the Bank is intended for small-scale producers.

In project appraisals, it was reported that agricultural credit operations during fiscal 1969-73 would benefit over 900,000 small farmers with holdings of five hectares or less. In addition, 300 cooperatives were beneficiaries, which included small farmers among its members. Almost 80% of the farmers holding less that five hectares and benefiting from Bank funds are in India and Ethiopia. Bank/IDA credits to India go to 300,000 small farmers, or about 0.7% of the estimated 42 million smallholders in the country. The loans, mostly for wells, pumps and motors, are for an average amount of approximately $1,000, of which the Bank provides about $650. The Bank's commitment to these loans is $185 million and constitutes 65% of the volume of all Bank funds flowing to small farmers in the form of credits.

Another 400,000 small farmers in Ethiopia receive Bank assistance as part of the Agricultural Minimum Package Project. The average loan size is approximately $25, of which $12.50 is provided through Bank lending. These loans are for seasonal inputs, such as seeds and fertilizers. Although the number of small farmers benefiting from Bank-supported programs has grown in recent years, it constitutes at best only 1% of the 100 million small farmers in the developing world.

The country and regional pattern of World Bank agricultural credit activities (shown in Annex 7) brings out the prominent role Latin America has played in past World Bank operations of this kind. Only in fiscal 1969-73, did Asia approach this volume of lending and the number of projects. The table also points up the Bank's limited involvement in agricultural credit in Western Africa. This reflects the difficulty of expanding credit projects in that region, where traditional cultural practices predominate and many countries did not achieve independence until fairly recently. Two countries, India and Mexico, together received nearly two-fifths of all World Bank lending for agricultural credit during fiscal 1969-73.

A review of the contribution made by World Bank financing to the total costs of agricultural credit projects (see Annex 8) clearly shows that in fiscal 1969-73 significantly higher proportions of project costs went to low-income countries. Also, local cost financing has tended to be more important for low-income countries than for those in the highest brackets. By fiscal 1969-73, countries with a per capita GNP of $150 or less had, on average, nearly two-fifths of local costs covered by Bank financing. The ability to provide local cost financing has been a key element in expanding the scope of World Bank participation in agricultural credit, particularly in countries with the lowest incomes and at the earliest stages of development.

Categories of Bank Lending

Information on the types of credit projects assisted by the Bank (see Annex 10) shows that total lending in each category has increased in the three periods covered between 1948 and 1973. However, the rates of expansion by project type and by region differ considerably and indicate the changes in Bank policy. Lending for livestock operations continues to be the single most important type of credit activity, although its relative share in Bank credit commitments has declined slightly. Livestock loans constitute nearly one-third of all Bank agricultural credit projects and over 70% of those in Latin America. This region, in turn, has been receiving the largest number of World Bank credit loans. Within Latin America, at least in earlier years, most of the funds have gone for the development of large-scale commercial ranches. More recently, the trend in Africa and the Middle East, and in Latin America as well, has been toward developing smaller-scale livestock operations.

The second largest number of loans in this category have been credits in support of general agriculture. The nature of such projects is quite varied and includes mixed farming, general on-farm improvements, such as land-leveling, and the purchase of nonmechanized implements, such as plows.

In fiscal 1969-73, agro-industrial credits have been third in importance. Classified by the Bank under agricultural loans, they are not intended for crop or livestock raising but for processing plants, storage and marketing facilities, and for aerial spraying of crops. Next in importance are loans for minor irrigation projects, mostly for wells and low-lift pumps. In recent years, this type of operation has been limited to Asia. It is often used to provide the water control essential for growing the new varieties of wheat and rice.

Lending for crop development—essentially such export crops as tea, oil palm and cocoa—and integrated agricultural development have both emerged as important credit activities in fiscal 1969-73. Reliance on these types of projects in Eastern and Western Africa reflects the specialization of commercial agriculture in these regions, necessitating the packaging of credit together with extension and infrastructure.

Loans for buying farm machinery were among the earliest to feature in the Bank's agricultural credit activities. They frequently involved financing imports of machinery and using the counterpart funds for on-lending to farmers. Although lending for this purpose has continued to expand, it has done so at a slower rate than lending for other agricultural purposes and is now concentrated in Asia rather than in Latin America. There is an awareness in the Bank that too rapid mechanization of agriculture may have adverse social effects and cause dislocation of labor.

Problems of Agricultural Credit Markets

Agricultural credit institutions tend to be treated in isolation rather than as a segment of the rural financial system. But they provide only a fraction, and in most countries only a small fraction, of the credit used by farmers. If farm savings are included, the institutions provide an even smaller part. A recent study in India reported that more than half of the farm households did not have any debt. Farmers who borrowed still financed 95% of household expenditures, 90% of operating outlays and 50% of investment costs out of their own resources. Of the funds borrowed, only 30% came from institutions, and institutions financed only 1% of total farm outlays. Institutional credit programs must, therefore, be designed to operate within the overall rural finance situation.

Some of the major problems in rural finance stem from the fragmentation of financial markets. In some countries, funds do not flow readily, either between markets or even among borrowers within a market. This situation can lead to: (1) lack of competition among lenders, leading to usurious interest rates; (2) an inelastic supply of funds, slowing the investment process when the demand for development funds is increasing rapidly; and (3) the use of surplus funds whether for consumption for land purchase (exacerbating the land tenure problem) or for other investments that are not related to increasing productivity. Each of these difficulties is basically associated with a different stage of agricultural development, although a monopoly of credit supplies can be a problem at any stage.

Limitations of Informal Sources

In traditional agriculture with a stagnant technology, the output of farmers is stable or expanding slowly, and investment is low. This is so not because farmers are too poor to save or interest rates too costly, but because farmers have over time acquired the amount of capital which is consistent with their technology, the size of their holdings and the number of their workers.[2] In a traditional setting, some poor farmers use credit regularly to pay for their household requirements in the months before the harvest. But most farmers borrow only when their crop has been poor or if they are faced with unusual expenditures, often for a family ceremony such as for a birth, a wedding or in case of death.

Much of the borrowing is from other farmers—neighbors, friends and relatives. They charge a nominal rate of interest and expect comparable financing when they themselves need credit. Many small farmers, especially those who borrow regularly, obtain loans from merchants, middlemen and moneylenders—and pay high interest rates. In some places, such lenders compete with each other and charge rates which are roughly equivalent to the high cost of lending to small rural borrowers, including a realistic risk premium and the opportunity cost of the funds. Other moneylenders have a monopoly position and are able to charge rates greatly in excess of competitive market levels.

[2] In this paper, the term "capital" is used to refer to fixed and working capital, while "credit" is used to mean a transfer in cash or kind with an obligation to repay.

In countries of Asia and Africa for which figures are available, friends and relatives provide 50% of the loans; in Latin America, this is only 10% (see Annex 2, "Non-Commercial" lenders). On such loans, interest is not charged or is nominal. Nevertheless, some farmers, and a disproportionate number of them are probably small farmers, are forced to borrow from moneylenders, middlemen, landlords and merchants. On average, these lenders provide 27% of the total agricultural credit (see Annex 2, "Commercial" lenders), much of it at very high rates of interest. In Africa particularly, the rates on commercial loans are very high (see Annex 9), but the volume of commercial lending is very small. The interest rate figures, however, may be misleading since they represent an annualization of monthly rates. Most loans at high rates are for short durations, seldom longer than for three months.

Exploitation is made possible through ignorance, poor communication, the absence of alternative lenders, established trading patterns and differences in economic and political power. By offering an alternative source of funds, public credit programs can help those who until now have dealt with a credit monopolist. But monopoly power may not be the only, or even the most important, reason for high interest rates on agricultural loans in developing countries. Rates on commercial loans may be high in part because of monopoly, but also because capital is scarce, because farm loans are costly to administer, because the rate of defaults is high, because much of the demand for credit is seasonal, and because in many countries there is substantial inflation.

The following illustration suggests the level of interest rates which might be achieved only by the most efficient private lenders. They would have the possibility of investing their capital during the whole year, and holding their administrative costs and defaults to only 3%.[3] To earn 15% in real terms, these lenders would have to charge a real interest on loans in excess of 21% per year.[4] This is a competitive, nonmonopolistic rate. On a monthly basis, it is about 1.8%. Even at this high rate, the cost to a farmer of financing half his total expendi-

[3]Merchant lenders usually invest their capital in loans over a period of the year. In seasonal agriculture, there is in effect a symbiotic switching, over the year, of working capital between the farmer and the merchant who is a crop-buying agent. The merchant requires substantial working capital after the harvest to carry the crop. Over the year, as he sells out his position, his need for working capital is diminished, freeing funds for lending just when farmers are running low on money and need loans to purchase household supplies. This seasonal shifting of funds between merchant and farmer makes for an efficient use of capital over the year.

[4]The calculation is as follows: For an annual return of 15% on his capital, the lender must collect $15 on every $100 lent, plus $3 for administrative expenses and $3 for losses—that is, $21. This must be earned from the actual capital recovered—that is, $97 over a period of 12 months. The lender must, therefore, charge a real rate of about 21.6%.

tures for four months through borrowing would be about 1% of his annual expenditure. Data on India indicate that few farmers actually borrow this much. The figures for Africa and selected countries of Asia and Latin America show that the interest rates charged by commercial lenders are in excess of 32% in real terms. In these areas, there may be some monopoly in the credit markets, but shorter loans, higher administrative costs or more delinquencies than assumed in the example would justify higher competitive rates. In other countries, the moneylenders' monopoly power appears to be quite limited.

Only a few studies throw light on the question of informal market interest rates. The studies indicate that in Ecuador, India, Indonesia, Thailand and the Republic of Viet-Nam average interest rates on commercial loans are not out of line with competitive rates. But in Malaysia and Chile, the high rates are to a substantial extent due to the monopoly held by moneylenders.

The object of government policy should be to eliminate not the moneylender, but his monopoly profit. The most effective way of reducing interest rates and exploitation is to increase both the alternative sources and the volume of credit in agriculture. This can be done either by establishing government credit agencies or by pursuing policies that encourage private institutions to lend to agriculture, by allowing them to charge interest rates high enough to make lending to farmers profitable.

Many governments attempt to limit interest rates charged by the private sector through usury laws. If this could prevent exploitation, such laws would be most desirable. But moneylenders and borrowers generally do not pay much attention to usury laws. If the maximum interest rate is set too low, usury laws discourage agricultural lending by private institutions, such as commercial banks, which usually obey the law. It is important for development to improve financial markets and to increase the flow of credit, both between and within sectors. Financial policy must pay due regard to intersectoral interest rates. Limits on interest charges which impede the flow of funds from institutions into agriculture and are unenforceable against the moneylender do little good.

Changing Credit Uses and Requirements

Modernizing agriculture requires various kinds of new technology: the introduction of a crop not formerly grown; the adoption of some practice which preserves yield levels, such as soil or moisture conservation or pest control; a yield-increasing technology in the form of new varieties of seeds, pesticides, fertilizer, machinery and crop strains more resistant to drought, heat or cold.

The various types of innovation have different financial requirements. Some require little additional capital. For example, a switch from one variety of seed to another can be made without much investment. The additional capital needed for others, such as the introduction of pesticides, can be financed by many farmers from savings. Evidence from such countries as Brazil, the Republic of China, the Republic of Korea, Pakistan and Zambia indicates that farmers have substantial savings capacity when they have attractive investment opportunities.

In addition to savings, many farmers need borrowed funds, especially when the investment is large relative to their income. In modernizing agriculture, credit is less likely to be available among farmers, as in all likelihood any surplus funds will be used for the same purpose.

Nor are local landlords, merchants and moneylenders likely to be an important source of additional agricultural finance, since their supply of funds is quite inelastic. These lenders finance only short-term production credits. Lumpy, longer-term investments almost always need to be financed elsewhere. Furthermore, in the event of the introduction of land reform, this source may well disappear.

New technological opportunities can lead to financial stringency when they require more resources than traditional sources are able to provide. It is at this point that access to credit from external institutions becomes critical. Without it, the investment strategy of farmers, especially of small farmers, will be biased toward marginal variations within traditional technology.

Mobilization of Savings

One method of increasing the flow of funds within the agricultural sector is to tap the surplus funds of those who have successfully adopted the new technology. To realize this potential, an appropriate savings transfer mechanism must be established. If credit (and savings) institutions can offer successful farmers attractive financial returns, a high rate of savings may be maintained. The resources so mobilized may then be re-lent to farmers who are at an earlier stage of development. To the extent that agricultural credit institutions may become the foci of local financial markets by mobilizing and distributing savings, they will have the effect of lessening the dependence of the agricultural sector on outside sources of finance.

The mobilization of savings, however, will not automatically lead to an increased flow of funds to agriculture unless the returns there are commensurate with those elsewhere in the economy. Traditionally, savings mobilized in rural areas have been re-lent primarily in urban areas, where higher interest rates prevail.

Constraints on the Role of Credit in Development

Credit—that is, money—can by itself grow nothing. To expand production, borrowed funds must be spent by farmers on physical inputs—fertilizer, seeds, pesticides, labor. The surplus output must then be transported to market and sold to domestic or foreign consumers. This is a complex process. Credit puts in the farmers' hands funds that can be used to purchase productive inputs, but whether this will be done or not depends upon technology, markets, infrastructure, information and attitudes.

In most developing countries, growth rates in agricultural output have been the slowest of all major sectors: farm production, generally, has been increasing by less than 3% per year. This has been coupled with a low level of capital formation in the countryside. Many credit programs are predicated on the assumption that, in large part, a shortage of funds is responsible for the slow rates of investment and growth in agriculture, particularly in the case of small farmers. The factors, which are essential complements of credit in promoting agricultural development, are identified in the following section.

Limited Applicability of New Technology

There are many opportunities for putting credit to productive use in agriculture. They range from merely spreading fertilizer where none was used before, to utilizing the more advanced elements of the technology associated with the "green revolution," including multiple cropping. But the latter are often limited to farmers in specific regions or to areas with particular natural endowments. Although dramatic increases in yields were experienced after the successful introduction of new technology in some areas of the world in the 1960s, the applicability of these practices has been geographically limited. Through 1970-71, apart from Mexico, the "green revolution" was highly concentrated in Asia—South and West Asia for wheat, and South and East Asia for rice. Small quantities of the higher-yielding varieties of wheat were also raised in North Africa and of rice in Latin America. In fact, outside Mexico, 86% of the total area planted to the new varieties of wheat was in India and Pakistan. The production of high-yielding rice was not quite so concentrated, but 60% of the land planted to the new varieties was in India.

The introduction of high-yielding and/or multiple-cropping techniques is presently limited to irrigated and high rainfall areas with mild temperatures, which probably do not represent more than 30% of the world's potential arable land. For many other areas, it is possible to

131

develop yield-preserving, rather than yield-increasing, technologies. But more basic research is urgently needed to open new technical horizons for agriculture in developing countries. Similarly, there are limits on the availability of uncultivated land. Although there are areas of cultivable but unused land in Latin America and Africa, and to a lesser extent in Asia, experience suggests that the expansion of cultivated land in developing countries is unlikely to exceed 1% per year. That rate is far short of the population growth in the developing countries.

Economic and Social Constraints

Technical opportunities, even where they exist, may not be economical to implement. New grain varieties, although they may produce larger harvests in physical terms, have sometimes sold at a discount because local consumers consider them inferior to native grains. Profitability of new investment opportunities resulting from new technologies or from opening up new lands is clearly not guaranteed, and it would be misleading to assume that all new technologies made available to the small farmer will be profitable to him. Where opportunities for new technology do not exist, governments should give priority to developing conditions which will facilitate increased output on economic terms, or, where feasible, take steps to bring additional land under cultivation.

Some of the recent improvements in technology involve "indivisibilities" which make them less suited for adoption by small farming units. For example, the new seed varieties are much more productive when water application can be controlled. Yet, the minimum size tubewell or low-lift pump available in most areas is larger than that required by small farmers to irrigate their land. In some areas, it has been possible to group small farmers to share a single pump or tubewell, but where farmers cultivate several tiny parcels, this kind of organization becomes more difficult. On the other hand, fertilizer, pesticides and new seed varieties are almost perfectly "divisible." In the Punjab of India and Pakistan, where irrigation was already available, the new grain technology appears to be as well suited to small farmers as to large, and the new practices were adopted to a similar degree by both groups. When "indivisibilities" are important, the new technology tends to be less profitable for smaller farmers, giving the larger ones advantages in the market place.

Many agricultural innovations present risks. For example, the new seeds show a greater yield variation than the varieties they displace. Under ideal conditions, output may be twice as large or more so, but under adverse weather conditions the new seeds may yield even less than the traditional varieties.[5] Many of the traditional varieties have evolved over time, or were consciously developed through early research work, to grow under wider extremes of climatic conditions. The risks associated with the new technologies may threaten economic survival, especially of small farmers in marginal ecological areas who live close to subsistence levels. This reduces the attractiveness of the new practices.

Such practices also may be disturbing to local culture, traditions, attitudes and values. Profitable changes in practices may not be adopted if they involve work considered to be demeaning, if agriculture is only a secondary occupation in areas where the primary orientation is toward nonagricultural employment, or if societies impose sanctions against progressive farmers.

The absence of an adequate marketing infrastructure may make investment unprofitable. A number of studies—of Ecuador, Ghana, India and Malaysia—report that a lack of infrastructure makes the marketing of additional output unduly costly. Price policies, such as unrealistic export exchange rates, export duties or artificially low prices designed to favor urban consumers, may also reduce the profitability of marketing additional output. Experience shows that satisfactory delivery and marketing systems and pricing policies greatly facilitate credit operations and minimize credit requirements.

Adoption of the new practices may also be constrained by a lack of inputs. For example, new seeds and pesticides may be available, but fertilizer may be in short supply. Because the success of the new technologies depends on a balanced application of several inputs, the absence of any one may adversely affect the benefits to be gained from using the others. An investment in a tubewell may fail if the farmer cannot obtain the fertilizer required. The small farmer is at a definite disadvantage in acquiring essential inputs if their supply is limited to a degree which requires rationing. Steeply rising prices may keep limited supplies away from small farmers. Even where prices are controlled (and sometimes subsidized), the wealthier and more influential farmers seem better able to capture what is available.

Farmers may be ignorant of the economic opportunities open to them, or they may misjudge the potential returns from new practices. In many cases, the recommended procedures appear to be only imperfectly adopted. Farmers may use new seed but no fertilizer, or use fertilizer in seed beds but not in their fields. For various reasons, including the great effort required to reach a large number of small

[5]The new wheat varieties introduced into Morocco from Mexico were found to be highly susceptible to rust—a problem which had never occurred in the somewhat different Mexican climate.

farmers, extension agents spend less time visiting smaller farm units. The result is that the latter are less informed about new practices. A study in Zambia concluded that small farmers need to be educated regarding both the potentially commercial nature of farming and the profitability of innovation.

Noncredit Policy Requirements

To be successful in expanding production, government policy must seek to relax the constraints, whether financial or nonfinancial. For example, where the constraint is ignorance, the government's program should incorporate some form of extension service. Where it is a lack of experience with a particular input or crop, the program might include a subsidy on the input or a support price for the output to make farming more profitable. If the constraint is an aversion to risk, crop insurance may be used to reduce losses from low yields, or a support price may reduce the risk of price declines.

There are also various techniques for shifting more resources into agriculture. In addition to institutionalized credit programs, alternatives include cutting taxes on agriculture, particularly export levies, or improving the terms of trade between agriculture and other economic sectors. Many countries discriminate between the prices established for agricultural and for industrial commodities. These countries raise the prices of the latter through protective tariffs and depress those of the former by price controls on domestic foodstuffs and through taxes on export commodities. In countries that pursue such policies, improving the terms of trade for agriculture should be given the highest priority and would probably have a very substantial impact on output and, consequently, on the demand for credit.

However, it must be recognized that credit is but one facet of economic policy. Increased availability of credit may have little effect on production if other economic policies militate against the profitable use of credit. In such a situation, credit will become effective only if those policies are modified.

Credit and alternative programs of the kind indicated compete for scarce funds to achieve basically the same objective, i.e., to encourage farmers to adopt new agricultural practices. The choice of means, or combination of means, should depend upon a careful analysis of the nature of the constraints in a specific situation. The choice should also depend on costs of alternative programs and their political and administrative feasibility. The costs and the ability of the government to deliver services to a target group, especially in the case of small farmers, can differ markedly among programs.

For the very poor in rural areas, agricultural credit programs are of limited application. Many of the very poor in the countryside are landless laborers, or the aged or infirm. For them, credit will be of little direct benefit. But even owners of very small holdings may have either no productive opportunities or only require such small amounts of capital that grants would be more economical than the cost of collecting loans.

To help these underprivileged groups, programs other than credit have to be adopted. Agrarian reform is important. Programs aimed at improving the productive opportunities of small farmers will also help. So far, most agricultural research has been directed at mono-cultural practices. Litttle has been done to improve methods of inter-cropping, typically employed by very small farmers. In addition, programs not directly connected with agriculture, such as health and education schemes, are likely to improve farm productivity. But, in the end, many in these groups will improve their lot only by leaving agri-culture and finding employment elsewhere.

Chapter 2: AGRICULTURAL CREDIT PROGRAMS AND POLICIES

The success of credit operations depends not only on the condi-tions under which farmers use institutional credit to expand produc-tion, but also on the agricultural credit agencies themselves. Institu-tions present three key problems: (1) the design of credit programs; (2) the financial viability of the credit agency; and (3) the structure of the credit delivery mechanism. In order to discuss these issues, however, some conceptual clarifications are required.

Firstly, for purposes of exposition, this paper divides farmers into two classes—large farmers and small farmers. There is, however, actually an infinite variety of farm sizes, and the problems of the medium-sized farmers cannot be ignored. Experience has shown that the most progressive farmers—who are the real innovators—most often come from this class. Secondly, land quality is as important as land size. Three hectares of irrigated lowland may be far more pro-ductive than 25 hectares of arid or mountainous land. Thirdly, invest-ment opportunities vary. The point was made earlier that investment programs would succeed only if the farmer had profitable investment opportunities. To take advantage of some opportunities requires only additional working capital, while others need more expensive fixed investments. Because of differences in the size of holdings, the quality of land and the nature of the investment opportunity, there is a substantial range in the additional capital required by farmers. This amount cannot be precisely identified with farm size, and certainly not with the oversimplified terms, small and large farmers.

For the design of credit programs, what matters is not so much the size of landholdings, but the scale and type of the farmers' loan requirements. For example, costs of administration rise as the average size of loans declines. A small farmer seeking to finance the acquisition of a tubewell may require more funds than a large farmer borrowing for the purchase of fertilizer. Also, the availability of credit personnel and the level of their salaries greatly influence the type of credit program that can be administered economically. Where salaries are low, it is, of course, possible to service smaller loans. For example, on the rich alluvial lands in certain areas of Asia, it may be economical to have credit programs serving farmers with much smaller landholdings than in the mountains of Latin America. In the latter case, because of the poorer land quality, the different nature of the investments and the higher salaries of credit officials, the costs of credit service for farmers of a similar size would be much higher.

Designing Credit Programs

Separation of Programs for Different Borrowers

Experience with both World Bank and other programs has shown that, when a single credit agency serves both large and small farmers, most of the funds go to large farmers. In part, this is a political problem. At the local level, it is the larger farmers who have the political and social influence with the credit agents. In addition, lending to large farmers involves lower costs and lower risks. As will be discussed later, administrative costs on small loans to widely dispersed farmers are high. Institutions are often unable to charge interest rates high enough to cover the costs of small-farmer lending. Because it is more difficult for small farmers to generate a marketable surplus, the risk of default on small-farmer lending is also greater. Finally, many credit agencies require some form of security from farmers, and small farmers have little or no security to offer. Since the misuse of funds for consumption, high default rates and an inability to recover costs are usually considered the hallmarks of a poorly administered credit program, managers of credit institutions attempt to hold down the amounts of small-farmer loans to avoid these problems.

In order to increase the probability that funds intended for small farmers actually reach them, it seems advisable that the Bank should support separate credit programs for large and small farmers in areas where landholdings differ markedly in size. But, since credit institutions utilize scarce human and capital resources, it is often not economical to have completely separate and parallel lending organizations for the two categories. In such cases, different programs should be created within a single institution largely utilizing the same facilities and personnel, but keeping the financial accounts separate. Where small and large farms cannot be clearly distinguished, other criteria, such as income, will have to be adopted to differentiate between the two.

Providing Credit for Particular Purposes

The World Bank's agricultural credit projects have generally been oriented toward funding specified production activities (hence their classification into livestock, mechanization, general agriculture and other categories). But the items covered are often not exclusively of a single type. All components of a production package should be, and usually are, financed under such schemes. In some instances, this has unfortunately not been the case. For example, in cash crop projects in Africa, credit was provided for inputs for the cash crop (mainly fertilizer) but not for the subsistence crop, though the cash crop can be grown on many farms only if land is released from subsistence crops by increased yields. In a number of agricultural credit projects, as in India, short-term credit for incremental working capital needed because of permanent improvements and the adoption of modern technologies has not always been made available. Lack of coordination between two separate cooperative systems, which provide either short- or long-term credit, was to blame. Clearly, there is a need to think of production packages for the farm as an entity and to finance all complementary components of a new technology package, if the goal of rapid innovation is to be attained. Further, there is a need for related long-term financing plans which project farmers' overall financial requirements and recognize the necessity for sustained financial support for on-farm development and working capital.

Terms and Conditions of Lending

In the past, the World Bank has financed credit programs for lending to farmers for investments in fixed capital. The Bank believed this type of lending to be most appropriate, since it is the lumpier investments with longer-term payoffs that farmers have the most trouble financing from their own savings or from commercial sources. (The latter usually provide only relatively short-term credits.) Many of the longer-term investments in fixed capital are not suitable for small farmers because of size "indivisibilities." However, this constraint could be reduced by creating farmer groups which would share capital investments for such installations as tubewells and pumps. A further reduction in the scale of investments might be achieved by developing smaller-scale equipment and irrigation systems. At present, however, much of the investment requirements of smaller farmers are seasonal—to take advantage of new technology comprising seed, fertilizer, pesticides and the like.

Most of the credit from public agricultural credit institutions is for short duration loans for working capital. Annex 11 shows that in Africa and Latin America, 75% of the institutional loans are for two years or less. In Asia, that figure is 65%. Certainly, a similar proportion of small-farmer credit needs will be short-term. The World Bank has, for the most part, followed a policy of financing a working capital revolving fund only when it constitutes an essential part of investment under a project and meets two conditions: it is incremental start-up working capital, and such financing is not available from other sources. The Bank's approach has been essentially pragmatic, however, and in recent years the policy toward seasonal lending has been relaxed. One of the first cases of such a change in policy was in Tanzania. There, the Bank financed a substantial portion of a permanent working capital revolving fund for cooperatives to purchase and distribute fertilizer and pesticides to their members. In the future, the Bank's increased emphasis on small-farmer projects will necessitate more lending to credit institutions that finance seasonal activities. Farmers most need credit of this kind to produce a marketable surplus.

The small size of individual loans is one reason for the high administrative costs in most small-farm lending programs. These programs can ill afford to fragment further into separate long-term and short-term components. Consequently, small-farmer credit agencies should be responsible for the delivery of both long-term and short-term credit. These agencies should supplement long-term financing with working capital when needed, as well as provide short-term loans for small farmers with only seasonal credit needs.

Provision of Complementary Services

A shortage of capital is not the only constraint preventing the adoption of a new technology. Often the farmer lacks other important ingredients—a knowledge of technology, inputs such as fertilizer and seed, and sometimes the ability to sell his crop. To make the credit program a success, the government must provide the complementary inputs that the market system or other channels do not provide, or provide poorly. Usually, various specialized agencies supply the auxiliary services of extension, sale of inputs and marketing. Often, however, several separate services are delivered jointly in what has been called a package program.

The package approach is to be preferred since it provides the farmer with credit plus all the ancillary services he requires, even though some of the benefits of specialization are thereby lost. Several of the smallholder projects which the Bank has supported in Africa are of the integrated variety. They include the Lilongwe and Shire Valley projects in Malawi, tea projects in Kenya, Tanzania and Mauritius, the Wolamo project in Ethiopia, the Casamance project in Senegal, and the cocoa and palm oil projects in the Ivory Coast. These projects have been a success. On the other hand, in several credit programs in Latin America in which the credit agency assumed responsibility for performing noncredit functions not directly related to the purposes of the loan, the quality of lending and the credit institution's financial position deteriorated.

Whether a single agency should be responsible for delivering several services or specialize in only one depends on each situation. In countries rich in manpower and institutions, there are some advantages in specialization. In less well endowed countries, it is possible to separate functions at the apex level but combine them at the local level where the availability of staff is thinnest and application most costly. Where administrations are least developed, it is necessary to utilize whatever distribution channels exist. Sometimes this will mean credit officers providing extension. In other cases, organizations developed by private companies to ensure adequate supplies of such crops as tobacco, tea, cotton and groundnuts may be used to provide the needed services. Finally, area or crop development organizations, such as those being assisted by the Bank in Africa, may perform these functions.

In sum, the scope of activity best suited to credit agencies will depend upon the availability of trained personnel and the feasibility of using or creating separate administrations to provide the additional services required to stimulate farmer development. If a multiservice approach is adopted, the credit agency should keep costs and income from various activities separate and be reimbursed for the costs of services not related to the administration of the credit program. If a clear division of costs is not established and if there is no compensation for ancillary services, it will not be possible to judge the financial success of the credit program. Then, losses incurred by providing ancillary services may lead unjustifiably to abandoning the entire program.

The most common ancillary service provided and financed by credit agencies is farm supervision. The degree of supervision employed varies widely. It ranges from simple provision of basic crop information (a service roughly equivalent to extension) to the specification of inputs (sometimes provided in kind to prevent the misuse of loans), to almost complete control of farm operations by supervising officers. Supervision is designed to help the farmer but also to prevent loan funds from being misused for financing consumption and to ensure repayment. Improved supervision can encourage the effective use of credit.

But supervision to prevent the use of loans to finance consumption can be only partially successful. Farmers, particularly small farmers, seldom divide their operations between production and consumption. Farm life is integrated and much of a farmer's production is used for household consumption. Due to the inherent fungibility of credit, supervision can never completely eliminate increases in consumption following the receipt of loans, even when credit is provided in kind. Because supervision is costly, it must be subjected to careful evaluation and planning in terms of number, purpose and scope of visits by the supervisory officer, to assure that benefits justify costs. Essentially, expanded supervision appears to be warranted as a means of reducing defaults.

Financial Viability of Credit Institutions

Throughout the period of the World Bank's involvement in agricultural credit, a major concern has been to strengthen the credit institutions within the borrowing countries, and particularly to ensure their financial viability. The main reason is that institutions without financial viability, if they survive at all, depend on annual appropriations from governments to help cover costs and are, therefore, susceptible to political influence. In fact, without substantial subsidies, few existing credit institutions would have been able to survive. For most of them, costs have exceeded revenues, and inflation plus defaults have eroded their capital structure.

Loan Delinquencies

Failure of farmers to repay their debts on time, or to repay them at all, is a serious problem for most agricultural credit institutions. The data on delinquencies and defaults, by country and program, are shown in Annex 12. The table presents two measures of arrears where available: unpaid loans as a percentage of the total portfolio and as a percentage of payments coming due and those overdue. The latter percentage is called the arrears rate. The figures cited should not be used to make invidious comparisons among countries or programs because they reflect a wide variation in definition and in the quality of information. Nevertheless, the import of the data is clear. In most programs, delinquency rates are very high, frequently as much as 50% of amounts due. Some agencies are thought to have even higher rates of arrears than reported in the Annex, but these are concealed, primarily through the refinancing of unpaid debts.

Data on actual defaults are scanty. But experience shows that, except for a few countries, recuperation of large portions of arrears is usually possible over a number of years. On Bank-assisted projects, losses resulting from defaults have seldom exceeded 5% of loans outstanding. Nevertheless, loan delinquency is serious for most agricultural credit institutions because it results in a waste of manpower, higher administration costs and slow turnover of resources. In recent years, projects supported by the Bank have experienced serious collection problems in Colombia, Pakistan, Senegal, Tanzania and in certain Indian states.

There are three general reasons for overdues. The first stems from the farmer's failure to use borrowed funds for productive purposes. Secondly, overdues may result from the investment having gone bad rather than from a failure to apply the loan proceeds as expected. Causes include bad harvests, natural disasters of various kinds and changes in economic conditions followed by a drop in farm prices. Some loans have been made on the basis of unrealistically favorable assumptions about the results. At other times, the terms of loans were ill-suited for the purpose, e.g., short-term loans for medium-term activities. Although much of this can be prevented by improved planning and a better appreciation of the real developmental potential in specific situations, along with consideration of the borrower's repayment capacity, many overdues will continue to occur for reasons that cannot be foreseen at the time the loans are made.

The third reason for delinquency or default is related not to an inability, but to a refusal, to repay. Whether a debtor has the funds to repay a loan is, of course, not always clear-cut. Some funds usually are available and farmers have to establish priorities for their use. Apparently, repaying public sector credits is accorded low priority. In some cases, farmers have the impression that credit is a gift made to ensure their loyalty and future support. Governments sometimes do little to change this attitude, and may even encourage it in times of political uncertainty. Low interest rates may also encourage delinquency, especially if new credit has to be obtained at a higher rate.

The farmer's lack of enthusiasm toward repayment is worsened by the unwillingness of governments to impose sanctions, through their credit institutions, on those whose debts are overdue. If land is pledged as collateral, government credit institutions rarely foreclose. Denial of new loans is the usual penalty for failure to repay. This is often a weak sanction, especially for short-term credit, since the farmer has less incentive to repay when the size of a recurring loan levels off. This is reflected in lower repayment percentages as programs mature. Lack of proper records and effective collection procedures also contribute to poor repayment performance.

Cases have arisen where nonrepayment has been the result of a concentrated effort to cheat the credit institution, which is sometimes encouraged by landowners and moneylenders who fear the competition. At times, nonpayment stems from corruption within the credit institution itself. Some officials are more interested in bribes from borrowers than in the difficult, and personally less remunerative, task of recovering the overdues.

Failure to repay is common to large and small farmers alike. Small farmers appear to be more prone to delinquency stemming from the first two causes. Small farmers are more likely to use borrowed funds for consumption and, in poor crop years, are less able to generate the marketable surplus needed to repay their loans. On the other hand, in several countries, including Bangladesh, Bolivia, Colombia, Costa Rica and Ethiopia, there is evidence that larger farmers actually have poorer repayment records. In many of these countries, it appears that delinquencies by large farmers are deliberate as they use their political power to protect themselves against penalties. Overdues also occur where agrarian reforms are expected or are already in effect, and repayment of past loans is stopped in the hope that a debt adjustment or moratorium on repayment will be forthcoming.

From the overall economic point of view, defaults are transfer payments to the defaulting farmers. But it is one of the least desirable or equitable forms of transfer. It destroys the financial viability of the credit institution, and farmers who know they will not be required to repay are more likely to use the borrowed funds for consumption purposes. From a social viewpoint, this is one of the most costly aspects of the default problem.

Reducing the levels of delinquency and default is the most important issue in seeking to make public sector credit programs financially viable. Traditionally, credit agencies have required that borrowers pledge some collateral, usually land, to secure their loans. Although this practice is feasible when lending to large farmers, small farmers often lack certified titles to their land and tenants have no title. Moreover, it is frequently difficult and expensive for the small farmer to obtain the appropriate legal instruments. For its part, the World Bank has consistently emphasized that the productive capacity of a farmer's holding should substitute for security as the essential criterion in loan decisions.

In many cases, it is too costly to foreclose on assets pledged by small farmers, making security instruments poor protection against default. Lending only to those with investment opportunities sufficient to produce a significant marketable surplus is perhaps the best way to reduce the level of default. In the Puebla project in Mexico, and such programs as that of the Instituto Colombiano de la Reforma Agraria (INCORA) in Colombia and of the Associação de Credito e Assistencia Rural (ACAR) in Brazil, where the use of credit was followed by a large increase in output, the problems of default and delinquency have been noticeably reduced. Delinquencies have also been reduced when repayment has been coordinated with the marketing of crops that are centrally processed, e.g., tobacco, cotton, cocoa, tea and coffee. The use of chattel mortgages and liens on crop production has been effective as a low-cost method of protection against default.

Following a bad harvest, credit agencies frequently adjust repayment terms, either through renewals or postponement of maturity dates. However, most of the available data indicate that once a loan is in arrears, collection is both difficult and costly. This suggests that in areas where output is highly variable, it might be possible to employ contracts whereby the credit agency would be paid a percentage of the farmers' output rather than a fixed amount. Such sharecropping arrangements are quite common for land rentals. Crop insurance is a possible way to protect both the borrower and the credit agency against the vagaries of nature. Both approaches involve difficulties of administration and, in the case of crop insurance, may prove costly.

If the incidence of delinquency and default associated with poor harvests and a failure to use borrowed funds for production could be reduced, credit agencies could afford to deal more strictly with the remaining source of overdues, i.e., farmers who have the funds but refuse to repay. The onus attached to attempts by public credit agencies to take court action would be greatly reduced if such efforts were confined to deliberate defaulters. This becomes largely a matter of attitude and political will. If external lenders were to withhold funding where that will is lacking, it might strengthen the government's hand.

Costs of Agricultural Credit

Credit programs are costly to operate. The administrative costs of agricultural credit institutions vary considerably, as shown in Annex 13. In part, the variation in reported costs reflects a difference in concept and in the responsibilities of the institutions involved. The costs of supervision and other ancillary services vary, but it has not been possible to eliminate these items to achieve comparability among agencies. In some cases, the cost figures cited encompass the entire credit delivery mechanism, while in others the costs refer only to one element among many in a chain of credit delivery. In addition, cost accounting procedures, especially for reserves and write-downs of defaulted loans, vary widely. For the group of institutions shown, the median figure for administrative costs as a percentage of the total portfolio would be around 5%.

The administrative costs of agricultural credit institutions tend to be high in relation to most other types of lending institutions. Because borrowers in rural areas are widely dispersed, credit distribution is more costly there than in urban areas. Also, collection costs are higher because of the high level of overdues inherent in agricultural credit.

Administrative costs, of course, depend upon the size of loans and their duration. For an efficient institution making medium- and long-term loans to large farmers, the costs of administration are about 3% of the total portfolio.[1] The costs rise if the institution provides ancillary services or has to mobilize funds through deposits.

Although a general study of costs in credit programs supported by the World Bank has yet to be undertaken, a recent analysis of administrative costs of credit agencies in India funded by Bank loans and IDA credits may serve as an example. At the level of the land development banks, the administrative costs were 3% of the total portfolio. Adding the costs of the apex bank raised administrative costs to 4% on outstanding credits. However, in India a portion of the total costs of credit administration were borne by the state government departments of cooperatives; if these costs were included, total administrative costs would be higher. In addition, the land development banks handled only medium- and long-term loans, going principally to medium-sized and large farmers. They provided no extension or supervisory services, and benefited from a salary scale that was low. All these factors helped keep costs down.

The costs of administration rise as the size of loans falls, as the duration of loans shortens, and as the amount of ancillary services provided increases. Also, costs tend to be greater in wealthier countries where credit officers are paid higher salaries. For an efficient credit institution providing a mix of short- and long-term loans to

---

[1]This is somewhat higher than the administrative costs of development finance companies (DFCs), which grant medium- and long-term loans to private industrial enterprises. It is somewhat lower than the costs of efficient commercial banks in developing countries that lend to large urban corporate customers on a short- and medium-term basis but have to incur the substantial costs of mobilizing savings through deposits.

small farmers, administrative costs would be between 7% and 10% of the total portfolio.[2] This assumes that the institution would bear all costs associated with credit delivery, but would exclude extension and other ancillary services. The actual cost would depend upon size and type of loan and salary scale. There is a trade-off between administrative costs and delinquencies and defaults. The more carefully the institution scrutinizes applicants, supervises loans and pursues delinquents, the lower the delinquency and default rates—but the higher the administrative costs. However, no amount of appraisal or loan supervision can reduce defaults much if they arise from political misuse of the credit institution or if the failure to repay is quietly condoned. With sufficient political will, it should be possible to reduce complete defaults to 5% or less in a well-run credit institution.

The cost of the capital used by the credit agency is an additional factor to be taken into account. Some public credit institutions receive government loans on which they are required to pay little interest. Others operate on government-provided equity funds. Whatever the financial charge for capital, however, there is an opportunity cost of using funds for agricultural credit rather than for some alternative program. There is a substantial amount of literature on the opportunity costs of capital in developing countries. These estimates are seldom less than 8% in real terms, approximately the level required to mobilize savings effectively.

In sum, the forgone opportunity costs of using funds for agricultural credit are at least 8% per year in real terms. Administrative costs for institutions making long-term loans to large farmers may be as low as 3% per year, while short-term loans for small farmers will average at least 8% per year. "Normal" defaults can be expected to add another 4% to costs. Excluding supervision and ancillary services, total costs in real terms for an efficient institution would range between 15% and 20%, depending upon the nature of the operation and the average size of loans.

Interest Rates

Credit programs, in the past, were aimed at protecting small farmers from exploitation by moneylenders. Consistent with this goal, interest rates were set quite low. It would be fair to say that these programs were not expected to be self-financing. Governments, at least implicitly, recognized that the loans contained a large element of

---

[2] *In developed countries, consumer credit institutions which lend relatively small amounts primarily for short and medium terms have administrative costs of between 6% and 12% of the total portfolio, depending on the term, collateral and credit risk involved. Defaults average around 2%.*

subsidy. Although the original program objectives have changed over time, interest rates charged have remained relatively low in nominal terms. In some countries with substantial rates of inflation, they have become negative in real terms. Institutional interest rates are low compared with those charged by commercial lenders. Institutional rates are also low relative to the cost of funds as determined by supply and demand in the market, and low as compared with agency costs.

The nominal rates charged farmers by institutions (see Annex 9) fall between 5% and 30% per year. Half the institutions charge between 9% and 12%, with the remainder about equally divided between those charging more and those charging less. Interest rates, corrected for inflation, range from -16% to $+16\%$. The nominal rate charged by institutions averages about 10% and the real rate above 3%.

From the point of view of the farmer, institutional credits involve other costs in addition to the rates cited. Detailed studies of the true costs to the farmer of official agency credit in Bangladesh, Brazil and various countries in the Middle East showed that the combination of application fees, travel and "entertainment" costs, and working days lost in arranging loans greatly diminished the attractiveness of public credit as compared with private borrowing. Information from other countries suggests that significant "informal" charges on public credit are not confined to these areas. Nevertheless, even allowing for the hidden costs, institutional credit in most countries is notably cheaper than loans from commercial lenders.

The level of interest rates on loans to subborrowers and the spread available to credit institutions are recurrent points of discussion between the World Bank and many borrowers. It could be argued on economic grounds that interest rates should reflect the true cost of capital. This argument rests on an assumption that even though capital and credit markets are imperfect, the interest rate influences resource allocation, savings mobilization, the financial viability of the credit institution and equity.

Resource Allocation: The Bank is lending to institutions with a production orientation and assists in the financing of investments with a high expected rate of return. If productive opportunities exist and capital is scarce, low rates should not be necessary to stimulate investment. On the other hand, if farmers cannot afford to pay adequate rates because the investments open to them have low yields, it is questionable whether these investments constitute the best use of scarce resources. Low interest rates lead to higher capital-output ratios on the farm. In countries with surplus labor, this is a questionable policy.

146

Savings Mobilization: Agricultural credit agencies have attempted to mobilize rural savings in the form both of deposits and of equity participations. Countries that have succeeded in mobilizing voluntary savings in the rural areas have paid high rates for deposits. These countries include Japan, where deposits in cooperatives amount to 84% of working capital, and the Republic of China, where the comparable figure is 76%. The savings mobilization effort in other countries without high deposit rates, such as India, Peru and Senegal, has been much less successful.

Some institutions offer equity participation as a means of mobilizing capital. In several countries (e.g., Ecuador, Thailand and Tunisia), borrowers are required to purchase shares in the cooperative in proportion to the size of the loans. Farmers regard such purchases as compensating balances whose effect is to raise the rate of interest. In most countries, however, the difficulty of redeeming shares, the absence of dividends and the poor operating record of many of the cooperatives discourage farmers from voluntarily purchasing shares.

Financial Viability: Financial institutions charging rates which are insufficient to cover costs cannot be financially self-sufficient. If they must rely upon government transfers for survival, they become susceptible to political influence. If governments are unwilling to provide adequate transfers, or if politicization of the institution results in high default rates, the credit agency runs the risk of paralysis and ultimately of reorganization or closure. Financial institutions represent an investment in organization and human capital that few developing countries can afford to lose.

Equity Considerations: If charges on institutional loans are set unduly low, large farmers almost always garner a disproportionate share because of their greater political power. In fact, if cheap credit is available in excess of investment needs, large farmers may utilize institutional loans to purchase land, thereby exacerbating the land tenure problem. Evidence from Colombia and Ethiopia shows that this is a serious matter. Unless rates are high enough, even for small farmers, the financing institutions' resources will not be replenished and fewer farmers will have access to credit.

A number of major considerations, however, may in practice require substantial departures from using an interest rate that covers the real cost of lending. These include:

1. *Comparative intersectoral interest rates.* In practice, real rates throughout most economies are likely to be well below the rate that would cover the real cost of lending in agriculture (especially to small farmers). Forcing up interest rates for agriculture alone can lead to an

uneconomic diversion of resources and considerable leakage between sectors. The problem for agriculture cannot be separated from that of the economy at large, and a solution rests on restructuring lending rates under a national policy on interest rates.

2. *The level of interest rates and the psychological impact on borrowers.* A substantial rise in interest could have a deleterious impact on borrowers. Sharp rises may well deter small-scale farmers, or farmers moving into the cash economy, from borrowing the resources needed to sustain the production of a marketable surplus. Interest rates would have to be increased gradually to avoid discouraging this class of borrower and would probably have to remain low over a fairly long period of time.

3. *Low levels of interest rates and discrimination against agriculture.* The terms of trade are often weighted against agriculture. Low interest rates are advocated as a means of offsetting the discrimination from adverse terms of trade between agriculture and industry or between agriculture and the rest of the economy. Using interest rates for this purpose may have merit. However, by the same token, modifying interest rates to offset the terms of trade may further distort the economy. In this event, it may be preferable to go to the heart of the matter, wherever possible, and change the policies that discriminate against agriculture. These might include tariff policies that lead to high-cost domestic production of manufactured goods or policies that penalize agricultural exports.

4. *Low interest rates help to fulfill social objectives.* Subsidized interest rates—especially to small farmers—can help redistribute income in favor of the low-income groups in the agriculture sector. Given the extreme inequalities in income distribution, there may be considerable merit in using subsidized interest rates for income redistribution. However, there are also arguments against the use of subsidized or differential interest rates for social purposes:

(a) It has been pointed out that lower interest rates lead to higher capital-output ratios on the farm. Low interest rates may be questionable when there is surplus labor since they may discourage the expansion of employment.

(b) Experience indicates that subsidized or differential interest rates are open to considerable abuse. Frequently, leakage occurs and larger farmers obtain loans at subsidized rates. Subsidized interest rates also provide opportunities for corruption and political manipulation. It is difficult to ensure that low-interest loans reach the groups for which they are intended. It is not uncommon to find that subsidized loans have been diverted to nonagricultural uses or have been used in ways that contribute little to a rise in output of small farmers.

(c) If it costs 15% to 20% to lend money and the rate charged for lending is half this amount (as it frequently is), then each loan made by an institution will contribute to a depletion of its resources. This, in turn, will diminish the "reflow" of funds into the system for institutional lending. The lending ability and the financial viability of the institution will be weakened. Reliance on budgetary support to maintain financial viability diminishes the institution's independence and can make it susceptible to pressures that may reduce its effectiveness.

(d) Subsidizing interest rates may not be an effective means of redistributing income, since institutional credit may reach only a minority of small farmers. It is questionable whether income distribution can be improved substantially by further subsidizing small farmers who already benefit from access to institutional credit when this reduces the resources available to the lending institution for other small farmers. In addition, subsidized interest rates would not help the large group of landless laborers nor farmers whose holdings are so small that they cannot qualify for credit. Redistribution of income often can be implemented more effectively by means other than subsidizing interest rates for small farmers.

(e) Subsidized interest rates have been advocated as a means of encouraging technological change in agriculture. Low-cost capital may induce farmers to adopt changes in methods of production, but subsidies to encourage change are usually most effective when they are linked to a particular technology. Thus, when the use of an input, such as fertilizer is to be encouraged, it is preferable to subsidize the fertilizer rather than the cost of credit *per se*. Furthermore, subsidizing an input such as fertilizer, has the advantage that the subsidy can be modified as the input gains acceptability and so can be varied, depending on the rate of acceptance of the new input. Subsidized interest rates, on the other hand, have a pervasive effect and so cannot be varied according to the rate of acceptance of a given input or change.

(f) A subsidy that might be effective would be one to cover the added administrative costs of lending to small farmers. Such a subsidy could be used to equalize interest rates so that all loans of equal duration would carry the same charge whether for the use of large or of small farmers. A unified interest rate would avoid the leakages and opportunities for corruption that might stem from differential rates. In addition, uniform interest rates would help foster optional resource allocation, especially if they reflect the true cost of capital.

This discussion indicates that there is no simple or unique answer to the question of what constitutes an appropriate interest rate for agriculture, especially for small farmers.

It follows that there is no unique answer to the question of what might be an appropriate interest rate on a Bank-assisted agricultural credit project. Many considerations will have to be brought to bear. It is difficult for the Bank to press for interest rates that are different from those charged by others on similar projects. This is especially the case in regions where other external lenders have accepted the plea that interest rates should be heavily subsidized. In such situations, the Bank seeks to work with other external donors and the borrowing government to develop a common policy consistent with the best interests of the national economy.

In general, the World Bank strives toward the objective that institutions should lend at positive interest rates which reflect the costs of capital and of providing the capital. Such an objective should be seen as a long-term goal. An intermediate objective might be to set the interest rate at a level which at least covers the opportunity cost of capital. If subsidies are used, these should generally be limited to cases where they can be clearly justified and are likely to be effective in view of the pattern of farming in the project area.

Lending in an inflationary situation presents a special problem. In recent years, the Bank has made loans, particularly in several Latin American countries, where the rate of inflation has been both high and variable. On several occasions, the Bank declined to make new loans until inflation was brought under a semblance of control. Where it did lend, it insisted either on rates sufficiently high to cover the expected price increases or on indexing the principal of the loan and/or the interest charges. This procedure has now been used by the Bank in nine countries.

If indexing is applied only to agricultural credit and not to other kinds of lending, it disrupts the allocation of resources. It is inequitable if only farmers or, worse still, small farmers have to pay indexed rates while others do not. Further study of the problem of inflation as it relates to credit is necessary, but it is a problem which affects all lending, not in agriculture alone.

The choice of an appropriate price index to which interest rates may be tied, presents difficulties. Various indices have been used, including the price of livestock (for livestock projects), consumer price indexes and the exchange rate. All have deficiencies. If indexing is to be used in the future, detailed studies of suitable measures should be made. In some cases, a catch clause allowing for an increase in interest on, say, three months' notice, may be an effective approach. However, when the inflation rate is variable, inflationary expectations differ. High nominal rates, particularly when set only on certain loans (for instance, institutional loans in agriculture), may deter borrowers rather than promote development.

Finally, it must be borne in mind that credit is only one element in the package of inputs and services necessary to raise the productivity of small farmers. Frequently, it may not be the most important element. Thus, the attitude of the Bank on the issue of interest rates will have to be determined by the extent to which a project overall is achieving the objective of increasing the productivity of small farmers and giving them a satisfactory rate of return. The significance of a proper interest rate must be seen in the perspective of the many-faceted requirements of raising incomes of the mass of potentially viable, small-scale agricultural producers.

Chapter 3: SYSTEMS FOR DELIVERING AGRICULTURAL CREDIT

Policy Making and Administrative Issues

The implementation of a credit program involves strategic, tactical and day-to-day decisions. The first category covers questions of priority: budgetary allocation to agriculture as against other sectors and, more specifically, to credit as against other developmental tools. This process covers borrowing from organizations such as the World Bank, and setting the key conditions of credit policy, such as the interest rate. Because government credit covers only a limited number of farmers, strategic considerations also include the decision on the characteristics, broadly defined, of those to be financed. This may represent a choice among regions, among income classes or among crops. In most governments, such decisions would be made at the ministerial level.

Normally, the tactical decisions would be handled by the organization responsible for administering agricultural finance. These functions include the detailed design and organization of the credit program; the choice, training and supervision of staff; the handling of funds and accounting procedures; and the coordination of activities with agencies responsible for providing ancillary services. In design, credit institutions are usually pyramidal. At the top is an apex financial institution, under which are several layers of bureaucracy, sometimes within one institution and sometimes organized into separate agencies. At the bottom is the widely dispersed organization which actually delivers credit to farmers. The bottom layer is responsible for day-to-day operations. These include adapting the credit program to local conditions; choosing borrowers or organizing credit groups; coordinating activities with other agencies at the local level; and granting, supervising and collecting loans.

The process is complex and problems may arise at any stage in the credit delivery system. However, there seem to be issues which, while not found in all credit organizations, are common to many. The first is the politicization of the credit delivery mechanism. This process can hardly be avoided in some form when dealing with the distribution of an input such as credit which is in short supply and is channeled through a government bureaucracy. Because large farmers have greater political influence, they have usually been able to garner most of the government-provided credit.

In many countries, politics has invaded the tactical and even the operational level of credit delivery. The choice of directors for the credit institution, and sometimes even of the staff, may be made on grounds of political loyalties rather than qualifications. And, in some cases, politics spills over into the choice of individual loan recipients and the degree to which sanctions against defaulters are enforced. While the strategy of credit cannot be completely divorced from politics, it is obviously desirable to insulate actual operations from political interference as much as possible.

The second problem common to many credit programs is over-centralization with subsequent cumbersome and inflexible procedures for obtaining loans. An organization delivering credit to farmers, especially where many small loans are involved, has to be widely dispersed. Furthermore, at the local level the staff is usually thin and inadequately trained. To control such an operation is difficult, and the procedure typically adopted is to centralize the decision-making processes. Loan decisions often must be passed on to higher levels in the bureaucracy. The result is a credit program costly to administer, beset by paper work and red tape, and not well adapted to local conditions. Illiterate farmers are subject to preaudits and postaudits. The actual delivery of credit is slowed. Few agencies can process loan applications in less than 60 days, and many take up to 90 days to provide funds after receiving a request. For long-term investment loans, this time element is not so important. But for small farmers who do not plan their credit requirements in advance, such delays in obtaining seasonal credit often mean that they receive the funds only after the need for them has passed.

Studies of farmer attitudes have shown that farmers often are so disenchanted with the red tape and delays of centralized credit programs that they prefer to borrow from moneylenders. The latter can operate more quickly and flexibly, though they charge higher interest rates. Farmer alienation is increased when, as a result of inflexibility and the lack of a proper feedback mechanism, the credit program is poorly adapted to local requirements. The problem of poor staffing at the local level is a real one, but overcentralization is clearly not the solution. Institution building and staff training are needed. The use of farmer groups and cooperatives may also help reduce the problem of overcentralization. There is great scope for innovation and modification to improve the borrowing procedures for small farmers.

Channels of Agricultural Finance

As noted previously, noninstitutional sources provide most of the credit used by farmers in developing countries. On the institutional side, the main lenders are agricultural or development banks, usually established by the government and partially or, more frequently, fully government-owned; cooperatives or farmers' associations, often government-organized; and private or nationalized commercial banks. Many central banks are involved in various ways and degrees in the delivery of agricultural credit. Central banks primarily serve as a rediscount facility but also are involved in developing and enforcing lending policies and the sectoral allocation of resources. In a few countries, such as India, the central bank has played a considerable role as promoter of agricultural credit through research, guidance, supervision, and the establishment and financing of agricultural credit agencies.

The funds provided by the World Bank for agricultural credit are usually loaned or passed on initially to an apex financial institution which then re-lends, either directly through its own network of branches or through independent intermediaries, to the ultimate borrowers. The Bank's funds have, therefore, currently been handled at the top level of government agricultural or development banks and central banks, or by special agricultural refinance institutions, usually closely associated with central banks. The World Bank's experience has been that central banks are well suited to serve as conduits for credit agencies. Where the objective of the Bank is to lend to farmers through many institutions, principally commercial banks, the use of the central bank for refinancing is appropriate. However, central banks should not be associated too closely with administering agricultural credit programs, especially with making loans to ultimate borrowers. This might divert them from their primary responsibilities for financial and monetary policy. In some cases, the borrowing government on-lends or passes on the Bank's funds to a government agency or a special entity responsible for carrying out a project which re-lends the funds to the participants in the projects. The use of such channels, and also of central banks, should not obscure the need for building specialized agricultural credit institutions.

The volume of World Bank funds passing through the various channels which deliver credit directly to farmers is summarized in Annex 14. Commercial institutions, primarily banks, were the most important final channel utilized by the Bank in fiscal 1969-73, accounting for roughly 38% of agricultural loans. The bulk of the funds were for livestock projects in Latin America. Agricultural banks, once the most important channel, recently have become less important, but still distribute 25% of Bank loans to farmers. In recent years, cooperatives have emerged as an important final channel. Lending through cooperatives is concentrated in India, but has also been used by the Bank in the Republic of Korea, Niger and Tanzania. The channel "Project Authority, Ministry or Special Entity" in Annex 14 consists of the agencies or administrations, primarily government organizations, which are mainly in charge of regional integrated development, land settlement or development of a particular crop. The last channel, "Development Banks," represents a type of institution which, in addition to financing other sectors, lends to agriculture, mostly commercial agriculture.

Agricultural Credit Agencies

Agricultural and Development Banks

In many countries, governments have established specialized credit institutions, mostly state-owned or with majority government participation, for lending to agriculture. The World Bank has lent to farmers through these institutions in such countries as Afghanistan, Jordan, Kenya, Pakistan, Peru and Bolivia. The institutions lend primarily to large farmers, although their original purpose was often to benefit small farmers. Agricultural banks are operated through highly centralized bureaucratic structures, which tends to make them ill-suited for lending to large numbers of highly dispersed small farms.

Excessive centralization, when dealing with small farmers, often results in increased administrative costs, an inability to adjust programs to local conditions and political interference.

From experience, there seems to be a definite advantage in having specialized agricultural banks instead of multisectoral development banks extending short-, medium- and long-term credit. The latter are inclined to favor other sectors and confine lending principally to long-term credit. Development banks are also centrally operated and thus, like agricultural banks, are ill-suited to carry out credit programs for small farmers. Both types of institution may, however, lend to groups or cooperatives to make their credit accessible to the small farmer.

Farmer Groups and Cooperatives

To overcome problems associated with excessive centralization, many developing countries have tried to establish farmer groups and farmer cooperatives in order to reach small farmers. The idea is that when the group or cooperative is the final mechanism for delivering credit, it represents a form of organization which embodies decentralization of control and decision making, and incorporates local knowledge and responsibility.

The terms "cooperatives" and "farmer groups" cover a wide range of organizational forms. Farmer groups are usually informal in character, organized around a village, kinship or common economic interest; they typically have about 10 to 20 members. The groups include farmers' associations, village societies and peasant societies. If they grow too large, they tend to lose their social cohesiveness. In some cases, the only real function of the farmer groups is that they are jointly responsible for the repayment of members' loans. Other functions for delivering credit are retained by the financial institution which provides the funds. More authority is transferred when the group is made responsible for the division of funds among members and for the collection of loans. Further development takes place if the group manages a joint investment such as a tubewell. The group may also become a political organization for the small farmer, whereby he gains power vis-à-vis larger farmers and can participate in the decision-making process of the credit institution from which the group obtains its funds.

Formal cooperatives are usually larger-scale organizations, built around such functions as distributing credit, supplying inputs, marketing output, and managing joint investments such as storage facilities or processing plants. Credit cooperatives are financial institutions that usually hire their own professional staff. Farmers are required to make a financial commitment to the institution through the purchase of equity shares and sometimes also through deposits. In some cases, the credit cooperative is restricted to credit distribution, and separate organizations are created to manage joint investments or handle marketing. In other cases, one multipurpose cooperative is responsible for all of these functions. To be successful, cooperatives must have a certain minimum size and carry out a certain minimum volume of operations. The trend has been toward an increase in the size of these institutions for economic reasons, usually with adverse effects on their social cohesiveness.

Sometimes, informal farmer groups work in conjunction with formal farmer cooperatives. Some responsibilities, such as joint signing for loans and collection of repayments, are relegated to the farmer groups. Other functions, such as the choice of members and the decision on loan applications, may be retained by the cooperative. There are also cases where farmer groups deal directly with financial institutions of a noncooperative character. In Thailand, for example, commercial banks lend directly to farmer groups, and in the Western State of Nigeria, farmer groups borrow directly from the Agricultural Credit Corporation.

When functioning properly, the use of groups and cooperatives to deliver credit to small farmers has numerous advantages. Decentralization of the day-to-day aspects of management increases the adaptability of credit programs to local conditions and reduces the time required to process loan applications and make other decisions. Local knowledge can be used to assess the risk of lending to a particular farmer and his investment opportunities. This, plus group responsibility for repayment and equity participation in the cooperative, should reduce default. Furthermore, organizing farmers into groups raises the average size of loans—thereby reducing costs—and increases the political influence of the small farmer.

The cooperatives considered to be most successful are those in Egypt, areas of India, Israel, southern Brazil, the Republic of Korea and the Republic of China (Taiwan). Some have combined informal village groups with financial institutions operating on a cooperative basis. This was quite successful for a time at Comilla in Bangladesh. In most cases, however, although the so-called cooperatives have been effective in delivering credit and other inputs to the farmer, they have operated much like centralized credit bureaucracies.

The system of cooperatives in the Republic of Korea is a case in point. Almost all farmers are members, and almost all are small farmers. The one institution involved, the National Agricultural Cooperative Federation, is organized into three tiers—at the national, county and village or township levels. Overall, this system may be judged to be quite efficient, providing ancillary services as well as credit with relatively low administrative costs. Arrears also have been kept at manageable levels, averaging only 7% of the total portfolio in recent years. However, the system is tightly structured and highly centralized, and farmers have virtually no voice in its operations.

Institutions such as these are cooperatives only in the sense that a financial commitment in the form of shares or deposits is required of members. In other respects, they are quite similar to specialized agricultural banks and many suffer from the same problems. Cooperatives and farmer groups which are truly locally controlled have proved to be difficult to establish. Many societies are quite individualistic and small farmers everywhere tend to shy away from being organized. Moreover, in many countries both the government and the wealthy farmers who are the local leaders have discouraged the growth of representative organizations of small farmers. Cooperatives have tended to work best in areas where landholdings have been homogeneous, tenant farmers have equal status, some social cohesion exists at the grass roots, and where literacy has attained a reasonable level. Grouping small farmers into cooperatives and farmers' associations has great promise, but developing these organizations and adapting them to local conditions inevitably takes time and requires a strong commitment from the government. The World Bank expects to foster the development of appropriate conditions, but should avoid pursuing a single or rigid concept of cooperative organization since many forms of association can be effective.

Project Authorities

Special project authorities or project units have often retained the responsibility of extending credit to participants for on-farm development and working capital. These agencies have been established to execute various projects of regional integrated development, land settlement, crop development and irrigation. In many instances, farmers had no alternative credit sources because no agricultural credit system was available or the existing one was unsatisfactory. In some cases, there were clear advantages in associating credit closely with other services provided by the authority. The project authorities are government departments, public boards or statutory corporations, funds set up by special acts, or companies organized under special or general legislation. Project authorities generally have established special units with expert staff to deal with agricultural credit operations. Especially when authorities were set up to develop a specific cash crop or to carry out a regionally integrated development project, the arrangements have achieved close integration of credit operations and ensured productive use of credit and satisfactory repayment records. Cooperatives and farmer groups are, in some cases, intermediaries between farmers and the project authority. But there is a need to develop apex institutions which can promote, oversee and service such enclaves within national programs.

Most of the World Bank's experience with crop or regional project authorities is in Africa. Countries there generally have not had suitable nationwide administrative mechanisms to provide various services and credit. Projects falling in this category include the Lilongwe and Shire Valley projects in Malawi; tea projects in Kenya carried out by the Kenya Tea Development Authority; the Wolamo project in Ethiopia; the Casamance project in Senegal; tea projects in Malawi and Mauritius; and cocoa and palm oil projects in the Ivory Coast.

Noninstitutionalized Commercial Channels

In regions where institutional credit systems are inadequate, it may be possible to deliver credit through existing noninstitutional commercial channels. In most areas, these serve far more small farmers than do credit institutions. By working through merchants, middlemen and moneylenders, existing credit agencies can increase the volume of credit available to farmers by taking advantage of their greater flexibility, their speed in lending, and their lower administrative costs and default rates. Increasing the supply of funds of noninstitutional lenders may also reduce interest rates. Lending through merchants has an added advantage. By splitting the overhead costs associated with distribution between two functions—the delivery of goods and of credit—merchants are able to deliver credit in small amounts more cheaply than other channels.

Such schemes, however, have a number of disadvantages. It is difficult to prevent misuse of funds. Small farmers usually require inputs and services other than credit, which would be more difficult to coordinate when credit is distributed through noninstitutional lenders. (An attempt to incorporate noninstitutional credit into the Muda project in Malaysia has been abandoned.) The effectiveness of public schemes to use noninstitutional sources has yet to be demonstrated. Furthermore, the idea of using such conduits is politically unacceptable in many countries because of their past exploitation of farmers. On the other hand, contractors of farming operations—such as custom tractor enterprises, suppliers of farm inputs, processors and intermediaries in the marketing of farm products—have provided an increasing amount of credit to commercial farmers. Under strict safe-guards, these sources might be useful in a credit delivery system where no realistic alternative is available.

Institutional Commercial Channels

Commercial institutions represent an additional channel for lending to farmers. Many have an extensive branch network spreading into rural areas. They are generally more efficient than government agencies, and less prone to abuse and political pressure. In general, they are properly organized, keep adequate records and are audited by independent auditors. They usually obtain better repayment performance by borrowers than do government banks since the mechanism is efficient and policies for loan collection are strict. Because of the nature of their resources, commercial banks tend, however, to concentrate on short-term lending, and to avoid credit to small farmers where costs are high.

In the Philippines, through government efforts and the use of incentives a private rural banking system has been developed by local capitalists who established banks for the purpose of meeting the current credit requirements of rural communities, including small farmers. Although the rural banks are partially government-owned, they are nonetheless private institutions operated according to commercial principles. They have experienced steady growth in the past 20 years. They continue to expand their activities and now provide a significant proportion of the institutional credit for agriculture in the country. Two World Bank loans have been channeled by the central bank through these institutions for on-lending of medium- and long-term credit to small farmers, which were types of loans not extended previously. Rural banks lend to commercial farmers owning up to 50 hectares of land. A significant portion of their lending has reached farmers with three to 10 hectares. However, smallholders with less than three hectares, who comprise 73% of all farmers and cultivate 39% of the land, have received less than 1% of the credit extended. To encourage lending to this class of farmers, the authorities have had to make the lending program of rural banks similar to that of the more traditional public agricultural credit programs. Additional subsidies have been introduced for small-farmer lending, including an 85% government guarantee of repayment on such loans. The Philippine experience suggests that specialized institutions of a commercial type, if they charge positive rates of interest and receive some government encouragement, can lend to medium-sized farmers. Experience has also shown that in the absence of farmer groupings, heavy subsidies or significantly higher interest rates, these institutions

159

will not extend finance to the smallest farmers. A rural banking system along the same lines is being duplicated in the Republic of Viet-Nam.

In Thailand, private commercial banks have also lent to small farmers. This activity was concentrated principally in one institution, which lent to farmer groups organized by the bank itself. The operation did not produce a profit and ceased to expand several years ago. A state-owned general purpose bank in Indonesia, the Bank Rakyat, is providing credit directly to small farmers. The recently nationalized commercial banks of India have also started lending to small farmers. As a general rule, to be successful in lending to large numbers of small farmers, commercial institutions will need to rely on the same elements as public institutions, such as farmers' groups and government financial support. They also require properly trained management and personnel, bureaucratic decentralization and some degree of insulation from political influence.

Since commercial banks constitute the core of financial markets in most developing countries, several governments, such as those of Bangladesh, India and Mexico, are now experimenting with using commercial banking systems as a channel for reaching small farmers. Where commercial banks already have an extensive network of rural branches, the costs and delays associated with building new institutions are eliminated. But the costs to banks rise appreciably when loans to small farmers are added to their activities. Commercial banks have been induced to lend to small farmers only through some form of government intervention, such as compulsory investment quotas, or through such incentives as special rediscount facilities and loan repayment guarantees. Special rediscount facilities or repayment guarantees are preferable to investment quotas because the former are more easily adapted to small-farmer programs.

World Bank lending for agricultural credit through commercial banks, via the central bank or a special fund, has proved satisfactory from a managerial and control standpoint, and has been effective both technically and in reaching the clientele of large borrowers. Commercial banks hold little promise of dealing with small farmers directly, because of high administrative costs, lack of borrower collateral and restricted access due to their location. Government regulations prescribing quotas for lending to agriculture and special incentives for loans to small farmers have had little effect. Commercial banks are bound by the same kinds of limitations as agricultural and development banks; they would also need to use intermediate channels such as cooperatives or farmers' groups to reach significant numbers of small farmers.

160

Guidelines on Delivery Systems

Large-farmer Channels

It has been recommended earlier that credit programs for large farmers should be separate from those for small farmers. The basic principles behind lending to large farmers should be essentially commercial. Resources should be allocated to large farmers only if the opportunities they offer are more productive than those found in other sectors of the economy. Programs for large farmers should charge realistic interest rates and achieve financial viability.

Private financial institutions, if adequate, can be used to finance commercial agriculture. Unfortunately, in many developing countries, commercial banks are biased against agriculture, even large-scale farming; they prefer to lend to urban-based sectors, such as trade and industry. To counter this bias, some governments have attempted to channel the loans of commercial banks into agriculture through compulsory lending requirements. The advantages of such an approach are deceptive. Compulsory lending requirements reduce the ability of the banking system to allocate resources efficiently. If coupled with low interest charges for agricultural borrowers, this results in low deposit rates, which lessen the ability of the banking system to mobilize savings. Commercial banks should be encouraged to innovate and to move away from their traditional orientation. The best way of achieving this is through persuasion, through preferential rediscount rates used on a temporary basis to familiarize commercial banks with agricultural lending, or through the creation of new commercial institutions which specialize in agricultural credit.

Small-farmer Channels

Lending to small farmers is considerably more complicated than lending to large farmers. The large number of small loans, coupled with geographical dispersion, make small-farmer credit considerably more expensive to administer. A number of distributive systems have been tried, including specialized agricultural banks, cooperatives and commercial lenders, both organized and unorganized.

No one approach is the best. To a large extent, the choice will depend upon the specific conditions in each country, or even regions within a country. While different programs have been used in different countries, few governments have experimented with more than one delivery system. It is feasible to use alternative delivery systems at the local level while at the same time maintaining a single apex structure. Experimentation should be encouraged to determine which systems are most economical and most compatible with local social and economic conditions.

Principles

Although much experimentation has yet to be done with alternative channels for particular situations, certain principles have emerged from experience which may serve as guidelines. They may be summarized in 10 basic points:

1. *Accessibility:* The approach via branch offices has not always proved effective in reaching small farmers for several reasons. Small farmers have difficulty reaching branches because of limited transportation facilities. They are unfamiliar with, and intimidated by, offices and office procedures. Branch staff tend to isolate themselves from the problems of farmers. Consequently, it is necessary for the institution to go to the villages or even individual farms, to cooperative meetings or to small informal groups to make contacts. The use of field agents who can visit small farmers in their own surroundings has proved successful. So has the use of mobile units or village offices that operate periodically, e.g., on market days.

2. *Packaging:* Credit alone is of little consequence. To be effective in increasing smallholder productivity, it must be supplemented by detailed information on proven new technology, and accompanied by a timely supply of inputs.

3. *Distribution in kind:* This has proved to be the most effective means of delivering credit for productive purposes to small farmers, even in the case of loans for livestock. While the approach may seem excessively paternalistic, it is unrealistic to expect farmers who are not accustomed to having a cash surplus or to using purchased inputs to adjust automatically to making the necessary transactions. This may be true even if the required inputs are readily available.

4. *Timing:* When credit is provided in kind, it is vital that inputs be made available at the time they are needed. Since smallholders seldom have adequate storage space, too early delivery often results in wastage of inputs such as seed and fertilizer. Delivery too late for seasonal requirements is, of course, pointless. Many smallholder development projects have failed because the inputs have not been provided in time.

5. *Selection:* Smallholder borrowers should be chosen on the basis of creditworthiness, just as any other borrower. But the appropriate criteria for assessing creditworthiness of small farmers might differ. Three elements seem important: the reputation of the individual

within his community; the technical feasibility of the proposed investment in the context of his farm situation; and the expected cash flow that is generated by the investment.

6. *Individual liability and group responsibility:* While the repayment of a loan should be the individual borrower's responsibility, the strong sense of community in many rural societies can be used effectively to reinforce the honest performance of individuals. If transactions are made in public—the opposite of conventional financial practice—and the whole village or cooperative society is made aware of the implications of an individual default (either in a damaged reputation or in some form of penalty), group responsibility can become an important influence in ensuring repayment.

7. *Control:* It is unreasonable to expect people who have no knowledge of financial practices suddenly to conform to institutional lending regulations. Payments and repayments need to be geared to liquidity conditions. If this is done, the supervision of even large groups can become more orderly.

8. *Flexibility:* This is necessary to permit the rescheduling of loans in times of crop failure or other unexpected events. Also, often changes in individual circumstances may require some adjustment of part of the program. Many things may go wrong in any program and this is aggravated as the complexity or required precision of the scheme increases. Flexibility in lending criteria is essential, since no two communities or farmers are exactly alike.

9. *Continuity:* Many programs fail to continue beyond the pilot stage, generally a single year, and often leave slow repayments outstanding. This encourages mistrust and poor discipline. Continuity of services is essential if programs are to have a positive impact.

10. *An open-ended approach:* Since programs need to be tailored to meet local conditions, no fixed prescription can be established. A process of trial and error is necessary, beginning with a simple package and small numbers of borrowers, after which the program may be consolidated and replicated to reach the whole target group. An open-ended approach is also needed because agricultural modernization is a continuing process. As with agriculture in the industrialized countries, each new round of technical innovation may be expected to require increased amounts of capital. It is unlikely that a single injection of credit will ever create sufficient liquidity to make continuing modernization self-sustaining. Thus, programs should be planned to provide for continual adjustment and evolution.

AGRICULTURAL
CREDIT
ANNEXES

Abbreviations for Institutions

AFRICA

CADU	(Ethiopia)—Chilalo Agricultural Development Unit
ADB	(Ghana)—Agricultural Development Bank
GMR	(Kenya)—Guaranteed Minimum Return (program)
AFC	(Kenya)—Agricultural Finance Corporation
SOCAP	(Morocco)—Société de Crédit Agricole et de Prévoyance
CNCA	(Morocco)—Caisse Nationale de Crédit Agricole
CLCA	(Morocco)—Caisse Locale de Crédit Agricole
WRFC	(Nigeria)—West Region Finance Corporation
FAID	(Nigeria)—Fund for Agricultural and Industrial Development
ABS	(Sudan)—Agricultural Bank of Sudan
BNT	(Tunisia)—Banque Nationale de Tunisie
COOP	(Uganda)—Cooperative Credit System

ASIA

ADBA	(Afghanistan)—Agricultural Development Bank of Afghanistan
ADBB	(Bangladesh)—Agricultural Development Bank of Bangladesh
ADB	(Bangladesh)—Agricultural Development Bank
BKB	(Bangladesh)—Bangladesh Krishi Bank
COOP	(Bangladesh)—Cooperative Credit System
IRDP	(Bangladesh)—Integrated Rural Development Program
KTCC	(Bangladesh)—Kotwali Thana Central Cooperative (association)
PCCS	(India)—Primary Cooperative Credit Societies
PLDB	(India)—Primary Land Development Bank
BIMAS	(Indonesia)—Acronym for "Bimbingan Missal" meaning "Mass Guidance"
ACBI	(Iran)—Agricultural Cooperative Bank of Iran
ADFI	(Iran)—Agricultural Development Fund of Iran
ACC	(Jordan)—Agricultural Credit Corporation
BCAIF	(Lebanon)—Lebanese Credit Bank for Agricultural and Industrial Development
BAAC	(Thailand)—Bank for Agriculture and Agricultural Cooperatives
SCP	(Turkey)—Supervised Credit Program
NACF	(Republic of Korea)—National Agricultural Cooperative Federation
TRAB	(Turkey)—Turkish Republican Agricultural Bank

LATIN AMERICA

ACAR	(Brazil)—Associação de Crédito e Assistencia Rural
INDAP	(Chile)—Instituto de Desarrollo Agropecuario
CAJA AGRARIA	(Colombia)—Caja de Crédito Agrario, Industrial y Minero
INCORA	(Colombia)—Instituto Colombiano de la Reforma Agraria
BCR	(Costa Rica)—Banco de Costa Rica
BNCR	(Costa Rica)—Banco Nacional de Costa Rica
DACP	(Ecuador)—Directed Agricultural Credit Program
DAPC	(Ecuador)—Directed Agricultural Production Credit (program)
ABC	(El Salvador)—Administración de Bienestar Campesino
BNF	(Honduras)—Banco Nacional de Fomento
FONDO	(Mexico)—Fondo de Garantía y Fomento para la Agricultura, Ganadería y Avicultura (Guarantee and Development Fund for Agriculture, Livestock and Poultry)
NBN RUR. CRED.	(Nicaragua)—National Bank of Nicaragua Rural Credit (program)
NBN	(Nicaragua)—National Bank of Nicaragua
ADB	(Peru)—Agricultural Development Bank

Institutional Lending for Agriculture, in Selected Countries

Country	Loans outstanding (US$ millions)	New loans (US$ millions)	Debt per capita of rural population (US$ millions)	Year of observation
Africa				
Ethiopia	18.0	6.0	1.0	1970
Ghana	19.0	6.0	4.0	1971
Kenya	131.0	—	12.0	1970
Morocco	130.0	65.0	13.0	1971
Tunisia	53.0	15.0	20.0	1970-71
Uganda (COOP only)	—	3.0	—	1971
Asia				
Afghanistan	2.0	1.0	1.0	1971
Bangladesh	130.0	4.3	1.0	1972-73
China, Republic of (Taiwan)	409.0	225.0	3.0	1971
India	2,400.0	1,380.0	3.0[1]	1971
Indonesia (BRI only)	72.0	—	1.0[1]	1971
Iran	159.0	127.0	9.0	1970
Jordan (ACC only)	17.0	2.0	17.0	1971
Korea, Republic of	236.0	206.0	55.0	1971
Malaysia	200.0	—	0.2[1]	1971
Pakistan	—	33.0	26.0	1967-68
Philippines	523.0	443.0	4.0	1971
Sri Lanka	30.0	9.0	74.0	1970
Thailand	73.0	42.0	20.0	1970
Turkey	414.0	—	2.0[1]	1967
Viet-Nam, Republic of	—	32.0	—	1971
Latin America				
Argentina	555.0	—	111.0	1968
Bolivia	15.0	5.0	8.0	1971
Brazil	—	1,500.0	40.0[1]	1969
Chile	—	264.0	106.0[1]	1969
Colombia	416.0	319.0	52.0	1970
Costa Rica	110.0	—	126.0	1968
Dominican Republic	57.0	—	24.0	1968
Ecuador	—	48.0	13.0[1]	1968
El Salvador	—	78.0	36.0[1]	1970
Guatemala	52.0	—	18.0	1968
Honduras	—	59.0	35.0[1]	1971
Mexico	1,671.0	—	84.0	1971
Nicaragua	100.0	—	77.0	1970-71
Panama	23.0	—	31.0	1967
Paraguay	33.0	—	22.0	1968
Peru	160.0	—	25.0	1967
Uruguay	18.0	—	36.0	1967
Venezuela	448.0	—	179.0	1968

[1] Per capita value of new loans extended during the year rather than the per capita debt outstanding.

Note: Loans outstanding represent the portfolio of the lending institutions at the end of the fiscal year. As few credit agencies write off bad debts, this figure is inflated by defaulted loans.

New loans represent the amount of lending by institutions in the fiscal year under consideration and not the change in outstanding balances at year end. Since most credit is meant to be short-term, a low ratio of new loans to outstanding debt probably indicates that the institution's portfolio contains a substantial amount of defaulted debt.

Not all country figures are complete. For some countries, figures were not available for all institutional lenders.

Distribution of Agricultural Loans by Type of Lender, in Selected Countries
(Percentages)

Country	Institutional		Noninstitutional	
	Public	Private	Commercial	Noncommercial
Africa				
Ethiopia	----------- 7 ----------		--------- 93 ---------	
Ghana[1]	75	25	—	—
Kenya[1]	60	40	—	—
Morocco[1]	23	77	—	—
Nigeria (Western)	—	40	25	35
Tunisia[1]	90	10	—	—
Zambia	—	—	1	99
Asia				
Bangladesh	14	—	34	52
China, Republic of	12	53	--------- 35 --------	
India	26	4	51	19
Iran	---------- 57 ----------		--------- 43 ---------	
Jordan[1]	90	10	—	—
Korea, Republic of	34	—	20	46
Malaysia[1]	54	46	—	—
Pakistan	14	—	23	63
Philippines	16	26	51	7
Sri Lanka	20	—	45	35
Thailand	7	1	36	56
Turkey	38	2	----------60----------	
Viet-Nam, Republic of	23	—	4	72
Latin America				
Brazil	66	17	11	6
Chile	73	12	--------- 15----------	
Colombia	27	69	3	1
Costa Rica	70	—	20	10
Ecuador	26	64	----------10----------	
El Salvador[1]	15	85	—	—
Honduras[1]	23	77	—	—
Mexico[1]	72	28	—	—
Nicaragua[1]	83	17	—	—
Peru[2]	23	4	49	24

[1] For these countries, information is available only on the division of loans within the institutional sector between public and private institutions.

[2] The distribution is based on number rather than value of loans.

Note: This table reflects the division of outstanding credit balances among four types of lenders: public institutions; private institutions, such as commercial banks; commercial lenders, such as storekeepers, middlemen, landlords and moneylenders; and noncommercial lenders, such as friends and relatives. The available information for some countries was not adequate for a breakdown of funding sources into the four classes. In some cases, it was difficult to decide on the appropriate classification. For example, should the rural banks in the Philippines which are privately owned but publicly funded be considered public or private? Should friends who charged interest on loans be considered commercial or noncommercial lenders? In these two cases, the rural banks in the Philippines were considered to be private; private lenders who charged more than nominal interest rates were considered to be commercial lenders.

The figures are based on information gathered from a small sample of farmers, except in the case of India where the survey on credit was nationwide.

Farmers Receiving Credit from Institutional Sources, in Selected Countries

(Percentage of all farm families)

Country	Percentage	Country	Percentage
Africa			
Ethiopia	1	Sri Lanka	14
Ghana	1	Thailand	7
Kenya	12	Turkey	23
Morocco	10	Viet-Nam, Republic of	21
Nigeria (Western)	1		
Sudan	1	**Latin America**	
Tunisia	5	Bolivia	5
Uganda	3	Brazil	15
		Chile	15
Asia		Colombia	30
Bangladesh	15	Ecuador	18
China, Republic of (Taiwan)	95	Guatemala	2
India	20	Honduras	10
Jordan	8	Mexico	15
Korea, Republic of	40	Nicaragua	20
Malaysia	2	Panama	4
Pakistan	5	Paraguay	6
Philippines	28	Peru	17

Note: These numbers suffer from an upward bias. Some farmers borrow from more than one institution, but it was not possible to eliminate such duplication. Also, some of the statistics represent potential rather than actual borrowers, as is the case for the Republic of China and the Republic of Korea, where coverage exceeded 30 percent of farm households. For example, in Korea all farmers are members of the NACF, the major source of institutional credit. However, in any one year perhaps no more than one-third of farmers actually borrow from the NACF. Furthermore, some of the statistics are based not on national data but on a sample survey. If the sample was taken in an area where an institution was active, as often appeared to be true, there would be overestimation of coverage.

World Bank Agricultural Credit and Total World Bank
Commitments for Agriculture, by Per Capita Gross National Product Group, FY1948-73

Per capita GNP of borrowing countries[1]	FY1948-63			FY1964-68			FY1969-73		
	Total amount of agricultural lending (US$ millions)	Agricultural credit (US$ millions)	Agricultural credit as percentage of total	Total amount of agricultural lending (US$ millions)	Agricultural credit (US$ millions)	Agricultural credit as percentage of total	Total amount of agricultural lending (US$ millions)	Agricultural credit (US$ millions)	Agricultural credit as percentage of total
Less than $150	272.3	10.2	3.7	152.3	63.9	42.0	1,045.0	535.5	51.2
$151-$375	85.6	41.9	48.9	165.3	54.8	33.2	831.4	289.6	34.8
$376-$700	82.2	24.2	29.4	251.2	107.7	42.9	532.2	469.9	88.3
Over $700	28.0	13.1	46.8	52.0	52.0	100.0	180.3	127.2	70.5
Total	468.1	89.4	19.1	620.8	278.4	44.8	2,588.9	1,422.2	54.9

[1] *World Bank Atlas*, 1972. The countries with agricultural credit projects under each income category are shown in Annex 7.

World Bank Agricultural Credit Operations, by Funding Agency and Per Capita Gross National Product Group, FY1948-73

(Amounts in US$ millions)

	FY1948-63						FY1964-68						FY1969-73					
	Number of operations		Loan/Credit		On-lending portion		Number of operations		Loan/Credit		On-lending portion		Number of operations		Loan/Credit		On-lending portion	
	No.	%	Amount	%	Amount	%	No.	%	Amount	%	Amount	%	No.	%	Amount	%	Amount	%
Bank																		
Less than $150	2	10.5	10.2	14.7	10.2	15.6	–	–	–	–	–	–	4	10.8	28.0	3.9	20.5	3.0
$151-$375	5	26.3	21.9	31.5	20.1	30.8	4	26.7	35.7	18.3	35.2	18.8	9	24.3	91.8	12.8	75.6	11.2
$376-$700	7	36.9	24.2	34.9	24.1	37.0	7	46.6	107.7	55.1	103.2	55.1	15	40.6	469.9	65.6	455.8	67.5
Over $700	5	26.3	13.1	18.9	10.8	16.6	4	26.7	52.0	26.6	48.8	26.1	9	24.3	127.2	17.7	123.1	18.3
Subtotal	19	100.0	69.4	100.0	65.2	100.0	15	100.0	195.4	100.0	187.2	100.0	37	100.0	716.9	100.0	675.0	100.0
IDA																		
Less than $150	1	100.0	20.0	100.0	8.2	100.0	8	61.5	63.9	77.0	51.7	74.8	39	65.0	507.5	81.8	409.2	82.0
$151-$375	–	–	–	–	–	–	5	38.5	19.1	23.0	17.4	25.2	21	35.0	113.0	18.2	89.8	18.0
$376-$700	–	–	–	–	–	–	–	–	–	–	–	–	–	–	–	–	–	–
Over $700	–	–	–	–	–	–	–	–	–	–	–	–	–	–	–	–	–	–
Subtotal	1	100.0	20.0	100.0	8.2	100.0	13	100.0	83.0	100.0	69.1	100.0	60	100.0	620.5	100.0	499.0	100.0
Bank/IDA blend																		
Less than $150	–	–	–	–	–	–	–	–	–	–	–	–	–	–	–	–	–	–
$151-$375	–	–	–	–	–	–	–	–	–	–	–	–	5	100.0	84.8	100.0	78.5	100.0
$376-$700	–	–	–	–	–	–	–	–	–	–	–	–	–	–	–	–	–	–
Over $700	–	–	–	–	–	–	–	–	–	–	–	–	–	–	–	–	–	–
Subtotal	–	–	–	–	–	–	–	–	–	–	–	–	5	100.0	84.8	100.0	78.5	100.0
Total																		
Less than $150	2	10.0	10.2	11.4	10.2	13.9	8	28.6	63.9	22.9	51.7	20.2	43	42.2	535.5	37.7	429.7	34.3
$151-$375	6	30.0	41.9	46.9	28.3	38.6	9	32.1	54.8	19.7	52.6	20.5	35	34.3	289.6	20.4	243.9	19.5
$376-$700	7	35.0	24.2	27.1	24.1	32.8	7	25.0	107.7	38.7	103.2	40.3	15	14.7	469.9	33.0	455.8	36.4
Over $700	5	25.0	13.1	14.6	10.8	14.7	4	14.3	52.0	18.7	48.8	19.0	9	8.8	127.2	8.9	123.1	9.8
Total	20	100.0	89.4	100.0	73.4	100.0	28	100.0	278.4	100.0	256.3	100.0	102	100.0	1,422.2	100.0	1,252.5	100.0

On-lending to Farmers and Number of Beneficiaries in World Bank Agricultural Credit Operations, by Size of Farm, FY1969-73[1]

	On-lending to farmers		Beneficiaries	
	(US$ millions)	Percentage	Number	Percentage
Eastern Africa				
0-5 hectares,	17.7	30.5	483,580	97.9
of which Ethiopia[2]	(5.2)	(9.0)	(400,000)	(81.0)
5.1-10 hectares	—	—	—	—
10.1-100 hectares,	4.2	7.2	9,150	1.9
of which Ethiopia	(2.3)	(4.0)	(350)	(0.1)
Over 100 hectares: Private,	11.4	19.7	855	0.2
of which Ethiopia	(3.8)	(6.6)	(245)	[3]
Government	21.8	37.6	121	[3]
Cooperatives	2.9	5.0	43	[3]
Subtotal	58.0	100.0	493,749	100.0
Western Africa				
0-5 hectares	8.4	26.7	100,500	25.4
5.1-10 hectares	13.7	43.5	70,000	17.7
10.1-100 hectares	9.4	29.8	225,000	56.9
Over 100 hectares: Private	—	—	—	—
Government	—	—	—	—
Cooperatives	—	—	—	—
Subtotal	31.5	100.0	395,500	100.0
Asia				
0-5 hectares,	206.4	57.6	320,090	79.5
of which India	(184.6)	(51.5)	(295,800)	(73.5)
5.1-10 hectares,	40.5	11.3	38,610	9.6
of which India	(32.8)	(9.2)	(36,000)	(8.9)
10.1-100 hectares,	106.8	29.8	43,870	10.9
of which India	(58.4)	(16.3)	(17,600)	(4.4)
Over 100 hectares: Private	1.7	0.5	63	[3]
Government	3.0	0.8	9	[3]
Cooperatives	—	—	—	—
Subtotal	358.4	100.0	402,642	100.0
Europe, Middle East and North Africa				
0-5 hectares	9.1	4.8	12,000	12.3
5.1-10 hectares	—	—	—	—
10.1-100 hectares	104.0	55.0	79,815	81.6
Over 100 hectares: Private	49.4	26.1	5,696	5.8
Government	—	—	—	—
Cooperatives	26.7	14.1	254	0.3
Subtotal	189.2	100.0	97,765	100.0
Latin America and Caribbean				
0-5 hectares	—	—	—	—
5.1-10 hectares	—	—	—	—
10.1-100 hectares,	147.7	40.3	44,025	60.2
of which Mexico	(117.0)	(31.9)	(32,900)	(45.0)
Over 100 hectares: Private,	218.8	59.7	29,075	39.8
of which Mexico	(101.7)	(27.8)	(11,100)	(15.2)
Government	—	—	—	—
Cooperatives	—	—	—	—
Subtotal	366.5	100.0	73,100	100.0
All Regions				
0-5 hectares	241.6	24.1	916,170	62.6
5.1-10 hectares	54.2	5.4	108,610	7.4
10.1-100 hectares	372.1	37.1	401,860	27.5
Over 100 hectares: Private	281.3	28.0	35,689	2.5
Government	24.8	2.5	130	[3]
Cooperatives	29.6	2.9	297	[3]
Total	1,003.6	100.0	1,462,756	100.0

[1] Based on anticipated results, as noted in appraisal reports.
[2] Ethiopia Agricultural Minimum Package Project.
[3] Less than 0.1%.

World Bank Agricultural Credit Operations, by Country and Per Capita Gross National Product Group, in Selected Countries, FY1948-73[1]

(US$ millions)

Country and GNP group	FY1948-63	FY1964-68	FY1969-73
Eastern Africa			
Less than $150:			
Botswana	—	—	1.7 (1)
Ethiopia	—	—	37.2 (4)
Kenya	10.2 (2)	3.6 (1)	9.6 (2)
Malagasy Republic	—	—	2.8 (1)
Malawi	—	9.7 (2)	17.1 (2)
Sudan	—	— (1)	16.3 (2)
Tanzania	—	5.0 (1)	39.6 (4)
Uganda	—	3.4 (1)	7.0 (2)
Zaire	—	—	8.5 (1)
Subtotal	10.2 (2)	21.7 (5)	139.8 (19)
$151-$375:			
Rhodesia	5.6 (1)	—	—
$376-$700:			
Zambia	—	—	14.0 (2)
Total Eastern Africa	15.8 (3)	21.7 (5)	153.8 (21)
Western Africa			
Less than $150:			
Dahomey	—	—	6.1 (1)
Gambia, The	—	—	1.3 (1)
Niger	—	—	0.6 (1)
Nigeria	—	—	7.2 (1)
Upper Volta	—	—	6.2 (1)
Subtotal	—	—	21.4 (5)
$151-$375:			
Ghana	—	—	9.8 (2)
Ivory Coast	—	—	7.5 (1)
Senegal	—	—	17.9 (3)
Sierra Leone	—	—	4.3 (1)
Subtotal	—	—	39.5 (7)
Total Western Africa	—	—	60.9 (12)

[1] Figures in parentheses denote the number of operations.

(continued)

**World Bank Agricultural Credit Operations, by Country and Per Capita
Gross National Product Group, in Selected Countries, FY1948-73**[1] (continued)

(US$ millions)

Country and GNP Group	FY1948-63	FY1964-68	FY1969-73
Asia			
Less than $150:			
India	—	42.2 (3)	306.9 (1)
Indonesia	—	—	19.9 (4)
Pakistan	—	—	30.0 (1)
Subtotal	—	42.2 (3)	356.8 (16)
$151-$375:			
Korea, Republic of	—	—	17.5 (2)
Papua New Guinea	—	—	11.5 (3)
Philippines	—	5.0 (1)	31.6 (3)
Subtotal	—	5.0 (1)	60.6 (8)
$376-$700:			
China, Republic of	—	13.7 (2)	—
Malaysia	—	—	25.0 (1)
Subtotal	—	13.7 (2)	25.0 (1)
Total Asia	—	60.9 (6)	442.4 (25)
Europe, Middle East and North Africa			
Less than $150:			
Afghanistan	—	—	14.0 (2)
Yemen, People's Democratic Republic of	—	—	3.5 (1)
Subtotal	—	—	17.5 (3)
$151-$375:			
Jordan	—	6.0 (2)	—
Morocco	—	10.0 (1)	34.0 (1)
Tunisia	—	—	19.2 (3)
Turkey	20.0 (1)	—	45.5 (3)
Subtotal	20.0 (1)	16.0 (3)	98.7 (7)
$376-$700:			
Iran	—	—	20.5 (2)
Yugoslavia	—	—	31.0 (1)
Subtotal	—	—	51.5 (3)
Over $700:			
Finland	—	—	20.0 (1)
Iceland	2.4 (2)	—	—
Ireland	—	—	25.0 (1)
Israel	—	—	20.0 (1)
Spain	—	—	25.0 (1)
Subtotal	2.4 (2)	—	90.0 (4)
Total Europe, Middle East and North Africa	22.4 (3)	16.0 (3)	257.7 (17)

[1] Figures in parentheses denote the number of operations.

**World Bank Agricultural Credit Operations, by Country and Per Capita
Gross National Product Group, in Selected Countries, FY 1948-73**(1)   (continued)

(US$ millions)

Country and GNP Group	FY1948-63	FY1964-68	FY1969-73
Latin America and Caribbean			
Less than $150:	—	—	—
$151-$375:			
Bolivia	—	2.0 (1)	8.2 (2)
Colombia	10.0 (2)	16.7 (1)	43.4 (3)
Dominican Republic	—	—	5.0 (1)
Ecuador	—	4.0 (1)	16.8 (3)
Guatemala	—	—	4.0 (1)
Guyana	1.3 (1)	—	2.2 (1)
Honduras	—	—	2.6 (1)
Paraguay	5.0 (1)	11.1 (2)	8.6 (1)
Subtotal	16.3 (4)	33.8 (5)	90.8 (13)
$376-$700:			
Brazil	—	40.0 (1)	116.7 (4)
Costa Rica	6.5 (2)	3.0 (1)	9.0 (1)
Jamaica	—	—	3.7 (1)
Mexico	—	25.0 (1)	250.0 (3)
Nicaragua	2.7 (2)	—	—
Peru	15.0 (3)	26.0 (2)	—
Subtotal	24.2 (7)	94.0 (5)	379.4 (9)
Over $700:			
Argentina	—	15.3 (1)	—
Chile	2.5 (1)	19.0 (1)	—
Panama	1.2 (1)	—	4.7 (1)
Trinidad and Tobago	—	5.0 (1)	—
Uruguay	7.0 (1)	12.7 (1)	21.5 (3)
Venezuela	—	—	11.0 (1)
Subtotal	10.7 (3)	52.0 (4)	37.2 (5)
Total Latin America and Caribbean	51.2 (14)	179.8 (14)	507.4 (27)

	FY1948-63		FY1964-68		FY1969-73	
All Regions	US$ millions	Percentage	US$ millions	Percentage	US$ millions	Percentage
Less than $150	10.2	11.4	63.9	22.9	535.5	37.7
$151-$375	41.9	46.9	54.8	19.7	289.6	20.4
$376-$700	24.2	27.1	107.7	38.7	469.9	33.0
Over $700	13.1	14.6	52.0	18.7	127.2	8.9
Total all regions	89.4 (20)	100.0	278.4 (28)	100.0	1,422.2 (102)	100.0

(1) Figures in parentheses denote the number of operations.

Contribution to Project Costs by World Bank Agricultural Credit Operations, by Per Capita Gross National Product Group, FY1948-73

	FY1948-63					
	World Bank/IDA					
	Project		Total loan/credit		Project local cost	
Per capita GNP[1] of borrowing countries	Total cost (US$ millions)	Local cost (US$ millions)	Amount (US$ millions)	As percentage of total project (%)	Amount (US$ millions)	As percentage of local cost (%)
Less than $150	24.7	14.5	10.2	41.3	—	—
$151-$375	102.0	73.9	41.9	41.1	13.8	18.7
$376-$700	49.9	25.7	24.2	48.5	—	—
over $700	27.8	14.7	13.1	47.1	—	—
Total	204.4	128.8	89.4	43.7	13.8	18.7

	FY1964-68					
	World Bank/IDA					
	Project		Total loan/credit		Project local cost	
Per capita GNP[1] of borrowing countries	Total cost (US$ millions)	Local cost (US$ millions)	Amount (US$ millions)	As percentage of total project (%)	Amount (US$ millions)	As percentage of local cost (%)
Less than $150	153.7	103.8	63.9	41.6	19.0	18.3
$151-$375	102.1	63.7	54.8	53.7	16.9	26.6
$376-$700	228.6	166.1	107.7	47.1	44.8	27.0
over $700	143.5	97.0	52.0	36.2	5.5	5.7
Total	627.9	430.6	278.4	44.3	86.2	20.0

	FY1969-73					
	World Bank/IDA					
	Project		Total loan/credit		Project local cost	
Per capita GNP[1] of borrowing countries	Total cost (US$ millions)	Local cost (US$ millions)	Amount (US$ millions)	As percentage of total project (%)	Amount (US$ millions)	As percentage of local cost (%)
Less than $150	912.4	587.6	535.5	58.7	227.5	38.7
$151-$375	552.0	318.1	289.6	52.5	62.5	19.7
$376-$700	1,154.3	861.5	469.9	40.7	174.8	20.3
over $700	381.1	275.3	127.2	33.4	21.5	7.8
Total	2,999.8	2,042.5	1,422.2	47.4	486.3	22.9

[1] *World Bank Atlas,* 1972. The countries with credit projects under each income group are shown in Annex 7.

Interest Rates to Farmers, by Source of Loans
(Percentage per year)

Country	Nominal rates		Real rates	
	Institutions	Commercial lenders	Institutions	Commercial lenders
Africa				
Ethiopia	12	70	8	66
Ghana	6	70	0	64
Ivory Coast	10	150	6	144
Kenya	7	—	7	—
Morocco	7	—	5	—
Nigeria	6	200	−2	192
Sudan	7	120	7	120
Tunisia	7	—	4	—
Uganda	12	—	1	—
Asia				
Afghanistan	9	33	—	—
China, Republic of	10	—	3	—
India	10	25	0	15
Indonesia	14	40	3	28
Iran	7	—	5	—
Jordan	7	20	2	15
Korea, Republic of	16	60	5	49
Malaysia	18	60	16	58
Pakistan	7	30	4	27
Philippines	12	30	6	22
Sri Lanka	12	50	6	44
Thailand	11	30	9	28
Viet-Nam, Republic of	30	48	2	20
Latin America				
Bolivia	9	100	5	96
Brazil	15	60	−7	39
Chile	14	82	−16	52
Colombia	12	41	4	33
Costa Rica	8	24	4	20
Ecuador	10	—	7	23
El Salvador	10	25	8	38
Honduras	9	40	6	53
Mexico	10	60	7	—
Nicaragua	13	—	8	—
Peru	12	—	5	—

Note: The nominal interest rate reported for institutions represents an average rate for different types of loans and for different institutions. The element of uniformity is that private institutions tend to charge about 3 percentage points higher than public institutions. The information on the rates charged by commercial lenders should only be considered as suggestive. At best, this information was based on sample surveys. Often, it represents only hearsay evidence which authors chose to report. In practice, most commercial loans are short-term, one to three months being typical. Multiplying monthly rates by twelve exaggerates both the cost to the borrower and the income to the lender.

Nominal rates were converted to real rates by deducting the average rate of inflation between 1967 and 1970 from the nominal rates, except in a few cases, such as Indonesia, where the inflation rate between 1967 and 1970 clearly did not reflect current levels of inflation.

World Bank Agricultural Credit Operations, by Major End Use and by Region, FY1948-73

Major end use	Eastern Africa		Western Africa		Asia		Europe, Middle East and North Africa		Latin America and Caribbean		TOTAL	
	Number of operations	Amount (US$ millions)	Number of operations	Amount (US$ millions)	Number of operations	Amount (US$ millions)	Number of operations	Amount (US$ millions)	Number of operations	Amount (US$ millions)	Number of operations	Amount (US$ millions)
General agricultural credit												
FY1948-63	1	5.6	—	—	—	—	—	—	1	1.3	2	6.9
FY1964-68	2	8.6	—	—	—	—	2	13.0	2	18.0	6	39.6
FY1969-73	2	11.5	3	14.8	5	107.4	6	76.7	3	29.7	19	240.1
Subtotal	5	25.7	3	14.8	5	107.4	8	89.7	6	49.0	27	286.6
Livestock												
FY1948-63	—	—	—	—	—	—	2	2.4	1	7.0	3	9.4
FY1964-68	—	—	—	—	—	—	—	—	10	145.8	10	145.8
FY1969-73	8	41.9	—	—	3	16.1	4	75.0	19	373.6	34	506.6
Subtotal	8	41.9	—	—	3	16.1	6	77.4	30	526.4	47	661.8
Crop development												
FY1948-63	—	—	—	—	—	—	—	—	—	—	—	—
FY1964-68	1	3.4	—	—	—	—	—	—	—	—	1	3.4
FY1969-73	4	35.3	5	35.5	3	14.3	1	20.0	—	—	13	105.1
Subtotal	5	38.7	5	35.5	3	14.3	1	20.0	—	—	14	108.5
Irrigation												
FY1948-63	—	—	—	—	—	—	1	20.0	—	—	1	20.0
FY1964-68	—	—	—	—	1	5.2	1	3.0	—	—	2	8.2
FY1969-73	—	—	—	—	4	141.0	—	—	—	—	4	141.0
Subtotal	—	—	—	—	5	146.2	2	23.0	—	—	7	169.2

	No.	Amount	No.	Amount	No.	Amount	No.	Amount	No.	Amount	Total No.	Total Amount
Farm machinery												
FY1948-63	1	5.6	—	—	—	—	—	—	12	42.9	13	48.5
FY1964-68	—	—	—	—	3	42.0	—	—	—	—	3	42.0
FY1969-73	2	16.3	—	—	3	92.5	—	—	—	—	5	108.8
Subtotal	3	21.9	—	—	6	134.5	—	—	12	42.9	21	199.3
Fisheries												
FY1948-63	—	—	—	—	—	—	—	—	—	—	—	—
FY1964-68	—	—	—	—	2	13.7	—	—	—	—	2	13.7
FY1969-73	—	—	1	1.3	2	15.1	2	5.5	1	5.3	6	27.2
Subtotal	—	—	1	1.3	4	28.8	2	5.5	1	5.3	8	40.9
Agribusiness												
FY1948-63	—	—	—	—	—	—	—	—	—	—	—	—
FY1964-68	—	—	—	—	—	—	—	—	—	—	—	—
FY1969-73	2	10.7	1	3.7	3	26.0	3	60.5	2	84.0	11	184.9
Subtotal	2	10.7	1	3.7	3	26.0	3	60.5	2	84.0	11	184.9
Integrated agricultural development												
FY1948-63	1	4.6	—	—	—	—	—	—	—	—	1	4.6
FY1964-68	2	9.7	—	—	—	—	—	—	2	16.0	4	25.7
FY1969-73	3	38.1	2	5.6	2	30.0	—	—	2	14.8	9	88.5
Subtotal	6	52.4	2	5.6	2	30.0	—	—	4	30.8	14	118.8
Forestry												
FY1948-63	—	—	—	—	—	—	—	—	—	—	—	—
FY1964-68	—	—	—	—	—	—	—	—	—	—	—	—
FY1969-73	—	—	—	—	—	—	1	20.0	—	—	1	20.0
Subtotal	—	—	—	—	—	—	1	20.0	—	—	1	20.0
Total	29	191.3	12	60.9	31	503.3	23	296.1	55	738.4	150	1790.0
Percent of total (Number of operations)	19		8		21		15		37		100	
Percent of total (Amount)		11		3		28		17		41		100

Duration of Loans Made, by Selected Institutions

(Percentages)

Country	Institutions	Duration		
		Less than 2 years	From 2 to 5 years	More than 5 years
Africa				
Ethiopia	All	100	—	—
Kenya	All	26	31	43
Morocco	All	73	27	—
Tunisia	BNT	62	38	—
Uganda	COOP	100	—	—
Asia				
Bangladesh	ADB	44	48	8
China, Republic of	All institutions	50	28	22
India	COOP	76	24	—
Iran	ACBI	30	70	—
	ADFI	—	10	90
Jordan	ACC	25	75	—
Korea, Republic of	NACF	90	10	—
Malaysia	BPM	60	40	—
Pakistan	COOP	88	12	—
Philippines	Rural banks	93	7	—
Sri Lanka	All institutions	95	5	—
Thailand	All institutions	71	28	1
Turkey	SCP	23	53	24
Viet-Nam, Republic of	Rural banks	100	—	—
Latin America				
Brazil	Federal banks	78	19	3
Bolivia	Agricultural banks	95	—	5
Chile	INDAP	70	30	—
Colombia	Caja Agraria	42	39	19
Costa Rica	State banks	40	60	—
Ecuador	DACP	100	—	—
El Salvador	All institutions	96	4	—
Honduras	BNF	43	37	20
Mexico	FONDO	90	5	5
Nicaragua	NBN	82	18	—

Note: This table shows the cumulative distribution of loans by duration for specific institutions. Production credits constituted the bulk of all short-term loans. In some cases, the institution initially made longer-term loans but unpaid loans were usually rescheduled for one year. Thus, the short-term nature of the portfolio partly reflects the degree of rescheduling as well as the emphasis on production credits.

Measures of Loan Delinquency of Selected Institutions
(Percentages)

Country	Institutions	Arrears to portfolio	Arrears[1] rate
Africa			
Ethiopia	Wolamo[2]	—	3
	CADU[2]	—	50
Ghana	ADB	—	55
Ivory Coast	BNDA	—	15
Kenya	GMR	25	33
	AFC[2]	51	36
Malawi	Lilongwe[2]	—	2
Niger	CNCA[2]	11	29
Nigeria	WSACC	52	80
	FAID	—	95
Morocco	SOCAP	—	50
	CNCA[2]	13	5
Sudan	COOP	—	26
	ABS	—	13
Tanzania	NDCA[2]	28	50
Tunisia	BNT[2]	66	50
	Local credit unions	—	50
Uganda	COOP	10	—
Asia			
Afghanistan	ADBA[2]	37	77
Bangladesh	AB	43	76
	IRDP	—	40
India	PCCS	34	7
	PLDB[2]	12	20
Iran	ACBI	—	44
Jordan	ACC[2]	41	82
Korea, Republic of	NAFC[2]	7	15
Malaysia	BPM	6	21
Pakistan	ADB[2]	36	65
Philippines	Rural banks[2]	20	18
Sri Lanka	New credit scheme	50	41
Thailand	BAAC	—	50
Turkey	ABT	29	43
Viet-Nam, Republic of	Rural banks	—	5
Latin America			
Bolivia	Agricultural bank[2]	1	68
Chile	INDAP	16	60
Colombia	Caja Agraria	19	—
	INCORA[2]	4	16
Costa Rica	BNCR, BCR	35	—
El Salvador	ABC	37	81
Honduras	BNF, Sup. Credit	10	18
Jamaica	ADB	31	10
Peru	Plan Costa	33	—
	BFA[2]	30	—

[1] The arrears rate is equal to 100 minus the repayment rate.

[2] Institutions involved in World Bank-assisted projects.

Note: These measures have various shortcomings. Most agencies consider rescheduled loans as having been repaid. A low ratio of arrears to portfolio may not mean much when loans are expanding rapidly and not yet due, while at the same time the repayment rate on previous loans is poor.

Administrative Costs for Selected Institutions

Country	Institutions	Cost as a percentage of new loans	Cost as a percentage of total resources
Africa			
Ghana	ADB	10.0	10.0
Ivory Coast	CNCA	—	9.0
Kenya	AFC[1]	—	3.0
Morocco	CNCA[1]	10.0	3.0
Senegal	BND	—	3.0
Uganda	COOP	50.0	—
Asia			
Bangladesh	KTCC	17.0	10.0
	BKB	—	3.0
China, Republic of	Farmers Association	—	2.5
	Coop. Bank	—	(2.5)
	Land Bank	—	(1.5)
India	LDB[1]	—	3.0
Indonesia	BIMAS (improved)	25.0	—
Jordan	ACC[1]	30.0	3.0
Korea, Republic of	NACF[1]	6.0	4.0
Lebanon	BCAIF	—	3.0
Malaysia	BPM	20.0	—
Pakistan	ADB[1]	—	3.0
Philippines	Rural banks[1]	5.0	5.0
Thailand	BAAC	13.0	8.0
Turkey	SCR	5.0	2.0
	BAT	—	6.0
Latin America			
Brazil	ACAR	10.0	—
Colombia	INCORA[1]	10.0	7.0
Costa Rica	BNCR	7.0	3.0
Ecuador	DAPC	4.0	—
El Salvador	ABC	16.0	11.0
Mexico	FONDO[1]	3.0	1.0
Peru	ADB	—	6.0

[1] Institutions involved in World Bank-assisted projects.

Note: Capital and, wherever possible, supervisory costs have been excluded. However, it was not possible to obtain comparable figures for different institutions. The very low cost figures reported by such institutions as the KTCC in Bangladesh reflect only the cost of the final lender and not that of the entire agricultural credit system. On the other hand, institutions with very high cost figures are probably providing more services to farmers, the cost of which could not be eliminated from the available data. Other reasons for high costs are that programs are new and of small size but the institutions have already hired the staff that will enable them to expand, as in the case of the BPM in Malaysia, for instance.

World Bank Agricultural Credit Operations, by Lending Channel to Ultimate Borrower, FY1948-73

	FY1948-63				FY1964-68				FY1969-73			
	Operations		Amount		Operations		Amount		Operations		Amount	
	Number	Percentage	US$ millions	Percentage	Number	Percentage	US$ millions	Percentage	Number	Percentage	US$ millions	Percentage
Commercial channel	4	20.0	14.7	16.5	6	21.4	101.0	36.3	27	26.5	546.5	38.4
Agricultural banks	9	45.0	53.0	59.3	15	53.6	129.4	46.5	33	32.3	354.9	25.0
Cooperatives	—	—	—	—	—	—	—	—	11	10.8	266.9	18.8
Project authority, ministry or special entity[1]	4	20.0	9.6	10.7	2	7.1	8.9	3.2	14	13.7	136.5	9.6
Development banks	3	15.0	12.1	13.5	5	17.9	39.1	14.0	17	16.7	117.4	8.2
Total	20	100.0	89.4	100.0	28	100.0	278.4	100.0	102	100.0	1,422.2	100.0
Average size of operation			4.5				9.9				13.9	

(1) British Guiana: Credit Corporation; Korea: Dairy Beef Company; Malagasy Republic: Ranch State Farm; Spain: Instituto de Credito a Medio y Largo Plazo; Sudan: Mechanized Farming Corporation; Zaire: The National Ranching Development Authority.

LAND REFORM

LAND REFORM
CONTENTS

Page

Introduction   191

Summary   193

Chapter 1: Characteristics of Land Reform   203

    Man and Land   203

    Context of Land Reform   204

    Dimensions of Land Reform   208

Chapter 2: Land Reform and Economic Development   213

    Implications for Productivity   215

    Land Reform and Employment   217

    Land Reform and Equity   218

    Effects on Marketed Surplus and Savings   219

    Tenancy Reform   222

    Implementation Issues   223

Chapter 3: The World Bank and Land Reform   226

    Changing Concerns   226

    Technical Assistance   226

    Lending Operations   228

    Major Policy Options   234

Annexes

    1. The Context of Land Reform   237

        Ratios of Population to Land   237

        Population and Production   240

        Distribution of Land   243

        Tenants and Farm Laborers   248

        Landless Workers   250

    2. Experiences with Land Reform   252

        Republic of China   252

        Republic of Korea   252

        Japan   253

        India   254

        Iran   255

        Morocco   256

        Yugoslavia   258

        Kenya   259

        Mexico   259

        Peru   260

INTRODUCTION

Land reform is concerned with changing the institutional structure governing man's relationship with the land. At present, the livelihood of more than half of mankind depends directly on agriculture. Nine-tenths of this total agricultural population is in the developing countries, where questions of access and rights to land are of paramount interest to more than 2,000 million people.

Land is one of the basic factors of production for food and other agricultural products. With food production rising in the developing countries at about the same rate as population, there is growing pressure on land resources to increase output. Much of this increase will have to come from higher output per hectare. Changing the pattern of landownership and redistributing land can contribute to increases in output in some countries but will make little difference in others.

Conditions governing agriculture vary enormously in developing countries. But one characteristic that is common to all is a very rapid growth in rural population. Thus, while pressure on the land is increasing, the average man-land ratio is worsening. At the same time, nonagricultural employment opportunities are not expanding rapidly enough to provide adequate incomes for all those entering the labor market. Some countries have prospects for expanding the frontier of cultivation to absorb more labor. In other countries, more labor could be employed in the rural sector through a redistribution of land, while in yet others changing the rights to land will make little direct contribution toward absorbing more labor.

Distribution of land in terms of size of holdings varies from country to country. The greatest disparities are found in Latin America. Where the pattern of land control is skewed, the distribution of income is generally uneven, although to some extent it is the poorer land that makes up the larger holdings. In Asia and the Middle East, maldistribution is reflected in the landlord-tenant problem; the population is more evenly spread, but rights of access to land are restricted. Much of Africa presents a different problem, as the traditional pattern of group ownership and communal rights is eroded in favor of individual ownership with varying degrees of equality.

In terms of land reform policy, therefore, one is confronted with a range of cultural and political situations—based on different patterns of social organization and customs—and with different levels of development. As shown in Chapter 1, at least six land-tenure situations can be delineated. The differences among these types point to the varying reforms necessary to achieve more equitable land access and improved productivity in specific country situations. Accordingly, while it is possible to identify the need for land reform, it is difficult to make general prescriptions with regard to the form of landholding or pattern of distribution necessary to achieve the multipurpose objectives of development.

Further, one is dealing with a dynamic situation, where rural population growth and changing technology interact with the existing institutional structures of rural society. The manifestations of this interaction are seldom benign for the majority of the land-based population. A situation that has seemed relatively stable and equitable for decades can become untenable. This dynamism means that a solution which was appropriate ten years ago may be inappropriate today. Not surprisingly, therefore, many developing countries are experimenting with a variety of possible solutions—with different forms of rural organizations, ranging from communes to private ownership.

While recognizing the broad context of the land reform issue, this paper focuses on a much narrower aspect—the appropriate role of the World Bank.[1] In pursuing this question, Chapter 1 looks at the characteristics of land reform in terms of both its rural context and its component elements. Chapter 2 examines the economic implications of land reform in relation to the goals of development. Chapter 3 reviews the Bank's policy in relation to land reform. The quantitative background to land reform in terms of population patterns and land distribution is outlined in Annex 1, while some experiences with land reform programs are summarized in Annex 2. The policy guidelines are presented at the end of the Summary.

---

[1]All references to the World Bank in this paper are to be deemed to refer also to the International Development Association, unless the context requires otherwise. The fiscal year (FY) of the two institutions runs from July 1 to June 30.

SUMMARY

Land reform involves intervention in the prevailing pattern of land-ownership, control and usage in order to change the structure of holdings, improve land productivity and broaden the distribution of benefits. In practice, land reform is pursued in response to political pressures for socioeconomic change arising from factors such as increased population, pressure on a limited land base or an ideology of egalitarianism based on more even distribution of land or income. Land reform, by its very context, has interlinked political, economic and social dimensions which in turn have significant implications for development.

The systems of land control in developing countries can be classified into six types, as presented in Chapter 1, although in many countries examples can be found of more than one type. Three of the six types are found in a traditional context: the feudalistic landlord and tenant system of some Asian countries; the feudal Latin American system of large farms; and the communal landownership patterns of many tribal groups (especially in Africa). The other three major types have a modern context: the private ownership of land common in most market economies; the state or collective ownership of socialist countries; and the plantation or ranch type, which is often interspersed with other forms of tenure.

Land reform necessarily implies many different kinds of adjustments in an array of situations where there are great variations in individual equity and agricultural productivity. In most instances, social or equity considerations are the main concerns. Thus, when there are exploitative landlord-tenant systems of the Asian or Latin American feudal type, reform incorporates changes in the rights of tenants, redistribution of ownership to existing tenants, or the replacement of the landlord by the tribe or the community. When individual ownership of the market economy type is the norm but the distribution of land is skewed, reform may require subdivision of large holdings or transfer to the state. In contrast, reform in states with extensive government control may involve the transfer of some land from the state to individuals.

Other variations of land reform focus more on the economic use of resources than on equity. Where holdings are fragmented, an appropriate reform might involve consolidation of holdings without change in the patterns of ownership of land. Where communal lands are eroded or depleted, the appropriate reform might involve a program of supervised cooperative land management without changing the distribution of land. Elsewhere, land reform might involve changing tenancy arrangements with emphasis on providing security of tenure so as to encourage on-farm investment. Again, these do not require redistribution but eventually lead to a more economic use of resources.

The typology outlined in Chapter 1 makes it clear that there are situations where land reform is a necessary precondition for modifying the structure of a society and raising agricultural output. However, while land reform in itself may be necessary, it alone is not sufficient for improving land productivity and distribution of income. Changes in patterns of landownership will not automatically lead to an increase in output or technological change in agriculture. These will come about only if adequate provision is made for the supply of necessary inputs and mandatory services to the users of the land. Indeed, as stressed in Chapter 2, the organization of the supply of inputs to accompany any land reform program is essential, especially where the process of reform leads to a breakdown of the institutional structure of agriculture and leaves nothing in its place.

Finally, it must be recognized that a policy for land reform for a given situation cannot be stated in simple terms. Any policy involves fundamental judgments about the adequacy of an existing system and the most appropriate alternative. The judgments of policy makers differ. The case studies in Annex 2 show that reform-minded governments, such as in Kenya and Peru, have pursued different approaches. Some governments favor individual ownership of land; others favor communal or collective control over land. Clearly, the policies followed are not a matter of economics alone. They also reflect politics and ideology, and reach far beyond any purely economic calculus.

Distribution of Land and Income

Although few data are available, the distribution of landownership is known to be skewed, the degree of concentration varying with the types of tenure situation. The Asian and Latin American feudal types, and the plantation ranch types, have high degrees of property concentration. The socialist and traditional communal types have low concentrations. The market economy type falls somewhere in between. Individual countries are classified on the basis of landownership concentration in Annex 1, Table 1:9.

The distribution of land by size of holding is highly skewed throughout the world. As shown in Annex 1, Table 1:6, an estimated 80% of all holdings are less than five hectares in size, with about 40% less than one hectare. These holdings account for approximately 20% of all cultivated land, and only 7% of all land in holdings. Considered separately, the pattern in Latin America is particularly skewed. Less than 20% of holdings (those over 50 hectares) account for over 90% of the total area in holdings, and more than one-third of all holdings (those less than five hectares) account for only 1% of the area held (see Annex 1, Table 1:8). In Asia, by contrast, 40% of the land (accounting for almost 80% of holdings) is in holdings of less than five hectares.

The distribution of holdings by size is frequently used as a first approximation in estimating the distribution of wealth and income in the agricultural sector. The skewness of the distribution of holdings, however, does not reflect precisely the patterns of distribution of wealth or income. This is because, firstly, all land is not homogeneous; a concentration of large holdings in a semiarid region may reflect a smaller concentration of wealth than a concentration of small holdings in an irrigated area. Secondly, the distribution of holdings by size is not the same as the distribution of ownership of land; in general, there is a greater concentration of landownership than of holdings, as evidenced by widespread tenancy, especially in parts of Asia (see Annex 1). The distribution of income in these regions will depend largely on the contractual arrangements between owners and tenants or sharecroppers. But, in most cases, the distribution of income will be more skewed than the pattern of holdings. Frequently, the income of sharecroppers and tenants may be little different from that of landless labor.

Social and Economic Issues

The rural population in developing countries continues to increase by more than 2% per year, adding to the already heavy population pressure on the land. Except in a few places, there is no virgin cultivable land left, so that absorption of more people into agricultural activity requires more intensive cultivation of land already in use. The need to absorb more people in the rural areas differs among developing countries. In many, massive rural underemployment is accompanied by high rates of open unemployment in the cities and growing inequality in the overall distribution of income. Where the problems are most acute—as in parts of Asia—the emergence of large numbers of landless laborers in rural areas suggests that the family farm system as a means of spreading work among family members may be breaking down.

The extreme poverty of many who live on the land, and the increasing pressure on the land through population growth highlight the double challenge of rural development: to raise productivity and income in agriculture and, at the same time, to provide more employment. Access to land, and the conditions that govern access, are questions of major importance in these circumstances. Where land is marketable, increasing population pressure will inevitably drive up the price of land, thus benefiting those who own land. Where land-ownership is skewed, this will tend to exacerbate inequalities in income distribution.

These same circumstances (relating to employment and income distribution) give rise to questions about the efficiency of land use under existing arrangements. For various reasons, landowners often prefer to underutilize land, either by working it themselves on an extensive basis instead of through tenants on an intensive basis, or by leaving it unused. In other cases, tenancy arrangements are such that landlords are discouraged from making investments and tenants from applying variable inputs, because half the benefits will go to the other party. In some situations, the fragmentation of holdings causes great inefficiencies in land use associated with transportation, irrigation and mechanized operations (even on a small scale). In general terms, increases in the population of working age create additional demands for work and income. At the same time, however, the additional labor available, if used productively, could serve to augment output. A strong case can be made for land reform (including tenancy reform and consolidation) in situations where land would otherwise be underutilized in terms of its production potential.

Evidence on the effects of changing farm size (examined in Chapter 2) indicates that the productivity of land—defined as yield per hectare—is generally higher on smaller holdings than on larger holdings. The main reason is that smaller holdings are worked with bigger inputs of labor than are large holdings. The economic benefits, however, often depend on the effectiveness of new technology when used on small as compared with large farms; mere redistribution of land may not suffice to raise farmer output substantially without accompanying agrarian reforms and new services.

These effects on output may be reinforced by some of the possible side effects following land reform. Smallholders tend to consume more of their own produce and, therefore, market less, per unit of output, than do large farmers; this may necessitate food imports to meet the needs of urban consumers. On the other hand, the additional food consumed by small farm families might have otherwise been purchased if members of the family had moved to the city. The consumption of food by poor growers may also be less costly than the consumption of imported or capital-intensive consumer goods by the better-off farmers. Small farmers may also save less per unit of

196

income. The evidence suggests, however, that small farmers save proportionately *more* than urban dwellers, and that in the aggregate they may also have larger savings than large farmers, though these may be directly invested in the smallholding.

A program based on the prescription that "the benefits should go to those who till the soil" is often reasonable in an agrarian society. But in a partly urbanized setting, those who do not work on the land still require and should have some rights of access to the products of the land. The food and fiber needs (and the spatial requirements) of the nonfarm population are not infrequently overlooked by the advocates of land reform. In this respect, attention should be paid to both a minimum and maximum farm size. These sizes might be designed, firstly, to ensure that smallholdings are large enough to provide food sufficient to meet with a high degree of certainty the minimum physiological needs of the farm family; and, secondly, to ensure a scale large enough to provide a salable surplus to meet the needs of urban consumers, especially for fresh produce. Few land reform programs provide for such a minimum limit despite evidence, from many areas, that allowing farms to become too small (relative to the best available technology) may be just as unsatisfactory in terms of equity and efficiency as an uncontrolled tenancy situation.

Recent Experience with Land Reform

Experience with land reform in the past points to the overriding importance of the political factor in securing meaningful change. The concentration of control over land provides a power base for many groups in developing countries. Land is a symbol of authority and a source of political power, especially where the landowner controls the access of peasants to their only source of security—land. A meaningful land reform program will inevitably destroy or limit the power base of many persons. It is not surprising, therefore, that land reform is often a central issue in political debates, and that these debates are often couched in terms of redistributing political power as well as wealth. Ambitious programs of land reform will seldom be implemented unless there are shifts in political sentiment and power. Many countries have legislated land reform, but only a few can be said to have implemented it. And in these cases the reforms were implemented only when there was a change in government in circumstances that favored drastic change, as in the Republic of China, Japan, Kenya and Mexico.

A second factor of importance in making reform effective is the creation of institutions to implement the reforms once legislated, and to press for continuing development. This has usually involved organizing the beneficiaries to create follow-up pressure. For example, in Japan, Taiwan and Venezuela suitable institutions were established to ensure that land was indeed transferred. In other countries, a community of interests between landowners and officials, combined with an absence of organized pressure from the beneficiaries, largely nullified positive reform efforts. The land reform experience in much of Asia and Latin America suggests that some form of rural organization, especially involving local representation, may be a critical condition for successful land reform.

A third conclusion is that land reform is rarely undertaken without considerable upheaval and loss of production, although there is evidence to suggest that these costs can be kept small and temporary. The restructuring of landholdings is often accompanied by the destruction of traditional delivery systems for input needs and marketing, since these systems are almost always tied to the operations of the larger farmers who are dispossessed. Because of this, rather than because of any deficiency inherent in the small relative to the larger farmers, land reform has often proved costly in terms of lost output. Minimizing such costs necessitates the provision of services concurrently with reform implementation, incorporating as much forward planning as feasible.

A fourth consideration relates to the problem of perspective, over time, in assessing the effects of land reform. As the country experiences summarized in Annex 2 reveal, the effectiveness of land reform may be relatively limited in the short run, and many socioeconomic benefits, such as are associated with greater social mobility and improved political stability, emerge only in the longer run and accrue for many years subsequently. The cases of Japan and Mexico are particularly significant in this respect. While the direct short-run effects of the land reforms in these countries have not been considered wholly beneficial, there is little doubt that the long-run effects for their total societies have been overwhelmingly favorable, contributing substantially to the ultimate economic development of both countries.

The World Bank and Land Reform

The World Bank has taken an active interest in land reform on a number of occasions. Concern has usually been focused on new or improved possibilities for production following changes in the tenure situation, with emphasis on security of tenure being a particularly important theme. More recently, the extent and gravity of the employment problems and income disparities in developing countries have caused a new concern over land reform, from an equity as well as a productivity standpoint.

The Bank's experience through project financing of land reform has been very limited. In part, this may be because there have been relatively few cases of land reform, particularly in areas where the political situation was reasonably stable and otherwise conducive to World Bank involvement. But also relevant is the fact that the financial requirements of land reform tend to be relatively limited. Even where the land transferred is purchased from the previous owners, the amounts involved are usually small, especially where payments are in the form of bonds. In addition, such payments usually constitute an internal transfer (unless foreign owners are involved) and, thus, are not attractive for external financing. Some examples of World Bank involvement in land reform programs, notably in Malawi and Tunisia, are discussed in Chapter 3.

In general, this report concludes that land reform is consistent with the development objectives of increasing output, improving income distribution and expanding employment, and that the World Bank should support reforms that are consistent with these goals. However, it is recognized that the Bank cannot force structural change; it can only support appropriate efforts within existing structures. Although the Bank's direct action must be limited, its preferences regarding national policy choices and those which are considered consistent with the Bank's development goals are set out below as country guidelines. These same conclusions are reflected in the subsequent Bank policy guidelines.

Country Guidelines

1. Governments which accept a basic commitment to land reform should consider three components: (i) redistribution of landownership to reduce the present maldistribution; (ii) tenancy reform; and (iii) consolidation, where necessary.

2. A commitment to land reform implies simultaneous action to create or develop an input supply system to meet the special needs of the beneficiaries of land reform. This may require either the creation of new institutions, or special branches or fund allocations within existing organizations to supply credit, inputs and technical services, including research and extension.

3. In sparsely populated regions or countries, specially structured settlement schemes can serve as second-best substitutes for, or supplements to, the redistribution of land currently in use.

4. It should be recognized that a small farm structure can generate employment to absorb underemployed labor in crowded regions where there is no short-term prospect of absorbing it in nonfarm or large farm employment. With a seed-water-fertilizer technology now available that is neutral to scale, such a structure can produce at least as much per unit of land as a large farm structure.

5. Equity-oriented land reform should be so programmed that (i) the effective ceiling on size of holdings is low; (ii) the beneficiaries belong to the poorest group; (iii) the extension and (nonland) input distribution system favors the beneficiaries; and (iv) owned and self-operated land, as well as leased land, is redistributed.

6. Where efficient large-scale plantations or ranches exist, these need not be broken up, but it should be accepted that in such cases the objectives of reform can only be realized if the enterprises are covered by a progressive tax system and the workers participate adequately in the benefits of the enterprise.

7. Research should be organized to evolve a low-cost settlement policy. Wherever settlement policy is used to supplement land reform, settlement schemes should be planned to have approximately the same effects as the redistribution of existing holdings. These effects can accrue if (i) the settlers are the really poor small farmers or landless workers and an input supply system is available to support their operations; (ii) the size distribution of the new holdings is equitable; and (iii) tenancy is discouraged, and allowed only under specified types of contracts.

8. Where the shortage of land is so acute that even with a low ceiling both smallholders and landless workers cannot be given minimum holdings, preference should be given to smallholders in the allotment of land, and a rural works program should be organized for the landless.

9. Experience in East Asian and some Latin American countries clearly shows that the organization of beneficiaries, both before and after the enactment of reform, is an indispensable condition for its success.

10. It should be recognized that landless recipients of land who take up independent farming for the first time may need to be provided with their entire short-term and long-term credit requirements and perhaps some consumption credit for three or four initial crop seasons. There may also be a need for special training facilities, research activities and field demonstrations in such circumstances.

11. The abolition of tenancy may not be feasible in many countries or regions where the demand for land by the landless and small farmers far exceeds the available supply. In such cases, regulation of

tenancy might be a more efficient policy. Generally, fixed cash-rent contracts are superior to crop-sharing contracts because they encourage the use of inputs to the optimal level. But where crop sharing cannot be eliminated because it provides risk insurance to sharecroppers, it can be made more efficient and equitable if it is combined with cost sharing. Such contracts should be promoted with a system of incentives and deterrents. The incentives can include the accrual of legal rights in land and the availability of credit and other inputs only if preferred types of tenancy contracts are implemented.

12. When the land-labor ratio becomes favorable, the conversion of tenants into owners of the land they cultivate, preferably against very low compensation payments, should be undertaken because, in general, owner-operated farming is likely to be more efficient and equitable than tenant farming.

World Bank's Policy Guidelines

1. The World Bank will give priority in agricultural lending to those member countries that pursue broad-based agricultural strategies directed toward the promotion of adequate new employment opportunities, with special attention to the needs of the poorest groups. The Bank will support policies of land reform designed to further these objectives.

2. The Bank will make it known that it stands ready to finance special projects and programs that may be a necessary concomitant of land reform, so long as the reforms and related programs are consistent with the objectives stated in the previous paragraph. These programs would include credit, technical services and infrastructure projects designed to meet the special needs of land reform beneficiaries.

3. The Bank will cooperate with the Food and Agriculture Organization of the United Nations (FAO), the United Nations Development Programme (UNDP) and other organizations to provide support and assistance to member governments seeking help with the specification and design of land reform programs where these are in keeping with the Bank's objectives. This support will include financial and technical aid with cadastral surveys, registration of land titles and similar services.

4. The Bank will continue to explore, through its agricultural and rural development projects, ways of providing for a distribution of benefits consistent with the goals outlined under (1) above, including appropriate tenurial arrangements and projects designed to serve the needs of small farmers and settlers.

201

5. The Bank will intensify its efforts through sector and country economic work to identify and draw attention to the need and opportunities for land reform with respect to existing tenurial situations and their economic effects.

6. The Bank will support and encourage research related to the economics of land reform in its broadest aspects, including its social dimensions. It will continue its support for programs of economic and technical research directed toward the special needs of the type of small farmer likely to emerge from land reforms.

7. The Bank will undertake studies of the costs and benefits of settlement projects, with particular attention to developing approaches which will lower the cost per family settled.

8. The Bank will not support projects where land rights are such that a major share of the benefits will accrue to high-income groups unless increases in output and improvements in the balance of payments are overriding considerations; in such cases, it will carefully consider whether the fiscal arrangements are appropriate to ensure that a reasonable share of the benefits accrues to the government.

9. In circumstances where increased productivity can effectively be achieved only subsequent to land reform, the Bank will not support projects which do not include land reform.

10. Where land is held under some form of tenancy, the Bank will foster the adoption of tenancy conditions and sharecropping arrangements that are equitable and conducive to the optimal use of resources.

11. Where land is communally held without regulation of access, the Bank will encourage subdivision, if sedentary forms of agriculture are possible, or pursue land usage and access arrangements that are compatible with the long-run productivity of the land and the welfare of the resident population.

12. The Bank will pay particular attention to the consequences of the interaction of new technology and the prevailing institutional structures, as reflected in the pattern of landownership, in order to avoid adjustments which will increase the maldistribution of income and cause economic hardship.

Chapter 1: CHARACTERISTICS OF LAND REFORM

Man and Land

Man's relationship to land, and patterns of landholding and land use, are shaped by the interaction of a complex of forces—climatic, economic, cultural, religious and political. In Eastern Africa, for instance, physical conditions in the temperate areas are suited to sedentary agriculture, whereas the more tropical and arid areas are better suited to shifting cultivation or livestock herding. As a result, different systems of land management and patterns of holdings have emerged in adjacent zones. Similarly, laws and customs governing inheritance have an effect on the distribution of land. Where land is inherited by the oldest heir and not subdivided, the pattern of holdings is less fragmented than in societies where the custom is to divide holdings equally among all heirs. In addition, many socioeconomic factors affect customs of usufruct, traditions of crop sharing and other arrangements surrounding land use in varying situations.

The political ideologies of governments also have a bearing on the relationship between people and the land. The right of the individual to own, sell and accumulate private property—including land—is one of the cornerstones of the market economy. While this right might be constrained in the public interest, land can in general be exploited, held and traded by individuals for private gain. Under some other ideologies, individuals do not have the opportunity to acquire and accumulate land; the right to own land may be vested solely in the state or in semipublic institutions, and it is the state which organizes and controls the land according to its own criteria. To the extent that the state controls the land, the allocative process may serve any number of ideological ends. Some governments have used control over land to implement policies of geographical separation of racial groups. The People's Republic of China, on the other hand, has changed rights to land and the organization of work several times over the past 25 years as part of a drive to eliminate rural inequality.

The level of economic development of a country has a strong influence on attitudes toward land. The more industrialized a country, the smaller the proportion of the population in agriculture and the less significant the role of land in the economy. In countries with mobile populations which have ample opportunities for employment, land is often seen merely as one factor of production in a highly developed commercial agriculture. However, in less developed countries with large rural populations, limited alternative opportunities and increasing pressure on the land, access to land may provide at least a sub-sistence income. In these circumstances, producers see land as more than a factor of production; it may well provide the margin between destitution and subsistence.

The established pattern of landownership is basic to both the social organization and institutional structures in rural areas. The social hierarchy in most agrarian societies reflects the kinds of access that different groups have to land, while individual status within these groups depends on the amount and quality of land commanded. The institutional structures which formalize the various means of control and the relationship between categories of land users, also determine the accessibility of external institutions and services to the various groups.

Context of Land Reform

The many complex factors that influence the patterns of land-ownership and land use in different regions of the world may be summarized as: (1) the political system and situation; (2) the structure of the economy; (3) the social system; (4) the legal system; (5) the demographic situation; (6) the agricultural system; and (7) the national resource base. When these interacting elements are taken into account, it is possible to delineate six main categories of land tenure and land use. These are characterized as follows:

1. *Feudal Asian Type*

High property concentration.
Great social inequality.
Great economic inequality.
Low land productivity.
Low labor productivity.
Low level of technology.
Mainly operated by sharecroppers.
High labor intensity.
Low capital intensity.
Production mainly for subsistence.
Land very scarce.
Institutional structure centralized.

2. *Feudal Latin American Type*

High property concentration.
Great social inequality.
Great economic inequality.

Low land productivity.
Low labor productivity.
Low level of technology.
Labor provided by squatters, neighboring smallholders and
  migrant workers.
Capital-extensive.
Labor-extensive.
Operated by owner or manager plus hired labor, serfs
  or sharecroppers.
Production for subsistence and export.
Institutional structure highly centralized.

3. *Traditional Communal Type*

Low property concentration—sovereign rights vested in community.
Decentralized cultivation—usufruct rights for members of group.
Moderate or high socioeconomic equality.
Low labor productivity.
Low land productivity.
Low level of technology.
Medium labor intensity.
Low capital intensity.
Production for subsistence.
Supporting service structure underdeveloped.

4. *Market Economy Type*

Medium property concentration.
Decentralized cultivation.
Medium socioeconomic inequality.
High land productivity.
High labor productivity.
High level of technology.
Capital-intensive.
Labor-extensive.
Market production oriented.
Institutions and services dispersed.

5. *Socialist Type*

Property right vested in the state or a group.
Centralized or decentralized cultivation.
Low, medium or high socioeconomic equality.
Low, medium or high land productivity.
Low, medium or high labor productivity.
Medium level of technology.

Production for market or subsistence.
Supporting systems centralized.

6. *Plantation Ranch Type*

High property concentration—owned by state or foreigners.
Great social inequality.
Great income inequality.
High land productivity.
Low or medium labor productivity.
Medium or high level of technology.
Operated by manager plus wage labor.
Production mainly for export.

In a traditional context, extremes in the pattern of land control are exemplified, on the one hand, by the feudalistic landlord-tenant system found in some Asian and Latin American countries and, on the other, by the communal landownership pattern of certain tribal groups in Africa. In the landlord-tenant system, landownership is vested in an elite minority with the majority having access through tenancy arrangements of various kinds. The ownership of property is generally highly concentrated, more so than the pattern of land-holdings. However, since holdings (the only category for which the Bank has data) involve leasehold units for which rent is paid on a share basis, the distribution of income is also highly skewed (see Annex 1, Tables 1:6 and 1:8). In the communal system, by contrast, land is common property and access to it is relatively unrestricted. Whereas in the feudalistic system the distribution of landownership and benefits are highly skewed and class differentiation is marked, the communal system has relatively egalitarian land access and class differentiation is less marked.

Both systems are relatively stable under favorable conditions, but face difficulties as the man-land ratio declines through population growth, unless there are offsetting changes in technology. In the landlord-tenant system, land pressures are reflected in a growing army of landless people and widening income differentials (see Annex 1, Table 1:11). The communal system manifests the same pressures by compressed fallow periods and declining soil fertility, over-grazing and increased erosion, accompanied by extensive poverty and vulnerability to seasonal effects.

The two systems differ in their ability to respond to changing external conditions and especially to new technology. The landlord elite, by virtue of its privileged position and power, can, and often does, become educated and innovate both through experimentation and the adoption of external ideas. (In doing so, however, its primary concern may be to promote its own narrow interests in terms of wealth and power, for instance, by displacing tenants through mechanization.) The communal system generally lacks such an institutional mechanism and tends to be both static in its technology and relatively insular, but such communities seldom manage to remain completely isolated from external influences.

In a modern context, the extremes in patterns of land control are seen respectively in the private ownership of land, which is a fundamental aspect of the market economy and common in most Western countries, and the state or collective ownership characteristic of socialist countries. Under private ownership, land is held by individuals and, while usually subject to special restrictions, can be bought or sold like any other commodity. Such holdings are typically operated as family units with little hired labor. However, a range of subtypes exists within this category which reflects a gradation in size from the predominantly subsistence smallholdings of many developing countries to the broad acres of North America and Australia. Although similar in legal and institutional respects, these differ significantly in their technology and input mix as well as in the degree of market orientation.

In the socialist system, on the other hand, little or no provision is made for individuals to acquire or accumulate land, this right being vested in the state, with control determined in accordance with the objectives of the state. But some variations remain within many socialist systems, often providing for the existence of private smallholdings in parallel with larger social units. A special type found in a modern context is one which includes the plantations and large ranches that often operate in developing countries as well as in some developed countries. These form, in some respects, a special category of the market economy type, but the tendency toward a corporate legal structure and dependence on hired labor differentiate them from privately owned family farms.

While private ownership has generally been compatible with technological progress and the economic adjustment of agriculture, it has often created inequities as people have been compelled to give up rural pursuits or have been squeezed into land-scarce rural enclaves. Generally, private control has been most satisfactory where population pressure could be offset by colonizing virgin land or moving people out of the rural sector. It has been most unsatisfactory where ownership patterns have become skewed because of the growth of large farms, combined with limited opportunities for people to move out of agriculture, and the subsequent emergence of economic dualism. State or communal control has led to fewer interpersonal inequities, although in most cases not without some broader economic inefficiencies.

Land reform raises issues of equity in the context of both the traditional landlord-tenant relationship and the modern skewed ownership pattern. In both these contexts, it is often a highly political concern, especially in the traditional feudalistic and communal systems. In many situations, the prevailing tenure conditions are the major impediment to development. For example, a high level of fragmentation can make canal irrigation virtually impossible and seriously impede mechanized operations even when on a very small scale. In other cases, the contractual share arrangement is such that neither landlord nor tenant are able to introduce new technology because, on the one hand, the landlord cannot capture a profitable share of the return on his investment, and on the other, the tenant cannot find the capital for investment or lacks the security of tenure that would guarantee a return from it. Further, in some situations, the social environment is characterized by inequity and oppression to the extent that it destroys human motivation to improve productivity or to resolve any problem within existing structures. In such circumstances, land reform may become a prerequisite of development. But, whether primarily an equity or a production concern, it is clear that land reform will involve different changes in different types of situations.

Dimensions of Land Reform

Land reform is thus concerned with the interrelated aspects of productivity and equity of land use. It is frequently pursued as a goal in itself, but in a development context is usually seen as a part of agrarian reform or of rural development programs. Land reform differs from political, administrative, fiscal or monetary reforms in that it normally relates to one sector and involves changes in control of a tangible asset that not only is fixed in supply but also provides the basic factor on which most of the people in developing countries depend for their livelihood.

Land reform can involve varying degrees of change, including some or all of the following:

1. Redistribution of public or private land in order to change the patterns of land distribution and size of holdings. Usually, this involves an increase in the number of small- or medium-sized farms and a reduction in the number of large holdings. Alternatively, all land can be nationalized and regrouped into state-owned holdings, all of which might be large.

208

2. Consolidation of individual holdings, thereby reorganizing the physical pattern of control. Fragmented holdings can be regrouped into contiguous blocks of land. This can be done with or without changing the distribution of landownership in terms of acreage or value belonging to each individual.

3. Changes in landownership and tenurial rights, with or without physical redistribution of land. Redistributed land can be allocated to new owners or to farmers working on the land. Alternatively, land need not be redistributed but tenants or workers can be made owners of the land they work. In that case, the result is generally a redistribution of income away from the former owners of the land to the new owners. The new owners may farm cooperatively or as individuals.

4. Changes in conditions of tenure without changing ownership or redistributing land. The rights of those working on the land can be safeguarded by law without a change in ownership. Changes in conditions of tenure would include providing security of tenure, introducing equitable crop-sharing arrangements, cooperative land management, and so forth. These changes would also include the conversion from customary to legal rights to land.

Structural Change

In the main, land reform is seen as a means of bringing about structural changes in the agricultural sector, thereby altering the size distribution of holdings or the distribution of income. By definition, therefore, pilot projects cannot be considered to be land reform for they operate within an existing structural framework, even though they might be useful in identifying problems of management, or the economics of various "models," or arrangements that might be part of a subsequent reform. Similarly, land settlement on the frontier does not usually constitute land reform, although land settlement might be a means of bringing unused land into production. Land settlement, by itself, may or may not have an impact on the structure of landholdings in a country, depending on the manner in which the settlers are selected and the size distribution of the new holdings. The kind of structural change involved depends on the prevailing tenure type and the proposed alternative. As reflected in the country experiences summarized in Annex 2, most changes involve a shift from traditional to modern types. Thus the Republic of China, the Republic of Korea and Japan moved from a "feudal Asian" to a "market modern smallholding" type; India and Iran moved from a "feudal Asian" toward a "market modern" type, with some traditional farms retained and some "plantation ranch" type variations in certain areas. Kenya and Morocco redistributed the large-scale, alien-owned "market economy" type holdings of their colonial eras, some going to smallholdings of the "market economy" type and some to "plantation ranch" type units. Mexico and Peru moved from a "feudal Latin American" type to a "market modern mixed large and smallholding" type, and a mixed "market modern" and "socialist" type structure, respectively. These changes in tenure systems were in all cases accompanied by changes in related organizations and services.

Fiscal Measures

Land taxes and preemptive taxes on income earned from land are often cited as instruments that will obtain the same ends as land reform. An effective land tax may have an impact on land use but its main purpose is usually to encourage more intensive production by making it costly either to leave productive land idle or to use it below its productive capacity. On the other hand, such taxes may provide a disincentive to investment with the potential of increasing productivity or bringing new land into production. In any event, the use of a fiscal instrument, such as a land tax, will not lead to structural changes in agriculture—at least not in the short run. A more likely fiscal instrument to encourage structural change is a graduated estate tax which would force estates to dispose of land to meet their financial obligations. But this is likely to bring about structural change only over a long period of time. While land taxes and estate taxes are often considered significant elements in fiscal policy intended to redistribute income, they cannot ensure the same degree of structural reform as can land reform and have, in general, been quite ineffective. In situations where fiscal measures—whether of a redistributive kind or a type which provides a return to the state on its investment—are found to be ineffective, land reform may be the only alternative option if economic development is to be pursued.

Agrarian Reform

Agrarian reform is a much more comprehensive concept than land reform, since it involves modification of a wide range of conditions that affect the agricultural sector. These modifications might include changing price policies so as to turn the terms of trade in favor of the agricultural sector; increasing allocations to the agricultural sector in order to expand research, extension, training and storage facilities; making physical supplies, such as fertilizers, available and increasing credit for their purchase; or providing infrastructure to facilitate agricultural production. Agrarian reform may or may not include land reform; in some instances, there may be no need for land reform since land is already evenly distributed. In other cases, it may not be politically feasible to have land reform—although it might be both

210

politically and economically feasible to raise output through the measures involved in agrarian reform. The point is that land reform may be a necessary condition for agrarian reform, but it is seldom a sufficient condition for increasing agricultural output, since land is only one factor of production.

Rural Development

Broader still is the concept of rural development, because it embraces all dimensions of the rural sector (agricultural and nonagricultural) and is more concerned with the welfare of rural people than with agricultural output or productivity as an end in itself. Since it has significant equity implications, land reform may be a necessary concomitant of successful rural development, depending on the prevailing pattern of land control. Where the ownership of land directly affects the nature of local institutions and the participation in them by the majority of rural people, land reform may be essential. However, in terms of implementation, in some situations establishing local institutions and smallholder services may be a prerequisite of land reform rather than vice versa. Where the existing service systems and administrative structure is geared to working with large-scale farmers, land reform without concurrent rural development activity might cause hardship and economic losses which would outstrip the equity gains associated with land redistribution. Tenancy reform, on the other hand, insofar as it stabilizes the existing relationship between landowners and renters, may be a useful precursor of rural development programs.

Political Dimensions

Substantial reform of the structure of holdings and the distribution of income from the land cannot be achieved without political action. For instance, where semifeudal conditions prevail, patterns of land rights and tenurial conditions have been established by tradition, and these cannot be changed through market operations, as there is virtually no organized market for land. Elsewhere, large landholders have accumulated capital and expanded landholdings acquired through the market; in most market-oriented economies with a skewed distribution of land, the tendency is for the skewed distribution to worsen. Whatever the prevailing situation, it can seldom be changed without actions that emanate from outside the market. Since these actions are based on policies deliberately intended to alter the distribution of land and change tenure, the implementation of the policies depends on the political will of the policy makers and the ability of the administrators to execute this will.

The concentration of control over land provides the base for powerful elements in many nonindustrialized societies. Where groups derive authority from their land, a meaningful land reform program will inevitably destroy or limit the power base of these groups. Land reform can change the political balance and the power structure in a country. Reforms have stripped large landholders, whether they were military, religious or private, of their power. It is not surprising, then, that land reform is often a central issue in political debates and that these debates are often couched in terms of redistributing political power as well as wealth. The political implications of land reform must be taken into account; ambitious programs of land reform will seldom be implemented unless shifts are made in political sentiment and power. Many countries have legislated for land reform but relatively few have achieved it—and these only with a change in government.

Frequently, the implementation of massive reform legislation has depended on the effective organization of the beneficiaries. In Japan, the Republic of China and Venezuela—to name three countries— suitable organizations were established to ensure that land was indeed transferred. In other countries, such as India and Pakistan, the official bureaucracy was the only implementation agency contemplated by the reformers. Because of the community of interests between the bureaucrats and the landowners, and the absence of organized pressure from the beneficiaries, the massive legislation has produced no significant reform. Experience in much of Asia and Latin America suggests that effective popular participation of rural people may be a critical condition of successful land reform.

Implications for Social Justice

The imbalance between the distribution of control over the land and the numbers dependent on it has historically led to increasing pressures for change. While the focus on land reform is related to economic development, the concept of an overriding social function of land justifying the imposition of limitations on private rights appears to be gaining the support of many groups, including the Catholic Church. Formerly one of the largest landholders in the world, the Church in Europe as well as in Latin America has increasingly put its weight behind this new concept, both in precept and in practice. The Church's new philosophy regarding the relationship between man and land declared that "private property does not constitute for anyone an absolute and unconditional right." And the immediate extension of this postulate to the world's agrarian problem is that "if certain landed estates impede the general prosperity because they are extensive, unused or poorly used, or because they bring hardship to peoples or are detrimental to the interests of the country, the common good sometimes demands their expropriation."

A further facet of land reform that warrants consideration in this respect is the potential of a new societal structure following a reform. Mexico, and more recently Bolivia and Egypt, had semifeudal societies similar to many which still prevail in other parts of the world. In these societies, large numbers of tenants and laborers were tied to the land and were held in forms of human bondage; this arose from custom, tradition or sheer indebtedness to landlords. The reforms which have taken place in these countries have changed the situation. The reform in Mexico broke a system that denied many people any range of choice in the pursuit of a livelihood. If the experience of Mexico—which has had the longest period of reform—is any indication of the long-run outlook, the reforms have led to an increase in social mobility.

Land reform is a complex subject. The issues involved are diffuse and appropriate reform measures vary according to the situation. Land reform is in practice predominantly a question of equity and, therefore, one that is often highly political. Nevertheless, it has significant implications for economic development, and these in turn are relevant concerns in the formulation of the World Bank's policy.

Chapter 2: LAND REFORM AND ECONOMIC DEVELOPMENT

Economic development has three basic objectives: rapid economic growth, full employment and distributive justice. Some policies and related investments, such as those affecting power plants or large-scale industry, are primarily growth oriented; others, such as those for rural works, are employment oriented; still others, such as those related to land reform, are essentially equity oriented. Each set of policies and investments aimed toward one objective has important repercussions with regard to the other two objectives, and these must be taken into account when weighing the potential impact of particular policies on economic development. For this reason, it is important to determine to what extent land reform might be costly in terms of growth and employment.

Many problems arise in assessing the costs and benefits of land reform. These include the definition of an acceptable time frame for measuring the effects of the related structural change in the agricul-

213

Table 1

Productivity, Employment and the Distribution
of Land, in Selected Countries

Country	Data year	Farm GDP per hectare (US$)	Farm GDP per worker (US$)	Employment per hectare	Size of average holding (hectares)	Gini's Index of Land Concentration
Europe						
Greece	1961	424	848	0.50	3.18	0.597
Spain	1962	90	980	0.09	14.85	0.832
Central America						
Costa Rica	1963	83	951	0.09	40.70	—
Dominican Republic	1971	129	463	0.28	8.64	—
El Salvador	1961	186	489	0.38	6.95	—
Guatemala	1964	144	492	0.29	8.17	—
Mexico	1960	22	569	0.04	123.90	—
Nicaragua	1963	55	580	0.09	37.34	—
South America						
Argentina	1970	18	1,903	0.01	270.10	0.873
Brazil	1960	14	285	0.05	79.25	0.845
Chile	1965	18	692	0.03	118.50	—
Colombia	1960	67	663	0.10	22.60	0.865
Paraguay	1961	11	479	0.02	108.70	—
Peru	1961	50	477	0.10	20.37	0.947
Uruguay	1966	14	1,333	0.01	208.80	0.833
Venezuela	1961	31	925	0.03	81.24	0.936
Asia						
China, Republic of	1960-61	841	410	2.05	1.27	0.474
India	1960	172	141	1.22	6.52	0.607
Indonesia	1963	323	149	2.17	1.05	—
Iran	1960	187	581	0.32	6.05	0.624
Korea, Republic of	1970	1,085	377	2.88	0.85	—
Japan	1960	1,720	1,188	1.45	1.18	0.473
Nepal	1961-62	352	138	2.54	1.23	—
Pakistan	1960	240	249	0.96	2.35	0.607
Philippines	1960	250	200	1.25	3.59	0.580
Sri Lanka	1962	376	337	1.12	1.61	—
Thailand	1963	166	137	1.21	3.47	—
Turkey	1963	155	243	0.64	5.03	0.611
Viet-Nam, Republic of	1960	355	127	2.79	1.33	—
Africa						
Botswana	1969-70	168	142	1.18	4.75	—
Egypt, Arab Republic of	1960-61	681	360	1.89	1.59	—
Kenya	1969	183	140	1.31	4.20	—
Malagasy Republic	1961-62	293	88	3.32	1.04	—
Mali	1960	98	48	2.06	4.35	—
Morocco	1961	144	295	0.49	4.62	—
Senegal	1960	209	174	1.20	3.62	—
Togo	1961-62	189	180	1.05	2.62	—
Tunisia	1961-62	42	341	0.12	15.41	—
Uganda	1963-64	167	198	0.84	3.29	—
Zambia	1960	68	101	0.67	—	—

Sources: Columns 1 and 3 are based on FAO, *Production Yearbook 1971*, pp. 10-11, 21-23, and column 4 on UN, *Monthly Bulletin of Statistics*, XXVI, No. 4, April 1972, and XXVII, No. 11, November 1973. For currency exchange rates, see *ibid*, and IMF, *International Financial Statistics*, XXVI, No. 8, August 1973. Gross Domestic Product (GDP) in agriculture shown here includes, unless otherwise indicated, agriculture, hunting, forestry, and fishing.

ture sector. The available evidence suggests that a well-designed land reform program need not entail unacceptable costs in terms of other objectives; its contribution to output and employment—as well as to equity—depends on the speed and effectiveness of the reform and complementary investments. However, the effects of land reform can best be examined by focusing on particular measures, such as the effects of farm size on productivity, equity and employment as well as on savings and market surplus. These measures are interrelated but, for analytical convenience, are treated separately here.

Implications for Productivity

The effects of land reform on productivity might best be isolated by comparing productivity in a given area before and after reform. Unfortunately, this is not possible as there is no situation where change has occurred in only one variable—size of farm—over time. The nearest alternative is the comparison over a defined period of the productivity of groups of different-sized farms in a given area. The ideal measure for comparison would take into account the contributions of all factors of production and so measure total factor productivity. Since data are not available to derive this measure, changes in yields per hectare are considered to be the most appropriate substitute.

Several comparative multicountry analyses have been made of the effect of differences in distribution of size of holdings on yields. One 13-country study undertaken by the FAO analyzed the relationship among size of holding, concentration of land and productivity. A similar study of 40 countries was undertaken by the Bank (see Table 1). Both studies indicated that a smaller average size of holdings and a lower concentration of landownership were associated with an increase in output per hectare.

Similar findings can be cited from cross-section studies in a number of individual countries. In Sri Lanka, for example, in 1966-67, the yield of paddy averaged 36 to 37 bushels per acre on farms of up to one acre and 33 to 34 bushels on larger holdings. In central Thailand, yields were reported to decline from 306 kilograms per rai on holdings of two to six acres, to 194 kilograms per rai on holdings of 140 acres or more (1 rai equals 0.4 acre). Small farms in the Philippines—that is, farms of less than two hectares—produced 2.9 tons of paddy per hectare, while farms of more than four hectares produced 2.2 tons per hectare. In a systematic analysis of the differences between large "multifamily" farms and small "subfamily" farms in Argentina, Brazil, Chile, Colombia, Ecuador and Guatemala, output per hectare was

Table 2

Agricultural Output per Hectare and per Worker,
by Farm Size, in Latin America

Country	Year	1 Smallest subfamily farms	2 Largest multifamily farms	3 Ratio of col. 1 to col. 2
		National monetary unit per agricultural hectare		
Argentina	1960	2,492	304	8.20
Brazil	1950	1,498	170	8.80
Chile	1955	334	41	8.20
Colombia	1960	1,198	84	14.30
Ecuador	1954	1,862	660	2.80
Guatemala	1950	63	16	3.90
		National monetary unit per worker		
Argentina	1960	40	192	0.21
Brazil	1950	1,197	8,237	0.14
Chile	1955	268	1,171	0.23
Colombia	1960	972	9,673	0.10
Guatemala	1950	74	523	0.14

Source: Barraclough and Collarte. *Agrarian Structure in Latin America*, a resume of the CIDA Land Tenure Studies of Argentina, Brazil, Chile, Colombia, Ecuador, Guatemala, Peru. xxvi, 351 p. Studies in the Economic and Social Development of Latin America. Lexington, Massachusetts: Lexington Books, 1973.

found to be three to 14 times greater, on the average, on the small farms than on the large farms (see Table 2).

There is other evidence to support these findings, including the results of Bank-sponsored analysis in Mexico, as well as studies on Japan and the Republic of China. However, there is no claim that all conditions were identical; the studies simply indicate that yields were higher on small farms than on large farms.

The important implication is that reductions in either the size of holdings or land concentration need not be associated with a reduction in output per hectare. On the contrary, it appears that under controlled circumstances output per hectare is likely to be higher. There are two associated reasons for this assumption. Firstly, there are limited economies of scale in most agricultural production. Secondly, small-scale producers tend to maximize output by applying labor intensively, while large-scale operators tend to maximize profits by using hired labor only until incremental production covers incremental costs. This is usually short of the output per hectare that would be produced if the goal were maximization of output.

In broad terms, land reform can be consonant with development from a point of view concerned purely with productivity, with output per hectare as the relevant criterion. Output per worker, however, is likely to decrease for the simple reason that, as pointed out below, smaller farms would employ more labor per hectare. In other words, the larger income would be shared by an even larger number of families. This decline in labor productivity only reflects the employment and equity benefits of land reform: the same land would supply more people and the income generated would be more widely shared.

Land Reform and Employment

Evidence exists that the use of labor per hectare is greater on smaller holdings than on larger ones. The cross-sectional analysis of the 13 countries previously mentioned shows that manpower per hectare of agricultural land is significantly correlated with the size of the holding—the smaller the holding, the greater the input of manpower. This cross-sectional evidence of the higher productivity of small farms indicates their long-run equilibrium potential. But the realization of this potential is contingent on the supply of nonland inputs being increased as soon as farm size is decreased.

A limited number of studies in Asia and Latin America have also confirmed these findings. In the Ferozepur district in Punjab (India), for example, in 1968, labor absorption varied between 33 and 39 man-days per acre on holdings of less than 30 acres. On larger holdings, it ranged from 20 to 23 man-days per acre. In Colombia, man-years per hectare declined steadily from 2.7 on small holdings (less than 0.5 hectare) to 0.17 on large farms (500 to 1,000 hectares) in 1960. In other Latin American countries (Argentina, Brazil, Chile and Guatemala), the number of workers per hectare of agricultural land on the smallest farms (subfamily units) has been estimated to be 30 to 60 times greater than on the largest (multifamily) farms.

More intensive labor use is the main reason why small farms are able to produce more per unit of land than the larger farms. But inputs other than labor are also likely to be applied more intensively on small farms, unless access to these inputs is blocked by institutional arrangements. Unfortunately, the relationship between these other inputs and farm size cannot be studied in many developing countries for want of data. It is interesting to note, however, that in the cross-section of *developed* countries, in 1961, fertilizer consumption and gross fixed capital formation per unit of land were relatively higher in countries with smaller average holdings.

In developing countries, too, small farms undoubtedly need much more nonlabor input in order to raise productivity. The mere redistribution of land and increase in employment may not suffice to raise output substantially. Therefore, the organization of an effective extension-*cum*-input supply system for small farmers must accompany land reform. Where there is such a system—as in Japan, the Republic of Korea and the Republic of China—the absorptive capacity of agriculture tends to be high even though holdings are small; at the same time, output per hectare is high. Small holdings can yield high returns to labor provided output per hectare is high—a condition that can only be fulfilled by the application of high-yielding, labor-intensive technologies.

Land Reform and Equity

The more radical the land reform and the more important the share of agricultural land in relation to total tangible wealth, the larger will be the equity effect of the reform program. In the rural areas, agricultural land accounts for such a large proportion of total wealth that it is usually the single most significant determinant of the distribution of both income and power. Evidence of this can be seen in many Latin American and Middle Eastern countries where the large landowners often dominate both commerce and government. There, land reform could have a major equity impact. However, where much of the wealth exists in the form of financial assets, real estate and other investments apart from farmland, and commodity stocks in the hands of traders, the redistribution of farmland alone may not improve the distribution of total wealth substantially. Landowners may easily change the composition of their assets on the eve of land reform if agricultural land alone is the target of redistributive zeal.

If rural and urban areas are considered together, the limitations of redistributing farmland alone appear even more serious. The distribution of real estate, financial assets and commodity stocks in the urban areas is even more skewed than the distribution of farmland in the rural areas. If, therefore, urban property reform or highly progressive taxation on urban wealth does not accompany land reform in countries with a substantial and prosperous industrial-commercial urban sector, land reform alone is not sufficient. By itself, it not only may not decrease the inequity of the distribution of total wealth in the country as a whole. It may even increase the inequity—in particular, the inequity between the town and the village—since it will freeze the maximum permissible ownership of the main rural asset, without freezing the maximum permissible ownership of urban assets.

Even with this broader focus, the equity effect of land reform will be significant only if: (1) the effective ceiling is low; (2) the beneficiaries belong to the poorer groups; (3) the extension and (nonland) input distribution system favors the beneficiaries; and (4) owned and self-operated land as well as leased land is redistributed.

The Population Factor

Opportunities for the redistribution of land depend to a great extent on the existing pattern of distribution of holdings and population density. As will be shown later, there are some countries, notably in the Americas, where land distribution is skewed and population is not dense. In such countries, there are ample opportunities for redistributing land so that inequalities can be diminished and the recipients of the land can generate an acceptable minimum income. In other areas, however, the pressure of population is such that there is not enough land to meet the minimum requirements of all claimants. The density of the farm sector is so high in some countries in Asia that, even if holdings above a certain size were completely eliminated, not enough land would be available either to raise the acreage of the minifarms to a tolerable minimum or provide for the landless.

In India, even if the maximum holding was 20 acres, the available land (43 million acres) would be barely sufficient to bring up the size of miniholdings to a minimum of five acres, and no land would be available for the landless (20-25 million households). In Bangladesh, a low 10-acre ceiling would not suffice even to bring all miniholdings up to a minimum two-acre size. The millions of landless families could not be provided for at the same time. In Sri Lanka, too, even with a low ratio between the ceiling and the floor holding (5 to 1), there would be enough land only to give two acres to each minifarmer. In Haiti, only 1.5 hectares is available for the average rural family of five. The solution to rural poverty clearly cannot be found exclusively in the agriculture sector. In these situations, it might be wise to give land only to the minifarmers and to attack the poverty problem of the landless by means of a massive rural works program. (Settlement of the landless on new land, where available, and their migration to urban areas, when possible, are the other obvious alternatives.)

Effects on Marketed Surplus and Savings

The redistribution of land can have a pronounced impact both on the availability of a marketable surplus and on aggregate savings in the agricultural sector. Although the total effect of the redistribution process will depend to a large extent on the costs of increased output after the redistribution, the change in the size distribution of holdings will shift the distribution of the source of the marketable surplus and savings. As the marketed surplus generates agricultural incomes and so potential cash savings, it determines the size of the rural market for domestically produced industrial products. The marketed surplus also represents the supply of agricultural products, mostly food, for the urban population. Thus, a fall in the surplus could necessitate imports and put an added strain on the balance of payments. But increasing the marketed surplus will not necessarily increase savings. Where it does, the savings need not be monetized, but may take the form of increased on-farm investment in such items as improved housing, wells and access roads.

Marketed Surplus

A reduction in land concentration through land reform could lead to a fall in the marketed surplus—at least in the short run. Small farm households tend to consume a larger proportion of their small output than do households which have a large enough acreage to produce in excess of domestic requirements. Thus, the ratio of marketed surplus to production falls as farm size decreases. Data from India show, for example, that small farms (2.5 acres or less) sell only 24.5% of their output, whereas large farms (50 acres or more) sell 65.4%. But these farm groups produce only 9.5% each of the national output. If output remained the same but, hypothetically, farms above a certain size were eliminated and their land transferred to the small class, the surplus-output ratio would probably decline. The rate of decline, however, might not be very great given that the largest and the smallest farm-size groups account for only small proportions of the total output.

The surplus-output ratios of different farm-size groups, however, and their shares of total output and sales can differ widely across countries and regions. Sixty-one percent of the maize farmers in Puebla (Mexico), for example, sell no maize at all; and another 16% sell 25% or less of their output. In Chile, on the other hand, a typical sharecropper sells as much as 43% of his output. In Mexico, 6.6% of the marketed surplus comes from 70.7% of the farmers; and 55.4% comes from only 1.7%. In India, 48% of the farms (less than 2.5 acres) contribute only 6% of sales, 1% (more than 50 acres) contribute 16%, and 51% (with 2.5 to 50 acres) contribute the bulk (78%) of the total surplus.

These differences would determine how much the surplus ratio would fall after land reform; but there can be no doubt that it *would* fall, with adverse effects on the economy. However, this decline in the market surplus ratio need not result in a decline in *total* surplus, *provided that there is a compensatory increase in total output.* Since per acre yields on small farms can be higher than on large farms, there may be a sufficient increase in output if, after reform, the necessary conditions are fulfilled whereby small farms can realize their full production potential. In addition, from the welfare point of view, a decline in the market surplus ratio has a direct distributive dimension which should be offset against the decline. As the surplus-output ratio falls, the subsistence consumption of small farmers increases—the extra consumption in kind representing a direct increase in their incomes (nutrition). Insofar as the productivity of small farmers was previously constrained by inadequate nutrition, there should also be a positive effect on productivity.

Savings

In considering the productivity effect of land reform, it is necessary to examine the implications of a change in farm-size structure on the aggregate savings rate of the farm sector as a whole, since the savings rate represents the contribution of the sector to the long-run growth of both its own productive capacity and that of the rest of the economy. Although the evidence on savings rates of different classes of farm households in developing countries is scant, it can be expected that the behavior of the savings rate will be similar to that of the marketed surplus. At the lowest end of the farm-size scale, the subsistence farmers can be expected to be net "dissavers" (for instance, by running down the existing soil fertility). As farm size increases, the savings rate can be expected to become positive and increase along with it (although large farmers can be "dissavers" too, by using capital for consumption). A recent study in the state of Haryana (India) tended to confirm this: the savings ratio was found to be —0.24% for small farmers, 8.5% for medium farmers and 16.3% for large farmers. In a further study in Orissa (India), there was no direct measure of the savings made, but the ratio of net capital formation as a proportion of income was found to be 5.5% in the smallest farm-size group (0 to 2 acres) and 19.3% on the larger farms (8 acres and above). For unirrigated villages, the corresponding figures were lower —2.6% on the smallest farms, and 11.2% on the larger ones.

It follows that a reduction in concentration of land will reduce the average savings rate of the farm sector. But, again, if a compensatory increase in total income can be secured by intensifying inputs per unit of land soon after land reform, the aggregate savings can be prevented from falling. This adds to the urgency of introducing effective agrarian reform (including improved technology and services) along with land reform.

A policy implication, from the foregoing, is that the farm-size structure created by any land reform program should fix a minimum as well as a maximum farm size. The minimum farm size clearly should

221

be determined on the basis of the current national norm of minimum family income. But one of the criteria for determining the minimum income itself should be that it should at least enable the smallholder to cease to be a "dissaver." An analogous criterion can also be derived from the known behavior of marketed surplus: the smallholder should have at least enough land for positive sales.

Tenancy Reform

The most successful land reforms include those whereby tenants become owners of the land they operate, as in Japan, Taiwan and some parts of Europe. Ownership control and income from the land is thus redistributed. However, if landlords are allowed to retain land that might be self-operated, and tenants become owners of the land that they operate, then the size distribution of operational holdings may not change. With the conversion of tenants into owners, security of tenure is greater and incomes for the farmers are larger. This, in turn, encourages increased savings and, hence, on-farm investment and higher output.

The conversion of tenants into owner-operators generally leads to a more efficient and more equitable form of production organization than tenancy. This is seen not only from the reforms in Japan and Taiwan, but also from experience in parts of Africa where "customary" tradition is converted into freehold. In Kenya, the provision of security of tenure, especially in the temperate production areas, has increased on-farm investment and helped raise output.

There may be situations where tenancy reform aims at stabilizing the position of tenants with respect to rent paid, security of tenure and labor objectives, without transferring ownership rights to them. Here, the problem is to promote more efficient types of tenancy, with contracts having well-defined incentives and deterrents. The expert consensus is that fixed cash-rent contracts are superior to the more common crop-share contracts, since the whole income in excess of the fixed rent accrues to the actual cultivator. Sharecroppers, however, often have a preference for crop sharing because it provides risk insurance. Crop sharing can be made more efficient and equitable if it is considered with cost sharing. There is growing evidence from the Philippines, for example, that since the seed-fertilizer technology began to spread, landlords and sharecroppers have spontaneously begun trying to combine cost sharing with crop sharing because the combination is profitable to both.

Tenurial reforms, whether through the distribution of the land to those working it or the provision of greater security of tenure and improved rental contracts, have an effect on development. Such reforms improve income distribution by shifting income away from the landlords to small-scale producers, often those among the lowest income groups. The more secure producers tend to invest part of their higher earnings in their holdings—thus raising the level of investment in agricultural production—whereas absentee landlords frequently invest in off-farm activities. Finally, greater security enables tenants to benefit from appropriate technological changes, instead of being displaced when landlords find it to their advantage to adopt a different technology. The financial returns to the landlord from using machines and hired labor may be high, but the returns to the economy are usually higher from labor-intensive operations undertaken by smallholders.

Implementation Issues

If reforms are to generate the benefits expected of them, several important considerations must be taken into account. Firstly, since agriculture is a private sector activity in most countries, production and investment decisions are made by millions of individuals operating in their own interests. Very often the greater part of national output comes from medium-scale farmers. These farmers, like prudent investors, weigh the risks as they perceive them before making on-farm investments—the major component of total investment in agriculture. Sustained uncertainty about a government's intentions with regard to the distribution of land adds to the risk of investment and can hamper capital formation and production. In some instances, continued uncertainty has led to disinvestment in agriculture by owner-operators and a flight of capital from the country. It follows that the more specific the plans and the more clearly defined the policies regarding land reform, the less likely the acceleration of disinvestment by landowners and, so, the lower the "cost" of the reform.

Logistical Support

Secondly, the introduction of a major land reform program usually disrupts the system of logistical support from the commercial sector to the farmers. In most countries in the world, there is a well-established link between commercial bankers and suppliers in the private sector and the larger agricultural producers. This linkage is based on mutual interests and, often, on long-standing business association. The redistribution of land frequently leads to a breakdown of this system. Often, there is a long interval before the public sector can undertake the role previously filled by the private sector, or before the private sector adjusts to the new situation. Without an appropriate organization for the provision of inputs, productivity will decline and output will fall. Thus, the reduction of the costs of a land reform program—in terms of production forgone—depends on the rapid reorganization of the input supply system.

Nature of Organizations

Thirdly, the nature of the organizations providing for both the supply of necessary inputs and the marketing of production surpluses is crucial in a post-reform period. There are many different forms of organization: cooperatives, agricultural development banks, special credit institutions, marketing authorities, and the like. Whatever the organizations that prevail, it is essential that they be designed specifically to assist the beneficiaries of reform. In many instances, the institutions that have provided services in a post-reform period have continued with a bias in favor of larger-size operations. Part of the reason is that these institutions have not been able to adapt their methods of operation to the needs of large numbers of small farmers. Unless this is done, the beneficiaries of the reform may not be in a position to increase their output. Indeed, the appropriate organization of supplies and the evolution of a low-cost delivery system to reach small-scale producers is a *sine qua non* for a sustained increase in productivity.

Adaptation

Fourthly, under certain conditions land reform programs might need adaptation if they are to fulfill the objectives of development. When land is fully utilized and yields are already high, the impact of redistribution of land on productivity and employment may be in question. In this context, it is important to determine the reasons for high yields. In much of agriculture, most of the inputs are "divisible," thus reducing the importance of scale of operations as a factor in raising productivity. In some situations, high yields and efficient operations may be directly associated with a system organized to function on a large scale (as in certain types of sugar plantations). The breaking up of such holdings may well reduce yields and lower output. A more realistic approach to obtaining widespread benefits would be to leave such operations intact and redistribute the profits from the enterprise. This can be done through taxation, by raising the wages of the workers, or—as in Peru—converting the operation into a worker-owned corporation and distributing dividends, out of profits, to the participating stockholders.

Structural Change

Finally, land reform leads to structural changes within the agricultural sector. The post-reform structure will depend on the ideology of the government. In some instances, the number of small-scale owner operations will increase; in others, producer cooperatives or communes or large-scale state farms will emerge. The pattern that evolves may also be tailored to fit the economic environment: the organization might be based on a system which can use surplus labor for direct capital formation; other organizations (such as large-scale state farms) might be intended to save labor. Experience has indicated, however, that:

1. Government reorganization can generate enthusiasm and provide opportunities for mobilizing workers, but raising output depends on more than land and labor. There must be an appropriate supply of other inputs.

2. No matter what the structure, an appropriate system of management is necessary which enables the managers of land to make decisions in a timely fashion—a most important condition in agriculture and one that is dependent on weather. This is a condition, however, that is often unfulfilled in rigidly controlled societies.

3. There must be an adequate system of incentives and rewards if productivity in agriculture is to be increased. This applies both to the agricultural sector as a whole and to the units in which beneficiaries of reforms are organized. Many communes, producer cooperatives and other units of production have floundered in developing a system that reflects both equity and incentives. The creation of adequate incentives is particularly important in a situation where labor is the major input.

Land reform, although equity oriented, can be consistent with all the goals of economic development: raising productivity, increasing employment and providing wider equity. In the long run, land reform need not lead to a reduction in marketed output or savings. Tenancy reforms can redistribute incomes and, by providing security of tenure, can encourage increased on-farm investment. However, sustained increases in output depend on complementary investments and policies. The most important of these concern the organization and provision of an adequate supply of inputs for the beneficiaries and the creation of incentives to use these inputs to raise production.

Chapter 3: THE WORLD BANK AND
LAND REFORM

Changing Concerns

The position of the World Bank in regard to land reform has changed over the past decade, reflecting a reconsideration of the objectives of development and the most appropriate strategies for attaining those objectives. The objectives are now generally accepted to be increased productivity and employment, and social justice. Land reform can be consistent with these objectives and, in some situations, may well be a necessary condition for their realization.

In the early years of the Bank's operations, the focus was on providing adequate infrastructure for increasing agricultural production. In the early 1960s, the approach to agricultural development was widened to include the provision of rural credit and on-farm inputs. Problems of tenure were seen to have an indirect bearing on production, mainly because they influenced on-farm investment decisions and determined the efficiency of resource use, especially irrigation water. By the end of the 1960s, however, concern was growing about distribution of income in the rural areas and the relationship between land distribution and income distribution. This was reflected in the Agriculture Sector Working Paper of June 1972, which recognized a relationship between land distribution and equity. The paper stated:

> "In developing countries, land represents a much higher proportion of total wealth than in developed countries, and inegalitarian patterns of landownership are a major source of income inequality. Furthermore, the owners of land usually possess political and economic power which can be exercised in ways that harm the interests of the bulk of the rural people."

The paper went on to affirm that:

> "It is clear that agricultural development cannot do all it might to improve rural life if the distribution of landownership is highly skewed."

This concern has been reflected both in the technical assistance offered to governments (especially in sector survey and economic reports) and in the types and components of projects in the lending program.

Technical Assistance

The Bank has been concerned with problems associated with land distribution and land reform since the beginning of its operations. One of the first major economic surveys undertaken was that of Colombia in 1955. The mission identified the patterns of land use and

226

land distribution by size of holding to be major obstacles to accelerating agricultural development. Large stretches of fertile land were held by large-scale producers for livestock raising, while intensive agriculture was practiced by "minifundios" on land that was less suited for crop production. The mission recommended to the government that it introduce a graduated land tax as a means of intensifying land use. A subsequent agriculture sector mission in 1956 confirmed that the systems of land tenure and land use were barriers to increasing output. This mission recommended that the government adopt a presumptive income tax to encourage the more productive use of land.

The two missions to Colombia were concerned with increasing productivity and intensifying land use. The missions were not concerned with the redistribution of land as a means of encouraging greater equity, nor did they consider redistribution as a means of intensifying production. Rather, they took the view that the distribution of land was a matter of national policy and internal politics, and that the Bank—as an external lending agency—should adhere to the existing policy and not advocate a rapid redistribution of land. It did, however, recommend a vigorous policy of settlement on reclaimed and cleared land.

Since that time, missions and sector surveys have been conducted in almost all the countries served by the Bank. Many of these have pointed to patterns of land control and insecurity of tenure as obstacles to raising agricultural productivity. More recently, there has been a growing emphasis on the problems of distribution of land and the rights to land as factors that influence equity as well as productivity. Thus, missions to Ethiopia and Morocco have drawn attention to the relationship between the land tenure situation and the distribution of benefits from growth. In Morocco, the mission emphasized the possibility of redistributing land as a means of increasing both output and equity. In Ethiopia, the problem was seen as one of uneven land distribution and insecurity of tenure; security of tenure was considered to be especially significant in the light of the distribution of potential gains from new technology being introduced into the country. Landlords were finding it increasingly profitable to displace their tenants as machine technology provided higher returns.

Despite this trend, many reports do not give appropriate emphasis to issues related to land reform and development. The Bank needs to be better informed about conditions governing rights to land and related institutions in member countries. More needs to be known about the distribution of land, conditions governing tenancy, and the policies and programs instituted to influence the distribution of land and rural incomes. It is only through a thorough analysis of conditions within member countries that the Bank will be in a position to discuss policy options with member governments. At present, many reports still do not address these problems; however, new guidelines are being developed which can form a basis for discussing the issues in a systematic way in sector and economic reports.

Lending Operations

The Bank's lending for agricultural development has increased very rapidly in recent years. Loans and credits have been made to countries with widely differing social and political structures. These have included socialist countries, such as Yugoslavia and Tanzania, as well as countries that follow capitalism, such as Argentina and Thailand. Loans and credits have been made for agriculture operating under different forms of tenure—for kombinats in Yugoslavia, kibbutzes in Israel, individual holdings in India, cooperative production units in Tunisia and group farmers in Kenya. Funds have also been provided for large-scale livestock producers, large-scale plantations and small-scale producers; these have benefited absentee landlords, large land-owners, small landowners, tenants and farm workers. On the other hand, the Bank has not been totally indifferent to structural and income distribution aspects, and the record shows an increasing awareness of the implications reflected in more frequent use of measures to improve them.

Nevertheless, few projects have supported land reform as such. In general, external financing, whether multilateral or bilateral, has played a minor role in the financing of land reform programs. One reason is that the process of reform in itself may only require relatively small outlays of public funds, as expenditures for a redistributive reform depend mostly on the levels and forms of compensation that are set for the former landowners. Public discussion of land reform financing is generally dominated by this issue. When land is confiscated as part of a revolutionary process—as it was in Mexico and Bolivia—clearly little, if any, public expenditure is involved. The compensation issue tends to be more important in such countries as Colombia and Venezuela where land is purchased. Even so, the actual amounts involved are not substantial, especially where, as is usually the case, payment is mostly in bonds. It is estimated that, in the Latin American countries which followed nonconfiscatory reforms, only some 9% to 15% of total reform-related cash budgets went for land-owner compensation—though in other cases the figure could be much higher.

Compensation paid for land is a "transfer payment" from the public sector to the landholding groups. Without doubt, compensation can have serious implications for income distribution, consumption and investment—but it does not of itself create any new productive capabilities in the country. Partly because of this, international lending institutions have refrained from using their resources for financing land purchases. It has been suggested that the international agencies might guarantee bonds issued to compensate landlords. If financing were to be through international maintenance-of-value guarantees of bonds and for compensation, this would have the paradoxical effect of giving land bonds greater stability than that enjoyed by the currencies of issuing countries.

The Bank has provided general support for at least one far-reaching land reform program. This was in Tunisia where the Bank provided a loan of $18 million intended to back a major agrarian reform relating to former French-owned estates, which occupied the most fertile land in that country. The nationalized land was to be converted into "units of production" which were to be farmed on a cooperative basis; each unit of production was to be self-financing and, *inter alia,* was to pay a guaranteed minimum cash wage to the workers out of the farm profits. However, the scarcity of trained manpower and the rapid pace adopted in establishing new cooperatives made it difficult for the production units to start on a sound basis and generate a large enough cash flow to meet their objectives. In addition, the system had built-in disincentives because wages were not paid according to work. The Bank successfully pressed for substantial improvements in the conception, design and implementation of the agrarian reform. It was unable, however, to influence the major political decision either to take all the land in Tunisia under state management or to put it all under the control of cooperatives. The extension of reform strained the limited administrative capacity, and the reform program collapsed. Smallholders opted for private farming and were supported by landowners who resisted the takeover of their lands. The Bank subsequently canceled half of the loan.

The problems encountered in financing the Tunisian program underscore some of the difficulties in lending for reform-related projects. The financial viability of these projects depends to a great extent on the managerial capacity of the beneficiaries of the reform and the development of an efficient service system for them. Very often the managerial capacity of the beneficiaries may be untried; the agencies created to deliver the inputs are usually new, have limited technical capacity and are of questionable financial viability. Furthermore, these institutions often provide inputs that were formerly provided by the private sector, and the whole delivery system changes from one based on the profit motive to one based in the first instance on social consideration. This directly affects their financial viability, especially in that cash flows generated by reform projects tend to be less immediate than in other projects, and many investments in social overhead are not self-liquidating in the short run.

Another Bank project provided direct financial assistance to facilitate the implementation of land reform as part of the Lilongwe development scheme in Malawi. It was recognized during the preparation of the Lilongwe project that there was an opportunity to change the existing land tenure pattern of customary right of usufruct. The need for change to a more secure and lasting tenure system was evident as almost all uncultivated land had been taken up; individual holdings were of the order of about five acres per family, and fragmentation of holdings had occurred on a substantial scale. Five acres was deemed to be the minimum holding size capable of providing a family with subsistence at present levels of technology.

As a consequence, the Malawi Government introduced three Acts of Parliament which provided for the allocation, consolidation and registration of holdings, and the issuance of either family or individual freehold titles. These Acts also provided for the regulation of the subsequent sale, mortgage or transfer of registered land through the establishment of Land Boards. To date, some 200,000 acres have been allocated and titles issued on 60,000 acres. IDA credits are being used for the land survey (both topographical and cadastral), the provision of allocation and registration staff, vehicles, equipment, and the construction of housing and land registry. The amount involved will be approximately US$1 million by the end of the second phase. The Lilongwe project indicates that Bank assistance can play a role in assisting governments in the "mechanics" of land reform and in the drafting of legislation.

A number of other projects have been financed by the Bank involving some change in distribution of land or in tenurial rights within the area encompassed by the project. These include projects for land settlement, outgrower schemes, irrigation, and rural credit.

Land Settlement

The Bank has financed a number of settlement projects in which infrastructure was made available together with other services for families settled in the project area. Table 3 gives information on ten projects located in Brazil, Colombia, Ethiopia, Kenya, Malawi and Malaysia. Seven of the projects were established on public land and so did not involve any change in the size distribution of existing

Costs of Selected Settlement Projects Assisted by the World Bank

Table 3

| Country | Project | Total project costs (US$ millions) | Bank or IDA finance | | | Number of families[1] to be settled | Estimated project costs per family[2] (US$) | Average farm size (hectares) | Settlement on |
			Amount (US$ millions)	Loan or credit	Date				
Brazil	Alto Turi Land Settlement Project	12.6	6.7	loan	1972	5,200	2,423[3]	40.0	Public land
Colombia	Atlantico No. 3 Irrigation	15.7	9.0	loan	1967	2,500	6,280[4]	4.0[5]	INCORA land (involved appropriation of private land)
	Second Atlantico Development	9.7	5.0	loan	1972	1,800	5,389	11.0	
	Caqueta Land Colonization	21.6	8.1	loan	1971	6,300[6]	3,429	n.a.[7]	
Ethiopia	Wolamo Agricultural Project	2.3[8]	3.5	credit	1969	1,050	2,214	6.0	Public land
Kenya	Land Settlement and Development	6.9	3.9	credit	1969	5,200	1,327	14.3	European-owned land
Malawi	Karonga Rural Development	7.8	6.6	credit	1972	2,830	2,756	6.0	Public land
Malaysia	Jengka Triangle	29.1	14.0	loan	1968	2,770	10,505	4.8	Public land
	Second Jengka Triangle	41.0	13.0	loan	1970	3,000	13,667	4.3	Public land
	Third Jengka Triangle	43.3	25.0	loan	1973	4,000	10,825	4.5	Public land

Source: World Bank and IDA appraisal reports.

(1) Except for Kenya, figures represent goals rather than actual state of settlement.
(2) Project costs, as estimated in the appraisal reports, do not necessarily reflect total economic costs of settlement.
(3) The cost to the government is $1,700 per family settled. This excludes expenditures on health, education, research and related studies. These cost expenditures are being reviewed and are expected to be considerably higher than originally expected.
(4) The cost per small farmer settled is estimated to be $17,000, whereas the cost per middle-size farmer remaining in the project area is $100,000.
(5) The original goal was to settle 2,500 landless peasants and develop 9,900 hectares. The project is behind schedule.
(6) Includes 2,800 new settlers and 3,500 partially established settlers.
(7) Although 2,800 new settler families are scheduled to be settled on some 280,000 hectares, no data on the farm size of 3,500 partially established settlers are given.
(8) Excludes $2.73 million used for agricultural development on the highlands.

231

holdings. Thus, settlers were allocated holdings of from three or four hectares in Malaysia to 40 hectares in Brazil. Each holding was deemed adequate to provide a livelihood and full employment for the settler and his family.

There are severe limitations on settlement as a means of reaching large numbers of landless people or relieving pressures on the land. Although the costs per family in a settlement project can be misleading, the data in Table 3 indicate the limitations on settlement projects —as presently conceived. The ten projects were intended to settle no more than 35,000 families; the total cost was expected to be $190 million, the Bank's contributions being almost half that amount. The capital requirement of more than $5,000 per family limits the prospects of the approach. Clearly, the whole approach to capital-intensive settlement requires reexamination considering the magnitude of the problem outlined in Annex 1 of this paper.

Outgrower Schemes

The problems of distributing the gains from plantation development were mentioned earlier. It was suggested that the benefits be distributed through the raising of wages and the payment of dividends to the workers. In this area, the Bank has made a substantial contribution toward a novel form of tenure through the development of "outgrower" schemes. These schemes involve the production of tree crops on smallholdings rather than on large-scale plantations. The smallholdings are established around the nucleus of either a processing plant or a plantation. The central unit provides technical assistance, inputs and marketing services for the outgrowers who, in turn, sell their products through the central organization.

The Bank has participated in nine such projects costing $125 million, of which the Bank has contributed $68 million and affecting some 120,000 families. These have included tea projects in Indonesia, Kenya, Mauritius and Uganda, rubber in Indonesia and Malaysia, cocoa in the Ivory Coast, and oil palm in Nigeria. The average holding in each project has ranged from 10 hectares in Senegal to one acre in Kenya. In the main, the size of holdings for outgrowers is small, although large enough, under labor-intensive cropping systems, to employ a family and produce enough of a high unit value commodity to yield an income well in excess of that earned by producers of staple commodities who have holdings of a similar size. While this system has made a valuable contribution toward establishing viable smallholders, it is only effective when there is a commodity that can be handled through a central processing system.

232

Irrigation

The Bank has invested about $1,450 million in irrigation, flood control and drainage projects. While these projects covered many facets of water storage and distribution, most were intended to improve the use of water and bring more land under intensive cultivation. To this end, the Bank has worked with various governments in determining the most appropriate size of holding for the beneficiaries of each project. For example, 11 projects costing $342 million (incorporating a Bank investment of $190 million) are expected to improve 810,000 hectares and benefit more than 500,000 families. The average size of holdings in the irrigated areas ranges from 10 hectares in Iraq to one hectare in Korea, Pakistan and Sri Lanka, or an average of 1.6 hectares per family over all the projects.

In many instances, irrigation projects are subject to special regulations or laws regarding the size of holding that can be held by the beneficiary. Thus, in Mexico the Bank-supported projects have conformed to the law which limits the size of irrigated holdings to a maximum of 10 hectares. Elsewhere, problems have arisen because there is no legal provision regarding size of holding or because the law has been ignored. In some instances, the Bank has insisted on special legislation giving tenants security of tenure. But, in practice, this has been difficult to enforce.

Rural Credit

While in itself farm credit is an important instrument for reaching groups of a particular size in agriculture, access can be restricted by tenurial arrangements if lending criteria specify that registered land titles be used as collateral for borrowing. Bank-assisted projects have provided more than $1,000 million for rural credit. Most of these resources have aided larger commercial producers, although in recent years there has been a pronounced trend toward lending for smaller producers. By the end of 1973, an estimated $250 million had been allocated for small farmers.

In some instances, the Bank has made loans on the condition that the recipient government takes steps to ensure that the intended beneficiaries do indeed gain from the investment. However, in several instances, the governments concerned have not fulfilled obligations regarding the provision of security for tenants or the allocation of land to low-income groups. In other instances, governments have failed to implement conditions provided for by existing legislation on rights to land; or they have failed to introduce legislation which would have met the conditions specified in the loans. This highlights one of the major dilemmas confronting an international lending agency concerned with promotion of land reform as an instrument of economic development. That is, to what extent can the Bank influence the course of events regarding distribution of land, and income from the land, in the sovereign states that are members of the Bank?

Major Policy Options

The Bank has to recognize that its leverage is limited as it seeks to redefine its position with regard to land reform. Using Bank finance to gain a developmental impact through land reform involves highly complex issues at the project level, while the potential for using the Bank's influence to press or even force the issue of structural reform on member countries is severely circumscribed. Such political decisions are not amenable to ready negotiation with governments in the same way as are other institutional questions—such as, for instance, the setting of public utility rates.

The Bank would seem to be left with only two options. Firstly, in countries that are interested in pursuing land reform the Bank can give support in the form of technical assistance and finance for reform-related projects. It should give overt priority in lending to those countries and projects which meet land reform criteria. Secondly, in countries where governments are not interested in land reform the Bank should:

(1) study the situation in all cases;

(2) call the attention of the governments to the problems associated with the existing tenure system, and enter into a dialogue on the subject;

(3) support land reform proposals when they are made officially; and

(4) not lend for projects if tenurial arrangements are so bad that they frustrate the achievement of the Bank's objectives.

These options are reflected in the policy guidelines provided in this paper.

LAND REFORM
ANNEXES

THE CONTEXT OF
LAND REFORM

Ratios of Population to Land

The total land area of the globe is about 13,393 million hectares, made up of 1,456 million hectares of cropland, defined as arable land and land under permanent crops (10.8%); 2,987 million hectares under permanent pasturage (22.8%); and 4,041 million hectares under other uses (36.4%). Of the arable land, approximately 32% is in Asia; 19% in North and Central America; 16% in the USSR; 15% in Africa; 10% in Europe; 6% in South America; and 3% in Oceania.

The world's population was estimated at approximately 3,617 million in the early 1970s. This represents an average of 3.7 hectares of land, or close to 0.40 hectare of cropland, per person. The world's agricultural population—defined as population depending on agriculture for its livelihood—is estimated at 1,851 million, or 51% of the total population. On the basis of these global figures, there is an average of 0.78 hectare of cropland per person in agriculture.

The relationship between population and land in all major regions and for 52 selected countries is shown in Annex Tables 1:1 and 1:2, respectively. Among other things, the tables show that:

1. More than 70% of all rural people live in Asia, which has approximately 32% of the world's cropland. The ratio of cropland to agricultural population is the lowest in Asia among all the major regions, averaging 0.35 hectare per person. Together, the People's Republic

Table 1:1

Regional Distribution of Land, Cropland, Agricultural
Population and Area per Person in Agriculture

Region	Land area (million hectares)	Cropland (million hectares)	Cropland Distribution (%)	Rural population (millions)	Rural population Distribution (%)	Agricultural population as percentage of total population	Cropland area per rural person (hectares)
Europe	493	145	10.0	89	4.8	17	1.63
USSR	2,240	232	15.9	77	4.2	32	3.01
North and Central America	2,242	271	18.6	54	2.9	17	5.02
South America	1,783	84	5.8	74	4.0	39	1.14
Asia	2,753	463	31.8	1,314	71.0	64	0.35
Africa	3,031	214	14.7	239	12.9	67	0.90
Oceania	851	47	3.2	4	0.2	4	11.75
Total	13,393	1,456	100.0	1,851	100.0	51	0.78

Source: FAO. *Production Yearbook 1972.*

Cropland in Relation to Population, by Country

Country	Cropland (000 hectares)	Total population (000)	Agricultural population (000)	Hectares of cropland per person of:	
				Total population	Agricultural population
Africa					
Angola	900	5,501	3,568	0.16	0.25
Ghana	2,835	8,832	4,840	0.29	0.59
Ivory Coast	8,859	4,916	3,986	1.80	2.22
Nigeria	21,795	76,795	45,423	0.32	0.48
Rwanda	704	3,609	3,277	0.20	0.21
Uganda	4,888	8,549	7,342	0.57	0.67
Zaire	7,200	17,493	13,701	0.41	0.53
Asia					
Bangladesh	9,500	71,000	60,000	0.13	0.16
Burma	18,941	27,584	17,570	0.69	1.08
China, People's Republic of	110,300	850,406	568,921	0.13	0.19
China, Republic of	867	14,520	6,171	0.06	0.14
India	164,610	550,376	372,605	0.30	0.44
Indonesia	18,000	119,913	83,230	0.15	0.22
Japan	5,510	103,540	21,329	0.05	0.26
Korea, Democratic Republic of	1,894	13,674	7,275	0.14	0.26
Korea, Republic of	2,311	32,422	17,300	0.07	0.13
Malaysia	3,524	10,931	6,176	0.32	0.57
Nepal	2,090	11,040	10,112	0.19	0.21
Pakistan	24,000	60,000	35,000	0.40	0.69
Philippines	8,977	38,493	26,752	0.23	0.34
Thailand	11,415	35,814	27,398	0.32	0.42
Viet-Nam, Democratic Republic of	2,018	20,757	16,108	0.10	0.13
Viet-Nam, Republic of	2,918	18,332	13,620	0.16	0.21
Europe					
Denmark	2,678	4,921	595	0.54	4.50
German Democratic Republic	4,806	17,257	2,133	0.28	2.25
Germany, Federal Republic of	8,075	61,682	3,514	0.13	2.30
Hungary	5,594	10,310	2,484	0.54	2.25
Italy	14,930	53,667	9,735	0.28	1.53
Poland	15,326	32,805	9,940	0.47	1.54
Portugal	4,370	9,630	3,523	0.45	1.24
Romania	10,512	20,253	10,503	0.52	1.00
Spain	20,601	33,290	11,222	0.62	1.84
Sweden	3,053	8,046	754	0.38	4.05
United Kingdom	7,261	55,711	1,540	0.13	4.71
USSR	232,809	242,768	77,322	0.96	3.01
Yugoslavia	8,205	20,527	9,651	0.40	0.85
Latin America					
Argentina	26,028	24,353	3,704	1.07	7.03
Bolivia	3,091	4,931	2,873	0.63	1.08
Brazil	29,760	93,565	40,869	0.32	0.73
Chile	4,632	9,780	2,484	0.47	1.86
Colombia	5,258	21,117	9,541	0.25	0.55
Cuba	3,585	8,407	2,755	0.43	1.30
Guatemala	1,498	5,180	3,246	0.29	0.46
Haiti	370	4,867	3,754	0.08	0.10
Mexico	23,817	50,670	23,617	0.47	1.01
Peru	2,843	13,586	6,189	0.21	0.46
Puerto Rico	236	2,784	387	0.09	0.61
Uruguay	1,947	2,886	482	0.67	4.04
Venezuela	5,214	10,997	2,887	0.47	1.81
North America					
Canada	43,404	21,406	1,712	2.03	25.4
United States	176,440	205,395	8,216	0.86	21.5
Oceania					
Australia	44,610	12,552	1,049	3.55	42.53

Source: Dovring, Folke. *Land Reform: Ends and Means.* A Background Study prepared for the World Bank.

of China and India have an agricultural population of close to 1,000 million, while Indonesia, Bangladesh and Pakistan have a further 178 million. Of the Asian countries, in terms of hectares per person, Burma has the most favorable ratio of cropland to rural population (1.08), followed by Pakistan (0.69), Malaysia (0.57) and India (0.44), compared with Indonesia (0.22), the People's Republic of China (0.19) and Bangladesh (0.16). The least favorable ratio is in the Republic of Korea and the Democratic Republic of Viet-Nam (each with an estimated 0.13). It is notable that the Republic of China (Taiwan) and Japan have ratios of 0.14 and 0.26 arable hectares per person in agriculture. Japan is the only developed country with such a low ratio— well below the 1.63 of Europe and 5.02 of North and Central America.

2. South America accounts for 4% of the world's agricultural population and 5.8% of the world's cropland. Although 13% of the land area of the world is in South America, almost half of that area is in forests and woodlands, 20% is in pastureland and only 5% or 6% is in cropland. However, as only 39% of the population is in agriculture, there is an average of 1.14 hectares of arable land per rural person. Argentina and Uruguay have high ratios of agricultural land to rural population, the most favorable in the developing world (7.03 and 4.04, respectively). Venezuela, Chile, Bolivia, Mexico and Cuba have ratios of more than 1 hectare per person in agriculture; Brazil, Colombia, Peru and the crowded Central American republics have ratios of less than 1 hectare per rural person. Haiti with 0.10 hectare per person in agriculture appears to have the most unfavorable ratio in the world.

3. Africa has 13% of the world's rural population and close to 15% of the world's cropland, with an average of 0.90 hectare of cropland per person in agriculture; 67% of the population depends on agriculture, a higher proportion than in any other region. The most favorable ratio in tropical Africa appears to be in the Ivory Coast, with 2.22 hectares per person in agriculture. Uganda, Ghana, Nigeria and Zaire have between 0.50 hectare and 0.70 hectare per person in agriculture. Rwanda, with 0.21 hectare per person in agriculture, is one of the few countries in tropical Africa where the pressure on land resources is greater than the average in Asia.

This brief summary indicates the wide range of population densities in rural areas in different regions and countries of the developing world. The data show that, by and large, countries with a high proportion of population in agriculture have less favorable ratios of population to land. They are also among the poorest countries. Further, they are the countries in which population is increasing rapidly and where it is particularly difficult to raise agricultural output.

Population and Production

The population in the rural areas of developing countries, while declining relative to total population, is increasing in absolute numbers. Despite rapid migration out of agriculture, and despite the explosive growth of population in certain areas, the rate of growth of the rural population has increased in all regions of the world other than Africa. Table 1:3 shows the trends in rates of growth between 1950-60 and 1960-70, with overall growth rates rising from 1.9% to 2.1%, and the largest regional rate of increase being the one from 1.8% to 2.1% in East Asia (where population density is already great in rural areas).

Table 1:3

Rural Population Growth, by Region

	Annual percentage rate	
	1950-60	1960-70
Latin America	1.4	1.5
East Asia	1.8	2.1
Middle East	1.8	1.8
Africa	2.4	2.2
Total all regions	1.9	2.1

Source: Davis, Kingsley. *World Urbanization, 1950-70*, Vol. I, 1969.

The larger number of people has added to the pressure of population on the land. Historically, this pressure has been relieved through the expansion of acreage along a frontier of cultivation. Indeed, it was the expansion of the frontier in the new lands of North America, Argentina, South Africa and Australia that helped relieve population pressures in the first period of generalized population growth in the late eighteenth century. In these areas, population growth was accelerated by an influx of migrants to rates comparable to those found today in many of the poorer countries. However, since the frontier is fast disappearing in most of the poorer countries, so are the opportunities for low-cost expansion of acreage under cultivation. The changing situation is difficult to document at an aggregate level, but Table 1:4 gives some perspectives on trends in the expansion of cropped areas and production.

The rate of expansion in acreage fell, in the aggregate, in the 1950s and the 1960s. The only exception is Latin America where the acreage under cultivation grew from a rate of 1.8% to 2.5% per year. In all other areas, the expansion of acreage slowed down, halving in the

Cropped Area and Production Trends, by Region

| | Average annual growth rate | | | |
| | 1953-55 to 1962-63 | | 1961-63 to 1969-71 | |
	Production	Area	Production	Area
Latin America	3.1	1.8	2.9	2.5
East Asia	2.5	1.9	2.8	1.1
Middle East	3.8	2.2	2.7	1.1
Africa	3.0	1.7	2.6	1.2
All regions	2.8	1.9	2.8	1.4

Source: FAO. *Report on the 1960 World Census of Agriculture*. Rome: 1971.

Middle East from 2.2% per year to 1.1%. When the rates of population growth are compared with rates of increase in acreage under cultivation, it appears that the rural population increased at about the same rate as the cropped area during the 1950s, but increased more than one-and-a-half times as fast as the cropped area during the 1960s.

As shown in Table 1:4, production increased at the same rate during the 1950s as during the 1960s. A rate of increase in output consistent with an increase in rural population indicates a decline in the rate of growth of output and incomes from 0.9% per year in the 1950s to 0.7% per year in the 1960s. At the same time, as average per capita income was increasing at a declining rate, yields per acre rose very moderately—in this instance, an increase of around 0.4% a year in the 1950s and 1960s.

The increase in population and slow expansion of the area under cultivation have caused a deterioration in man-land ratios. This deterioration, arising from constraints on the low-cost expansion of acreage under cultivation, makes it increasingly difficult to accelerate growth rates of output and income in agriculture. This is because raising yields requires a higher level of technology and management as compared to increasing output or expanding acreage under cultivation. It is only in recent years that a concerted effort has been made to develop technologies to raise yields of staple crops grown in the developing areas. Hitherto, these efforts have been confined to a handful of crops, and the successes attained have been limited to a relatively small area of the developing world. In some fortunate countries, such as Nigeria, some land resources are still available for future development through an expansion of acreage under cultivation. But many other countries have little or no unused land, so the situation is correspondingly worse. The emphasis in the latter countries will have to be placed more and more on raising yields per hectare.

The increasing pressure of population on the land highlights the issue of absorptive capacity in agriculture. Most developing countries have considerable opportunities for increasing employment and production in this sector. This applies to the more densely populated regions as well as to others. Table 1:5 shows the startling differences in input of agricultural labor and output per hectare in developing countries of Asia on the one hand, and in Japan on the other. Japan

Table 1:5

Agricultural Labor Force and Production in Selected Asian Countries, 1970

Country	Agri-cultural workers per 100 hectares	Indices Japan = 100	Net agri-cultural produc-tion per hectare (US$)	Indices Japan = 100	Output per worker (US$)	Indices Japan = 100
Burma	48	25	71	9	148	37
India	92	48	115	15	150	38
Indonesia	224	117	283	37	126	32
Khmer Republic	75	39	146	19	194	49
Korea, Republic of	261	136	440	58	169	43
Laos	153	80	119	16	75	19
Malaysia	74	39	366	48	492	124
Nepal	229	119	220	29	96	24
Pakistan	101	53	218	29	215	54
Philippines	113	59	178	23	158	40
Sri Lanka	107	56	286	38	266	67
Thailand	119	62	179	23	150	38
Viet-Nam, Republic of	242	126	241	32	100	25
Japan	192	100	762	100	397	100

Sources: Column 1: International Labour Office. *Labour Force Projections.* Pt. 1-V. Geneva: 1971.
Columns 3 and 5: FAO. *The State of Food and Agriculture,* p. 99. Rome: 1972.

is a country of small holdings and has approximately two workers per hectare with an average output of $397 per worker and $762 per hectare. Several other countries have a higher ratio of workers to the land than Japan, while one country, Malaysia, has a higher output per worker in agriculture than Japan. However, the point to be emphasized is that if the level of labor intensity of two workers per hectare prevailing in Japan could be attained in countries such as Pakistan and India, the agricultural sector in these two countries could absorb all the labor force expected by 1985. This kind of labor intensity is not likely to be reached, however, because of the small size of the irrigated areas in Pakistan and India and other constraints related to technology, resource base, land tenure and capital formation.

It is reasonably clear that whatever is done will only partially satisfy the ever-rising demand for work and income in the many developing countries that are faced with the general problems of high population growth, low incomes and increasing unemployment. With very few exceptions, the poverty and unemployment problems of the developing countries are unlikely to have any long-term solutions that would not include a reduction in population growth, urban as well as rural. Nonetheless, even if effective birth control could be introduced overnight, special and possibly extraordinary measures would have to be taken to satisfy the expanding demand for work and income from today's children. Such measures include those related to land reform.

Distribution of Land

The ratio of population to land tells us nothing about the distribution of land among the rural population: countries with dense rural populations may have a more even distribution of land than countries with sparse populations. The most recent data on distribution of holdings by size is given in the worldwide census of agriculture held in the early 1960s. This covered 83 countries, including all of the larger countries that are members of the Bank, except Afghanistan, Bolivia, Ecuador, Nigeria and Romania.

The census provides a breakdown of distribution by size of 138.3 million holdings in the 83 countries. There is also a breakdown of the distribution of land and cropland by size of holding for 64 countries (which account for all but 9% of the land in the 83 countries covered in the census). Table 1:6 combines the two sets of information to give an indication of the distribution of land and cropland by size of holding. It shows that:

1. About 53.9 million holdings, or 39% of the total number, are under 1 hectare in size. If the pattern in the 83 countries is the same as in the 64 countries for which there are data on distribution of size and distribution of land, then these holdings occupy 1.1% of the land area and 3.4% of the cropland.

2. About 109 million holdings, or 78.8% of the total number, are less than 5 hectares in size. Based on the same assumption as above, these holdings account for approximately 6.8% of the total land area and 20.7% of the cropland.

Distribution of Holdings by Size and Percentage of Total Holdings: Distribution of Holdings by Percentage of Land and Cropland

Size distribution (hectares)	Number of holdings		All farmland in holding (%)	Cropland in holding (%)
	(millions)	Percentage distribution		
Under 1	53.90	38.90	1.10	3.40
1- 2	26.55	19.20	1.70	5.30
2- 5	28.73	20.70	4.00	12.00
5- 10	13.24	9.60	4.20	11.50
10- 20	7.27	5.20	4.40	10.70
20- 50	4.40	3.20	5.80	11.80
50- 100	1.97	1.40	5.80	9.80
100- 200	1.40	1.00	6.60	11.00
200- 500	0.67	0.48	8.60	11.50
500-1,000	0.23	0.16	6.50	5.90
1,000 and over	0.23	0.16	51.30	7.10
Total	138.59	100.00	100.00	100.00

Source: FAO. *Report on the 1960 World Census of Agriculture,* pp. 34-36. Rome: 1971.

3. One million holdings of 200 hectares or more represent less than 0.8% of all holdings in the 83 countries. In the 64 countries surveyed, farms of this size group account for 66% of the total land area and nearly 25% of all cropland.

These data confirm that, when viewed in the aggregate, the distribution of land and cropland is highly skewed. If the distribution of holdings by size in 83 countries represents a global picture, and if the distribution of 91% of the land reflects the pattern of distribution of all the land, then holdings above 50 hectares in size, which represent 3.2% of all holdings, account for 78.8% of the total farmland area and 45.3% of all the cropland. That is, roughly 3% of all holdings (in the aggregate) account for slightly less than half of the arable land and land under permanent crops, and more than three-quarters of all farmland. Conversely, 97% of all holdings account for less than one-quarter of all farmland and slightly more than half of the area under crops.

The information on distribution of holdings by size refers to the 83 countries, both developed and developing, covered by the census. There were an estimated 16 million holdings of less than 5 hectares in the developed world: 6 million in Japan and 10 million in Europe. Thus, of 122 million holdings in the developing countries, 92 million were less than 5 hectares in size; approximately half of these holdings were less than 1 hectare and the remainder were between 1 and 5 hectares in size.

It is safe to conclude that well in excess of 100 million holdings are less than 5 hectares in size in the developing world at the present time. This conclusion is derived as follows: The 1960 census indicated that there were approximately 92 million smallholders in developing countries, excluding those in Nigeria, Afghanistan, Ecuador and Bolivia. Together, at the time of the census, these countries had an agricultural population estimated to be close to 50 million people, or 10 million families, most of whom were farming on units of less than 5 hectares in size. Thus, it is highly likely that close to 100 million holdings of less than 5 hectares existed in 1960. Between 1960 and 1970, the agricultural population in the developing countries increased by a reported 190 million persons, or by more than an estimated 35 million farm families. Preliminary indications are that the fragmentation of holdings has increased in many of the more densely populated countries as well as in countries where the distribution of land is skewed. Consequently, it is safe to assume that the census forthcoming in the 1970s will reveal that there are well in excess of 100 million smallholders in the developing world; in all probability, more than half of their holdings are less than 1 hectare in size.

The 1960 census data also provided information on holdings by size and land area for different regions and countries. The most comprehensive regional and national analysis for the 83 countries deals with holdings of 1 hectare or more in size and pertains to 84.4 million holdings covering 2,242 million hectares. Obviously, this is not a complete coverage, since it excludes holdings of less than 1 hectare. However, it does provide an insight into the patterns of distribution of holdings within the major regions. The results are summarized in Table 1:7.

Table 1:7

Distribution of Holdings above One Hectare, by Size and Area

	1-5 hectares		5-50 hectares		50 hectares	
	% holdings	% area	% holdings	% area	% holdings	% area
Europe	50.0	13.0	47.4	52.3	2.4	34.7
North and Central America	23.4	0.5	39.4	8.0	37.2	91.5
South America	36.4	1.0	45.5	8.5	17.8	90.5
Asia	78.2	40.7	21.6	50.2	0.2	9.1
Africa	73.2	3.7	23.7	6.3	3.1	90.0
Oceania	5.5	—	27.7	0.5	66.0	99.5

Source: FAO. *Report on the 1960 World Census of Agriculture.* Rome: 1971.

The analysis indicates the vast differences in patterns of land-holding and land distribution between Asia and the other regions. The contrast between Asia and the Americas is highlighted by the fact that 78% of the holdings larger than 1 hectare in Asia are less than 5 hectares in size and occupy 40.7% of the land. The 36.4% of holdings in South America and 23.4% in North and Central America that are less than 5 hectares in size occupy only 1% and 0.5%, respectively, of the area under farms. Only 9% of the area in Asia is in holdings of more than 50 hectares. As much as 34.7% in Europe, and more than 90% in North and Central America, South America and Oceania, is in farms of more than 50 hectares in size.

The data for Africa, as presented in the census, are misleading. This is because coverage of that continent in the 1960 census was poor, with the data on the distribution of holdings by size and acreage for the 18 countries surveyed heavily weighted by the results in South Africa and Southern Rhodesia, while the sampling in Zambia was confined to European holdings and in Tanzania to commercial holdings. If these are excluded from the sample, then the land held by smallholders owning under 5 hectares is much more than 50% of all land.

The analysis of the distribution of holdings by size on a regional basis points to the highly skewed distribution in the Americas; the pattern of holdings in the eight major countries in Latin America, as shown in Table 1:8, helps explain this. The information confirms that a very high proportion of all land—ranging from 86% to 97.5%—in the eight countries is in holdings of more than 50 hectares in size. At the other end of the spectrum, only 5% of the land in the eight

Table 1:8

Distribution of Holdings above One Hectare,
by Size and Area, in Selected South American Countries

	1-5 hectares		5-50 hectares		50 hectares	
	% holdings	% area	% holdings	% area	% holdings	% area
Argentina	14.9	0.1	38.5	2.4	46.6	97.5
Brazil	28.1	1.0	52.6	12.8	20.3	86.2
Chile	37.7	0.7	30.3	5.2	32.0	94.1
Colombia	50.3	4.1	40.6	10.1	9.1	85.8
Paraguay	43.5	1.1	51.0	6.6	6.5	92.3
Peru	73.8	4.2	22.9	8.0	3.3	87.8
Uruguay	14.7	0.2	49.2	4.6	36.1	95.2
Venezuela	36.3	1.3	42.9	6.7	20.8	92.0

Source: FAO. *Report on the 1960 World Census of Agriculture.* Rome: 1971.

countries is in holdings of less than 5 hectares (even though these holdings constitute between 14% and 74% of all holdings).

A further partial measure of concentration of holdings is given by the Gini coefficient—an index of concentration based on the departure of an existing pattern of holdings from an even distribution, as revealed by a Lorenz curve. The Gini coefficient has been estimated for 30 countries which have been grouped into three categories, as shown in Table 1:9. As can be seen, the Gini coefficient indicates a high concentration in six South American countries included in the sample. On the other hand, countries such as the Republic of China (Taiwan), Canada, Japan and Sweden have a low concentration of holdings. Clearly, the distribution of holdings by size varies widely in different parts of the world. The most skewed distribution appears to be in Latin America where the density of population is relatively low in rural areas. At the same time, the distribution of land appears to be much less skewed in many areas with a very high density of population, notably Asia and Europe. It is of special interest that two of the countries with a high density of population and very little concentration of landholdings are Japan and Taiwan.

The distribution of land by size of holdings is "a geographical phenomenon" and must be interpreted with caution in a socio-economic context. It may indicate little about the international distribution of wealth or income—5 hectares of irrigated land in Japan would certainly yield an income well in excess of that yielded by

Table 1:9

**Concentration of Land Ownership
in Selected Countries**

High concentration	Medium concentration	Low concentration
Argentina	Austria	Belgium
Brazil	Egypt, Arab Republic of	Canada
Colombia	India	China, Republic of
Iraq	Iran	Denmark
Peru	Ireland	Germany, Federal Republic of
Spain	Italy	Greece
Uruguay	Netherlands	Japan
Venezuela	Norway	Philippines
	Pakistan	Sweden
	Turkey	Yugoslavia
	United Kingdom	
	United States	

Sources: FAO. *Land-Tenure: World Agricultural Structure*, Study No. 2. Rome: 1961. Other data provided by FAO. US Department of Agriculture, Economic Research Service: *Changes in Agriculture in 26 Developing Nations, 1948 to 1963*, p. 36. Washington: 1965.

100,000 acres in parts of Northern Australia. Similarly, within countries, the pattern of distribution of land may not reflect the prevailing pattern of distribution of wealth or the socioeconomic conditions —2 hectares of irrigated land in the Medjerda Valley of Tunisia, producing tomatoes, yield a far greater income than do 1,000 hectares of land used for sharecropping in the semiarid parts of Tunisia's central area.

The caveats on quality of land and ecological conditions governing land-use patterns must be borne in mind. The evidence presented here (and elsewhere) indicates, however, that most of the agricultural land and cropland is concentrated in a relatively few holdings. It also indicates that the greatest skewness in distribution is in the Americas, and that this skewness is by no means confined to Latin America.

Tenants and Farm Laborers

The distribution of holdings by size and population densities gives no indication of the status of those who hold the land or the numbers of the landless. Only limited data on these are available. Table 1:10 gives some information on the number of renters and sharecroppers in 15 countries, and the percentage of farms and areas of farmland they occupy. Table 1:11 indicates the number of landless farm workers in 12 countries.

This limited sample indicates that renting and sharecropping are widespread in all the major regions of the world. In such countries as the Republic of Viet-Nam, Iran and Egypt, more than two-thirds of the farms, occupying much more than half of the land, are farmed by tenants or sharecroppers. However, in other countries, such as Guatemala and Tunisia, this is true of less than one-quarter of the farms. All in all, in the 15 countries, out of 82 million holdings, close to 29 million are worked by renters and sharecroppers.

Renting or sharecropping of land is a common practice in both developed and developing countries. In some parts of the world, the rights of those who rent land are protected by law or custom, and renters enjoy the same working conditions as owners of land. In other areas, however, renters and sharecroppers are in a very tenuous position when it comes to negotiating arrangements with the landlord, and they commonly give as much as half their output in return for the use of land and services provided by him.

The conditions that govern rental agreements and crop-sharing arrangements differ throughout the world. In most developing countries, where tenancy is widespread, there is heavy dependence on the landlord—usually an absentee landowner—for the provision of pur-

Tenancy and Sharecropping in Selected Countries[1]

	Renting and sharecropping as percentage of total		Number of renters and sharecroppers[2] (000)
	Number of farms[2] (%)	Farmland (%)	
Asia			
India	27.3	n.a.	13,350
Indonesia	35.9	25.9	4,392
Malaysia[3]	31.2	15.7	141
Pakistan[4]	43.4	57.0	5,271
Philippines	54.3	40.4	1,176
Viet-Nam, Republic of	70.3	70.0	1,334
Total	33.0	45.7[5]	25,664
Middle East and North Africa			
Egypt	62.1	57.2	1,020
Iran	66.7	73.4	1,253
Tunisia	23.3	32.0	76
Total	61.1	62.6	2,349
Latin America and Caribbean			
Chile	49.3	24.4	128
Colombia	31.5	13.5	381
Dominican Republic	28.9	n.a.	129
Guatemala	22.4	16.6	93
Nicaragua	26.3	n.a.	27
Trinidad and Tobago	49.5	32.8	18
Total	31.4	19.2[5]	776

[1] Data refer to latest available year in 1960s and, therefore, do not reflect land reform action on the one hand and changes in the work force on the other.

[2] Includes holdings operated under more than one tenure form (21.8%).

[3] 1960 estimates are for former Federation of Malaya.

[4] Includes both Pakistan and Bangladesh.

[5] Dominican Republic, India and Nicaragua are excluded, due to lack of data.

Source: FAO. *Report on the 1960 World Census of Agriculture,* Vol. 5, pp. 92-97. Rome: 1971.

chased inputs. Another widespread characteristic is the absence of written registered agreements governing the conditions of tenancy and the rights of tenants (even though there may be laws stipulating what these should be). Tenants and sharecroppers typically operate under conditions of great insecurity and are in a weak bargaining position vis-à-vis the landlord. Frequently, the tenants are among the lowest income groups in agriculture. The insecurity of tenants has been highlighted by their displacement on short notice when technological change has made it more profitable for landowners to mechanize their operations—as has happened in Ethiopia, India and Pakistan.

Landless Workers

The number of landless farm workers in developing countries is increasing. Approximately 100 million persons are farm wage workers

Table 1:11

Landless Farm Workers in Selected Countries[1]

	Number of land-less workers (000)	Landless workers as % of active population in agriculture (%)	Active agricultural population as % of total active population (%)
Asia			
India[2]	47,300	32	68
Indonesia	5,673	20	70
Pakistan[3]	8,013	29	70
Total	60,986	30	68
Middle East and North Africa			
Algeria	1,099	60	56
Egypt, Arab Republic of	1,865	38	55
Iran	903	25	46
Morocco	484	19	61
Tunisia	210	20	46
Total	4,561	33	58
Latin America and Caribbean			
Argentina	694	51	15
Brazil	3,237	26	44
Chile (1971)	378	66	28
Colombia	1,158	42	45
Costa Rica	122	53	45
Dominican Republic	179	25	61
Ecuador	391	39	54
Honduras	138	27	67
Jamaica	72	41	27
Mexico (1970)	2,499	49	39
Nicaragua (1971)	101	43	47
Peru	557	30	46
Uruguay	99	55	17
Venezuela	287	33	26
Total	9,912	35	39

[1] Except for India, data presented here are estimated from ILO, *Year Book of Labour Statistics 1971,* pp. 43-294, and *1972,* pp. 44-301. Unless otherwise indicated, data refer to latest year available in 1960s and, thus, do not reflect recent reform actions on the one hand and changes in the work force, on the other.

[2] Agricultural laborers as shown in India: Ministry of Agriculture, Directorate of Economics and Statistics. *Indian Agriculture in Brief* (11th ed., 1971), p. 14.

[3] Includes population now belonging to Bangladesh.

(including family members and heads of families with very small land-holdings) in the 22 countries for which data are provided in Table 1:11. This figure includes an estimated 47 million in India alone—about 32% of the active population in agriculture. There are about 10 million such workers in Latin America. Even in Argentina and Uruguay (with only 15% of the active population depending on agriculture), more than half of the workers are essentially landless. In the remaining countries of the region, the proportion ranges from a minimum of about one-fourth in Brazil and Honduras to a maximum of approximately two-thirds in Chile.

Almost no reliable estimates exist of the number of unemployed in rural areas. It is usually assumed that the labor force subsists off a holding and joins in some arrangement with the extended family whereby it shares work and output. The emergence of a landless wage-earning class confirms that a growing rural labor force has to rely on work outside the traditional sectors for its livelihood. This group is increasing in size, and the provision of employment for what is already a large rural proletariat may well be one of the greatest challenges facing national governments in the future.

There is a vast amount of underemployment in the rural areas of most countries of the world. The nature of this phenomenon has been discussed elsewhere. At this juncture, it should be pointed out that the redistribution of idle land can provide added employment, but that the prospect is limited for redistribution of land providing full employment for all the present and prospective populations in the rural areas of densely populated countries. Structural changes within agriculture can help alleviate underemployment and open unemployment, but the problems of reducing nationwide unemployment have to be seen in a national rather than a sectoral context.

251

EXPERIENCES WITH
LAND REFORM

The following summaries illustrate selected country experience in land reform over the last three decades. Their inclusion in this paper should not be taken as indicative of Bank judgment on what does or does not constitute land reform, nor should the statements be regarded as definitive. Land reform is a complex process in which several socioeconomic variables are changed more or less simultaneously. In most cases, the evidence is inadequate to allow identification of causal relationships between reform measures on the one hand and production, income and social effects on the other, even though it is often feasible to trace correlations, such as that between land distribution and a rise in productivity.

Republic of China

Taiwan's land reform program was implemented in three steps. A reduction of rents, in 1949, was followed by the sale of public lands. A land-to-the-tiller program completed the reform in 1953. The proportion of cultivated land under tenancy leases was reduced from 41% to 16%, while the proportion of farm families owning all land under their cultivation increased from 33% to 59%. On the land remaining under tenancy cultivation, written and secure leases were arranged at much reduced rental rates.

Following the reform, the productivity of agriculture has increased, income distribution has become more even, and rural and social stability have been enhanced. Land productivity is highest on holdings below 0.5 hectare. The share of total agricultural income that is consumed has increased only moderately, leaving intact enough income to achieve a fairly high agricultural savings rate.

The smooth implementation of the reform program in Taiwan was due to a stable sociopolitical climate and the many complementary development measures taken before and during the reform. The existence of a thorough cadastral survey, good agricultural research and extension services, a vast expansion of publicly sponsored farm credit during the reform period, and a gradually increasing involvement of tenant farmers in the administration of the program, all contributed to the success.

Republic of Korea

Land reform in South Korea after the Second World War consisted of: (1) a reduction of farm rents from 40-60% of production to 33%

in 1945; (2) a redistribution, in 1948, of Japanese property confiscated by the military authorities; and (3) a redistribution between 1950 and 1953 of land in excess of a ceiling of 3 hectares on Korean holdings. The terms of sale were similarly generous toward the buyer in both cases. Some 1.4 million acres (25% of the total farmland) were distributed to 1.6 million farmers (approximately 70% of all farmers).

It has been estimated that, before the reform, 19% of the farmers owned 90% of the land and more than 50% of the farmers were landless tenants. Afterward, 69% of the farmers owned all the land on which they worked and 24% were part-owners, while only 7% were tenants. Considerable sociopolitical stability has been achieved, together with income redistribution in favor of the poorer rural families. Yields did not fall as a consequence of the reform; by the 1960s, yields had far surpassed prereform levels. Labor productivity and rural employment increased. But the small size of most farms has now become a constraint on farm income.

Japan

The first Japanese land reform program, in 1868, laid the groundwork for Japan's social and economic transformation. The peasantry was freed from bondage, the power of the feudal lords to collect taxes from landowners was broken, and private landownership was reinforced for the purpose of cash taxation by the central government. Supplementary programs for infrastructure improvement, training and extension, credit services, and promotion of farm chemicals and new crop varieties were pushed on a large scale. Labor intensity and land productivity rose quickly, with the result that the agricultural sector could provide savings, cheap food and surplus labor to the industrial sector. The first reform did little, however, to distribute property ownership or reduce income inequality—rather it strengthened the landowner class.

Subsequent to the first reform, the tenancy problem grew gradually worse. Large numbers of smallholders lost their property in the agricultural depression at the turn of the century, partly because of heavy land taxes. In the late 1940s, a second land reform program was executed. Owners had to sell all land in excess of about one hectare to the government at confiscatory prices. The former tenants were given property rights at an extremely low real cost, which resulted in a thorough restructuring of rural society.

The second reform resulted in greater equity, and may also have removed a constraint on the growth of Japanese agriculture. The economic effects were not as enormous as those associated with the first reform. Land productivity did increase after 1947, but some observers regard this as essentially a continuation of a long-term trend (1895-1939) started by the first reform.

The second reform worsened, however, the problems of fragmentation and undersized farms. At the time of the reform, the tenancy problem had already been relieved through a reduction of excess rural population by the war and absorption into industry. The landlords who were forced to sell excess property were mostly smallholders themselves. Two-thirds of the owners were required to sell less than one hectare and only 6% more than five hectares. Although the reform increased income equality among farmers, it hampered equalization of rural and urban incomes. Part-time work outside the farm is an outlet, but the farmers concerned are often limited to low-skilled work. Rural incomes have, therefore, lagged behind, price supports notwithstanding. An attempt to create larger farming units through cooperatives has had little effect. Agricultural policy is now aimed at, among other objectives, an increase of farm income through diversification into horticulture and animal husbandry.

India

Land reform in India, pursued since 1950-51, is largely recommended and coordinated by the Central Government and the Planning Commission and executed by the individual state governments, with the result that policy implementation varies widely. The four major types of reform have been: (1) the abolition of the zamindari[1] system; (2) tenancy reform designed to fix maximum rents, to improve security of tenure and to give the right of purchase to the tenant; (3) ceilings on landownership and distribution of surplus; and (4) consolidation of fragmented holdings.

By 1961, the intermediary rent and tax collectors, most important of whom were the zamindars, had been abolished. Since tenants continue to pay revenue directly to the government, their economic position has not been greatly improved. The abolition of the zamindari system involved 173 million acres, more than half of the area occupied by holdings. A total of Rs. 4,350 million was paid in compensation, mainly in the form of bonds.

Under the tenancy reforms, 3 million tenants, subtenants and sharecroppers had, by 1961, acquired ownership under purchase agreements of 7 million acres. Security of tenure appears in general to have worsened, however. Actual rents have not come down; in

---

[1]The zamindars were revenue collectors during the Moghul period. Under the British, they gradually turned into powerful landlords.

some states they have even increased. Landowners have been permitted to resume land above legal ceilings for personal cultivation, which has allowed them to escape the reforms. Unreported casual tenancy and share agreements have multiplied.

Under the ceilings legislation, approximately 2 million acres have been taken over by the government in order to settle tenants and landless laborers. A further 4.2 million acres were formally pledged to the Bhoodan (gift) movement, but most of the donated parcels are still in the hands of the donors. Only about 1 million acres out of all gifted land have actually been given to landless laborers.

Consolidation of land parcels has been more successful and has resulted in a rationalization of holdings covering 69 million acres. It appears to have contributed to a growth in productivity in the northern states of Punjab, Uttar Pradesh and Haryana.

It is well recognized in India that the reform measures dealing with security of tenure and acreage ceilings are only partially enforced, and that many of the state legislatures are not anxious to have such radical land reform. Even if a ceiling is imposed, the land acquired is sufficient to give minimal holdings either to the minifarmers or the landless— but not both. There appears to be scope for some distribution which will also assist agricultural production because the yield per acre in India is higher on small farms. As long as population pressure continues, it will be unrealistic to try to abolish tenancy in the short run. Therefore, it will be better to legalize some forms of tenancy which exist on a large scale, and to promote more efficient types of tenancy contracts. All kinds of tenants should also be registered and given access to credit and inputs. A large extension of credit at reasonable terms, together with accessible marketing channels to small farms in general, and particularly to tenants with secure leases, is required. Provision of these facilities is as essential as further land distribution for attaining the income equity and productivity objectives of India's land reform, and is likely to present fewer problems.

Iran

Iran's land reform started in 1962. Before the reform, 56% of the holdings, covering 62% of the area under cultivation, were rented. Tenants were rotated annually, a practice which hampered agricultural investment and caused exploitative use of the soil. The largest estates occupied relatively more fertile lands, and owners were often absentee landlords who contributed little to agricultural production.

Former landowners were partly compensated upon expropriation by cash payments ranging from 10% to 20% of the estimated value

of their holdings, with the balance paid in bonds in annual install-
ments. The beneficiaries were to repay the government the expropriation price plus 10% to cover administrative charges. As these payments fell behind, the Central Bank funded the difference. The costs
to the Government were limited to those incurred in carrying over the
acquisition costs to the time of final reimbursement.

During the first stage of the reform, landownership was limited to
a maximum of one village per owner. Excess land was expropriated
and distributed to the tenants. In the second stage, the limit of one
village was reduced further to plots of 20-100 hectares (depending
on the nature and location of the land). The landlord had five options
for the area in excess of the maximum allowed to him, to wit: (1)
leasing to the tenants for 30 years; (2) selling to the tenants; (3) purchasing the tenants' rights; (4) dividing the land with the tenants in
the same ratio as the customary crop sharing; and (5) forming an
agricultural unit for joint operation by the owner and the tenants.

The third and final stage of the reform, which was practically completed in 1971, aimed at conversion of all 30-year leases into smallholdings. Virtually all of Iran's 50,000 villages have undergone land
reform and more than 3 million families have received land.

Although agricultural output increased by a total of 18% in the
first five years of the reforms, it is believed that the land reform program on balance had adverse short-run effects on output. It created
uncertainty which discouraged investment in improvements; there
was also considerable interference with the normal flow of irrigation
water from streams and storage places still controlled by landlords.

The reform favored tenants and sharecroppers insofar as it con-
ferred ownership on them or enhanced their security of tenure.
Because they were based on the existing distribution of holdings, the
reforms did not assist those who were landless. Continuation of the
existing inequities of land distribution was regarded as one of the
costs of ensuring a speedy enactment of the reform.

The ownership and tenancy reforms have been complemented by
rural cooperatives, credit and extension services, and increased supply of quality seeds and fertilizers. Many measures were set up in a
somewhat improvised fashion. The early accomplishments of the
credit program were striking; total lending by the Agricultural Bank
tripled between 1960 and 1965, but this growth leveled off after 1966.

Morocco

The Moroccan Government has undertaken a series of measures
aimed at land reform since independence in 1956. The objective of
these measures is to facilitate an increase in agricultural production

and to improve the distribution of rural incomes. Legislation passed in 1962, 1966 and 1972 provides for land consolidation and distribution of land to smallholders and landless families throughout the country. The Agricultural Investment Code, published in 1969, is aimed at facilitating the development of irrigated agriculture in well-defined development zones. It provides for the restriction of inheritance rights to limit fragmentation, an improvement in the tenure position of members of traditional collectives, and the adoption of modern cultivation techniques.

Land distribution is so far based mainly on former foreign-owned land, although some other state-owned land and traditional collective land is involved. At the time of independence in 1956, about 900,000 hectares were foreign-owned; of this area, about 300,000 hectares were sold privately to Moroccans, mainly before 1963, when legislation was introduced subjecting such transfers to Government approval. Thirty-one thousand hectares which were mainly used by foreigners for research purposes were recovered by 1960, and a further 220,000 hectares of "official colonization" lands were taken over by the Government between 1963 and 1965.

Distribution so far has been limited to land under field crops, while land under tree crops (mainly orange groves) remained under Government control and ownership. Distribution to smallholders and landless families was slow until 1967 and then gathered momentum up to 1972. By the end of 1972, 181,000 hectares (3% of the cultivated area) had been distributed to over 11,000 families. However, the impact of land distribution alone on the problem of rural poverty has been small; the number of beneficiaries so far is only about 1% of farm families with less than 2 hectares.

Through the establishment of cooperatives, intensified extension support and the provision of modern inputs, the beneficiaries of land reform have generally quickly achieved high yields and acceptable incomes. Land consolidation has also been successful and has so far benefited almost 200,000 hectares. The main constraint on the program has been the unavoidable complexity of supervising its implementation considering the Government's manpower resources. The Government's main priority now is to accelerate land distribution, while maintaining high technical standards of management on the distributed land. Remaining foreign-owned land, amounting to about 370,000 hectares, was recovered by the Government in 1973. The target for the third Five-Year Plan is to distribute 395,000 hectares of land under field crops, mainly formerly foreign-owned, between 1974 and 1977, and to seek a suitable formula for distributing land under tree crops. The achievement of the distribution target for land under field crops alone would, by the end of the plan, enable the program to cover 9% of cultivated area and 5% of farm families with less than 2 hectares.

Yugoslavia

The first land reform in Yugoslavia was undertaken in 1919. In the south and west, bondage was abolished, and the tenants of the Turkish landowners received ownership rights. In the north, the size of the large estates was reduced, but the former landowners were allowed to retain rather large holdings. The implementation took two decades, and resulted in a transfer of ownership of almost 25% of the farmland to more than 33% of the peasants.

The second land reform started in 1945, when all large estates, all land in excess of 25-35 hectares per farm, and the farm property of Germans and other aliens, were expropriated. Half of the seized land was distributed to the poor and landless, while the other half was retained as state property. The state and collective farms created in the late 1940s along Soviet lines expanded to approximately 25% of the total cropland. Collective farms were allowed to disband after 1952, however, and by 1956 accounted for only about 10% of all land under cultivation.

Aside from the socialist sector, the private sector of individual owners who cultivate their own land remains important, and vast tracts of mountain pastures are still under traditional, collective forms of usage. In 1953, a ceiling of 10 hectares of arable land or its equivalent was imposed on private holdings. The average holding in the private sector is now only 3.9 hectares. The socialist sector includes state farms, producer cooperatives and general cooperatives. The kombinats, which resemble the worker-managed industrial firms, form the largest and fastest-growing socialist element, whereas the producer cooperatives have declined. The general cooperatives are mainly associations for joint input purchases, equipment use and output sales, and have expanded to about 40% of all smallholdings.

The socialist sector is reportedly the most productive. This is related to the location of holdings on the better soils and its priority treatment in the allocation of inputs such as fertilizers, machinery and expertise. However, the bulk of agricultural output still originates from the large group of small farms, consisting of both the cooperatives and the farms outside the socialist sector. The reforms have resulted in a sizable redistribution of rural income and an increase in peasant participation in rural decision making, particularly since the mid-1950s.

Kenya

Land reform was initiated in Kenya by the colonial administration in 1954 and expanded by the Government after independence in 1963. The reform aimed at solving several problems at the same time. These included: (1) adjudication and consolidation of holdings under cultivation by African farmers; (2) resettlement of African farmers on the large farms previously owned by Europeans; (3) promotion of cash cropping and dairying, and increased production for the market; and (4) diversification of export output. More than 1 million acres of land formerly cultivated by Europeans were opened up to Kenyan small-holders, and the rights to about 7 million acres were adjudicated and consolidated.

The implementation and results of the reforms have been quite successful, notwithstanding political friction and a lack of qualified personnel. An active extension program has enabled smallholders to increase the production of coffee, pyrethrum, maize, wheat, dairy products and beef. The economic benefits of the adjudication and consolidation of holdings seem to have been greater than those of resettlement on large farms. Socially, the reforms have created a class of prosperous smallholders. In particular, those that were already relatively well-to-do have profited, while the poorest smallholders and nomads have benefited much less from the reform. It was esti-mated in 1973 that approximately 25% of all smallholdings were less than one hectare and about 50% less than two hectares, occupying altogether less than 4% of total arable land. The landless amount to approximately 16% of the rural population.

Mexico

Having its roots in the revolution of 1910-15, the agrarian reform in Mexico created village groups (ejidos) with usufruct rights to land. Most of the ejidos were formed in the late 1930s and have been oper-ated on an individual rather than collective basis by the ejidatarios. Close to 90 million hectares have been distributed between 1915 and 1972 to about three million ejidatarios. These primary beneficiaries of the reform represented 53% of all farmers and 26% of the rural labor force. Some three million landless rural workers remain and, despite the considerable concentration of ownership that persists in the pri-vate sector, 1976 has been planned as a terminal year for land reform.

Total production by the ejidos grew very slowly during the first decade of their establishment. Since then, the ejidos have increased output about as fast as has the private sector. Incomes of the ejida-tarios are almost certainly better than would have been the case with-out reform, but substantial regional differences persist in natural resource endowment and in the extent of public investment in complementary infrastructure. More such investment and a mechanism for selective consolidation of small farms will be required to ensure that the impact of the reform is maximized.

Following the land redistribution during the 1930s, the concentration of landownership increased again between 1940 and 1960. Since then, the concentration may have fallen back as a result of the distribution of another 35 million hectares during the last decade. Rural income distribution is still skewed. In 1967-68, 50% of the farmers earned only 20% of all farm income (including personal income from sources other than agriculture). Among ejidatarios, however, income was more evenly distributed. While the top 20% of private farmers received 60% of all private farm income, the top 20% of the ejidatarios accounted for only 45% of all ejido income.

Peru

Between the start of land reform in 1963 and 1972, a total of 4.7 million hectares has been expropriated. Over 100,000 families have been settled on 2.8 million hectares of this area. Expropriated lands that have not yet been resettled continue to be operated under direct government supervision until a cooperative or SAIS (Sociedad Agrícola de Interés Social) farm organization has been formed, to which the land title is then transferred. Despite the priority given by the government, implementation is well behind schedule. The target for the current Five-Year Plan is to expropriate 26,200 farm units containing 12 million hectares, and to redistribute these to 500,000 families. In 1972, about three-quarters of the target area still remained to be expropriated and reallocated before the end of 1975.

The agrarian reform law of 1964 concentrated on redistribution of inefficiently managed latifundia (large landed estates) in the Sierra. Well managed productive units were exempted. The more fundamental reform law of 1969 was the basis for the expropriation of the large, productive and profitable sugar complexes of the north coast. A limit was established on the size of holdings (150 hectares on the coast). The government bonds given to the former owners can be used for investment in industry to supplement their other resources.

Four different categories of farm organizations can receive redistributed land, but the bulk has been placed in the hands of worker-owned cooperatives. Only a small number of individual farms has been assigned to former tenants, while in a few cases land has been added to the holdings of Indian communities.

The SAIS is a unique form of farm organization, and is the basic unit of agricultural reform in the Sierra. The SAIS represents an attempt to solve the problem of providing agricultural and social development opportunities to the members of the traditional Indian communities without jeopardizing the relatively high production and economies of scale attainable on expropriated haciendas. Hacienda production is almost entirely based on extensive grazing of mountain pastures, and early experiences of land distribution in the Sierra indicated a high risk to production if haciendas were taken over as community land or subdivided into small sheep ranches.

In any attempt to meet social needs through redistributing land and income in the Sierra, therefore, the government is faced with problems of maintaining or raising productivity levels attainable only through exploitation of scale economies. The SAIS, the proposed solution to this dilemma, accounted in 1972 for 10% of the families benefiting from the agrarian reform program. It can be regarded as a second-degree cooperative whose members are social bodies instead of individuals. Membership of each SAIS unit consists of the cooperative of the production unit and of the communities surrounding it. Each group contributes to the capital of the enterprise on the basis of resources, population and economic potential; the share of each group is determined by the land reform agency. Management of the SAIS is in the hands of professional employees. Profits are allocated to each member community in relation to its share in the SAIS, and are to be used in community development projects involving schools, roads, power reticulation and housing. In this manner, surplus manpower is given employment, and the rather meager profits can be used in developing badly needed physical infrastructure.

The debt assumed by each SAIS unit is to be repaid from profits in 20 years following a five-year grace period. Debt repayment may become an onerous burden on those units whose profit potential is limited by their physical capacity to expand livestock numbers and by the need to employ high-quality technical services. Legally, the full market value of expropriated livestock has to be paid in cash while fixed capital is to be paid for largely in agrarian bonds.

The land reform program alone will not be able to solve the rural unemployment problem. Even if the optimistic targets for 1975 are met, employment opportunities in agriculture will increase only from 1.32 million to 1.6 million, while the number seeking work in agriculture will rise from 1.9 million to 2.1 million. Nearly 800,000 families with insufficient land to provide adequate subsistence are eligible to benefit through the land reform program. Even if all land which can be expropriated is redistributed, about 500,000 families, mostly in the Sierra, will still lack a minimum subsistence landholding. However, agrarian reform is providing the basis for social and economic change.

261

EDUCATION

FOREWORD

Developing countries have greatly expanded their educational systems over the past quarter of a century. But much of the expansion has been misdirected. The results are seen in one of the most disturbing paradoxes of our time: while millions of people from among the educated are unemployed, millions of jobs are waiting to be done because people with the right education, training and skills cannot be found.

Ever since the World Bank decided to enter the field of educational development in 1962, its aim has been basically one: to help developing countries reform and expand their educational systems in such a way that the latter may contribute more fully to economic development. The efforts and experience of the earlier years were reviewed in the first Education Sector Working Paper published in September 1971.

The present paper takes a fresh look at the problem. It states convincingly that educational systems in developing countries are all too often ill-conceived and are not adapted to their developmental needs. The educational policies themselves are not always at fault; they have tended to serve only too well the basically irrelevant development strategies they were supposed to uphold and sustain. These overall development strategies have come under close scrutiny in recent years. Today, government leaders and economists alike increasingly believe that to the developmental goal of economic growth must be added social dimensions without which the mass of the people cannot achieve a fuller, happier and more productive life.

Among the questions this paper raises, and attempts to answer, are: How can educational systems be reshaped to help the poorest segments of society? How can education contribute to rural development, and thus respond to the needs and aspirations of the vast majority of the poor living in the villages? How can educational opportunities be made more equal in order to promote social mobility in countries where educational systems have hitherto favored the urban dwellers and the relatively rich?

Rapid population growth, together with the misallocation of educational resources, has led to an increase in the number of illiterates in developing countries around the world. It is estimated that, if the trend continues, the number of illiterates will increase to 865 million by 1985. This disturbing phenomenon threatens not only the more equitable distribution of the benefits of development; it threatens development itself. This paper explores, therefore, how low-cost functional education can enable the poor to participate more effectively in the development process.

265

We recognize the prospect that not many countries may undertake soon the radical changes that are necessary. But we are encouraged by the fact that a small, though growing, number of countries have begun to look squarely and objectively at their total educational systems in terms of both internal and external efficiency.

The World Bank stands ready to help those countries which look and do not like all that they see. The most important service the Bank can render its borrowers is to help them in the diagnosis of their problems and provide assistance in solving them. Relevant lending programs and projects can be conceived only through a dialogue conducted between the Bank and its borrowers at the policy-making level. This dialogue can best be conducted through sector studies, some of which may be undertaken with the help of the Bank, but most of which, I hope, will come from the developing countries themselves.

In the five-year period 1974-78, the World Bank and its affiliate, the International Development Association, intend to increase their support for educational development. They will do so in the conviction:

• that every individual should receive a basic minimum education as soon as financial resources and the priorities of development permit;

• that skills should be developed selectively in response to specific and urgent needs, by training the right people, both urban and rural, for the right jobs—both in the modern and traditional sectors;

• that educational policies should be formulated to respond flexibly to the need to develop educational systems (nonformal, informal, and formal), so that the specific requirements of each society might be met; and

• that opportunities should be extended throughout an educational system for those underprivileged groups who have been thwarted in their desire to enter the mainstream of their country's economic and social life. This must include more equitable access to education for the poor, the ill-fed, women, and rural dwellers, and must provide, as well, a better chance to advance from the classroom to the place of work.

If economic progress is to be rapid and equitable, education will need to be supported by action in other fields such as agriculture, health, nutrition, and employment. Only in such a context can education be effective in strengthening the potential of those developing nations which wish to ensure productive participation by all in the development process.

Robert S. McNamara
President, World Bank Group

December 1974

EDUCATION
CONTENTS

Page

Foreword. 265

Summary. 269

Chapter 1: Trends in Education and Development to 1970. 276

Chapter 2: Education Development Strategy for the 1970's and Beyond . . . 280

  Poverty-oriented Development Strategy. 280

  Major Issues Facing Education Systems. 281

  Formation of Skills Corresponding to the Needs of Developing Countries . . . 286

  Development of Skills for Rural Areas. 289

  Ensuring Mass Participation in Education and Development. 293

  Education and Equity. 299

  Increasing Efficiency in Education. 302

  Improving Management and Planning Capacity. 308

Chapter 3: The World Bank's Education Lending Policy and Program. 313

  Bank Policy and Activities: 1963-74 315

  Objectives of Bank Lending for Education 318

  Bank Lending Programs and Possibilities 323

  Conclusion 327

Annexes

  1. Estimated Total Enrollment by Level of Education. 331

  2. Analysis of World Bank/IDA Education Lending, FY1963-74 331

  3. Student Places Provided or Improved through World Bank/IDA
    Education Projects, FY1963-74. 332

  4. World Bank/IDA Education Lending by Per Capita GNP of
    Borrowing Countries, FY1963-74. 332

  5. World Bank/IDA Education Projects Approved as of June 30, 1974 333

  6. Comparison of Education Efficiencies in Urban and Rural Areas in
    Latin America. 337

  7. Availability of Complete Primary Schools in Urban and Rural Areas 337

  8. Female Enrollment as a Percentage of Total Primary and Secondary
    School Enrollments 338

  9. Public Expenditure on Education as a Percentage of the Budget
    and GNP. 339

  10. School Textbook Production 340

  11. Education at the First and Second Levels: Student-Teacher Ratios 340

SUMMARY

This paper consists of three parts. The first chapter describes world-wide trends in educational development during the period from 1950 to 1970. The second chapter summarizes the state of education throughout the world at the beginning of the 1970's, and sets forth issues and problems which confront developing countries, together with different policies which might enter into their development strategies. The third chapter deals with the education lending policies and programs of the World Bank and the International Development Association (IDA).[1]

After rapid progress from 1950 to 1965, there has been a slowdown in the rate of educational expansion. This decline in enrollment increases, which coincides with the peaking of the population surge at the school levels, will be felt until the mid-1980's. It could lead to stagnation in the progress toward universal education. In a number of poorer countries, where already tight financial constraints have been made more severe by recent economic events, larger numbers and proportions of people would be left without even a minimum education.

Education systems have been irrelevant to the needs of developing countries during the last two decades because education policies were often keeping company with overall development strategies which were themselves irrelevant to the societies and conditions of developing countries. Emphasis on the development of the modern economic sector, providing employment to a small and intensively trained elite, leads to the neglect of the 60-80% of the population living in sectors characterized by traditionally lower productivity. Consequently, a large part—often more than 50%—of the resources is devoted to secondary and higher education, although the student enrollment at those levels is generally less than 20% of the total. Despite the substantial progress realized in both general development and education during these decades, the bright hopes of the early years are far from being realized.

The growing realization that equitable income distribution is not an automatic corollary of growth has helped turn attention to a development strategy which is directed to sharing the benefits of growth as well as to growth itself. Such a strategy, based on a different deployment of scarce capital throughout the economy, means a fuller use of available human resources—particularly in traditional and tran-

---

[1]All references to the World Bank in this paper are to be deemed to refer also to the International Development Association, unless the context requires otherwise. The fiscal year (FY) of the two institutions runs from July 1 to June 30.

sitional sectors of the economy. A broadening of development objectives implies that education also needs to adapt itself to the needs of people living in these sectors. A major implication is emphasis on mass education to ensure that all receive education and training of some kind as soon as resources permit and to the extent that the course of development requires. This perspective sets the framework for the analysis of the major issues facing education systems and the choices of policy to be considered.

Five basic issues are discussed, together with related policies:

(a) Development of Skills and their Relevance

The importance of educational credentials in getting access to wage employment generates social pressures for the expansion of formal education beyond the absorptive capacity of the modern sector. This increases the demand for increasingly higher levels of schooling, and distorts the content of education by making each cycle only a step toward the next. Education systems thus become dysfunctional, both for the economy and for the large majorities of school leavers.

Measures suggested to deal with the problems in the modern sector include increasing the demand for educated manpower, adapting education to job requirements, rationing secondary and higher education and changing the pattern of demand for education through suitable pricing. These measures require coordination of education, employment and labor market policies and cooperation of employers. A different set of recommendations for the rural sector includes an increasing emphasis on rural subjects in formal schools, development of nonformal schemes as parallel or alternative programs, and functional literacy schemes. Whatever the particular form adopted, rural education and training schemes should be designed as functional programs, integrated into the broader system of education and coordinated with other sectoral activities in the rural scene. Training management personnel for rural programs is of high priority.

(b) Mass Participation in Education and Development

In spite of the considerable efforts made by the developing countries, about half of their citizens, children and adults alike, are without a minimum level of education; and the prospects for the next decade are not promising. There will be significant increases in the total numbers of out-of-school children and illiterate adults if no remedial action is taken.

The provision of a minimum education is an essential condition for the effective participation of the masses in the development process. Low-cost, functional, mass education is required. In countries

270

with high primary enrollment ratios, mass education can be provided by the primary schools, supplemented by schemes designed to reach non-educated youths and adults. For poor countries facing serious problems in expanding primary enrollment, the concept of basic education is proposed as a more adequate approach to provide minimum learning packages. This could be effected by changes in the structure of the formal system as well as by parallel and complementary schemes. Such schemes, open to various age groups, would offer programs of varying content and length adapted to the different groups' needs, with corresponding changes in the training and the role of teachers. Despite the controversy around the issue of "duality", financial constraints may compel some of the poorest countries to adopt this approach if they are to meet the minimum learning needs of the masses within a reasonable time.

(c) Education and Equity

Educational systems and policies have a regressive character which favors urban populations and middle- and upper-income groups. These groups, therefore, have a definite advantage in terms of access to, and promotion within, the systems.

Equalizing opportunities for access to education is a necessary, but not sufficient, condition to ensure social mobility through education. Providing equal chances for achievement, both in and after school, is a more difficult objective, as factors which cannot be affected by educational policies play a significant role. Opportunities may be equalized somewhat by appropriate methods of selection and promotion, such as "quota systems,"or by improvements in the methods of educational finance. As a whole, however, equity through education can be achieved only within the context of broader social policies.

(d) Increasing Efficiency

Education systems are inefficient in using resources and often do not achieve their quantitative and qualitative goals. Failure to define objectives is a principal source of waste. The shortage of good teachers and the design and efficient use of learning materials are other major problems. Malnutrition and related illnesses also affect the performance of students. All these inefficiencies are first reflected in high dropout and repeater rates. In a number of countries, one-fourth of the education budget is spent on students who drop out before reaching Grade 4 without having received any lasting benefit from education.

Better specification of the education and training objectives and performance standards is a first step which needs to be followed by the identification of factors most likely to affect efficiency. These include a number of school-related factors (methods of teaching and promotion, language of teaching) as well as non-school factors (poor health, family income). Most measures to improve quality have serious implications for costs. It is important, therefore, to explore areas in which costs may be reduced. Recent research indicates possibilities for savings, for example, by some changes in class sizes. (It is now believed that class size may not be as closely associated with the quality of education as has been traditionally assumed.)

(e) Improving Management and Planning

New policies mean new challenges for educational management and planning. An inability among political decision makers and education managers to communicate with each other is a major source of confusion about objectives and programs.

A wider approach to planning is needed as the conventional practices, based on manpower and rates of return analysis, are inadequate to deal with the issues of broadly conceived education policies. "Cohort analysis" is suggested as an aid to planning. New education policies will require substantial changes in the organization and structure of education systems, improvement in methods of educational finance and, finally, an adequate flow of information and research for use in management.

The Bank's Program

A basic premise in the discussion of lending for education is that the World Bank's operations in this sector should reflect its overall policies. Those policies include an increasing concern with the problems and needs of low-income countries and the promotion of development strategies to improve the well-being of the lower 40% of the population through increased productivity and employment and improved income distribution. But these new features of Bank policy should not obscure the fact that the Bank will continue to assist countries which have moved to higher levels of development.

The following principles will govern the Bank's effort to promote balanced educational development:

(a) There should be at least a minimum basic education for all, as fully and as soon as available resources permit.

(b) Further education and training beyond the basic level should be provided selectively to improve, both quantitatively and qualitatively, the knowledge and skills necessary for the performance of economic, social and other developmental roles.

272

(c) A national education system should be viewed as a comprehensive system of learning, embracing formal, nonformal and informal education, all working with maximum possible internal and external efficiency.

(d) In the interests of both increased productivity and social equity, educational opportunities should be equalized as fully as possible.

A flexible response, adjusted to the variety of conditions in developing countries, will guide the Bank's activities in education. The differences between the lower-income countries and the relatively more developed ones will determine the proportion or "mix" of different areas and kinds of assistance. In the poorer countries, basic education and rural training are expected to receive emphasis, together with selective support for the further development of skills. The development of second and third levels of education would take a more central place in the education strategies of the middle- and higher-income countries.

Basic/Primary Education: The Bank's interest in basic education is closely related to its efforts to promote a broader approach to development. In countries where mass education can be achieved through the expansion of the primary system, the Bank will give particular attention to curriculum and other reforms which take into account the needs of the many who will not continue beyond the primary cycle. A review and revision of education structures will be encouraged to provide low-cost, minimum, mass education in poor countries with low primary school enrollment ratios. A variety of programs for youths and adults will also be supported as a follow-up or, when necessary, as an alternative to primary education.

Development of Skills: Assisting the borrower in meeting the need for critical skills for economic development continues to be a major objective. The Bank will continue to assist not only training institutions, but also educational systems as a whole. Project-related training is another method increasingly used by the Bank to meet requirements for skills in specific areas. It is expected that during the period from 1974 to 1978, training components in other than education lending, together with school construction in urban and rural development projects, will total about $350 million.

Efficiency: Effective and cost-conscious management, together with internal and external efficiency, will receive continuous attention throughout all phases of the dialogue with borrowers. Particular emphasis will be placed on policies which can be more directly linked with the Bank's lending operations.

Equity: Equity will be used as a criterion in all Bank operations. In its analysis of education systems and policies, the Bank will be concerned with such questions as where the funds go, who benefits most and who pays. Information on specific target groups will be sought during project identification and design to assess the equity of education programs. More specifically, a guidance and monitoring system will be developed to determine the beneficiaries of education projects.

Will developing countries be willing to accept the kind of general and specific policies suggested in this paper? What might the Bank do to encourage their receptiveness? Experience suggests that relatively few countries will undertake the radical changes which many consider necessary. At the same time, there is a growing recognition that significant changes are needed and an increased willingness to consider selective proposals for reform. Awareness of financial constraints may be a powerful inducement for change. If this is so, in some countries the unfavorable effects of the recent economic changes may encourage a critical and objective review of existing educational systems. Sector studies, carried out by the countries themselves, are major vehicles through which the critical issues raised in this paper may be tackled. The Bank will assist an increasing number of these, both financially and technically.

What are the risks involved in these policies? Will countries have sufficient managerial capacity to carry them out? It must be acknowledged that the risks involved in highly innovative action are substantial for the Bank and even more so for the borrowers, especially in such uncharted areas as rural- and poverty-oriented policies. But when the effects of continuing to neglect to act are foreseen as being more costly, a prudent but active course seeking to identify and minimize risks should be preferred. Improving management is, of course, a major priority.

Do the Bank's current policies, procedures and lending programs give effect to the direction and proposals put forth in this paper? How should they be changed or improved? The allocation of $1,075 million (in constant prices) covering 80 projects proposed in the lending program for 1974-78 is reasonable in view of the rapid expansion of education lending in recent years and the experimental nature of some of the new emphases in lending. This program would permit the necessary "tooling up" for a substantial expansion beginning in about 1978. The distribution of lending by areas (a substantial increase of up to 27% for primary/basic education and a proportional decrease for intermediate and higher education) reflects the new directions in policy. The Bank is making every effort to ensure that an equitable distribution—both inter-country and intra-country—in its lending activities will occur.

Implementation of the policies and programs proposed will require greater use of flexible procedures which already exist in the Bank but have not been fully utilized in the education sector. In order to give momentum to experimentation in such areas as basic education, the Bank can lend an appropriate part of the total costs of an experiment—both capital and operational—over a stated period of time. The capital and operational costs of training teachers and administrators should be financed by the Bank to ensure the development of an adequate human infrastructure for educational change.

The Bank's lending operations in any sector are part of a continuing relationship with its member countries which is rooted in agreement on an overall development strategy and on individual sectoral strategies such as education. Such strategies take their direction from the country's own definition of its developmental objectives and aspirations. In the context of a constructive dialogue with each of its borrowers, the Bank desires to contribute to policy making by clarifying the choices that its member countries face. Through such a dialogue, it is hoped that there may emerge for each country a unity of purpose and plan between it and the Bank.

Chapter 1: TRENDS IN EDUCATION AND DEVELOPMENT TO 1970

The first World Bank Education Sector Paper of 1971 noted the effect on educational expansion since 1950 of the movement for political independence, the quickening pace of economic development and the population explosion. These three forces continue at work, although the rate of educational expansion has slackened since the late 1960's. Throughout the expansion period of the 1950's and 1960's, there had been increasing concern in developing countries about the relevance of the education which was being widely replicated and the quality of learning provided by the largely borrowed formal school systems.

In addition to the continuing concern for relevance and quality, there is now the problem that the decline in enrollment increases (for reasons of financial constraint, difficulty in reaching rural populations, and perhaps disenchantment with the benefits of formal education) coincides with the peaking of the population surge at the school-age levels. Until the mid-1980's, when some relaxation is expected, the population pressure will manifest itself most sharply in the large number of children between the ages of 6 and 15. As a consequence, there is a prospect not only of stagnation in progress toward universal education, but even of a retrogression which would leave larger numbers and proportions of the populations of many countries without even a minimum education.

In a number of developing countries, the already tight financial constraints have been made more severe by the changes in the world economy associated with rapid increases in petroleum prices and other movements in the terms of trade. The World Bank estimates that 800 million people—whose per capita incomes average less than $200 per year—are likely to receive a severe setback. These are the people of the poorest countries, where education enrollment ratios, like other social indices, are still low and where rural populations are least affected by development forces. For them, the "setback" in education could be severe.

The challenge posed by these circumstances is heightened by changes in the definition of development itself during recent years. Questions of employment, environment, social equity and, above all, participation in development by the less privileged now share with simple "growth" in the definition of the objectives (and hence the model) of development toward which the effort of all parties is to be directed. These changes have their counterpart in the education sec-

276

tor, where the need is being felt for new educational policies responding to new objectives of development.

In general, new educational policies are less a sharp break with the past than a shift in emphasis and a broadening of benefits and beneficiaries. In this sector of limited resources and unlimited demands, we will continue to ask the same questions, namely: Who shall be educated? How? For what? At whose expense? And at what expense?

No single answer to any of these questions will serve for all, or even for several, of the developing countries. We will find similarities among them, and we will explore these common features to discover typologies which might ease the work of analyzing problems and proposing remedies. But either because of the conformation of factors within the education sector, or the relation of education to all other sectors, we continue to see each country as unique, requiring its own individual development strategy.

In recent years, there has been wide discussion—as in the first edition of this paper—about the lack of consistency between educational policies and systems and the development objectives they are assumed to serve. In almost all cases, it has been assumed that it was the educational policy that was irrelevant. It is no longer certain that this was always the case. In many respects, it seems that educational policies were simply keeping company with overall development objectives which were themselves irrelevant to the societies and conditions of developing countries. For this reason, and in search of a broader perspective, we begin this paper with a historical review covering, roughly, the two decades from 1950 to 1970.

For much of the developing world during these two decades, the transcendent event was the achievement of independence. There followed the slow process of nation building which, in many cases, sought to recast the diversity of ethnic, religious and cultural traditions into a new national formulation. And since political independence is more easily achieved than economic or cultural reconstruction, the practices and institutions chosen to replace the existing diversities were frequently those previously established by the colonial powers.

The changes in the political scene of developing countries were expected to be accompanied by a modernization process yielding a general and dramatic rise in the standards of living of the populations concerned. In many cases, the difficulties of transforming a traditional society into a modern one were underestimated. In already independent countries, similar great expectations were awakened. The idea of "catching up with rich countries" exerted a pre-eminent influence on the thinking of the leadership in the developing countries.

277

To a certain extent, that idea prevented the leadership from elaborating original and viable models of society for their countries. Perhaps nowhere was this demonstration effect more pervasive and successful in dampening local initiatives to adapt to the socioeconomic realities than in the sphere of education.

Investment in both industry and agriculture tended to flow toward a modern, capital-intensive, export-oriented subsector which provided employment to a relatively small portion of the labor force, the major part of which was either engaged in traditional subsistence farming or suffered increasingly from unemployment. Thus, in both the urban and rural sectors, relatively sophisticated technologies called for more intensive education and training of a small elite working force.

Conversely, the traditional sectors of lower productivity, comprising 60% to 80% of the population, are characterized by their reliance on indigenous resources and little investment. Enterprises are small-scale, often self-employing and family-owned, except in agriculture, where some form of landlord-tenant relationships may persist. The technology of these enterprises is labor-intensive and primitive, requiring ostensibly less education and training.

In their haste to modernize, many developing countries, in collaboration with bilateral and multilateral donors of development aid, focused too sharply on increasing the overall national income, and paid insufficient attention to the equitable distribution of that income, as well as to the social and cultural aspects of development.

Education was considered a major instrument for the political, social, cultural and economic modernization of the developing world in the 1950's and 1960's. Political and cultural leaders were convinced that a well supported, easily accessible educational system was an efficient means to make people politically and socially conscious, and, therefore, active participants in nation building and cultural processes. The education sector was enthusiastically, often simplistically, supported as the major supplier of skills for the economy. The more optimistic expected that education would, of itself, stimulate the creation of jobs and thus generate economic development.

The education systems of developing countries, however, did not offer a good base for national development, either quantitatively or qualitatively. In many developing countries, the system was simply an expansion of that of the former colonial rulers. In countries which have long been independent, such as those in Latin America, tradition still bound the education system to an earlier European model that was no longer an effective instrument for development.

Regional conferences of education ministers, held more than a decade ago, established quantitative goals which were sometimes over-ambitious and financially unrealistic and which finally were set back by population growth. Nevertheless, they lent support to an unprecedented expansion of school enrollments, as shown in Table 1. As one moves up the ladder from primary through secondary to tertiary education, the net increases in enrollments over the past two decades are impressive. The aggregate increases were 211%, 465% and 511%, respectively. If one divides the decade of the 1960's into two halves, however, a significant pattern emerges. The pattern across all levels shows a decreasing rate of expansion, indicating that the momentum of the first 15 years has weakened.

Table 1

**First, Second and Third Level Student Enrollments
and Annual Increases in Developing Countries[1]**

	1950 Students (Millions)	1950-60 Annual increases (%)	1960 Students (Millions)	1960-65 Annual increases (%)	1965 Students (Millions)	1965-70 Annual increases (%)	1970 Students (Millions)	1950-70 Aggregate increases (%)
First level	64.7	+6.4	118.9	+ 6.0	159.6	+4.8	201.4	+211
Second level	7.5	+9.3	18.2	+ 9.9	29.3	+7.6	42.4	+465
Third level	0.9	+8.9	2.1	+12.4	3.7	+8.4	5.5	+511

[1] See also Annex 1.

During the 1960's, education planners began to take their cue from manpower studies—often crude and superficial—which tended to emphasize the kinds of highly skilled manpower which only secondary and higher education could provide. A large part of education budgets—often more than 50%—was devoted to these levels of formal education, although the number of students in them was generally less than 20% of the total enrollment. An increased number of better educated people were needed. But high percentages of the graduates were in low priority fields (from a developmental point of view), and had no readily employable skills. Thus, in the countries in which the Bank has supported education projects, the median percentage of students in vocational education has been only around 10%, compared with close to 30% in the most developed countries (see Table 3).

In sum, general development strategies and their educational components during this period were more closely related than was commonly supposed. Substantial progress was made in both general development and education. But the bright hopes of the early years were far from being realized. A stagnation in enrollment has occurred.

279

In some countries, the original problems remain; and, in most, new problems that are sometimes the consequence of achievement are emerging.

Chapter 2: EDUCATION DEVELOPMENT STRATEGY FOR THE 1970's AND BEYOND

Poverty-oriented Development Strategy

Many developing countries are concerned that the relatively high economic growth rates recorded during the last decade have brought little benefits to the poorest strata of society. The growing realization that equitable distribution of income is not an automatic corollary of growth has helped turn attention to development strategies which are directed to the sharing of the benefits of growth as well as to growth itself.

Central to this new approach is the widespread inability of the modern sector of developing economies to make full use of the resources available to it—above all, the human resources. A number of countries, therefore, are considering a strategy based on a different deployment of scarce capital throughout the economy, and a fuller use of available human resources. Translated into development objectives, this means that the creation of productive employment is being recognized as an economic goal as important as the growth rate of gross domestic product (GDP).

Fuller and more productive employment could also mean a more equitable distribution of income to the extent that the main beneficiaries—the unemployed and underemployed—are usually found among the less privileged strata of society. As the overwhelming majority of the very poor are engaged in subsistence farming, a poverty-oriented development strategy assumes that an important proportion of the new productivity will be stimulated in rural areas. Such a change in income patterns would increase the demand for such goods as basic foodstuffs, clothing and low-cost housing—which are usually produced locally (with low import content) by labor-intensive techniques.

A broadening of development objectives also implies that significant changes are needed in educational policies and practices. If education is to contribute to the development of the rural and traditional sectors of the economy, it will have to adapt itself to the needs of these sectors.

An important implication of this expanded development strategy is that mass education will be an economic as well as a social necessity.[1] Education and training systems will need to be designed to enable the masses that have been unaffected by the growth of the modern sector to participate in the development process as more productive workers—by being able to play their roles effectively as citizens, family members, leaders and members of groups involved in cooperative community action, and in many other ways. This ultimately means that all parts of the population must receive education and training of some kind as soon as resources permit and to the extent that the course of development requires. The benefits of mass education will, of course, be greater when other conditions of development are present. Emphasis on mass education, particularly in rural areas, will first require a better distribution of educational opportunities between geographical areas, between urban and rural regions, between social groups, and between the sexes.

Instances of disproportionate distribution are common. In Kenya, the relative primary school enrollment varies by as much as a factor of nine between provinces. In Colombia, the number of students who successfully complete their primary school education is, relatively, ten times larger in urban schools than in rural schools, mainly because few of the latter provide complete courses. Despite improvements in female enrollments during the 1960's, only 38% of the students in primary schools and 28% of those in secondary schools are girls in the poorest countries. (See Annexes 6-8.) The new emphasis must also take account of diverse learning clienteles and, consequently, of alternative delivery systems. Education cannot be restricted to school-age youths. Other target groups such as adults, and especially women, must be included. Given the diversity of target groups and educational tasks, it would be advisable to make effective use of nonformal and informal education, in addition to the formal school system.

It is evident that the need to respond to poverty-oriented development strategies introduces important new dimensions in education policy.

Major Issues Facing Education Systems

An analysis of the issues facing the less developed countries can be made within a broad perspective, taking into consideration the major objectives of education policies and the critical factors determining the development and functioning of education systems. In this framework, the focal points of discussion will be: (1) formation

---

[1]For an analysis of the economic and social role of mass education, see Redistribution with Growth, by Hollis Chenery et al., pages 45 and 123. Oxford University Press, 1974.

of skills; (2) participation; (3) equity; (4) efficiency; and (5) planning and management.

In attempting to discuss education policies, account should be taken of the variety of conditions observed in different developing societies, including countries with yearly per capita incomes ranging from $70 to $1,500, with populations ranging from less than one million to 500 million, and with literacy rates varying from 5% to over 90%. These countries also differ in social stratification, cultural and political traditions, and physical resources. As a basis for the discussion, some characteristic data and trends are shown and analyzed in Table 2, which relates enrollment ratios to levels of per capita Gross National Product (GNP). Table 3, which follows, elaborates on the variety of conditions found in both developed and developing countries.

There are important conclusions to be drawn from Table 2. Despite the enrollment increases at all levels of education during the 1960's in developing countries, the gap between the poorest and the richest countries has increased at the secondary and tertiary levels. Twenty-five of the poorest countries have increased their enrollments at those levels by 1.0 and 0.1 percentage points, respectively, during the decade. A middle group, including the populous nations of India, Indonesia, Bangladesh and Pakistan, as well as the countries in the $121-750 bracket, have increased their enrollments by approximately 11 and 4 percentage points, while the most affluent countries have increased their enrollments by 25 and 13 percentage points.

Other implications follow from the difference between enrollment ratios at the lower and upper levels of education. Countries in Group I have 43% enrollment in primary and only 5% in secondary education. Thus, in comparison with others, these countries will have to absorb a higher proportion of the primary school leavers in their societies and labor markets. Such facts should be reflected in the curriculum of the first level of education.

Countries in different income categories show significant variations in their expenditure patterns. (This can be clearly seen in Table 4.) The table shows the widening difference between what governments in the poorest and in the richer countries spend for the education of a student. This gap does not reflect differences in the educational profiles of countries, namely, relative proportions of lower and higher levels, as the differences in per student expenditures at primary level are in fact even greater. The table also indicates that, in the poorest countries, there was only a negligible increase in public expenditure

282

per student which, if measured in constant prices, corresponds to an actual decline.

In the previous paragraphs, differences between groups of countries were explored. It should be emphasized, however, that wide divergencies also exist between countries in the same income groups, both as regards educational efforts and outcome. Among countries

Table 2

School Enrollment Ratios

Per capita[1] GNP	Number of countries	Total population in 1970 (Millions)	Enrollment ratios[2]								
			First level			Second level			Third level		
			1960	1965	1970	1960	1965	1970	1960	1965	1970
I—Up to $120 (excluding India, Indonesia, Pakistan, Bangladesh)	25	168	34	39	43 (31)	4	5	5	0.3	0.3	0.4
India, Indonesia, Pakistan, Bangladesh	4	802	43	56	71 (63)	9	11	18	1.7	2.6	4.3
II—$121-250	23	287	67	79	83 (68)	9	14	19	2.1	3.0	5.6
III—$251-750	38	433	73	83	97 (77)	11	17	25	1.9	3.3	5.3
IV—$751-1,500	9	112	90	93	97 (80)	33	44	49	6.2	8.4	10.5
V—Over $1,500	24	623	100	100	100	58	65	83	17.0	23.7	30.2

[1] Countries in each group are as follows:

    I—Afghanistan, Bangladesh, Botswana, Burma, Burundi, Chad, Dahomey, Ethiopia, The Gambia, Guinea, Haiti, India, Indonesia, Lesotho, Malawi, Mali, Nepal, Niger, Nigeria, Pakistan, Rwanda, Somalia, Sri Lanka, Sudan, Tanzania, Upper Volta, Yemen Arab Republic, People's Democratic Republic of Yemen, Zaire.

    II—Bolivia, Central African Republic, Cameroon, Equatorial Guinea, Egypt, Ghana, Kenya, Khmer Republic, Republic of Korea, Liberia, Malagasy Republic, Mauritania, Mauritius, Morocco, Philippines, Senegal, Sierra Leone, Swaziland, Thailand, Togo, Tunisia, Uganda, Republic of Vietnam.

    III—Algeria, Bahrain, Brazil, Republic of China, People's Republic of Congo, Colombia, Costa Rica, Dominican Republic, Ecuador, El Salvador, Fiji, Gabon, Guatemala, Guyana, Honduras, Iran, Iraq, Ivory Coast, Jamaica, Jordan, Lebanon, Malaysia, Mexico, Nicaragua, Oman, Panama, Papua New Guinea, Paraguay, Peru, Portugal, Romania, Saudi Arabia, Syria, Turkey, Uruguay, Yugoslavia, Zambia.

    IV—Argentina, Chile, Cyprus, Greece, Singapore, South Africa, Spain, Trinidad and Tobago, Venezuela.

    V—Australia, Austria, Belgium, Canada, Denmark, Finland, France, Federal Republic of Germany, Iceland, Ireland, Israel, Italy, Japan, Kuwait, Libya, Luxembourg, Netherlands, New Zealand, Norway, Qatar, Sweden, United Arab Emirates, United Kingdom, United States.

[2] The enrollment ratios have been obtained by dividing the total enrollment at each level with the appropriate age group. These "gross" enrollment ratios are inflated by over-age students. For 1970, it has been possible to exclude the over-age students and estimate "net" enrollment ratios at the first level. The net ratios are indicated in parentheses and show that the over-age students form 10-20% of the total student body at the first level.

in Group I, for instance, Rwanda allocates 10% of its national budget to primary education and has achieved an enrollment ratio of 60%, while Mali allocates 12% of its national budget to the same level, but has a primary school enrollment ratio of only 18%.

Comparative Education Indicators

Comparative education data are useful in the evaluation of various education systems and the analysis of relative stages of educational development between various countries. However, on the basis of the present data, cross-national comparison should be approached with great caution. Data presented in the following table have been collected largely by World Bank missions from government sources; the remainder are staff estimates or data from Unesco. Efforts have been made to standardize definitions and, within limits, to check the accuracy of the data. Nevertheless, such data are still imperfect in several respects and the Bank is working to improve them progressively during its operational work. In the use of these data, the following qualifications should be borne in mind.

(1) "Education", as defined in the table, includes all education and training, formal and nonformal.

(2) "Primary" education refers to education at the first level and "secondary" education refers to all education at the secondary level regardless of type (e.g., general, technical, agricultural).

(3) "Vocational" education (Col. 10) includes enrollments in technical, commercial, agricultural, vocational and home-economics courses.

(4) "Literacy rates" (Col. 3) are usually obtained from country censuses. In many countries they are only approximations and it is doubtful that any uniform definition of "literate" has been followed consistently.

(5) "Public expenditure in education" (Cols. 4 & 6) refers to all capital and recurrent expenditures devoted to education by public and quasi-public agencies.

(6) "Enrollment ratios" (Cols. 7 & 9) refer to school year and mean the percentage of eligible children enrolled full-time in the appropriate school, public and private, by level. They are often subject to a wide margin of error in the developing countries owing to variation in the accuracy of basic data (i.e., age-specific population and enrollments). Enrollment figures frequently are higher than the number of students actually in school. Over-age students whose inclusion is indicated by footnotes also can inflate the ratios.

	Year	Population (Millions) (1)	Per capita GNP at market prices (US$) (2)	Literacy rate (% of Adults) (3)	Public education expenditures per capita (market prices US$) (4)
ADVANCED					
Austria	1970	7.5 G	2,200 G	99	73
Canada	1971	21.6	4,140	98	352
Germany, Fed. Rep.	1971	61.3	3,210	99	149
Japan	1971	105.0	2,130	99	
Netherlands	1971	13.2	2,620	99	216
New Zealand	1971	2.9	2,470	99	110
Norway	1970	3.9 G	3,130 G	99	169
Sweden	1970	8.1 G	4,240 G	99	311
United Kingdom	1970	55.9 G	2,430 G	97	94
U.S.A.	1970	207.1 G	5,160 G	99	253
Europe					
1. Greece	1971	8.9	1,250	82 E	23 E
2. Ireland	1972	3.0 G	1,510 G	98	58
3. Spain	1970	34.0 G	1,100 G	94 D	20
Africa					
1. Algeria	1971	14.4	360	25 B	34 F
2. Cameroon	1970	5.8 G	200 G	...	6
3. C.A.R.	1970	1.6 G	150 G	...	6
4. Chad	1970	3.7 G	80 G	7	5
5. Congo, P. R.	1970	1.1 G	270 G	50 ?	14
6. Ethiopia	1972	25.3	80	7	9
7. Gabon	1973	0.5 G	700 G	...	33
8. Ghana	1970	8.8 G	250 G	...	13
9. Ivory Coast	1968	5.2 G	320 G	9 A	10
10. Kenya	1970	11.7 G	160 G	30 D	8 H
11. Lesotho	1973	0.9 G	100 G	40	4.1
12. Liberia	1970	1.6 G	210 G	15	8
13. Mali	1972	5.1 G	70 G	10	3
14. Mauritania	1970	1.2 G	170 G	10	2
15. Mauritius	1972	0.8 G	280 G	80	11
16. Morocco	1970	15.4 G	260 G	20	9
17. Nigeria	1971	56.5	140	...	3
18. Senegal	1971	4.0	250	10	11 P
19. Sierra Leone	1968	2.7 G	250 G	27	4
20. Somalia	1973	2.9 G	70 G	5	2
21. Sudan	1972	16.1 G	120 G	15	6
22. Swaziland	1972	0.46	90 G	28	18
23. Tanzania	1971	13.3	110 G	...	4
24. Uganda	1970	10.1 G	130 G	25 A	6
25. Upper Volta	1972	5.5 G	70 G	5	2
26. Zaire	1970	19.3 G	90 G	13	8
27. Zambia	1971	4.2	380	43	28
Central America & Caribbean					
1. Costa Rica	1971	1.7	590	89	30
2. Dominican Rep.	1972	4.1 G	430 G	51	11
3. El Salvador	1971	3.7	320	58 YA	9
4. Guatemala	1968	5.4 G	391 G	38 YA	6 B
5. Honduras	1972	2.6 G	300 G	52	11
6. Jamaica	1969	1.9 G	720 G	86	24
7. Mexico	1970	52.4 G	700 G	76	18
8. Nicaragua	1969	2.1 G	450 G	53	10
9. Trinidad & Tobago	1971	1.0	940	90	40
South America					
1. Brazil	1971	93.2 F	460 G	67 F	16 H
2. Chile	1969	9.9 G	760 G	90	32
3. Colombia	1970	22.3 G	370 G	74 H	12
4. Ecuador	1968	6.3 G	310 G	68 A	8 V
5. Guyana	1974	0.7 G	390 G	83 A	35
6. Paraguay	1970	2.4 G	280 G	79	5
7. Peru	1971	14.4	480	72	18
8. Venezuela	1970	10.6 G	1,060 G	81	45
Asia					
1. Bangladesh	1973	72.4 G	70 G	23	
2. China (Taiwan)	1973	14.9 G	430 G	82	19.3
3. India	1971	551.1	110	29	3 AV
4. Indonesia	1971	119.2	80	56	1 Q
5. Iran	1971	29.8	450	37	11
6. Iraq	1970	9.7 G	370 G	26	19
7. Jordan	1973	2.4 G	260 G	59	19
8. Korea	1971	31.8	290	85 B	13.0
9. Lebanon	1971	2.8	660	86 F	21 F
10. Malaysia	1972	11.1 G	400 G	60	32
11. Oman	1972	0.6 G	450 G	20	12
12. Pakistan	1972	62.7 G	130 G	39	1
13. Philippines	1972	37.9 G	240 G	72	6.3
14. Singapore	1972	2.1 G	1,200 G	75 F	46
15. Thailand	1973	39.8	234	82	8
16. Turkey	1969	36.2 G	340 G	49 A	9
17. Yemen Arab Rep.	1971	5.9	90	10	1 P
18. Yemen, P.D.R.	1972	1.5 G	120 G	10	6 G
SUMMARY FOR DEVELOPING COUNTRIES					
Number of Countries				59	64
Range				(5-98)	(1-58)
Quartiles: Upper				72	18
Median				52	10
Lower				20	5

Symbols:		Notes:	
...	Datum unavailable	A = 1965 or before	G = 1971
-	Magnitude nil or negligible	B = 1966	H = 1972
0	Magnitude less than half of unit employed	C = 1967	J = 1973
?	Questionable	D = 1968	M = Current prices
*	Includes part-time students	E = 1969	N = GNP
		F = 1970	P = Including foreign aid

284

Table 3

% of GNP devoted to education (public expenditures only) (5)	% of total public expenditures devoted to education (6)	Primary enrollment ratio net (7)	Primary students per teacher (8)	Secondary enrollment ratio net (9)	% Secondary enrollment in vocational schools (10)	Secondary students per teacher full-time equivalent (11)	% Higher enrollment in agriculture and engineering (12)	Annual output from higher education per 100,000 population (13)
4.3	9.9	99	24	46	60	12	24	77 B
8.2	21.1	98	24	82	...	17	9	630
4.2	14.2	91	33	91 Y	30	22	19	211
4.3	20.7	99	25	94	41 H	20	22	415
7.7	17.0	95	29	70	40	19	25	230 E
4.8 M	16.5 M	99	27	68		18	18	287
6.7	17.5	99	23	71 E	22 E	16	22	64 C
9.0	15.0	100	18	88	51	14	14	240
5.8	13.8	98	28	58	5 C	18	16	188 B
5.8	16.0	97	25	94	...	20	7	520
2.2	9.3 E	99 E	33 E	59 E	16 E	31 E	14 E	86 F
5.1	14.8	97	35	75	22	19	12	154
2.4	12.5 E	91	35	29	22 C	30	19	31 C
9.0 F	29.8 F	64	40	13	18	26	6	22
3.0	20.0	74	48	8	23	25	4	7
4.0 N	20.0	73 X	64	4 X	18	30	...	...
4.3 N	14.3 D	33	72	2	8	30	...	...
5.8	23.2	80 X	59	13	10	28	...	...
2.8	20.0	17	51	5	3	35	10	4
5.0	22.0		46 G	20 H	13 H	21 H		
4.7	21.7 Q	74	29	8	4	18	15 E	13 E
4.2 C	20.4	44	46	6	8	23	...	...
5.3 H	20.0	64	34	10	2	22	29 D	5 A
4.7	22.0	65	45	8	1	22	10.1	0.04
3.7	11.7	50 X	31	12 X	6	16	12 C	9 C
4.6 N	32.3	18	40	4	6	17	36	5
4.5	21.0	15 X	22	3	13	24	15	...
3.7	11.7	86	31	30	2	30	...	55
4.1 N	17.4	54	35	12	3	22	3	7 A
3.2 N		34 X	37	4	18	23	16	6
4.0 N	25.1 H	38 X	46	11 X	8	25	2 C	12
3.8	19.5 C	32	31	13	7 C	25	22	9 H
	7.0	13	35	4	2	25	14	1
4.5	13.2	38	45	9	3	20	17	23
4.3 F	19.7	88	38	18	4	20	0	0.05
4.5	16.4	37	45	2	6	29	11	3
5.2 N	24.3 Q	46 EU	36	4 U	11	21	10	5
4.0	27.6	10	45	2	5	23	6	1
5.7 N	19.0 E	78	44	8	20	24	10	2 B
5.6	17.4	80 X	50	12	5	17	8	2
5.2	22.7	84	29	26	8	25	11	...
2.5	8.4	80	54	13	7	24	22	...
3.2	26.6 Q	69	37	16	18		24	8
2.5 B	17.6	43	38	6	22	26	10	6
3.9	18.2	81 X	37	14 X	17	14	8	4 E
4.4	19.1	86 X	52	43	9 A	19	...	11 A
2.6	17.1 Q	71	46	19	23 C	23	26 C	22
2.4	19.8	80	36	13	8	23	20 F	15
5.1	18.9	95	35	49	11	25	19	14
3.0 H	12.0 H	84	31 E	16 E	17 E	...	18 C	35 C
5.4	29.0 F	90 F	40	35	31	32 A	28 C	41 A
3.7 N	10.9	99 X	36	19 X	21	14	29	30
3.2 V	21.5 C	71	38	18	29 D	13 A	29 C	21 C
5.8 N	14.7	92 X	33 X	60 X	1	24	31	...
2.2	14.0	89 X	26	17 X	2	15	12	31
4.5	21.1	80	37	30	15	22	23	111
4.9	22.0	80	33	35	32	22	18	59
1.2	20.2	56	48	13 X		28	4	30
3.3	14.0	98	40	61	23	26	32	299
2.6 AVY		79 X	43 A	28 X	6 AY	20 AY	11 AY	52 AY
2.6 NV	13.0 F	77 X	39	15 X	26	18 X	8	...
3.1	10.8	62	33	23	3	36 F	23	39 F
6.7	16.3	64	22	25	3	26	17	80
7.0	8.8	91 X	38	50 X	10	22	3	101
3.6	16.7	100 X	56	46	49	36	28	117
4.0	21.0	79	18 U	34	36	23	4	120
6.4	20.9	90 X	32	33 X	2	26	19	80
2.3	3.8	24 X	33	0.2 X	23	9	...	...
1.3	8.0	48	35	8	5	18 E	7 E	41 F
4.6	29.0	119 X	30	71	8	36	10	457
3.1 N	11.5	107 X	33	47	4	24	20	172
3.1	19.1	88 X	29	18 X	15	22	15	37 G
3.5	17.1	92 X	42	25 X	14	33	26	41
1.0 P	9.4 P	12 H	40 H	1 H	3 H	18 H	...	1 H
2.3 E	12.6 G	70 X	29	12 X	14	20	8	...
64	64	64	65	65	64	62	56	53
(1.0-9.0)	(3.8-32.3)	(6-119)	(18-72)	(.2-75)	(1-49)	(9-36)	(0-36)	(0.04-457)
4.7	21.0	86	45	29	20	26	23	41
4.0	18.2	74	36	13	10	23	15	16
3.0	14.0	46	33	8	5	19	8	6

Q = Central government only
U = Public only
V = Including private expenditure
X = Including over-age students
Y = United Nations Educational, Scientific and Cultural Organization (Unesco) sources

Sources: Columns (1) & (2)   : World Tables (World Bank) Provisional Figures
Columns (3)—(9) & (11) : Bank Missions
Columns (10), (12) & (13): Unesco Statistical Yearbook and Bank Missions

Table 4

Public Expenditure in Education per Student[1]

(U.S. dollars, current prices)

Countries grouped by per capita GNP	1960	1965	1970	Net change
I Up to $120	16	21	18	+ 13%
II $121-250	33	40	49	+ 49%
III $251-750	43	58	57	+ 33%
IV $751-1,500	114	165	179	+ 57%
V Over $1,500	338	504	749	+121%
Group V amount as a multiple of Group I	21	24	42	

[1] Annex 9 contains additional data on education expenditures.

Formation of Skills Corresponding to the Needs of Developing Countries

Major Issues

Serious imbalances are observed between the skills generated by education systems and actual needs of most developing countries. In some areas, the number of graduates surpasses the absorptive capacity of labor markets, while in others critical shortages of skills continue to create problems. These discrepancies between the supply of, and demand for, skills are caused by a complex set of social, cultural and political conditions and aspirations which condition the development of educational systems. The failure of the systems to respond to countries' needs is accentuated by the fact that educational institutions have been borrowed from developed countries and have not acquired an indigenous character.

In considering the policy alternatives which may be open to a particular country, it may be useful to describe briefly the principal conditions which affect these issues. Not every one of the following propositions is wholly applicable to every developing country. But each does apply in large measure to most of them.

(i) Since incomes for modern sector (wage) employment tend to be substantially higher than for traditional (non-wage) employment, and since jobs in the former are often allocated on the basis of formal

286

education credentials, there is a strong and constant pressure for expanding enrollments.

(ii) For many types of work, wages and wage employment (especially in the public sector) are commonly based on the amount of education and the level of the credentials held, rather than on the type of education and its relevance to job requirements or the individuals' demonstrable proficiency.

(iii) As primary enrollments increase, competition for wage employment intensifies and the demand for education increases. Employers choose job-seekers with more education, and they, in turn, demand fuller educational opportunities.

(iv) The upward push of demand reinforces the built-in tendency of education at any one level to be preparation for the next. As a corollary, the content becomes more theoretical and abstract and less practical; experience drawn on is more universal and less local; and cognitive, or purely mental, skills are emphasized over attitudes and manual, social and leadership skills.

(v) This education is dysfunctional for most types of employment—wage or non-wage—and for playing other roles needed in a developing society.

(vi) School enrollments in a developing country increase faster than job opportunities in the modern sector, giving rise to "educated unemployed" at increasingly higher levels of education.

(vii) Even with enrollments expanding beyond the absorptive capacity of the job markets, most students completing one cycle are not able to progress to the next. They feel a strong sense of failure, together with an alienation from their original environment. For those who are unable to find the job they expected after finishing a cycle, there is frustration which, in some countries (for graduates of upper cycles), has reached explosive proportions.

(viii) In the poorest countries, the rapid expansion of educational systems has been accompanied by rapid increases in the proportion of public expenditure devoted to education. While the acceptable percentage will vary from country to country, any proportion much over 20% begins to impinge upon the needs of other sectors and services and limits further increases in educational expenditure to the rate of growth of GNP and public revenue.

Policies

Manpower planning has been a major preoccupation of educational planners during the last decade. Efforts have generally focused on increasing the supply of trained manpower in those categories in which shortages existed. A re-examination of the problem is now in order, given the increasing rate of unemployment among those who have been to school.

A number of policies are being advocated to help find employment for school leavers. These policies reflect differences in the analysis of the causes of the problem.

Increasing the Demand for Educated Manpower: This approach assumes that unemployment is the result of a failure on the part of the economy to harness the nation's skilled labor. It advocates creating enough productive job opportunities to absorb the output of the education system. Although positive in its choice of solution, the approach has limited applicability, given the constraints on investment capital and the high cost of capital inputs required to create new jobs.

Adapting Education to Job or Role Requirements: Another view of the employment problem sees the issue not so much as a quantitative imbalance as a qualitative one. The argument is supported by the fact that shortages in skills are observed in specific categories, such as science and technology teachers, engineers, agronomists and managers, despite unemployment among school graduates. The observation suggests that the content of education must be reoriented to relate skills taught to jobs, thereby ensuring that graduates can be employed. Emphasis on vocational and technical schools and centers, and attempts to "vocationalize" the curricula of academic schools, are illustrations of efforts to achieve such a reorientation.

Rationing Secondary and Higher Education: A common response to the problem of unemployment among school leavers is to decrease or stabilize school enrollments. This response reflects the view that unemployment among the educated is the result of an over-expansion of the education system, particularly at the higher levels. A policy of rationing education is proposed by those who hold this view. Measures involved might include the use of controls to limit access to certain kinds and levels of education, and the selection of pupils based on assessments of ability. Safeguards to avoid discrimination against underprivileged groups are generally built into such measures.

Changing the Pattern of Demand for Education: Some analysts conclude that the employment problem is the result of high private rates of return on schooling. They point to large government subsidies to education and large income differentials between groups with different levels of educational attainment. Subsidies keep a pupil's costs low, while existing salary differences offer him the promise of substantial benefits if he can stay in school. The result is an expected large private rate of return which generates demand for schooling. Analysts who espouse this view argue that a decrease in a pupil's benefit-cost ratio will result in a decrease in the demand for education and a subsequent reduction in unemployment among the educated. They suggest transfers of some schooling costs to pupils and reductions in earning differentials between groups with different educational attainments. They indicate that reductions in earning differentials are more difficult to achieve, but that, in theory, they can be made by changing pay scales and fostering recruitment and promotion based on job-related ability tests rather than on school certificates. The armed forces and multinational firms operating in developing countries sometimes offer examples of this latter practice.

Of these policies, only the rationing of education and increasing school fees can be pursued in isolation by education officials. Adaptation of education to job requirements demands some cooperation from private and public employers, such as cooperation in determining the requirements for skills in jobs. More extensive cooperation is demanded from the non-education sectors if demand for manpower is to be increased or wage scales are to be altered. Policy development in these domains is complicated by the absence of a central policy-making body in the administration. Ministries of labor usually have a limited impact on employment and wage policies, which are determined at various levels of both the public and private economic sectors. Central planning organizations also have a limited impact in those domains. The scope for coordination between education and labor market policies is perhaps greater in countries where the government is the major employer. But, too often, the government's willingness to alter the prevailing system of rewards is tempered by its sensitivity to political issues, while economic constraints severely limit its ability to generate new employment. [2]

Development of Skills for Rural Areas

Most of the preceding discussion on education and employment is relevant to education oriented to the modern sector and to relatively higher levels. Policies for the rural setting raise a number of different questions. Among the approaches tried by the less developed countries to meet the educational and training needs of their rural populations are:

---

[2] For an integrated analysis of education and labor market policies, see the International Labour Office's World Employment Program Reports for Ceylon (1971) and Kenya (1972).

Modification of the Content and Methods of Formal Education in Rural Areas: The "ruralization" of conventional schools to increase the relevance of rural education has been a traditional policy response. In most cases, this has been an isolated action unsupported by the creation of productive jobs for school leavers. This explains why many of the efforts have been unsuccessful in keeping the school leavers in rural areas, or in improving their participation in productive activities. "Ruralization" of conventional schools may, however, prove efficient if conceived not in isolation, but as part of an integrated policy of rural employment and development. This has been successfully tried on a small scale in Botswana in the Swaneng Hill and Shashe River Schools, where academic subjects have been combined with practical training directly related to the creation of new opportunities for self-employment for school leavers.

Nonformal Schemes as Parallel or Alternative Programs to Formal Education: All less developed countries have a number of nonformal education and training schemes in rural areas. A recent Bank-sponsored study on nonformal education, *Attacking Rural Poverty,*[3] shows the diversity of these programs in terms of their purposes, target groups, coverage, institutional characteristics and educational technologies. These schemes are usually conceived in isolation and, unfortunately, are not designed as components of an integrated structure. Some schemes, such as the Rural Education Centers in Upper Volta, are closely linked with a national system of education, as well as with the local economy, by helping school leavers to engage in specific economic activities.

Functional Literacy Programs are another example of efforts in rural education. The United Nations Educational, Scientific and Cultural Organization (Unesco) has played a major role in promoting functional literacy through projects in a number of countries (the World Experimental Literacy Program). Functional literacy, which teaches reading and arithmetic as part of the training for skills for a particular job, is essentially a sound concept, although the results have been mixed. Some projects have suffered from organizational problems in relating particular literacy schemes to national programs, lack of guidance for experimentation, delays in evaluation and high costs. Some, however, have been established on more solid grounds. Such is the case in Mali, where the functional literacy program may become a

---

[3] *Coombs, Philip H., with Ahmed, Manzoor.* Attacking Rural Poverty: How Nonformal Education Can Help. *Prepared for the World Bank by the International Council on Educational Development. Baltimore and London: The Johns Hopkins University Press, 1974.*

part of the national educational system, and is closely linked with the groundnut and other programs at the national and local levels. These programs, conducted in the national languages, have generated interest and motivation at the grassroots level. Some preliminary estimates indicate that the cost of producing a literate person is lower than in primary schools. Brazil's experience with the MOBRAL (Movimento Brasileiro de Alfabetização) project, although not conceived as an exclusively rural program, provides an example of a massive, functional literacy movement. It is a nationwide scheme managed from a central office, but relying on community organizations and local participation. In its first four years (1970-73), MOBRAL has reached more than 6 million illiterates to produce about 4 million literate adults at low unit costs.

The Bank study on nonformal education and other surveys of rural education and training clearly indicate that many rural schemes are limited, and that small-scale operations have all too often not been integrated into nationwide systems. Uncoordinated proliferation of projects, promoted by different agencies with different interests, approaches and methods, is a common phenomenon. These experiments could be valuable sources of information in developing rural education, but their contribution would remain limited in the absence of an overall policy. The design of a coherent strategy for rural education should, therefore, be considered as a prerequisite for effective action in this field.

Some basic criteria for the design of rural education and training programs can be suggested.

(a) They should be functional. This means that they must serve well identified target groups (participants in particular crop or area development projects, health, population, nutrition programs, etc.) and meet their specific needs (improved production and management, adoption of new methods of child care, etc.). The Tea Development Authority in Kenya, for example, has been effective in combining the organization and marketing of smallholder tea production with the training of farmers in all relevant aspects of tea cultivation and marketing.

(b) Rural education projects should be designed as part of a total education delivery system. In Colombia, the SENA (Servicio Nacional de Aprendizaje) program is responsible for providing training for skills, on a national basis, for both adults and adolescents. It is governed by a council which includes the Ministries of Education and Labor, the National Planning Office, and management and labor organizations. Education projects can also become the focal points of coordinated action through the use of multipurpose centers to serve other activities, such as cooperatives, health and family planning services. This is being done in Tanzania at both the district and village levels through tne establishment of Rural Training Centers and Community Education Centers. Teachers can also be trained and used as multipurpose agents.

(c) Education in rural areas should be integrated with other rural development activities at both the national and local levels. At the national level, development of a common framework of policy for various rural development activities is essential, with emphasis on making productivity and welfare-oriented activities complementary. At the local level, coordination or integration is necessary to ensure that education programs are functional and adapted to the needs and opportunities of the local milieu. They may be geared to other sectoral activities through functional literacy programs, such as those developed by Unesco in a number of countries. They may form components of integrated rural development programs, such as PACCA (Program on Agricultural Credit and Cooperation in Afghanistan) in Afghanistan and the Comilla project in Bangladesh, which have combined functional literacy, agricultural extension, cooperative marketing and the provision of agricultural inputs and services.

(d) Rural education projects should be replicable in terms of their costs and managerial requirements. For example, the national vocational training schemes in Colombia and Thailand have reduced costs through the use of mobile training units. The Vocational Industrial Centers in Northern Nigeria have made use of existing facilities in the evening and have drawn on the staff of other educational institutions on a part-time basis.

One of the critical areas in which education and training can play an important role is in developing an effective organizational and managerial capacity for rural development. An inadequate structure of management, at both national and local levels, often thwarts the implementation of rural programs. These programs require the support of a network of nationwide or regional institutions, such as rural development banks and cooperative unions, as well as strong local managers and leaders. Thus, the expansion of rural development programs creates new training needs. A special effort in training for rural development activities will be needed, especially in countries launching large-scale programs. Meeting manpower requirements in this field will necessitate crash programs for training or upgrading the staff of credit institutions, adult education schemes for training local leaders and use of teachers for cooperative management and accounting rather than creating completely new institutions.

Ensuring Mass Participation in Education and Development

Major Issues

Despite the increasing burden they impose on the economies of less developed countries, many education systems generally fail to achieve effective mass participation in educational opportunities.

The education sector has now become a major claimant of governmental and private resources. In the 1960's, public expenditure on education increased at an annual rate of 11%. Despite a slowdown in this rate, education continues to absorb a growing share of total public expenditure and of GNP. In 62 dèveloping countries for which recent data are available, the median government spending on education is above 18% of total public expenditure, and the number of countries spending above 20% is increasing. The median public expenditure on education is about 4% of GNP. Again, there is a significant increase in the number of countries allocating 5% or more of their GNP to education.

All these efforts have been insufficient to provide education for more than about half of the children and adults in developing countries, and the projections for the next decade are not promising. Twenty-five of the poorest countries have only one-third of the primary age children enrolled. Although middle-income countries have achieved much higher enrollment ratios, the analysis shows that even there, more than one-fourth of the appropriate primary age group (excluding over-age children) does not attend school.

It is also important to realize that the numbers, both of those not attending school and of illiterates, will increase during the next decade if remedial action is not taken. Unesco has estimated the expansion of existing primary education systems in the developing world for the period up to 1985 based on most recent enrollment and population trends.[4] The projections of the in-school and out-of-school groups which are shown in Table 5 have drawn on this Unesco work.[5] It shows that school enrollments in the developing world may increase from 260 million to 350 million during the next ten years; in the lower-income countries of Groups I and II, enrollments may increase by 60 million, from 170 million to 230 million. The out-of-school groups may also increase from 290 million to 375 million, and from 220 million to 280 million, respectively.

---

[4] Educational Development, World and Regional Statistical Trends and Projections until 1985. A Unesco Background Paper prepared for the World Population Conference, Bucharest, 1974.

[5] The "out-of-school group" comprises those children in the age group 5-14 who have never attended school or who left school before completion.

Table 5

Projections of School Enrollments in Developing Countries
(In millions)

	1970	1975	1980	1985
5-14 age group population in all developing countries	481	550	630	725
Of whom in school	212	260	300	350
Of whom out of school	269	290	330	375
5-14 age group population in Group I and II countries	340	390	445	510
Of whom in school	141	170	200	230
Of whom out of school	199	220	245	280

While the overall literacy rate has increased during the 1960's from 41% to 50%, it is still as low as 26% in Africa. The number of illiterates in the age group above 15 increased during the decade from 701 million to 756 million, excluding the People's Republic of China. (See Table 6.) It is estimated that 470 million of those are in the Group I and II countries. The increase in the out-of-school group during the next decade will raise the number of adult illiterates in the developing world to 865 million.

The fact that a number of countries are now approaching the limits of their financial capability without having achieved even a minimum education for the majority of their populations raises some fundamental questions. These questions are related not only to the overall allocation of resources and their efficient use but, probably more importantly, to the redefinition of priorities within the education system and to the consideration of alternative strategies to meet educational needs within the limit of available resources.

Policy Alternatives

As has been discussed earlier, some form of mass education is a necessary part of any development strategy based on the fuller and more productive utilization of human resources. This is particularly important in lower-income countries where the provision of a minimum education is a necessary condition for the effective participation of the masses in productive life as well as in the social and political process. Mass education would also mean a step toward greater equity as it involves better distribution of educational opportunities to underprivileged groups.

In countries with high primary enrollment ratios, such as many in Latin America and Asia, mass education will be provided by the formal primary school system, supplemented by schemes designed to reach non-educated youths and adults. The major problems for these countries are: (a) to improve the quality and efficiency of the primary system, and (b) to increase its relevance for the majority of school leavers who will join the labor force. This may be a stage most developing countries will, in time, achieve. It would not be a feasible solution at present, however, for many lower-income countries— and most of the least developed ones—which face serious financial shortages at the very early stages of the development of their school systems. For example, when a country has achieved less than 40% enrollment of the primary school age group, but is already spending 15-18% of its total public expenditure on education, the expansion

Table 6

Estimated Number and Ratio of Illiterates in the Developing World, around 1960 and 1970

(In millions)

	Developing countries		Africa		Asia		Latin America	
Around 1960								
Males	295	50%	56	73%	224	45%	17	28%
Females	406	69%	68	88%	318	63%	23	37%
Total	701	59%	124	81%	542	55%	40	33%
Around 1970								
Males	306	40%	61	63%	231	37%	16	20%
Females	450	60%	82	84%	348	57%	23	27%
Total	756	50%	143	74%	579	47%	39	24%

Source: *Unesco Statistical Yearbook, 1972.*

of the conventional formal systems may not be financially viable. In such a case, governments should explore alternative approaches, at least as interim solutions.

Basic Education

Basic education is an attempt, despite severe resource constraints, to meet the needs of substantial portions of the population who do not have access to even minimum educational opportunities. It is a supplement, not a rival, to the formal education system, and is intended to provide a functional, flexible and low-cost education for those whom the formal system cannot yet reach or has already passed by. Although the primary cycle may be its principal vehicle in many countries, it differs from the conventional concept of "universal primary education" in three major respects:

(i) The objectives and content of basic education are functionally defined in terms of "minimum learning needs" of especially identified groups, and not as steps in the educational hierarchy (i.e., primary level).

(ii) The "target groups" of basic education are not necessarily school-age children. They may vary according to age (children, youths, adults) and socioeconomic characteristics (rural-urban groups, women, participants in particular development programs).

(iii) The "delivery systems" of basic education will take different forms in different countries (restructured primary schools, nonformal programs or various combinations of the two) adapted to the needs of different clienteles and to constraints upon resources. The costs will play a predominant role in the choice of educational technologies of basic education programs.

Minimum Learning Needs

A recent study[6] prepared for the United Nations Children's Fund (UNICEF) has defined "minimum learning needs" for individuals as a threshold level of learning required for participation in economic, social and political activities. These essential learning needs include functional literacy and numeracy (skill in using numbers), knowledge and skills for productive activity, family planning and health, child care, nutrition, sanitation and knowledge required for civic participation. They can be operationally defined as "minimum learning packages" to be attained by all, comparable to the term "poverty line" which refers to minimum family income. Minimum learning packages would vary according to the level and pattern of development and the relative poverty of each country.

The main features of the basic education programs for the low-income countries are:

(i) Formal primary schools are considered only as one part of a delivery system designed to reach children and youths in the earlier stages of their education. Other parallel programs such as the rural education centers in Upper Volta, which serve young people aged 15-20 years, can play an equally important role in providing education at that level. The use of traditional institutions is also possible, as in Mauritania, where the use of Koranic schools is being considered to provide basic education; or in Ethiopia, where village priests are being trained for educational work.

---

[6] Coombs, Philip H., with Prosser, R. C., and Ahmed, Manzoor. New Paths to Learning for Rural Children and Youth. New York: International Council for Educational Development, 1973.

296

(ii) Age of entry and length of study should be reconsidered, both for primary schools and other parallel schemes. A later start for a shorter course of study is seen as a way to reduce costs in order to broaden participation in education.

(iii) New and diversified programs are designed to take into account the terminal character of lower levels of education for the large majority of the participants.

(iv) Parallel changes are also introduced in teacher training, through the simplification of methods and localization of content and recruitment.

(v) There are cases where mass media, particularly radio, are used effectively in support of basic education programs.

(vi) In countries where teaching takes place in foreign languages, mother tongues are increasingly accepted as being more efficient learning vehicles for basic education.

Such an approach expresses a major principle of the report of the International Commission on the Development of Education, Learning to Be, that education should extend over lifetimes and not be confined to particular levels.[7] This approach will necessarily lead to significant changes in other parts of the educational system. It will, first, require a systematic effort to link education and work, through relatively short, nonformal, vocational, adolescent and adult training schemes, particularly for traditional and transitional sectors. Second, post-elementary education will need to be reoriented in order to match the changes introduced at the basic level.

It must be recognized that this approach frequently gives rise to controversies with important political and social dimensions. Objections are made that it creates a dual system—a standard primary school which provides access to higher levels of formal education, and a second-rate parallel structure which is terminal. This is considered a violation of the principle of equality of opportunity. Shortening the primary cycle and other cost-saving or simplifying proposals are opposed on grounds of educational quality. These objections are important, particularly since they are often supported by parents who perceive primary schools as being the only avenue for social advancement of their children.

These views are based, however, on an assumption that conventional primary schooling can accommodate all children within a reasonable time. This assumption is unrealistic for low-income countries which face a choice between a standard system serving only 30-40% of the children, and an alternative which aims at providing

---

[7] Faure, E., et al. Learning to Be. Paris: Unesco-Harrap, 1972.

some kind of education for all. Given this reality, the search for alternatives is both justified and probably inevitable. It is important, however, to avoid rigid definitions of structures, particularly as they relate to access to higher levels of education. Adequate methods and criteria of selection can be designed which preserve the chances for selective educational promotion of children and youths receiving nonformal basic education in proportions not too different from those in the formal primary cycle.

It may be possible to minimize or even eliminate the "dualism conflict" among the primary school age group by structural adjustments. Thus, a six-year primary cycle might be divided into two subcycles of four and two years. Most of the money available for primary education would be devoted to the first subcycle, thereby increasing the percentage of the age group receiving a minimum education. The remaining resources would be applied to the second subcycle, in the amount needed to prepare an equitably selected group for further education or training. As resources increased, enrollment percentages in this subcycle would also be increased until, ultimately, there was no rationing of opportunity at the primary level. It should be noted that, in this example, the content of the primary course would need to be revised so that instruction in each subcycle might be substantially self-contained. The broad estimates of worldwide needs and possibilities for primary basic education which follow are predicated on the possibility of modifying school structures in this way.

It has been shown earlier that school enrollments in the age group 5-14 of the country groups I and II with the lowest per capita GNP might increase from 170 million to 230 million during 1975-85 if the most recent trends in enrollment continue. Despite the increase, the out-of-school population would increase from 220 million to 280 million by 1985. It would be useful, therefore, to see how difficult it would be to reverse this trend, given two different assumptions.

Approximately 140 million new student places would be required by 1985 in primary education in the Group I and II countries to take care of the out-of-school group if the existing primary education systems of the world (averaging about six years for the cycle) were expanded without change. If we assume a four-year cycle of primary education, it might be possible to achieve the same aim by adding approximately 60 million new student places. An expansion of the primary education system without a structural change might require an average annual capital spending equal to about 18% of the total public expenditures in 1974 on education in the Group I and II countries. A restructured, four-year system might require capital expenditure equaling 8% of the same total. The annual recurrent increases in cost caused by the expansion would also be lower in a restructured primary system, and possibly average 2%, as against 5% in the traditional system.

The number of illiterates in the age group 15-44 increased during the last decade and will continue to increase. Unless existing adult education programs serving this age group and enrolling about 5 million students are expanded, the number of illiterates in Group I and II countries will continue to increase during the next decade from a current 355 million to 405 million.

Adult education is in its very early stages in most Group I and II countries. It is estimated, however, that all illiterates in the 15-44 age group could have an opportunity to participate in functional literacy or other basic education and training programs by the end of this century if programs for 12 million or 13 million adults per year were organized in addition to those already in existence. The programs would require capital expenditures of only about 1% of the total public education expenditures of Group I and II countries in 1974. The annual recurrent costs might be about 6% of their total public education expenditures.

Available data on costs are scarce and they vary considerably between countries. The above estimates should, therefore, be considered only as an illustration of the efforts needed to reach the population groups outside the current development sector and the existing education and training systems. They suggest that solutions are possible.

Education and Equity

Major Issues

The regressive character of educational systems and policies is a prevailing feature in most cases, irrespective of the level of development of countries. Educational systems not only fail to ensure mass participation, as discussed in the previous section; they also practice discrimination in their process of selection, promotion and future determination of careers. They show an elitist bias, favoring urban upper- and middle-income groups at the expense of the rural and urban poor. The appraisal of a recent sites and services project in Zambia showed that half the population of the capital was living in squatter areas, but all schools, with one exception, were located elsewhere. Consequently, the primary school enrollment was only 36% in the squatter areas, against 90% in the rest of the capital. Dropout and repetition rates were also higher among the squatters.

Students of higher-income origin have a greater chance not only of access to education, but also of promotion within the system. This is seen in the socioeconomic profile of the dropouts, repeaters and successful students, and in the fact that middle- and upper-income groups are particularly over-represented in higher education. In some countries, other factors, such as sex, ethnic origin or religion, play a role which is frequently combined with the effect of income levels. These inequalities are aggravated by differences in the quality of teachers, educational facilities and other inputs between schools serving different geographic areas and income groups. (See Annex 7.)

The system of educational finance reinforces the regressive character of education. Because of the combined effect of the tax systems and the pattern of distribution of education services, the concept of "free education", which is intended to assure equality of opportunity, in fact operates as a mechanism by which income is transferred from lower- and middle-income groups to upper-income categories. This is particularly true at the higher levels of education, where the public subsidy per student is particularly high. (The other implications of educational finance for such issues as demand management in education and ensuring a regular flow of resources into the system are discussed later.)

Policies

How to reach neglected target groups and equalize educational opportunities? Policies directed toward these objectives have traditionally been conceived only in terms of access to education. It is now evident that equalizing access to education is far from sufficient to ensure equal opportunity.

Equalizing access is, of course, a necessary first step. The appropriate location of educational facilities is a simple but effective instrument, particularly for lower levels of education where physical proximity is a major factor in determining enrollments. At higher levels, scholarship schemes and the provision of living accommodation can be used to reduce the barriers for the underprivileged.

Equalizing the chances for achievement is a more difficult objective. The important question here is the assessment of the school-related and other variables causing inequity and the identification of the factors which can be influenced by educational policies. Non-school variables, such as family characteristics, cannot be directly affected by educational policies. Schools can, however, be instrumental in providing to underprivileged children some of the elements lacking in their homes. A larger supply of good teachers, textbooks and reading and other learning materials would contribute to improving student achievement. These inputs, however, imply increased unit costs.

Methods of selection and promotion in education are among the school variables influencing student achievement. Examinations and diplomas are frequently criticized as factors reinforcing the regressive effects of education. Despite the progress noted in the use of more flexible aptitude and attitude tests, and notwithstanding some experience with the controversial "quota system" (i.e., introduction of quotas to equalize the chances for promotion of students from underprivileged areas or population groups), fully practical alternatives have not yet been developed.

The socioeconomic background of a student's family (income, parental attitude and level of education) appears to be a very important non-school variable influencing achievement. Yet it can only be partially affected unless changes are made in the overall income distribution pattern of a country. Even so, it would be useful to explore policies in areas such as parent education or school and community action which might compensate for the absence of an adequate home environment.

The financing of education is a powerful policy tool to achieve equity, as it determines the distribution of the financial burden of education. A modification of the regressive impact of public subsidies is essential. Subsidies should be used to increase the participation of underprivileged groups and not, as they are now, to support children from middle- and upper-income families. An income-related system of subsidies and fees can thus be instrumental in equalizing educational opportunities.

Equalizing educational opportunities should not be considered only in terms of the needs of the school-age children. Such policies should also address themselves to people who are already in the labor force in a way which goes beyond the conventional adult training programs. There are methods to provide working people with a "second chance" to continue or complete their education through full-time or part-time studies.

The preceding paragraphs deal only with the question of educational opportunities. They do not cover the broader issues relating education to income distribution and social mobility. Recent research and experience have raised a number of serious questions challenging some of the traditional assumptions about the effects of education on social mobility. Equalization of educational opportunities does not automatically generate significant changes in income distribution and social mobility. The impact of education on mobility appears to be determined essentially by the pattern of stratification and the socioeconomic system of rewards in each society. Knowledge of these relationships is fragmented and limited, particularly in developing countries, since most of the research has been done in developed countries. It is possible to state, as a general proposition, that in the absence of other supportive social and economic action, isolated efforts in education would have only a limited effect on mobility. To achieve significant results, educational policies should be formulated within the context of a broader social policy.

Increasing Efficiency in Education

Major Issues

Educational systems in most developing countries are inefficient in using resources and often do not achieve their quantitative and qualitative objectives. The shortage of good teachers has been and continues to be a major handicap. Though the number of primary teachers has so far been adequate, their training has left much to be desired. The problems caused by the low quality of teachers in secondary education are aggravated by quantitative shortages, particularly in science and technology. Many countries face serious difficulties in developing teacher training schemes which correspond to changing needs. Efforts to upgrade teachers are usually limited and fragmented. School systems are frequently managed without proper attention to the effective utilization and supervision of teachers. Effective utilization is particularly important, since teacher costs, which range from 75% to 95%, are by far the most important single factor determining education expenditures.

The findings of recent research tend to challenge some of the assumptions concerning the relationships between class size, level of training of teachers, and student achievement. In a study on student achievement in secondary schools in some 20 countries, including four developing ones, it has been reported that there was no significant correlation between class size (within reasonable ranges) and student performance in certain subjects.[8] Another study in a Latin American country indicates that students do almost as well when studying under normal school-trained teachers as they do when they are taught by university graduates. The implications for saving money are significant. These results should be interpreted with care to avoid hasty generalizations for less developed countries and those types of education, such as vocational training, which were not covered by the studies. They do indicate, however, that the scope for improve-

---

[8]*A survey organized by the International Association for the Evaluation of Educational Achievement (IEA).*

ment in the cost-effective use of teachers may be greater than was traditionally assumed.

The design and efficient use of learning materials and equipment constitute another problem, one which is caused by inadequate curricula and methods of learning. There are, however, serious problems in the production, distribution and utilization of equipment. In many developing countries, students and teachers do not have enough basic textbooks. In 11 countries with annual per capita incomes of under $250, the average annual production is less than one textbook per student (Annex 10). Those few textbooks which are available are often irrelevant. In view of their importance in improving student achievement, larger local production of textbooks, especially in mother languages, is of high priority. The supply of other equipment used in learning is even more limited. Total spending for textbooks and other learning aids is often less than 5% of the education budget; it might be about 10-15% to meet a minimum standard for effective learning. Imported equipment is usually too costly and too complex, and is not adapted to local conditions. Even when available, it frequently is unused because the knowhow required for maintenance and utilization is lacking. The local design, economic production and effective use of various types of learning materials are critical but neglected tasks.

One of the strongest reinforcements of poverty is the lack of adequate nutrition for both childbearing mothers and their children. The mental capabilities of children can be permanently impaired in the very early years by nutritional deficiency. Though feeding programs in schools are valuable to the improvement of student performance, they often come too late in a child's life to avoid early damage. The major contribution of education in the area of nutrition may be through the instruction of parents in matters of diet, food handling and other rudiments of home economics. It may also be expected that adult education in aspects of nutrition will be most effective when combined with food programs.

Malnutrition and related illnesses affect student performance by reducing the child's motivation and his ability to concentrate and learn. In a study carried out in four Latin American countries, it was found that children miss more than 50 days of school a year (25-30% of the scheduled school days) because of illnesses which may be related to malnutrition, compared with an average of 10 days or less per year in the developed countries.

These inefficiencies are first reflected in the performance of the school systems, and in dropout and repeater rates. According to Unesco statistics, the median dropout rate for the first level of education is 58% in Group I countries, against only 10% in Group V countries. In many countries, it takes more than 10 years to produce one graduate of the 5-6 year primary cycle, and about one-fourth of the education budget is spent on students who drop out in the first three grades. (See Table 7.)

The performance of educational systems is also assessed in measurements of student achievement. Most research in this area concerns developed countries. The IEA survey studies student achievement, but it covers only four developing countries. It is important, however, to encourage local research in developing countries to measure student achievement in relation to a range of socioeconomic goals and conditions.

Table 7

Internal Efficiency [1]

	Percentage of dropouts		
	Lowest	Median	Highest
I. Estimated percentage of dropouts in cohorts entering primary education around 1960			
A. Countries by per capita GNP			
I —Up to $120	27.9	57.5	81.3
II— $121-250	13.2	49.0	75.5
III—$251-750	8.8	45.1	74.7
IV —$751-1,500	6.7	45.7	60.6
V —Over $1,500	0.7	9.7	56.8
B. Countries in Major Regions			
Africa	26.2	54.0	81.3
Latin America	33.1	61.6	74.7
Asia	0.7	20.2	64.0
Europe	0.7	18.3	48.3
II. Estimated percentage of dropouts in cohorts entering senior secondary education around 1960			
A. Countries by per capita GNP			
I —Up to $120	5.0	43.2	47.9
II —$121-250	5.2	46.0	62.0
III—$251-750	5.0	28.3	69.1
IV —$751-1,500	11.4	13.9	23.4
V —Over $1,500	4.8	15.0	22.1
B. Countries in Major Regions			
Africa	7.5	41.9	61.4
Latin America	8.5	18.5	28.3
Asia	4.8	18.1	57.8
Europe	8.2	11.4	21.8

[1] The survey covered the educational systems of 58 countries for the years 1960-61 and 1967-68.
Source: Based on data compiled by Unesco.

Inadequate structures create other problems of efficiency. The education structure is often dominated by a formal system which is both chronologically graded and age-specific. Because of the hierarchical structure, formal education operates with rigid entrance and exit levels. Those who fail to enter at the specific levels may forever lose educational opportunities; those who do not leave with proper certificates at the exit levels are considered failures.

Policies

The first step towards improved efficiency would be to make more specific the educational and training objectives and the performance standards of formal as well as nonformal learning systems. What is the minimum level of reading comprehension or numeracy skill needed to fill a specific role in rural development? What are the bases—educational, social, psychological—which should determine what percentage of students, if any, should repeat a grade? What kinds of behavior should schools elicit in a developing society? Encouraging countries to provide answers to these types of questions would improve their prospects for achieving greater efficiency in education.

The second step is to identify the factors most likely to affect efficiency. What are the major factors responsible for high dropout and repeater rates? Are they school factors, such as the system of promotion, the distance to school, social tensions, the language of teaching, antiquated examination or testing systems, or a stultifying approach to teaching? Or are other factors more important, such as poor health, inability to pay fees or other expenses, or the need to work? It is essential for administrators to assess the causes of inefficiency in the particular social and educational environments of their countries and to design cost-effective measures to cope with them.

The level of training and remuneration of teachers may have important educational and financial implications. Overqualified teachers may not necessarily assure a better quality of education. Shorter periods of teacher training, supported by in-service training, could lead to significant savings, as could larger class sizes at the middle levels. Class sizes at those levels are generally not large now, and though an increase of 10-15% would not lower the quality of education, the savings achieved could be used either to reduce current costs by some 8-10% or to provide funds for activities known to improve learning. The type of teacher training institution also affects efficiency. In some cases, the smaller and locally based primary teacher training colleges can be more effective than large urban-

305

based schools in assuring a better deployment of teachers and an adaptation of the training to local conditions.

There are other measures which can save money or which can be implemented without increasing overall costs. Adapting the school calendar to the calendar of local economic activities may improve attendance. Flexible promotion methods, combined with multigrade teaching, could lead to more effective use of teaching resources. Teaching in national languages would improve learning rates and student attitudes to schooling.

Many measures, however, would have important cost implications. It is estimated, in a typical case, that the improvements educators traditionally recommend—smaller class sizes, better learning aids and more highly trained teachers—would increase annual recurrent costs by 75%. To counter this effect, for example, teachers could learn to prepare, by themselves or with the help of students, some of the teaching materials and apparatus. Essential but costly manufactured equipment may be kept in central facilities or mobile units which serve a number of schools.

Programs involving the use of such mass media as educational radio and television should be designed on the basis of careful analysis of costs and the capacity for the production of educational material. Emphasis should be placed on logistical problems, such as the distribution and maintenance of receivers, spare parts and other materials. The unit cost of radio or televised instruction can be very high for small numbers of students but declines sharply as the numbers increase. In the Ivory Coast's television project, for example, the estimated annual recurrent cost per student was $115 for 21,000 students and $6 for 700,000 students. It should also be remembered that where technical problems or costs make television prohibitive, radio may be a useful and cheaper substitute.

Preparing teachers to perform a new role in a changing educational technology is of crucial importance. Teachers are now expected to accept educational broadcasting not merely as a substitute for the blackboard, but as a vehicle to introduce improved curricula and new subject matter into the classroom. The best way to secure the co-operation of teachers is to involve them with the work of the broadcasting teacher in all phases of the program. Such cooperation will help secure a better product as well.

Better nutrition may be an important factor in increasing the return on educational investment. Feeding programs and others directed to improving the performance of those already in school—as well as programs aimed at pregnant mothers and younger children—may have a high rate of return. Nutrition influences the quality of education, and education can influence the quality of nutrition. Primary schools, teacher training colleges, agricultural training institutions, adult literacy programs and mass media can all provide nutritional education in their regular curricula.

There are, finally, ways to vary the structure of education systems so as to maximize both efficiency and educational opportunities. By varying the length and number of cycles in the formal system (and consequently the number of exit points), and by varying the progression rate from one cycle to the next, it is possible not only to broaden the base of enrollment, but also to respond more readily to the changing needs and possibilities in the system as a whole. To the traditional six years of primary, followed by three years of lower and three of upper secondary (6-3-3), a number of modifications can be made (e.g., 4-4-4 or 4-2-2-4). Each will serve different needs for schooling and initially larger percentages of the entering age group.

Structural variations may also be combined with patterns of school location to achieve a better distribution of education. In a 4-2-3-3 structure, the intermediate years—or part of them—may be provided in smaller, localized, satellite schools which feed into a larger school for the upper cycle, thus minimizing the need for boarding accommodations. This structure is now being introduced in Peru.

Close articulation between formal, nonformal and even informal systems can help to distribute the education workload more efficiently. It may be advantageous, for example, to upgrade the traditional (informal) systems of child care and preschool education by (nonformal) adult programs, thus avoiding expensive, formal, kindergarten instruction.

Once programs of basic education have been established, the critical task for many countries is the elaboration of follow-up vocational training in both rural and urban areas. This may take many forms—on or off the job—short courses at vocational or rural training centers, apprenticeship, youth groups, extension work, cooperatives, mass communication media and mobile training units. They may directly follow the completion of basic education or they may take place at intervals later. These nonformal "delivery systems" may prove to be more cost effective than the replication of formal education and training institutions at the lower and upper secondary levels.

Efficiency has so far been discussed in terms of structures and resources for educational institutions. Efficiency can also be discussed when choosing between alternative educational technologies, especially for vocational education and training. Attention has been focused on the comparison of vocational and technical schools with production-related or on-the-job training programs. Recent debates on "the vocational school fallacy" tend to create a bias in favor of on-the-job training programs, particularly for those with middle- and lower-level skills. This conclusion has not been substantiated by a Bank research project on the "Cost Effectiveness of Alternative Learning Technologies in Industrial Training",[9] which finds no evidence to support the claims for a clear-cut superiority of one technology over the other. Factors such as the "skill" category, the size of the target group, the teaching methods, and particularly the cost of equipment used for training, determine the efficiency and economy of the particular technology.

Improving Management and Planning Capacity

Major Issues

As enrollments, educational personnel, schools, and expenditures continue to increase, the management of education becomes a task of formidable magnitude and complexity. Experience reveals that educational planning, as understood only a decade ago, is inadequate, and that new approaches need to be developed. In most other respects—administrative structure, policy formation, operational procedures, research, information systems and evaluation—the elements of modern management are not yet available.

A major challenge faced by developing countries is to find better ways to channel private demand for education into socially beneficial areas. Countries must not only eliminate distortions between supply and demand, but also make educational systems more responsive to new development policies. It is evident that changes in the pattern of demand would require interventions not only in the education systems (structural and institutional reforms and changes in educational content and technology, etc.) but in other areas as well, such as the labor market. In orienting educational policy making toward social and economic utility, a comprehensive policy is needed to cover areas generally beyond the scope of conventional practices. Policy makers in education are usually not equipped to view their field in this broader context, especially in its interactions with employment and finance.

The structure of administration is another source of difficulty for the design and effective implementation of comprehensive educational policies. Educational responsibilities are often dispersed. Ministries of education, labor, agriculture, health, etc., control most educational training institutions. Their activities are seldom properly

---

[9] Zymelman, Manuel. Bank Staff Working Paper No. 169. December 1973.

308

coordinated. The lack of effective coordination at the local level causes further complications. Various agencies are directly linked to their respective ministries in the capital without being connected with other local units. A serious shortage of qualified middle-level managers in education hampers coordination within the administration. Poor communications with the public also create additional difficulties in generating popular support for new educational policies.

One fundamental issue in the effective management of education is political. The inability of political decision makers and education managers to communicate with each other is frequently a cause of failure in the implementation of educational policies and plans. It is important for both groups to have a clear idea of the objectives that education is expected to fulfill. Confusion about objectives or lack of consensus among educators and politicians have often been a major reason for failure. No planning method, however sophisticated, can substitute for a clear understanding of objectives. Planners must, however, take into account the political context within which educational policies have to be formulated. Political pressures generated by popular demand for certain types of education sometimes leave little scope for governments to consider other options. Designing politically feasible alternatives and preparing technical solutions which avoid political tensions are formidable challenges for educational planners.

Policies

(i) *New Approaches to Planning:* Two approaches to educational planning have customarily claimed attention—the rate of return approach and the manpower approach. The wide use of rate of return analysis in other sectors makes its use appealing in education since, theoretically, it could thus establish a basis for comparing and establishing intersectoral, as well as intrasectoral, priorities. Despite considerable efforts to develop rate of return analyses as an operational tool in education, it has so far been impossible to resolve many of the methodological and practical difficulties, either for sector or project analysis.[10] Estimates of manpower requirements have been more widely used although this method suffers from many of the same limitations. They include, notably, the limited reliability of its demand estimates given the long lead time required to produce the supply, the scarcity of knowledge about the ability to substitute skills and, more generally, about the behavior of the labor market.

---

[10] *Thias, Hans Heinrich, and Carnoy, Martin.* Cost-Benefit Analysis in Education—A Case Study of Kenya. *World Bank Staff Occasional Papers, No. 14. Baltimore and London: The Johns Hopkins University Press, 1972.*

The developments in basic and nonformal education foreseen in the next decade or so will raise further problems in the use of both of these techniques. Both methods are exclusively quantitative and are dependent upon data relevant to the modern sector, such as growth rates of GNP, wages, productivity, visible employment rates, occupations, and formal education costs. Though they can suggest how much (of the same type of) education is needed, they say nothing—as presently practiced—about who is to receive it. These methods, therefore, bypass the key questions of equalizing educational opportunities and participation, especially for people in the traditional sectors.

Despite these limitations, manpower planning can yield meaningful results in some specific areas. Occupational categories related to science and technology (and, more generally, all the skills for which no substitutes are readily available) can be subject to conventional methods of manpower analysis. A new and emerging economic activity for which no labor market yet exists could also be planned with the help of manpower considerations. A broader approach to planning is needed, however, to include analysis of both the demand and supply of trained manpower and of the socioeconomic environment within which the adjustment process between them takes place.

Though it has yet to be elaborated fully in practical terms, "cohort analysis" may become a useful tool for planning in the present context. While the unit of observation in conventional educational planning is the proportion of the population enrolled in and processed by the education system (the enrollment pyramid), cohort analysis is based on the idea of following the major steps in the life cycle of the total age group. This involves those who enter the system as well as those who are excluded. The steps include enrollment and promotion within the education-training systems, both formal and nonformal, and the absorption into the labor market (employment-unemployment, occupation, income, etc.) of all the groups, whether graduates or dropouts, leaving the system. This approach to planning provides a convenient way of viewing formal and nonformal education as a single learning system, and of analyzing its relationships with the labor market. It also embraces a longer time span than the age period of formal education, and is thus in line with the concept of "lifelong education."

Cohort analysis requires a broad information base covering not only the school population, but the educational and employment status of the whole age group. In some cases, such information can be obtained through special tabulations of available census data, school statistics and other survey results. But a fully fledged use of this approach may require the collection of new information, particularly in the area relating jobs to educational background. Tracer studies have been introduced in about ten education projects supported by the World Bank. A recent study in Thailand showed that while the vocational school graduates were readily employed and had no serious employment problems, an increasing percentage of them were entering higher institutions, and were taking subjects for which their vocational studies were less well suited. Tracer studies permit, therefore, a following of educational vocational careers of identifiable-age cohorts and of the impact on these of specific educational measures. It would, therefore, be useful to incorporate tracer systems into major educational programs.

More disaggregated analysis (by regions, economic sectors and social groups) is another essential feature of educational planning. Modern and traditional sectors cannot be grouped together in terms of their educational training requirements. Some specific social or occupational categories may need to be treated separately. Where, for example, it is government policy to improve the condition of a hitherto underprivileged group, or where the government wishes to test the impact of a new policy on different sectors of society, the disaggregated approach will have to be used.

(ii) *Educational Reform:* The implementation of new educational policies depends largely on substantial changes in the organization and structure of education systems. This implies that not only must existing institutions be changed, but that new ones must be created and developed as well. Political determination and effective management are essential for designing, initiating and implementing educational reforms. A critical question in considering reforms is the scope and pace of change on the basis of a realistic assessment of the country's readiness. Awareness by the public of the need for change is the starting point for the development of a climate conducive to reform.

(iii) *Educational Finance:* Educational finance raises questions of management affecting most aspects of educational policy. References have already been made to the implications of finance in such educational areas as supply, demand and equity. It would now be useful to present a more general picture of the role of finance as a policy tool for education.

An important function of the system of finance is to provide a regular flow of funds into the educational system to meet its current needs as well as its planned expansion. The critical issue is how to deal with the increasing burden of education on public finance. A number of ways can be suggested to broaden the sources of revenue for education beyond the limits of regular government budgets. They include various methods by which those who receive an education pay a greater share of its costs. Self-help is one way in which contributions may be elicited from whole communities. Earmarking certain revenues or tax levies on the total wage bill of business firms is another example, though it has usually been linked with specific types of education such as industrial training or adult literacy. Student loan schemes are also intended to lighten the burden of the government's education budget, although the available evidence suggests that the overall impact of student loans is rather limited.

The mode of financing can affect demand for education. The cost of education (fees, other expenses and income forgone), relative to the incomes of various segments of the population, is one factor determining demand. Subsidies and fees adjusted for different types and levels of education could, therefore, play a role in controlling the level and structure of demand. In some cases, the demand for certain types of education can be influenced by the use of nonmonetary contributions such as direct work schemes to encourage enrollments in vocational schools. Equity in education is also sensitive to alternative modes of financing.

Despite increasing knowledge about the relationships between education and finance, many financial measures need to be further developed and tested. The question, moreover, goes beyond the definition of specific policy measures or tools. These tools need to be related to each other to form a coherent education policy. A system of fees, if narrowly conceived, can, for example, defeat the principle of equal opportunity. There is, furthermore, the need for these measures to be consistent not only with education policies, but with overall finance policies as well. The earmarking of certain public revenues for education, while appealing to educators, may be an unsound fiscal practice.

(iv) *Research and Development for Education Policy:* In managing education systems, decisions must be made about a broad range of questions frequently not covered by traditional education policies or by available information and analysis. This means that some critical decisions will have to be made in uncertainty, without the benefit of past and current experience and, in many cases, without adequate research and information. In this context, policy making and implementation should be seen as a learning process conceived to improve one's knowledge about the behavior of education systems. Experimentation and feedback must be considered as regular components of major operations. Such an approach to policy making requires adequate research and development. Since research capability is limited and difficult to develop, a "research strategy" must be designed to establish priorities in the development and utilization of the resources of research. Policy-oriented research requires familiarity with local conditions. The development of local research capacity in less developed countries is, therefore, of high priority.

The creation of machinery for regular evaluation is essential for the effective management of education, as it is the main channel through which research and development can be introduced into decision making. Evaluation also contributes to the better design of educational schemes, by requiring a clear, operational formulation of their objectives. It plays an important role in the assessment of the results of various new measures, whether they are related to cost effectiveness, to internal efficiency and qualitative improvement, or to the contribution to development. Authorities on education have been increasingly aware of the need for independent machinery for formative evaluation which would be built into the educational system. Few countries, however, have so far established such regular mechanisms. A current Bank research project is aimed to help meet this need.

Chapter 3: THE WORLD BANK'S EDUCATION LENDING POLICY AND PROGRAM

Through its lending for education, the World Bank seeks to foster, in a variety of ways, developmental objectives tailored to the needs of its developing member countries. Under the circumstances that have been described—the great variety of conditions within developing countries and the uniqueness of each country's development strategy—the Bank's policy for education must have a high degree of diversity in its application. No single formula or strategy can meet the needs of all the Bank's borrowers. An analysis of educational profiles of countries with different levels of income and stages of development shows, however, some patterns which can help the Bank adjust its response to the differing priority needs of countries.

A basic premise is that the Bank's operations should reflect its overall policies. The Bank is deeply concerned with the problems and needs of low-income countries and with the promotion of development strategies designed to improve the well-being of the lower 40% of the population through increased productivity and employment and improved income distribution. The Bank's activities in lending for education increasingly reflect this concern. But while this is a new and dramatic feature of Bank policy, it should not obscure the fact that the World Bank will continue to assist countries which, although having moved to higher levels of development, still require help. A flexible response, adjusted to the variety of conditions in all developing countries, will govern the Bank's activities in education.

Meeting the minimum learning needs of the uneducated masses to ensure that they can both contribute to and benefit from economic and social development is a major task for the poorest countries. The development of low-cost and functional, basic education programs, through the restructuring of primary education and/or other methods, should be emphasized in such countries. In many cases, a necessary complement would include the concentration on rural training for related target groups within the framework of broader rural development schemes. Conversely, the development of upper levels of formal education should be selectively and carefully planned, taking into account both the limited absorptive capacity for labor in the modern sector, and the need for local leadership and technical skills in both the public and private sectors.

The development of secondary and post-secondary levels of education will take a more central place in the education strategies of the middle- and higher-income countries. Where first-level education is already widely available, the development of skills to meet the needs of increasingly sophisticated economies will have priority. In determining the rate of expansion of their education systems, as well as in defining their internal priorities and the choice of institutions and technologies, these countries will have major policy concerns of their own. They must strike a balance between the overall supply of and demand for educated manpower, matching the educational output with the particular needs of the economy and the efficient use of their resources. Middle- and higher-income countries must improve their planning capabilities (no less than the poorer countries), and they must place emphasis on educational reforms as well. These countries will have to pay increasing attention to providing educational opportunities for the urban and rural poor.

Differences in the educational strategies of developing countries will be heightened by the differing effects on their economies and development prospects of the recent changes in the world economy. At one extreme, it is estimated that the per capita GNP of seven members of the Organization of Petroleum Exporting Countries (OPEC) will increase by 8.4% per year during the period 1973-80. For such countries, financial constraints will be minor or non-existent. Indeed, it is clear that they intend to expand education as fast as possible. At the other extreme, ten countries with an annual per capita GNP of less than $200 are estimated to have growth rates during the same period of minus 0.4%. It is not yet clear whether such countries, faced with worsening economic prospects, will be able to stick to their goals of expanding educational opportunities, or whether their educational priorities will change. Their reactions to worldwide economic changes need to be followed closely so that the Bank can develop ways and means to respond to their needs in a timely and adequate manner.

These examples illustrate the differing considerations which must be brought to bear in framing lending programs for individual countries. It would be useful, therefore, to view these new considerations against the background of the Bank's earlier and more recent experience in this sector.

Bank Policy and Activities: 1963-74

By 1961, it had become clear to the World Bank that the lack of qualified manpower in developing countries was a serious obstacle to the successful implementation of many of its own projects in particular and to the process of economic development in general. As a result, the belief grew that investment in education was not only consistent with the Bank's objectives, but would be a desirable addition to its activities. In 1962, the first education project was presented to the Executive Directors. Later, in October 1963, a Memorandum from the President on "Proposed Bank/IDA Policies in the Field of Education" was issued in which the basic statement of policy with respect to the types of projects to be financed was set forth.

The major point of the policy statement was that "the Bank and IDA should be prepared to consider financing a part of the capital requirements of priority education projects designed to produce, or to serve as a necessary step in producing, trained manpower of the kinds and in the numbers needed to forward economic development in the member country concerned. In applying this criterion, the Bank and IDA should concentrate their attention, at least at the present stage, on projects in the fields of (a) vocational and technical education and training at various levels, and (b) general secondary education. Other kinds of education projects would be considered only in exceptional cases."

Adhering to this policy, the Bank concentrated on high-priority projects (usually related to the modern sector) within a country's educational development plan. Emphasis was placed on the training of critically needed types of manpower insofar as those needs had been identified.

With increased knowledge and experience, the Bank's approach to education widened in the late 1960's. In a Memorandum for the

Executive Directors in July 1970, the President reaffirmed the first sentence of his 1963 statement quoted above, but added: "In applying this criterion in future, we should broaden the scope of projects considered and we should determine priorities and select projects on the basis of a thorough examination of the education systems as a whole rather than by a priori designated areas of eligibility which may not relate to the particular country. We should continue to emphasize projects which, like vocational training, produce trained manpower directly but we should also consider for financing other types of projects . . . which should have important long-term significance for economic development." Such projects, the Memorandum added, would be "designed to encourage changes which improve the relevance, efficiency or economy of education systems."

As a consequence, the scope of the Bank's education operations increased to cover not only "hardware" projects in restricted subsectors, but a mixture of "hardware" and "software" projects. These projects were based on sector analysis and were aimed at achieving qualitative improvements, as well as meeting crucial manpower needs. Bank lending was also increasingly marked by experimental approaches, incorporating such innovations as educational television, production of learning materials, support for curriculum development and educational planning and management, mobile training units, and the training of health personnel.

These developments can be seen in the profile of the Bank's lending in education presented in Table 8.

The period covering the fiscal years 1963-71 was characterized by strong support for technical and vocational education (29%) and agricultural education and training (15%). Most lending (44%) went to general secondary education, largely in the form of comprehensive schools offering specialized options of pre-vocational education at the upper level in agricultural, industrial and commercial subjects. Teacher training institutions absorbed about 12% of the lending. Although a precise breakdown between rural and urban locations is not possible, urban groups preparing to work in the modern sector or act as modernizing agents in the rural sector were given priority in most instances. Other than teacher training, little was done in support of primary education, and with a few notable exceptions, universities were not assisted. A few projects for adult training— which would now be called nonformal education—were supported, but most Bank assistance went to the formal education system. Technical assistance amounted to less than 5% of the volume of lending.

A comparison of the lending during 1972-74 with the figures for 1963-71 shows that a shift began in the pattern of Bank educational financing. For example, the heavy concentration on the secondary level during the earlier period started to give way to greater support for primary and basic education and for the training of adults and youths. Technical assistance increased from less than 5% to over 7%. Moreover, the number of projects which included Bank-financed technical assistance rose from an average of 56% for the earlier period, to 90% in 1974. Relatively new items such as the production of learning materials, curriculum development and planning, which had only occasionally been assisted in the past, received more regular attention. They have more recently accounted for 5-10% of the funds. (See Annexes 2-5.)

The shift observed during the 1972-74 period is further confirmed in the projected lending program for 1974-78. Primary and basic education (which includes the education of youths and adults) is expected to absorb about a quarter of the total lending for education. Though the share of secondary, and especially higher, levels of education will decline, it will still account for about 75% of the total. The implications of the projected program for the Bank's objectives in lending for education will be analyzed later in this paper.

Table 8

Distribution of Education Lending [1]
(Fiscal years)

	1963-71 Actual (%)	1972-74 Actual (%)	1974-78 Projected (%)
By levels			
Primary and basic	5	11	27
Intermediate	72	48	43
Higher	23	41	30
	100	100	100
By curricula			
General and comprehensive	44	43	31
Technical	29	24	23
Agricultural	15	17	24
Teacher training	12	14	12
Health	—	2	10
	100	100	100
By outlay			
Construction	61	49	54
Equipment and furniture	34	44	37
Technical assistance	5	7	9
	100	100	100

[1] Through fiscal 1974, the World Bank and IDA had approved financial assistance for 99 education projects with a total project cost of US$1,936 million and a total lending amount of US$1,059 million. Of this lending, Eastern Africa, Western Africa, Asia (excluding the Middle East), Europe and the Middle East, and Latin America and the Caribbean absorbed 16%, 15%, 27%, 25% and 17%, respectively.

317

Objectives of Bank Lending for Education

The Bank seeks to promote balanced educational development based on the following broad principles:

(a) That there should be at least a minimum basic education for all as fully and as soon as available resources permit and the course of development requires.

(b) That further education and training beyond the basic level should be provided selectively to improve quantitatively and qualitatively the knowledge and skills necessary for the performance of economic, social and other developmental roles.

(c) That a national system of education should be viewed as a comprehensive learning system embracing formal, nonformal and informal education and working with maximum possible internal and external efficiency.

(d) That in the interest of both increased productivity and social equity, educational opportunities should be equalized as fully as possible.

Some considerations of particular importance in the pursuit of these objectives follow.

Dealing with Basic/Primary Education

The Bank's interest in basic education is closely related to its efforts in promoting a broader approach to development. Basic education is conceived as a means by which the minimum learning needs of the masses will be met so as to ensure effective participation in the development process by all. Basic education can thus be instrumental in increasing the productivity as well as improving the opportunities of underprivileged groups.

It is expected that most countries, particularly those with already high primary enrollment ratios, will meet the needs for mass education through an expansion of the formal primary system. For those countries, the Bank will give particular attention to curriculum and other reforms which take account of the needs of the many who will not continue beyond the primary cycle.

The Bank will encourage those countries having the lowest primary enrollment ratios and working under severe financial constraints to review and revise their education structures to meet the need for low-cost, minimum, mass education.

In all cases, the Bank will assist in the development of a wide variety of education and training for adolescents and adults, either as follow-up programs for those who have had primary education, or, in the more extreme cases, as a substitute for non-existent primary schools.

The Bank will encourage the integration of basic education with other rural and urban development programs. Education programs may be asked to serve different target groups whose development needs will be met through a combination of assistance programs. In Bank projects, the integration can take place by including education and training in comprehensive rural development or urban settlement projects. The education and training should, however, always be viewed as a part of a total education delivery system.

The Bank must guard against the serious danger of creating prototypes (multipurpose institutions serving whole communities, rural training centers) which are too elaborate and expensive to be replicable on the desired scale. The central purpose of basic education programs is to meet the minimum learning needs of the many within the limits of available resources. Standards for and costs of at least the first generation of institutional models should be consistent with this purpose.

Other important elements mentioned in the second part of this paper which contribute to a broader dissemination of basic and primary education, and to which the Bank will give particular attention, will be: (a) language planning and development for the greater use of mother language(s); (b) the use of electronic media and the production of learning materials for both formal and nonformal basic education; (c) improvement of the capabilities of local managers through appropriate administrative reorganization and/or training; such reorganization and training will often be needed for other sectors of rural development and might be assisted more effectively for all sectors together; (d) an essential corollary of (c) is the localizing of procurement and support through local taxation and other contributions, self-help construction schemes and the multiple use of qualified local people.

In Table 8 we have noted an increase from 11% in 1972-74 to 27% for 1974-78 in the estimated share of the Bank's education lending devoted to primary and basic education. Based on current estimates, the volume of lending for primary and basic education in 1974-78 would equal about $280 million in constant prices. To this figure should be added an estimated $90 million for education components included in rural development and "sites and services" projects. Total lending for primary and basic education may, therefore, reach the $350-400 million level. Though this amount should be manageable, it will challenge the capabilities of both the Bank and its borrowers, given the still highly experimental "state of the art."

The most important contribution the Bank could make during the next four years would be to use the period to "tool up" for a substantially greater attack on worldwide educational needs after 1978. This "tooling up" would embrace not only refinements of project criteria, planning, staffing and acquisition of experience within the Bank; it would also include a many-sided effort within the developing countries themselves to increase their capabilities and prepare for a major thrust to be launched in the later 1970's. It would include (a) operational research into demographic, social, geographical and economic conditions related to basic education; (b) development work in curricula, teacher training, institutional models, project design, physical facilities and the use of mass media; (c) planning, policy formation, legislation and budgeting by governments; (d) administrative reorganization and management training necessary to achieve the decentralized, yet coordinated, execution required by a major program; and (e) systematic monitoring and evaluation of ongoing operations.

The effort envisaged here should not be limited to the Bank and its borrowers alone. If the obstacles of mass illiteracy and ignorance are to be lifted from the path of development, the task will demand a common effort by interested educational assistance agencies, almost all of which are already giving the highest priority to meeting the need for basic education. Preliminary steps to form channels for cooperative action are now being taken. These channels can prove to be a potential vehicle for mounting a massive attack upon this most formidable problem of educational development. They can also provide an opportunity for the Bank to help crystallize sentiment for action among agencies and member countries.

The Development of Skills

There will continue to be a shortage of middle- and high-level manpower in specific areas in many developing countries. The Bank will, therefore, continue to support the development of skills to meet the needs of vocational and professional manpower in the urban and rural sectors. The Bank will utilize the experience it has gained in previous lending for the development of skills, and a major part of Bank funds for educational development will continue to flow into this sector up to 1978. The financing will cover secondary and post-secondary institutions, training centers and university institutions in agriculture, industry, science, commerce, management, pedagogy, health and other education and training sectors. The assistance will continue to include reconstruction of buildings, the purchase of equipment, development of curricula, the production and use of learning materials (including textbooks), and staff training. Technical assistance, utilizing local experts where possible, will be included.

The Bank has financed general secondary education, including comprehensive education projects, in the past. It will continue to do so to the extent that it supports the development of skills and the programs mentioned above. Comprehensive schools may often meet education needs in societies at a fairly advanced stage of development. They are, however, relatively costly, and the experience of Bank-assisted comprehensive schools indicates that the concept might be less relevant in poor countries with low school enrollments. It might sometimes be preferable to replace comprehensive education by a combination of general education and short, accelerated training courses.

The Bank will continue to use manpower analysis in assessing educational and training needs; it will, however, broaden the scope and perspective of such analysis to cover those categories (of skills and population, for instance) not covered by conventional manpower techniques. In this analysis, the Bank will continue to take account of the tendency of many education systems to generate surpluses of educated manpower and, as a result, will point out the need for explicit government policies on rationing and pricing secondary and post-secondary education. Wherever possible, tracer studies will be included in education projects.

The Bank will develop and apply new techniques for cost effectiveness analyses in the choice of alternative forms of vocational training. These techniques will be applied particularly in assessing the advantages and disadvantages of in-plant training institutions, as against the development of formal vocational schools.

The Bank will continue to finance training components in projects in agriculture, tourism, transportation, public utilities and other sectors at the post-basic level of education. Though there is no clear line between such project-related training provided as part of a system development, there are some criteria which can help to determine how to deal with a need for training which has been generated by project financing. Among such criteria are the urgency of the need, the degree of specificity of the skills and the length of the training period. As a general rule, training components attached to projects will result in more experience than if training were conducted as part of a regular education program. Its execution will require more Bank attention and manpower.

Efficiency

The Bank will continue to encourage efforts to increase cost-consciousness in the management of education and support the development of cost-effective education programs and projects. Methods

321

of learning which can save money will also be supported. The Bank will, therefore, assist in developing managerial abilities in education, and will provide technical assistance to develop local participation in educational activities in both rural areas and urban settlements.

The Bank will actively promote the best combination of high educational achievement and low costs in three specific ways:

(i) Encourage the application of substantial research findings which indicate that class sizes may be increased without a loss in student learning performance.

(ii) Encourage and finance the local design, production and distribution of learning equipment and textbooks.

(iii) Encourage the hiring of teachers with experience in fields other than education.

The Bank will back, through a systematic use of built-in evaluation systems in education projects, further efforts to identify and eliminate the main causes of high attrition and repetition rates. These evaluation systems can lead to improved curricula and selection, and better teaching and learning methods.

Wherever possible, the Bank will attempt to improve the nutrition of prenatal, infant and school-age children, believing as it does that proper nutrition is a crucial factor in the development of human resources. Such attempts can include improved nutritional education in teacher training colleges, in adult education programs and in the curricula of primary and secondary schools. This approach may be combined with feeding programs in schools.

The Bank will continue to emphasize the financial criteria of education projects and development strategies including:

(a) A sound balance of expenditure between components within the education system and between the education sector and other sectors of development.

(b) The implications of recurrent costs in both plans and projects, and the replicability of experimental activities.

Education and Equity

A final objective of Bank lending for education, as for other sectors, is the improvement of equity, the redressing of imbalances in educational and training opportunities among different geographical, ethnic, social, sex, income and age groups. Providing equality of opportunity is not a program which can be financed in itself; it is, rather, a major criterion which should suffuse all Bank operations.

In its analysis of education systems and policies, the Bank will want to know where the funds really go, who benefits most and how the financial burden is distributed. In some cases, special surveys may be needed to find the answers. The Bank will assist in such surveys and, based on their findings, will help design programs to improve the distribution of educational services. This help may be forthcoming even if the program is to be financed by others. One such study—in Colombia—has recently been published by the Bank[1]; others will follow.

In project identification and design, the Bank will seek to assess the degree to which education programs contribute to a rational policy balancing equity and other educational objectives such as efficiency and the development of skills. More specifically, the Bank will develop a guidance and monitoring system to determine the beneficiaries of education projects.

Bank Lending Programs and Possibilities

Having outlined the major objectives for the Bank's education lending and having defined the position the Bank would normally take on specific questions, three crucial sets of questions concerning the viability of these proposals arise:

(a) Will developing countries be willing to accept the general and specific policies suggested in this paper? What might the Bank do to encourage their receptiveness?

(b) What are the risks inherent in these policies? Will countries have sufficient managerial capabilities to carry them out?

(c) Are the Bank's own current policies, procedures and lending programs in harmony with the directions and proposals put forth in this paper?

Overall, experience suggests that the innate caution and conservatism of educational establishments will continue and that relatively few countries will undertake the radical changes which many external observers consider necessary. At the same time, there is a growing recognition that significant changes are needed and a willingness to consider, selectively, specific proposals for reform. A small but growing number of countries have begun to look objectively at their total educational systems in terms of both internal and external efficiency. Some factors which may encourage the growth of this highly useful practice of self-examination are suggested here.

Awareness of financial constraints may be a powerful inducement to considering alternative modes of education. For example, three countries—Ethiopia, Tanzania and Peru—which have faced their educational problems resolutely and with imagination were all previously

---

[1]Jallade, Jean-Pierre. Public Expenditures on Education and Income Distribution in Colombia. *World Bank Staff Occasional Papers, No. 18.* Baltimore and London: The Johns Hopkins University Press, 1974.

confronted by serious financial problems. Their examples may encourage a critical and objective review of existing systems by many of the poorest countries in the wake of the unfavorable effects of recent economic changes. For the more favored countries where growth prospects have substantially improved, there may be less inclination to experiment or question conventional practices. The need to plan for rapid expansion should, however, compel a searching review of existing conditions.

Change will normally begin through a comprehensive study of the sector as a whole which assesses broadly the degree to which the country's total learning system responds to its developmental objectives and needs. Such an assessment must perforce include a fresh look at accepted developmental objectives and an updating of the estimates of those needs.

These comprehensive sector studies must be undertaken at the initiative of, and carried out by, the country itself if the best results are to be achieved. Technical assistance and guidance may also be needed from the Bank, Unesco or some other source. The Bank has provided financial help for one such study, in Ethiopia, and has also assisted or cooperated in the formulation of such studies in Sierra Leone, Indonesia and the Philippines. It is financing a number of subsector studies, including a review of basic education in Mali and the role of the Koranic schools in Mauritania. During the next four years, we might expect that from eight to 12 countries might initiate comprehensive sector studies with the Bank's financial help. In addition, one can expect the Bank to help in preparing an indeterminate number of more specialized studies.

A second way of encouraging innovative attitudes is through technical assistance in the identification and design of projects as provided by the Bank's Cooperative Programs with Unesco and the U.N. Food and Agriculture Organization (FAO). Under these Cooperative Program agreements, signed in 1964 with Unesco and FAO, the Bank assumes 75% of the costs of a team of specialists in each agency which works exclusively on missions and studies involved in Bank lending. The teams may also complement Bank missions at any stage of the project cycle process, and they may call upon Unesco and FAO staff members outside the Cooperative Programs. As a result, the Cooperative Programs assure the Bank of the special experience of the two U.N. agencies.

Responding to the second question, it must be acknowledged that the risks inherent in embarking on highly innovative policies are substantial. In the face of the uncertainties involved, venturing into the relatively uncharted regions of educational development for rural dwellers and the poor will seem to many, including the politically accountable leaders of developing countries, to be a risky business indeed. But since the effects of continuing to neglect these needs would certainly be more costly, it is clearly preferable to pursue a prudent, but active, course while seeking to identify and minimize the risks involved.

It has been pointed out frequently in this paper and elsewhere that the major problem of development is management, and especially local management. Many have called for organizational reform, and, in all cases, for intensive training programs of all kinds. That continues to be a major recommendation.

Thirdly, it has been asked if the Bank itself is in a good position to help implement the proposals of this paper. The proposed lending program for 1974-78 allocated $1,075 million in constant prices for Bank/IDA lending to the education sector, compared with actual lending for the period 1969-73 of $947 million. The 1974-78 figure amounts to an increase of about 14%. During the 1974-78 period, 80 projects will be undertaken, compared with 66 projects in 1969-73. This amounts to an increase of 21%. In addition, nearly $350 million for educational and training components is expected to be included in lending for other sectors. This moderate increase is justified, given the rapid expansion of education lending during the previous five years (by nearly four times), the need for additional staff for project-related training and, above all, the experimental nature of some of the new emphases indicated in the lending profile (Table 8). This program would permit the necessary "tooling up" for substantial expansion beginning in about 1978.

In aggregate terms, the distribution of lending as shown in Table 8 does reflect the policy directions suggested here. This contention is generally supported by the content of projects approved for Bank/IDA assistance during fiscal 1974. In the future, however, a substantial increase (to about 27% of the total) in lending for primary and basic education, and a proportional decrease for intermediate and higher education, is projected. Lending for general education, including comprehensive schools, will decline, and support for technical education and teacher training will remain at approximately the same levels. Large increases for education for rural populations (agricultural plus a substantial part of primary and basic) are expected; support for the training of health personnel is expected to rise sharply, too. The estimated increase in technical assistance from 7% to 9% (it may, in fact, go higher) is also significant.

The Bank is making every effort to ensure that an equitable distribution of lending by income levels—both inter-country and intra-country—will occur. In drawing up these lending programs, however, the Bank must take account of those factors which tend to limit its ability to act in this regard: differences in a country's absorptive capacity for loans, educational technology, economic sophistication and levels of skills required, not to mention the greater availability of funds for Bank loans than for IDA credits.

Finally, in projects for basic education where capital expenditure is to be minimized and physical facilities are simple and locations widely scattered, international competitive bidding generally will not be appropriate. Greater resort to construction by negotiated contracts, force accounts or some form of self-help involving contributions of labor and materials from the community will be needed. In this connection, if building costs are truly to be low enough to be replicable and if local capabilities are to be brought into play, the Bank and its borrowers might reconsider what is a "proper" building for the Bank to finance. Instead of designing a structure to last 30 or 40 years, there might be many advantages, including those of cost, in designing first generation models which would last for shorter periods.

In some other respects, although no new policy issues appear to be involved, implementation of the policies and programs proposed here will require greater use by the Bank of flexible procedures for financing and procurement. Although those procedures already exist, they have not been fully utilized in the education sector. The Pearson Commission recommended in 1969, with agreement in principle by the Bank, that "greater resources for research and experimentation with new techniques" should be provided by World Bank lending. This was further defined as ". . . loans to finance: (1) research and experimentation with new curricula, methods, structures, materials, and plant design; and (2) the establishment and partial operation of new institutions based on the results." Since then, through its own allocations of money for research, and through loans and credits, the Bank has given increasing support to research and studies leading to improved techniques. But the effort can be greatly expanded. In particular, in order to give momentum to experimentation, the Bank can lend an appropriate part of the total costs of an experiment—both capital and operational—over a stated period of time. This policy should apply in all parts of the education sector, although in the immediate future it will perhaps be most widely used in basic education, where project models, criteria and standards are still being developed.

In view of the crucial role of the teacher in bringing about educational change (or in failing to do so), the capital and operational costs of the training of teachers and administrators—the human infra-structure of education systems—should be financed by the Bank and IDA, as was done in an Indonesian project for which an IDA credit of $13.5 million was extended in June 1973.

Conclusion

The Bank's lending operations in any sector are part of a continuing relationship which is rooted in agreement with its member country upon an overall development strategy and upon individual sector strategies such as education. Such strategies take their direction from the country's own definition of its developmental objectives and aspirations.

A recognition of the sovereign prerogative and the practical neces-sity for a country to determine its own affairs does not, however, pre-clude the possibility of a useful and constructive dialogue between it and the Bank. If there is no substitute for the borrower's own judg-ments regarding political and social issues, it may also be true that from its experience in development financing and its broad awareness of technical alternatives and their outcome in other countries, the Bank may help to illuminate the choices a country faces and help it to make better decisions. The Bank hopes to maintain such a dialogue, beginning with policy and strategy definitions and leading on through its lending operations to the implementation of projects and, ulti-mately, their evaluation. Through this dialogue, it is hoped there may emerge for each country a unity of purpose and plan between it and the Bank.

EDUCATION
ANNEXES

Estimated Total Enrollment by Level of Education [1]
(In millions)

	1950	1960	1965	1970
		First Level		
Developed countries	112.4	124.5	129.7	141.8
Developing countries	64.7	118.9	159.6	201.4
Africa	8.5	18.9	25.9	32.4
Asia[1]	53.3	87.7	113.9	138.8
Latin America	15.3	26.9	34.7	43.3
World[1]	177.1	243.4	299.3	343.2
		Second Level		
Developed countries	30.5	50.7	64.5	70.8
Developing countries	7.5	18.2	29.3	42.4
Africa	0.7	2.1	3.6	5.1
Asia[1]	12.7	21.3	30.7	36.3
Latin America	1.7	3.9	6.7	10.3
World[1]	38.0	68.9	93.8	113.2
		Third Level		
Developed countries	5.4	9.1	14.3	20.5
Developing countries	0.9	2.1	3.7	5.5
Africa	0.1	0.2	0.3	0.4
Asia[1]	1.1	4.0	5.0	6.2
Latin America	0.3	0.6	0.9	1.5
World[1]	6.3	11.2	18.0	26.0

[1] Not including the People's Republic of China, Democratic Republic of Korea and Democratic Republic of Vietnam.
Source: *Unesco Statistical Yearbook, 1972.*

Analysis of World Bank/IDA Education Lending, FY1963-74

	FY1963-71		FY1972-74	
	US$ million	%	US$ million	%
A. By levels				
Primary and basic	22.48	5	69.00	11
Intermediate	309.65	72	301.08	48
Higher	99.32	23	257.17	41
	431.45	100	627.25	100
B. By curricula				
General and comprehensive	190.77	44	269.72	43
Technical	126.48	29	150.54	24
Agricultural	63.03	15	106.63	17
Teacher training	51.17	12	87.81	14
Health	—	—	12.55	2
	431.45	100	627.25	100
C. By outlay				
Construction	262.17	61	307.35	49
Equipment and furniture	148.16	34	275.99	44
Technical assistance	21.12	5	43.91	7
	431.45	100	627.25	100

**Student Places Provided or Improved through World Bank/IDA
Education Projects, FY1963-74**

Student places pro-vided or improved	1963-71		1972-74		1963-74	
	Number	%	Number	%	Number	%
General and comprehensive	553,000	58	458,000	60	1,011,000	59
Technical	250,000	27	144,000	19	394,000	23
Agricultural	73,000	8	82,000	11	155,000	9
Teacher training	66,000	7	81,000	10	147,000	9
Total	942,000	100	765,000	100	1,707,000	100

**World Bank/IDA Education Lending by Per Capita GNP of
Borrowing Countries, FY1963-74**

Fiscal Year	Countries by per capita GNP					Total No.	Total amount	Average amount
	Up to $120	$121-250	$251-750	$751-1,500	Over $1,500			
	—(Number of loans or credits)—						—(US$ millions)—	
1963			1			1	5.0	5.0
1964	1	2				3	17.6	5.9
1965	1	2				3	29.5	9.8
1966	1	1	1	1		4	33.95	8.5
1967	1	3	2			6	51.8	8.6
1968	1	1	3			5	24.2	4.8
1969	2		7	1		10	81.8	8.2
1970		5	3	3		11	79.9	7.3
1971	5	2	6	1		14	107.9	7.7
1972	2	5	4	2	1	14	180.4	12.9
1973	7	3	6	2		18	293.55	16.3
1974	1	1	6	1	1	10	153.1	15.3
Total	22	25	39	11	2	99	1,058.7	
Average amount of loan or credit (US$ millions)								10.7

World Bank/IDA Education Projects Approved as of June 30, 1974

Fiscal year	Country	Main purpose	Total project cost	Amount of loan or credit Bank	IDA
1963	1. Tunisia I	Secondary general, technical and teacher training	9.2		5.0
1964	2. Tanzania I	Secondary general	6.0		4.6
	3. Pakistan I	University agricultural, post-secondary technical and teacher training (T.A.)	9.0		4.5
	4. Pakistan II	University agricultural, post-secondary technical and teacher training (T.A.)	17.0		8.5
1965	5. Philippines	University agricultural	11.7	6.0	
	6. Afghanistan	Secondary technical, agricultural and teacher training (T.A.)	4.7		3.5
	7. Nigeria	Secondary general, technical, adult and teacher training	30.0		20.0
1966	8. Chile I	Adult training	3.8	2.75	
	9. Morocco	Secondary general, technical and agricultural	16.2		11.0
	10. Ethiopia	Secondary general, technical and teacher training	10.7		7.2
	11. Pakistan III	University agricultural and post-secondary technical (T.A.)	21.7		13.0
1967	12. Kenya I	Secondary general, technical and teacher training	9.7		7.0
	13. Tunisia II	Secondary general and agricultural	19.8		13.0
	14. Jamaica	Secondary general, post-secondary agricultural, technical, adult and teacher training (T.A.)	19.4	9.5	
	15. Thailand	Secondary technical and agricultural (T.A.)	21.0	6.0	
	16. Uganda	Secondary general	14.3		10.0
	17. Malawi	Secondary general and teacher training	7.0		6.3
1968	18. Malagasy Republic	Secondary general, technical and teacher training	7.2	4.8	
	19. Nicaragua	Secondary general and teacher training	8.0	4.0	
	20. Gabon	Secondary general and teacher training	3.6	1.8	
	21. Sudan	Secondary general, post-secondary agricultural and teacher training (T.A.)	15.4		8.5
	22. Ecuador	Secondary general, agricultural and technical and teacher training (T.A.)	10.2		5.1
1969	23. Colombia I	Secondary general	15.2	7.6	
	24. Chad	Secondary agricultural and teacher training (T.A.)	2.1		1.8
	25. Trinidad and Tobago	Secondary general and teacher training	18.8	9.4	
	26. Guatemala	Secondary general, post-secondary agricultural and teacher training	12.6	6.3	
	27. Guyana	Secondary general and teacher training (T.A.)	10.0	2.9	2.9
	28. Zambia I	Secondary general, technical and teacher training	36.2	17.4	
	29. Malaysia	Secondary general, technical, agricultural and teacher training	16.4	8.8	
	30. Tanzania II	Secondary general and teacher training	7.2		5.0
	31. Korea	Secondary and post-secondary agricultural and technical (T.A.)	26.8		14.8
	32. El Salvador	Secondary general, technical and post-secondary agricultural (T.A.)	8.4	4.9	
1970	33. Cameroon	Secondary general, technical, agricultural and adult and teacher training (T.A.)	14.0		10.5
	34. Zambia II	University technical and teacher training	7.4	5.3	
	35. Sierra Leone	Secondary general, technical and teacher training (T.A.)	4.5		3.0
	36. Chile II	Adult industrial and agricultural training	3.0	1.5	
	37. Ivory Coast	Primary, secondary general, technical, post-secondary technical, agricultural and adult and teacher training (T.A.)	19.1	11.0	
	38. Chile III	Secondary agricultural and teacher training (T.A.)	14.0	7.0	
	39. Kenya II	Secondary technical, university agricultural and adult and teacher training (T.A.)	9.3		6.1
	40. Colombia II	Secondary general (T.A.)	13.0	6.5	
	41. China	Secondary and post-secondary technical and agricultural and teacher training (T.A.)	15.0	9.0	
	42. Pakistan IV	University technical (T.A.)	12.8		8.0
	43. Spain	Primary, secondary general and teacher training (T.A.)	24.0	12.0	

(continued)

333

World Bank/IDA Education Projects Approved as of June 30, 1974 (continued)

Fiscal year	Country	Main purpose	Total project cost	Amount of loan or credit Bank	IDA
1971	44. Iran	Primary, secondary general, technical and agricultural; teacher training; and university (education) (T.A.)	41.7	19.0	
	45. Indonesia	Secondary technical (T.A.)	7.6		4.6
	46. Greece	Post-secondary technical (T.A.)	24.0	13.8	
	47. Dominican Republic	Secondary general and teacher training (T.A.)	8.1		4.0
	48. Tanzania III	Nonformal rural training and post-secondary agricultural (T.A.)	4.7		3.3
	49. Jamaica II	General secondary; teacher training; vocational training; ITV (T.A.)	28.2	13.5	
	50. Congo (B)	Secondary general and technical teacher training; nonformal rural education (T.A.)	4.1		3.5
	51. Ethiopia II	Secondary general and secondary technical and agricultural	13.4		9.5
	52. Brazil	Secondary technical and agricultural, post-secondary technical (T.A.)	21.0	8.4	
	53. Chad II	Secondary technical and agricultural	3.1		2.2
	54. Somalia	Secondary general, technical; teacher training and nonformal agricultural (T.A.)	3.7		3.3
	55. Turkey	Secondary and post-secondary technical; technical teacher training; nonformal management and adult technical training; science equipment production; mass media (T.A.)	17.9	13.5	
	56. Senegal	Secondary general and secondary technical and agricultural	2.3		2.0
	57. Uganda II	Secondary general and technical; post-secondary and nonformal agricultural; health and medical training (T.A.)	10.4		7.3
1972	58. Ireland I	Secondary general and agricultural; post-secondary technical (T.A.)	33.0	13.0	
	59. Morocco II	Secondary general and technical; agricultural teacher training; university (agricultural); adult nonformal technical training (T.A.)	13.5		8.5
	60. Zaire I	Secondary technical; primary and technical teacher training (T.A.)	11.8		6.5
	61. Jordan I	Secondary general and agricultural; post-secondary technical; teacher training (T.A.)	9.8		5.4
	62. Singapore I	University (technical) (T.A.)	20.0	9.5	
	63. Indonesia II	Agricultural secondary; adult training (T.A.)	12.3		6.3
	64. Nigeria	Post-secondary general; teacher training (T.A.)	27.8	17.3	
	65. Malaysia II	Secondary technical; university (science); ITV	28.4	15.5	
	66. Liberia	Secondary general; university (agricultural); teacher training (T.A.)	9.6		7.2
	67. Central African Republic	Secondary general; post-secondary technical; teacher training (T.A.)	5.4		3.9
	68. Thailand II	University (agricultural) (T.A.)	28.3	15.4	
	69. Spain II	Secondary general; technical teacher training; university (technical) (T.A.)	152.5	50.0	
	70. Cameroon II	Secondary general and technical; teacher training; nonformal adult technical (T.A.)	11.4		9.0
	71. Iraq I	Secondary general and technical; post-secondary technical; nonformal adult agricultural and technical training; ITV	19.9	12.9	
1973	72. Greece II	University engineering and science; teacher training; technical and agricultural secondary; vocational training (T.A.)	43.9	23.5	
	73. India	Agricultural university, computer center, curriculum development (T.A.)	19.4		12.0
	74. Trinidad and Tobago II	General secondary, teacher training (T.A.)	19.7	9.3	
	75. Philippines	Agricultural university, agricultural secondary schools, technical and vocational institutions, development centers (T.A.)	17.7		12.7

World Bank/IDA Education Projects Approved as of June 30, 1974 (continued)

Fiscal year	Country	Main purpose	Total project cost	Amount of loan or credit Bank	IDA
1973	76. Paraguay	General secondary, technical post-secondary (T.A.)	7.3		5.1
	77. Lebanon	Basic and secondary general, teacher training (T.A.)	15.9	6.6	
	78. Thailand III	General secondary, university, teacher training (T.A.)	39.0		19.5
	79. Tanzania IV	Primary, general secondary, medical school (university), technical secondary (T.A.)	14.6		10.3
	80. Indonesia III	Teacher training, learning materials, development (T.A.)	39.2		13.5
	81. Algeria	Technical and agricultural post-secondary and university (T.A.)	10.2	6.0	
	82. Korea II	Engineering science and school of education at universities, teacher training, agricultural and technical secondary (T.A.)	70.2	23.0	20.0
	83. Zambia III	Paramedical, health training centers, agricultural school of university, farmer training centers, teacher training, general secondary, development (T.A.)	40.1	33.0	
	84. Bangladesh	University and post-secondary agricultural and technical, teacher training (T.A.)	36.4		21.0
	85. Mali	Technical teacher training, general secondary, technical education, development (T.A.)	5.5		5.0
	86. Nigeria	General secondary, teacher training (T.A.)	107.4	54.0	
	87. Upper Volta	General secondary, youth training, development (T.A.)	3.6		2.85
	88. Costa Rica	General secondary, adult training (T.A.)	9.4	6.2	
	89. Ethiopia	General secondary, agricultural training, university school of science, teacher training, development (T.A.)	12.7		10.0
1974	90. Yemen Arab Republic	Secondary general and agricultural, nonformal basis; teacher training (T.A.)	16.95		11.0
	91. Colombia IV	Primary agricultural; secondary general; post-secondary technical and teacher training, rural development center	33.50	21.2	
	Chad	Supplementary credit to Chad I and II			0.9
	92. Peru	General Secondary (T.A.)	40.00	24.0	
	93. Honduras	Vocational and agricultural training centers; teacher training (T.A.)	8.66	3.0	3.0
	94. Ireland II	Secondary general, post-secondary technical, university agricultural; teacher training (T.A.)	62.84	25.0	
	95. Mauritania	Secondary technical, community development vocational and teacher training (T.A.)	4.30		3.8
	96. Singapore II	University law, arts and science (T.A.)	42.00	19.5	
	97. Oman	Teacher training, agricultural secondary, youth training (T.A.)	11.10	5.7	
	98. Malaysia III	General secondary; post-secondary general and technical; teacher training	41.40	19.0	
	99. El Salvador II	Primary and basic education; youth training center (T.A.)	24.20	17.0	
	TOTAL		1,936.45	642.3	416.4

"(T.A.)" = Technical assistance

(continued)

World Bank/IDA Education Projects Approved as of June 30, 1974 (continued)

Summary of Education Lending by Fiscal Year, 1963-74

Fiscal year	Bank	IDA	Total
1963	—	5.0	5.0
1964	—	17.6	17.6
1965	6.0	23.5	29.5
1966	2.75	31.2	33.95
1967	15.5	36.3	51.8
1968	10.6	13.6	24.2
1969	57.3	24.5	81.8
1970	52.3	27.6	79.9
1971	68.2	39.7	107.9
1972	133.6	46.8	180.4
1973	161.6	131.95	293.55
1974	134.4	18.7	153.1
Total 1963-74	642.25	416.45	1,058.7

Comparison of Education Efficiencies in Urban and Rural Areas in Latin America

(a) Successful completers and dropouts in primary education

	Total country Successful completers	Urban Successful completers	Rural Successful completers
	---------------------------as % of entrances---------------------		
Colombia	27.3	47.3	3.7
Dominican Republic	30.4	48.1	13.9
Guatemala	25.4	49.6	3.5
Panama	62.3	80.7	45.3
Average percentage completers	39	51	22

(b) Efficiency of primary education

	Years taken to produce a successful completer				Input/output ratio		
	Ideal	Total country	Rural	Urban	Total country	Rural	Urban
Colombia	5	11	66	8	2.4	13.2	1.7
Dominican Republic	6	14	27	9	2.3	4.5	1.6
Guatemala	6	14	70	10	2.3	11.6	1.6
Panama	6	9	12	8	1.5	1.9	1.2

Source: Based on the Unesco report, *The Statistical Measurement of Educational Wastage.*

Availability of Complete Primary Schools in Urban and Rural Areas

Percentage of the total number of primary schools in each category (rural and urban) which offer the complete number of grades

	Number of countries	Complete urban schools as % of total urban schools	Complete rural schools as % of total rural schools
(a) Countries by per capita GNP			
I—Up to $120 (excluding India)	9	53	36
India		57	49
II—$121-250	7	72	32
III—$251-750	16	77	62
IV—$751-1,500	2	89	56
V—Over $1,500	6	100	99
(b) By major regions			
Africa	16	79	54
Asia (excluding India)	9	94	66
India		57	49
South and Central America	10	88	34
Europe	5	98	99

Source: Based on data in *Unesco Statistical Yearbook, 1972.*

Female Enrollment as a Percentage of Total Primary and Secondary School Enrollments[1]

	1960	1965	1970
Primary schools			
A. Countries by per capita GNP			
I—Up to $120	35%	37%	38%
II—$121-250	42%	43%	44%
III—$251-750	43%	44%	45%
IV—$751-1,500	48%	49%	49%
V—Over $1,500	49%	49%	49%
B. By continents			
Africa	37%	38%	40%
The Americas	49%	49%	49%
Asia[2]	38%	39%	38%
Europe	49%	48%	49%
Oceania	48%	47%	48%
Developed countries	49%	49%	49%
Developing countries	39%	40%	40%
World[2]	43%	44%	44%
Secondary schools			
A. Countries by per capita GNP			
I—Up to $120	19%	23%	28%
II—$121-250	27%	30%	29%
III—$251-750	37%	41%	41%
IV—$751-1,500	45%	44%	45%
V—Over $1,500	47%	47%	48%
B. By continents			
Africa	31%	30%	32%
The Americas	49%	49%	49%
Asia[2]	35%	36%	35%
Europe	45%	46%	47%
Oceania	42%	42%	44%
Developed countries	48%	51%	49%
Developing countries	31%	36%	35%
World[2]	44%	44%	43%

[1] Complete equity between the sexes would imply a female enrollment ratio of 49%.
[2] Not including People's Republic of China and Democratic Republic of Vietnam.
Source: *Unesco Statistical Yearbook, 1972.*

Public Expenditure on Education as a Percentage
of the Budget and GNP

Countries by per capita GNP	1960		1965		1970	
	Budget	GNP	Budget	GNP	Budget	GNP
I—Up to $120	6.7	1.8	9.6	2.3	13.2	2.9
(No. of countries)	(5)	(6)	(12)	(11)	(7)	(6)
II—$121-250	20.0	3.6	21.8	3.2	18.9	3.8
(No. of countries)	(3)	(10)	(14)	(17)	(7)	(7)
III—$251-750	15.3	2.3	14.6	2.9	13.5	3.0
(No. of countries)	(8)	(17)	(15)	(20)	(15)	(13)
IV—$751-1,500	6.1	2.1	8.3	2.2	10.1	3.1
(No. of countries)	(2)	(3)	(5)	(5)	(5)	(8)
V—Over $1,500	12.9	3.8	19.5	5.5	17.8	5.8
(No. of countries)	(4)	(14)	(14)	(14)	(10)	(12)

Public Education Expenditures Per Capita
of Population/Pupil
(In U.S. dollars. Current prices)

Countries by per capita GNP	1960		1965		1970	
	Population	Pupil	Population	Pupil	Population	Pupil
I—Up to $120	1	16	2	21	2	18
II—$121-250	5	33	6	40	9	49
III—$251-750	7	43	9	58	10	57
IV—$751-1,500	17	114	29	164	34	179
V—Over $1,500	67	338	113	504	168	749

Source: Based on data compiled by Unesco.

School Textbook Production[1]

Countries by per capita GNP	Number of books (000's)	Enrollment (000's)	Textbooks per student
Up to $250			
Ghana	19	1,518	0.01
Cameroon	30	956	0.03
Nigeria	340	3,871	0.08
Uganda	259	768	0.34
Kenya	592	1,404	0.42
Tunisia	1,580	1,070	1.48
Sri Lanka	4,229	2,653	1.59
Egypt	9,694	5,187	1.87
			Average 0.73
$251-1,500			
Chile	1,695	2,345	0.72
Argentina	3,973	4,359	0.91
Malaysia	6,945	2,274	3.05
Singapore	2,396	513	4.67
Spain	30,592	5,879	5.20
			Average 2.91

[1] School textbooks for primary and secondary education.
Source: *Unesco Statistical Yearbook, 1972.*

Education at the First and Second Levels: Student-Teacher Ratios

Countries by per capita GNP	1960		1965		1970	
	First level	Second level	First level	Second level	First level	Second level
I—Up to $120	39		42		42	
		19		21		21
II—$121-250	42		42		43	
		21		24		25
III—$251-750	37		36		37	
		15		14		19
IV—$751-1,500	31		30		36	
		17		18		15
V—Over $1,500	28		25		24	
		18		17		16

Source: *Unesco Statistical Yearbook, 1972.*

HEALTH

HEALTH
CONTENTS

	Page
Introduction	345
Chapter 1: Health Conditions in Developing Countries	348
General Measures of Health	348
Differences between and within Countries	350
The Disease Pattern.	351
Chapter 2: Causes of Poor Health	356
Demographic Factors	357
Malnutrition	359
Unsanitary Conditions and Housing	360
Causes of Improved Health	364
Chapter 3: Approaches to Health Policy	366
A Social Goal	366
A Productive Investment	367
Better Health for Socioeconomic Development	369
Role of Government	371
Chapter 4: Present Policies of Developing Countries	374
Expenditures on Health	374
Resources for Medical Care	375
Coverage of Official Health Services	377
Effectiveness of Official Health Services	380
Chapter 5: A Health Policy for the Future	382
Financing Extended Coverage	383
The Reformed Health Service	384
Increasing Effectiveness of Official Health Services	388
Chapter 6: World Bank Lending for Health-related Projects	389
Chapter 7: Policy Alternatives for the Bank	398
Conclusions	403
Annexes	
1. International Assistance for Health Programs	409
2. Measures of Health Status by Level of Per Capita Gross National Product (GNP) in Selected Countries	414
3. Health Expenditures in Developing Countries	416
4. Analysis of Government Health Expenditures in Selected Countries	418

5. Percentage Distribution of Health Expenditures
in Selected Countries, 1961 419

6. Health Resources in Developing Countries 420

7. Indices of Hospital Utilization 422

8. Population per Medical Doctor in Urban and Rural
Areas in Selected Countries 422

9. Distribution of Medical Doctors between the
Capital and the Remainder of the Country in
Selected Countries, 1968 423

10. Comparative Costs of Medical Education in
Selected Countries, 1965 423

11. Percentage of Deliveries Attended by a Physician
or by a Qualified Midwife in Selected Countries 424

12. Utilization of Official Health Services in
Selected Countries, 1962 424

13. Emigration of Medical Doctors to
the Developed World 425

INTRODUCTION

This is the first study published by the World Bank that is specifically addressed to health issues. Direct lending for health projects has not been part of the Bank's activities,[1] although its operations have influenced health conditions and some projects have included health services. Earlier papers have examined the Bank's policies in fields that significantly influence health conditions, such as water supply and sewerage, population planning and the environment. This paper now attempts a more comprehensive review of the policy relating to health. For this purpose, it:

- assesses the health situation in developing countries;
- examines the impact of poverty on ill-health, and of ill-health on economic development;
- analyzes the trends in health policy in member countries and offers suggestions for reform; and
- outlines the policy the Bank has decided to follow.

Health conditions in developing countries have improved considerably in recent decades. In general, the improvement has been associated with economic progress. But international differences in health levels remain substantial; within nations, differences in the health of the rich and the poor are no less wide. The evidence suggests, furthermore, that health conditions among poverty groups in different countries are basically similar, as the poor suffer from a core of fecally-related and air-borne diseases. Malnutrition increases the susceptibility to many of these diseases, and compounds their severity.

In developed countries, economic progress has reduced the threats to health by ensuring safe water supplies, sanitary waste disposal, adequate housing and improved nutrition. These improvements are essential for controlling disease; and until they are made, narrowly defined health care services will be largely ineffective. Even under very favorable circumstances, personal health care can do little to diminish the incidence of disease, although it can reduce its harmful effects. To improve the health of the poor in the developing countries, it is essential to devise programs which will improve sanitation and water supplies, housing, personal health practices and nutrition, and promote family planning and simple preventive health measures.

Improvements in health usually reduce mortality and tend, therefore, to accelerate population growth. In the longer term, once people perceive a reduction in infant and child mortality, they may want

---

[1]All references to the World Bank in this paper are to be deemed to refer also to the International Development Association, unless the context requires otherwise. The fiscal year (FY) of the two institutions runs from July 1 to June 30.

345

smaller families; but the interval between health improvements and this perception may be considerable. If the improvements are not accompanied by other measures to promote socioeconomic progress, faster population growth may offset the stimulus to economic development that better health could bring through reduced absenteeism, increased labor productivity and better exploitation of natural resources. The long-term effect of modernization and socioeconomic progress has historically been a fall in both mortality and fertility. Health programs, therefore, should not be isolated efforts, but should form part of a broad program for socioeconomic improvement designed to reduce mortality and fertility.

In many developing countries, health policies are inefficient and inequitable. Too large a proportion of public expenditures on health are allocated to impressive, but expensive, modern hospital facilities and sophisticated medical manpower. The allocations have resulted in a bias toward inpatient, curative care—a practice which barely touches health problems in areas beset with serious environmental hazards to health. Furthermore, the resources are typically concentrated on the needs of urban areas. Rural people are neglected; thus, only a small proportion of the total population is granted effective access to modern health care.

To increase the effectiveness of health resources and to ensure more equitable access to care, governments need to curtail their expenditures on hospitals and highly trained personnel, and devote more resources to the staffing of low-level health services in areas with few facilities, or none at all. The services would focus primarily on improving environmental and public health, personal health practices and nutrition. Further savings might be made by analyzing the cost-effectiveness of health care activities, and by better administration and more rational pricing policies.

Reforms in the service offered to the poorer people should concentrate on improving health at the community level. The objectives should include changes in living habits and attitudes, as well as household and community activities to improve water supply and sanitation. While the demand for curative care would not be denied, a more economical balance would be struck between measures to treat disease and measures to control its incidence.

The World Bank has initiated project lending in a number of areas that directly affect health. The number of health-related projects supported by the Bank has increased from four in fiscal 1969 to 22 in fiscal 1973. In the latter year, the total of such loans and credits was $500 million. Of this amount, $366 million was for water supply and sewerage, and $22 million was for population projects. The health components of education, rural development, irrigation and drainage, and sites and services projects totaled about $19 million.

The Bank has decided that, in the coming years, it will continue to strengthen its awareness of the health consequences of the projects it supports, and of opportunities for improving health that are available under present patterns of lending. In other words, while the health benefits of projects are expected to increase, the patterns of lending will remain basically unchanged.

Although this implies that the Bank will be less deeply involved in health than if it had decided to lend for basic health services, the scope and potential of the policy is not to be underestimated. It means that the Bank plans to:

- minimize any adverse side effects on health resulting from its lending operations in other sectors (such as projects for irrigation, drainage, land settlement, etc.);
- make a number of key interventions necessary for improving the health of low-income groups (for example, projects involving water supply, sewerage, nutrition, family planning, sites and services for low-cost housing, and training of health personnel);
- conduct field experiments to test selected elements of a reformed health-promotion system within rural development, population, and sites and services projects.

Chapter 1: HEALTH CONDITIONS IN DEVELOPING COUNTRIES

Health conditions in developing countries have improved considerably in recent decades. Generally, the improvements have accompanied socioeconomic progress. There is a marked association between the level of per capita income in a developing country and its health status. Superimposed on very substantial intercountry differences in health are equally notable variations within countries between rural and urban areas and between the poor, the middle-income and the affluent groups. Health conditions of the poor everywhere are basically similar. Their core disease pattern consists of the fecally-related and air-borne diseases and malnutrition. Socioeconomic development can reduce these hazards through improved nutrition and better health habits. In addition, sanitary water supply and waste disposal diminish the fecally-related diseases, and better housing and reduced crowding reduce the air-borne diseases. Sanitation has also contributed to reductions in another group of diseases—the vector-borne diseases—by destroying breeding and feeding areas for insects and small animals.

General Measures of Health

Life expectancy at birth and at selected ages is the most reliable measure of health status available. Although this measure does not take nonfatal diseases into account, it is closely correlated with many forms of morbidity and debility, and therefore provides an index to the range and intensity of health problems. For the developing countries as a group, life expectancy at birth is estimated to be about 49 years, compared with slightly over 70 years for the economically advanced countries (see Table 1). For the African continent, the estimate is 43.3

Table 1

Life Expectancy at Birth in Some Major Areas of the World

(In years)

	1935-39	1950-55	1955-60	1960-65	1965-70
Developing regions	32.0	41.7	44.4	47.0	49.0
South Asia	30.0	40.6	43.4	46.1	48.8
East Asia	30.0	44.8	47.1	49.6	52.2
Africa	30.0	36.4	38.6	40.9	43.3
Latin America	40.0	52.3	55.3	57.9	60.2
Developed regions	56.0	64.6	67.8	69.2	70.4

Source: World Bank. *Population Policies and Economic Development,* Statistical Annex Table 2. Baltimore and London: The Johns Hopkins University Press, 1974.

years for the period 1965-70. Since these values are averages, they do not indicate the health status of the poorest citizens of the developing countries.

The average life expectancy at birth for the developing world increased from 32 years before World War II to 49 years by the end of the 1960s. Starting from a very low level, the improvement in life expectancy was larger in both absolute and relative terms than in developed countries. The rate of improvement has declined, however—from 2.7 years in the periods 1950-55 and 1955-60, to 2.6 years in 1960-65 and to only 2.0 years in 1965-70. Further evidence on trends in life expectancy is presented in the Figure.

Life expectancy at various ages yields broader insights into health status than life expectancy at birth alone. Table 2 presents data for selected countries which show that, in countries with low life expectancy at birth, surviving the first year of life greatly increases the expected life span. In Cameroon, for example, life expectancy at birth is only 34 years, but those who survive to one year of age may expect to live 40 more years. This phenomenon results from the extraordinary risks of death encountered during the first year of life. Countries

Trends in Life Expectancy in Selected Countries

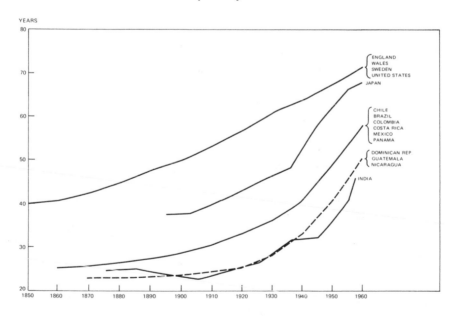

Source: Arriaga, E. and Davis, K. "The Pattern of Mortality Change in Latin America." *Demography* 6(3):223-242, 1969 (August 6) (Tables A-3 and A-4).

Table 2

Life Expectancy in Selected Countries for Males at Specified Ages

(In years of life remaining)

Country	Age					
	0	1	5	10	15	20
Cameroon	34	40	42	41	38	35
Central African Republic	33	40	41	38	n.a.	31
Chad	29	34	34	31	n.a.	31
Colombia	44	50	52	48	44	40
Egypt	52	56	61	57	52	48
Gabon	25	34	38	36	n.a.	29
Guinea	26	33	35	32	n.a.	29
India	42	48	49	45	41	37
Japan	68	69	66	60	56	51
Mexico	58	62	60	56	52	47
Nigeria	37	45	49	47	43	39
Sweden	72	72	68	63	58	54
China, Republic of (Taiwan)	66	67	64	59	54	49
United States	67	68	65	59	54	50

Source: United Nations. *Demographic Yearbook, 1968,* Table 21; and *Demographic Yearbook, 1970,* Table 20. New York: United Nations, 1969 and 1971, respectively.

with high life expectancies, however, have low rates of infant mortality; hence survival in the first years of life up to the age of five does not add significantly to the total expected life span.

Differences between and within Countries

A striking association exists between measures of per capita income and health status. Annex 2 shows the relationship between per capita income and life expectancy, infant mortality and the crude death rate, respectively. African countries, which have the lowest per capita incomes in the world, report the lowest levels of health, while the Latin American countries, which are among the wealthiest of the developing nations, report a health status approaching that of the developed world.[1]

Substantial intercountry differences in health are accompanied by equally notable variations within countries. These differences are pronounced between urban and rural areas in developing countries. The crude death rate for 1960 in the rural areas of the developing world was estimated by the United Nations as 21.7 per 1,000, compared with 15.4 for urban areas.[2] Data on infant mortality are especially pertinent as

---

[1]*The correlation coefficient for per capita GNP and life expectancy is 0.580 for the countries reported in Annex 20. If the United States is excluded from the analysis, the coefficient becomes 0.726.*

[2]*United Nations. Demographic Trends in the World and Its Major Regions, 1950-1970, Table 12. New York: United Nations, 1973.*

they refer to the population most vulnerable to health hazards. Absolute levels of infant mortality are probably grossly underreported in developing countries; the degree of underreporting is probably much greater for rural than for urban areas. Nonetheless, mortality rates, as reported, are much higher in the rural areas. These differentials are a consequence of the marked contrast in socioeconomic conditions between rural and urban areas. Such rural-urban differentials tend to disappear in advanced European countries, where living standards are much less disparate than in the developing countries.

Interestingly, the contrast between rural and urban health status in today's developing countries is opposite to that which prevailed historically in the advanced nations when they were becoming industrialized. In 1841, overall life expectancy for males in England and Wales was about 40 years, but in London it was only 35 years and in the industrial cities of Liverpool and Manchester, it was only 25 and 24 years, respectively.[3] Compared with rural people, the health status of urban dwellers in the now developing countries is better; this is because they enjoy higher incomes, better sanitation and water supply, higher school enrollment ratios, and superior environmental and personal health services.

The Disease Pattern

A comprehensive assessment of the health situation requires knowledge not only of death rates and life expectancy rates for all age groups, but also of the distribution, by cause, of mortality and morbidity. This study focuses on infectious and parasitic diseases—which are communicable—plus malnutrition as the core health problems of developing countries.[4]

Reliable information on patterns of disease is extremely difficult to compare on a countrywide basis for most nations.[5] Nevertheless, it is possible to convey a general idea of the difference in disease patterns on the basis of models developed by the United Nations (see Table 3). These models simulate the pattern of disease under specific assumptions regarding population characteristics, environmental conditions and socioeconomic circumstances. One model represents a population characteristic of a developing country: life expectancy at birth of

[3]*United Nations, Department of Economic and Social Affairs.* The Determinants and Consequences of Population Trends, *Vol. I, p. 133. New York: United Nations, 1973.*

[4]*The degenerative diseases—diabetes, hypertension, cardiovascular disease and malignancies—and accidents are excluded. It is believed that these problems are of lower priority because they make up a relatively minor part of the health burden of developing countries.*

[5]*Many problems arise in analyzing such data: underreporting is more common for some diseases than for others; multiple-causation leads to misreporting; and many deaths are registered without identification of causes (in Thailand, for example, such deaths account for 59% of the total reported, and in Iraq the proportion is 44%).*

Table 3

**Percentage Distribution of Deaths by Cause
in Selected Model Populations**

	Model developing country	Model developed country
All causes	100.0	100.0
Infectious, parasitic and respiratory diseases	43.7	10.8
Cancer	3.7	15.2
Diseases of the circulatory system	14.8	32.2
Traumatic injury	3.5	6.8
All other causes	34.3	35.0

Source: Adapted from *Population Bulletin of the United Nations,* No. 6, pp. 111-112, particularly Table V.33. See also pages 106-110 for a description of methods used in constructing these and other models. New York: United Nations, 1963.

40 years and a young age structure. The second model represents a developed country: an older age structure and a life expectancy at birth of 70 years. These statistics broadly indicate the different disease patterns of developed and developing countries.

The most widespread diseases in developing countries are probably those transmitted by human feces. The most common are the intestinal parasitic and infectious diarrheal diseases, but also included are poliomyelitis, typhoid and cholera. The spread of these diseases is easy in areas without community water supply systems. The category "bacillary dysentery and amoebiasis, enteritis, and other diarrheal diseases" was the leading identified cause of death in Paraguay (1971), Guatemala (1970) and El Salvador (1971). In Pakistan (1972), the category "all forms of dysentery" was the most frequently notified communicable disease.[6] In a case study in Punjab, India, a death rate of 3,446 per 100,000 infants from acute diarrheal diseases was reported.[7] In the Arab Republic of Egypt, Iran and Venezuela, the monthly incidence of diarrhea among children of preschool age has been estimated to be between 40% and 50%.[8]

Intestinal parasitic diseases are frequently chronic and debilitating rather than causes of acute illness or death. Their incidence in the developing world is often high. A World Bank case study of the labor force engaged in civil construction at three sites in West Java, Indonesia, found 85% infected with hookworm.[9]

---

[6]*World Health Organization.* The Fifth Report on the World Health Situation, 1969-1972—Part II, Review by County and Territory. *Geneva: WHO, 1974.*
[7]*Scrimshaw, N. S., Taylor, C. E., and Gordon, J. E.* Interactions of Nutrition and Infection. *WHO Monograph Series No. 57, p. 240. Geneva: WHO, 1968.*
[8]*Van Zijl, W. J. "Studies on Diarrheal Diseases in Seven Countries."* Bulletin of the World Health Organization 35:249-261, 1966.
[9]*Basta, S. S., and Churchill, A.* Iron Deficiency Anemia and the Productivity of Adult Males in Indonesia. *World Bank Staff Working Paper No. 175, p. 1. Washington: World Bank, April 1974.*

Possibly one of every four persons in the world is infected by round worms.[10] Case studies in Sri Lanka, Bangladesh and Venezuela found an average whipworm infection rate in preschool children of between 50% and 70% for both round worm and whipworm; at the age of six the infection rates for helminths were 95%, 97% and 93%, respectively, in Sri Lanka, Bangladesh and Venezuela.[11]

The second major disease group consists of the air-borne diseases. The group includes tuberculosis, pneumonia, diphtheria, bronchitis, whooping cough, meningitis, influenza, measles, smallpox and chickenpox. These diseases are spread by breathing the air-borne, respiratory secretions of infected persons. According to government statistics, they accounted for 24% of reported deaths in Bolivia in 1971, 29% in Guatemala in 1970, and 19% in Chile in 1972.

Table 4 presents an analysis of a recent study of various areas in Latin America where (excluding Jamaica) fecally-related diseases, air-borne diseases and malnutrition were the primary cause of death in over 70% of cases (excluding deaths from congenital anomalies and perinatal causes) among those below the age of five. The fecally-related diseases alone were responsible for over half of all deaths among children under five years of age in Chaco Resistencia, Bolivia; Ribeirao Preto Franca, Brazil; and San Salvador.

These three major disease groups account for the majority of deaths among the poorest people in developing countries, and particularly among children below the age of five. Other debilitating and fatal diseases are limited to particular geographical areas or particular ways of life. The water-borne diseases are the most significant of this group. However, direct contact with the exudate from infections is also an important transmission process for such diseases as syphilis, gonorrhea and leprosy. The contact diseases are generally of relatively minor significance except in limited areas. They are controlled largely by improved hygiene and changes in social habits.

Vector-borne diseases are less widespread and figure less prominently in mortality and morbidity statistics, but are nonetheless significant in the developing world. The most widespread of these diseases are malaria, trypanosomiasis (sleeping sickness), Chagas' disease, schistosomiasis (bilhärzia), and onchocerciasis (river blindness). In sub-Saharan Africa alone, about 270 million people remain exposed to malarial infection without any organized protection. In some areas, the malarial infection rate is 90% to 95%. Cases reported per 100,000

---

[10]Wilcocks, Charles, and Manson-Bahr, P. E. C. Manson's Tropical Diseases, Seventeenth Edition, p. 247. Baltimore: Williams and Wilkins, 1972.
[11]Van Zijl, W. J. "Studies on Diarrheal Diseases in Seven Countries," op. cit., Table 12.

Table 4

**Percentage of Deaths under the Age of Five (Not Due to Congenital
Anomalies or Perinatal Causes), for which Fecally-related
Diseases, Air-borne Diseases or Malnutrition
Were the Primary Cause of Death**

| | Deaths caused by | | | |
Areas	Fecally-related diseases	Air-borne diseases	Nutritional deficiency	Total
Chaco, Argentina, rural	40	36	2	79
San Juan, Argentina, central urban	38	32	3	72
San Juan, Argentina, suburban	34	38	8	80
San Juan, Argentina, rural	35	42	8	84
Chaco Resistencia, Bolivia, rural	52	27	6	84
La Paz, Bolivia, urban	29	55	3	87
Viacha, Bolivia, rural	25	65	0	91
Recife, Brazil, urban	42	41	5	88
Ribeirao Preto, Brazil, urban	49	36	2	87
Ribeirao Preto, Brazil, rural	50	29	3	81
Ribeirao, Preto Franca, Brazil, rural	55	20	7	82
Sao Paulo, Brazil, urban	40	33	5	78
Santiago, Chile, central urban	31	37	6	73
Santiago, Chile, suburban	33	38	3	74
Cali, Colombia, urban	44	25	15	84
Cartagena, Colombia, urban	38	23	17	78
Medellin, Colombia, urban	49	22	11	82
San Salvador, El Salvador, urban	52	28	6	86
San Salvador, El Salvador, rural	51	22	13	86
Kingston, Jamaica, urban	37	21	5	63
St. Andrew, Jamaica, rural	23	23	23	69
Monterrey, Mexico, urban	43	35	4	83

Source: Puffer, Ruth R., and Serrano, Carlos V. *Inter-American Investigation of Mortality in Childhood, Provisional Report*, Appendix Table I, pp. 133-154. Washington: Pan American Health Organization, September 1971.

were 15,247 in the Central African Republic (1972), 11,433 in Senegal (1972), and 10,439 in Upper Volta (1971). In Uganda in 1971, there were 1.6 million registered cases in a population of about 10 million.[12] The disease is endemic, and adults have acquired a higher degree of natural immunity through the process of adaptation. However, in the Indian subcontinent, epidemics break out periodically because adults have not achieved this level of adaptation. Malaria eradication campaigns launched in the 1950s and backed by international agencies were largely successful in 37 countries.[13] However, there is evidence of recent setbacks in Indonesia, Sri Lanka and the Indian subcontinent.

[12]Weller, T. H. "World Health in a Changing World." Journal of Tropical Medicine and Hygiene 77(4) Supplement: 54, 1974 (April).

[13]Weller, T. H. "World Health in a Changing World." Ibid., p. 54.

The number of persons living in areas where the eradication program is in the "consolidation phase" declined from 335 million in 1966 to 299 million in 1971.

Trypanosomiasis[14] occurs in a very wide band across the middle of Africa. It is generally fatal if not treated in its earliest stages. In the early twentieth century, as the movement of people was stimulated by colonization, the disease spread disastrously on the continent. In Uganda and the Congo, the population was estimated to have been cut in half. Between the World Wars, mobile health teams and enforced mass testing and treatment of populations substantially reduced the prevalence of trypanosomiasis; and, by the 1950s, it was under control in most areas. However, in some areas, control services were later dislocated, and in others, community-level support for control measures dwindled. The disease has started again to become more serious since the mid-1960s.[15]

The American form of trypanosomiasis, Chagas' disease, is concentrated in the rural areas. It is endemic in most countries of South America, and in much of Central America. The disease is typically chronic and can continue for years. Many cases show no symptoms, but heart troubles are a common sequel, and no satisfactory treatment exists.

Schistosomiasis is a debilitating disease of varying severity transmitted by snails. In arid regions, the disease is not a major problem since enough surface water is rarely available for large snail colonies. Large areas of slow-moving water and water vegetation provide an ideal habitat for the snails, and the most severe instances of the disease are found in East Asia. There are now perhaps 200 million clinical cases of schistosomiasis in the world, and its impact is growing.

Onchocerciasis, although less common in the world as a whole, is hyperendemic to Western Africa and parts of Central America. It is a debilitating, helminthic disease. Heavy infections of long duration produce clinical results which, even apart from blindness, can be very severe. In some areas, the disease has led to the depopulation of fertile river valleys. The vector, the simulium fly, prefers swift running water as its habitat. Although man-made lakes above dams tend to flood simulium breeding grounds, the turbulent water near the sluice gates can create ideal breeding conditions below the dam. Thus, the development of water resources may help spread the prevalence of the simulium fly and the incidence of the disease.

---

[14]Cattle are highly vulnerable to some forms of the trypanosome which are harmless to man. For a long time, much of sub-Saharan Africa did not have draught animals because of animal trypanosomiasis, and this was probably a major reason for slow technological development in the area.

[15]Burke, J., "Historique de la Lutte contre la Maladie du Sommeil au Congo." Colloque International sur la Lutte contre les Grandes Endémies, 1970, pp. 93-110. Antwerp: Prince Leopold Institute of Tropical Medicine, 1970.

In addition to these vector-borne diseases, tetanus is of real concern in many areas. Its prevalence is related both to specific occupations and practices. The disease is caused by anaerobic bacteria that live in dung or earth. In many areas of the developing world, tetanus in newborn children is a major danger, often because dung is used to stem the bleeding of the umbilical cord. Agricultural workers who wound themselves while working are also susceptible to tetanus. The use of animal manure as fertilizer may worsen the problem.[16] Induced abortion in unsanitary surroundings is a common cause of tetanus infection. Without sophisticated medical care for the disease, the fatality rate approaches 100%.

Chapter 2: CAUSES OF POOR HEALTH

Even though life expectancy is increasing and the incidence of specific diseases, such as malaria, has been reduced through eradication programs, poor health persists as a major problem in many developing countries. The conditions responsible for this situation need to be better understood if effective policies are to be formulated. Climate, cultural practices and life styles undoubtedly have an impact on health. However, the socioeconomic characteristics of a population have an even more pervasive influence.

Secular increases in health standards in Western Europe and North America were brought about much more by rising living standards and improving socioeconomic conditions than by medical care *per se.* For example, the incidence of cholera and typhoid fell in Britain and the United States long before effective methods of treatment were available; to this day, developed countries do not practice generalized immunization. In Sweden, death rates have been falling steadily since about 1800.[1] In the United States, tuberculosis deaths went down from 200 per 100,000 population in 1900, to 3 per 100,000 in 1967. Yet sanitoria and collapse therapy for treatment of tuberculosis were not widely available until the 1930s—when the death rate was already down to about 70. Chemotherapy became available only in the 1950s

---

[16]*In Kenya, the incidence of tetanus increased rapidly and was highest in areas where agricultural activity was greatest. See Fendall, N. R. E., "Agronomy and Health." Lancet: 648, 1965 (October 2).*

[1]*Scrimshaw, N.S. "Myths and Realities in International Health Planning." American Journal of Public Health 64(8):792–798, 1974. Scrimshaw argues that better nutrition has been the main factor in mortality declines in both developed and developing countries.*

when the rate was below 30.[2] It is the poverty of developing countries, with its accompaniments of rapidly expanding populations, inadequate nutrition, and crowded and unsanitary living conditions that is at the root of the health problems described in Chapter 1. The ways in which these elements of a low level of socioeconomic development interact and foster disease are explored in this Chapter.

Demographic Factors

A number of health risks derive from high fertility rates in developing countries. When large numbers of people live in poor households located in crowded, unsanitary surroundings, communicable diseases spread easily, and high mortality and morbidity rates result, particularly in the case of children. High mortality rates, in turn, induce families to have many children so they can assure themselves of surviving progeny. This circular pattern of high fertility rates and high mortality rates is difficult to break because lower mortality rates are followed slowly, and then only partially, by lower birth rates (see Table 5). In countries with high birth rates, children compose a relatively high proportion of the population. Children under five years of age make up 15% to 20% of the total population of developing countries, compared with about 8% in developed countries. Because children have less immunity to disease than adults, children's diseases predominate in developing countries, where half of all deaths are accounted for by children under five years of age.

High fertility rates imply high parity, and high parity directly affects maternal mortality—a sharp and steady increase in risk of death occurring after the third birth. Although the differentials are most marked where obstetric care is minimal, higher maternal morbidity due to toxemia, placental disorders, malpresentations and hémorrhage continues to occur in women of high parity after improved obstetrical care has reduced mortality.[3]

At a family level, population pressure increases the resort to abortion, a practice which can carry major health risks. Data on induced abortion are very difficult to obtain because the practice is illegal in most developing countries. Nevertheless, it is known that between 1958-60 in Chile, abortions accounted for 8% of all admissions to National Service Hospitals and 27% of blood transfusions; they were

[2]For a review of these issues, see Winkelstein, Jr., Warren. "Epidemiological Considerations Underlying the Allocation of Health and Disease Care Resources." International Journal of Epidemiology 1(1):69–74, 1972.

[3]World Health Organization, for the United Nations Economic and Social Council. Working Paper No. 8 for the World Population Conference, 1974: Health Aspects of Population Trends and Prospects, p. 17. New York: United Nations, 1973. This is an extremely useful paper on the interrelation of health and population.

Table 5

**Mean Rates of Decline in Infant Mortality Rate (IMR) and Crude Birth
Rate (CBR) in Developing Countries Since 1945–49 by Interval
Between Decline in Infant Mortality and Onset of Decline
in Crude Birth Rate**

Interval between decline in IMR and CBR	Number of countries	Rates of change since 1945-49 in:	
		Infant mortality rate	Crude birth rate
0 years	1[(1)]	−.0361	−.0178.
5 years	6	−.0196	−.0219
6–9 years	16	−.0373	−.0165
10–14 years	14	−.0353	−.0238
15–19 years	13	−.0327	−.0146
20 years	3	−.0288	−.0000
Total	53	−.0367	−.0178

[(1)]The Dominican Republic experienced a temporary rise in infant mortality after 1950-54, which has since reversed; the crude birth rate has been declining since 1950-54, so that the fall in birth rate appeared to precede the fall in death rate even though in 1950-54 the crude birth rate was 44.0 and the infant mortality rate was 79.7.

Source: World Health Organization, for the United Nations Economic and Social Council. *Health Aspects of Population Trends and Prospects,* E/CONF.60/BP/7, Table 1. Mimeo. New York: United Nations, 1973 (June 28).

responsible for over $1 million in hospital care expenditures in 1960. Studies in Turkey in the early 1960s estimated that, in a population of less than 30 million, 500,000 abortions were performed every year, and resulted in 10,000 deaths. One study in Turkey found 6.7 maternal deaths from abortion per 100 live births. The overall abortion rate in three metropolitan areas of Turkey recently was 56 abortions per 100 live births. For women over 30 years of age there were 1.1 to 1.5 abortions per live birth.[4] Studies of several areas have found the rate of abortion to be much higher among women who have already had several children.[5] Thus abortion can be interpreted principally as a response to untenable population pressure, at the family level.

Demographic factors may influence health at the community level as well as at the family level.[6] Population pressure on the land may lead to overcropping, soil degradation, and poor nutrition for an entire community. It may force people to migrate, with the resulting emotional and physical health problems of social disorganization. Population growth makes it more difficult to provide safe or sufficient water

[4]*Helpern, Milton, et al. "Abortion and Public Health."* Abortion in a Changing World, Vol. 2, Robert E. Hall (ed.), pp. 47-48. New York and London: Columbia University Press, 1970. *The figures should be regarded as approximate.*

[5]*Chow, L. P. "Abortion in Taiwan."* Ibid., Vol. 1, pp. 253-254. Requena, Mariano. *"Abortion in Latin America."* Ibid., Vol. 1, pp. 341, 345–346.

[6]*World Bank.* Population Policies and Economic Development, pp. 68–72. Baltimore and London: The Johns Hopkins University Press, 1974.

supply, garbage disposal and sanitation for the community. It increases the cost of providing adequately trained health manpower and medical facilities. When population pressure exists in a community, housing is likely to become congested; while high population density in a favorable social environment may not create major health problems, in an environment of poverty the probability that the infection will spread is very high.[7]

Malnutrition

Widespread malnutrition is a characteristic of poor nations which contributes to the incidence and severity of health problems. It poses a major threat to children and, in extreme cases, threatens their lives. Data presented earlier (in Table 4) underlined the role of malnutrition as a *primary* cause of death of children under five years of age in selected locations in Latin America.

In addition to being a primary cause of death among children in the developing world, malnutrition creates serious health problems by contributing to premature births and to abnormally low weight at birth. A major study of child mortality in Latin America—a comparatively well-fed part of the developing world—found that nutritional deficiency and immaturity (i.e., premature and/or underweight babies) were the direct cause of 6% of the deaths occurring before the age of five, with one or the other factor an associated cause in 57% of all deaths.[8]

Malnutrition is also a major contributing factor in infectious disease. Malnutrition impairs normal body responses to disease, thereby reducing acquired immunity. The importance of malnutrition as a contributing cause of illness and death has been widely documented. For example, it has been observed that, except where populations are malnourished or otherwise uncommonly susceptible to disease, the incidence of tuberculosis is significantly lower than would be expected by the widespread presence of the tubercle baccillus.[9] Diarrheal diseases have resulted in large numbers of deaths among undernourished children in Guatemala.

Similarly, it has been observed that mortality due to measles was 274 times as high in Ecuador as in the United States in 1960–61—before the

---

[7]Cassel, John. "Health Consequences of Population Density and Crowding." National Academy of Sciences, Rapid Population Growth: Consequences and Implications, pp. 462-478. Baltimore and London: The Johns Hopkins University Press, 1971.

[8]Calculated from data in Puffer, Ruth R., Serrano, C. V., and Dillon, Ann. The Inter-American Investigation of Mortality in Childhood, pp. 2-6. Washington: Pan American Health Organization/WHO, 1971.

[9]Scrimshaw, N. S., Taylor, C. E., and Gordon, J. E. Interactions of Nutrition and Infection, pp. 60-142. Geneva: World Health Organization, 1968.

development of measles immunization. At the time of the study, the incidence of the disease in the two countries was probably not significantly different. A more recent study of Recife, Brazil, identified nutritional deficiencies in 74% of measles deaths.[10]

Just as malnutrition can increase susceptibility to disease, so also can disease contribute to malnutrition. Epidemics of diarrheal diseases are often followed after a few weeks by outbreaks of nutritional diseases. This has been a well-documented and frequent occurrence in many countries, including Mexico, India, New Guinea and Brazil, etc.[11] Enteric infections inhibit the absorption of nutrients in the intestinal tract, thereby increasing the intake required to maintain nutritional status. Furthermore, fevers associated with infections increase the role of metabolism and thereby boost nutritional requirements.

The problem of inadequate nutrition is compounded by rapid population growth. Large family size and close spacing of births frequently preclude sufficient food and care for children.[12] Evidence of the correlation between malnutrition and large family size comes from Nigeria,[13] Thailand[14] and India.[15] Large family size and closely spaced births combine to make malnutrition a major cause of death among children under five years of age.

Unsanitary Conditions and Housing

The fecally-related or fecally-transmitted diseases found throughout the developing world share a common origin: the contamination of food, water or soil with human waste. If water is not safe for drinking, or is insufficient for personal hygiene and sewage disposal, diarrheal disease will spread more easily. Typhoid, dysentery and cholera are spread in this way, as are other intestinal infections which not only cause much illness among adults, but are also often fatal to infants or undernourished young children. Another disease related to poor sanitary conditions is trachoma. Although the exact transmission cycle is

---

[10]Puffer, Ruth R., and Serrano, Carlos V. Patterns of Mortality in Childhood. *Scientific Publication No. 262, Table 99. Washington: PAHO/WHO, 1973.*

[11]Scrimshaw, Taylor, and Gordon, op. cit., pp. 216-221.

[12]Aguirre, A., and Wray, J. "Estudios Epidemiologicos sobre Desnutricion en Candelaria" (unpublished paper, 1965), cited in Bryant, John, Health and the Developing World, p. 103. Ithaca: Cornell University Press, 1969.

[13]Morley, D. C., Bicknell, Joan, and Woodland, Margaret. "Factors Influencing the Growth and Nutritional Status of Infants and Young Children in a Nigerian Village." Transactions of the Royal Society of Tropical Medicine and Hygiene 62(2):164-195, 1968.

[14]Wray, J. D. "Population Pressure on Families: Family Size and Child Spacing." National Academy of Sciences, Rapid Population Growth, op. cit., Vol. 2, p. 408.

[15]Gopalan, C., and Rao, K. Visweswara. "Nutrition and Family Size." Journal of Nutrition and Diet 6(3):258-266, 1969.

still in dispute, trachoma is known to be closely related to poor hygienic conditions, particularly a lack of water for washing. Dusty conditions exacerbate the disease.

Surveys of water supply and sanitation facilities in the developing world have recently been conducted by the World Bank and the World Health Organization.[16,17] Data on the proportion of populations served by community water supply and sewage disposal facilities are presented in Table 6. These data are only approximate because of

Table 6

Estimates of Access to Water Supply and Sewerage[1]

	Per capita income in 1970 (US$)			
	Less than $100	$101 to $150	$151 to $450	Greater than $450
Number of countries	15	17	34	12
Percentage of population with access to water supply				
Rural, with reasonable access	13	8[2]	28	32
Urban, with public standpost	24	31	21	17
Urban, with pipe to house	21	36	58	63
Percentage of population with access to sewage disposal				
Rural, adequate	7	12	26	n/a
Urban, other disposal methods[3]	54	67	40	n/a
Urban, sewage system	6	14	24	n/a

[1]These estimates were obtained by calculating the population-weighted average of reported coverage within the group of countries. The definitions of coverage and of urban and rural are those developed by the individual countries and hence are not comparable. Furthermore, no attempt has been made to evaluate the quality of these statistics at the country level. The values reported in this table should therefore be interpreted only as crude "order of magnitude" indicators.
[2]This value is dominated by India and Pakistan which report 6% and 3% coverage, respectively.
[3]Buckets, pit privies and septic tanks not connected to public sewer system.
Sources: Pan American Health Organization. *1972 Annual Report of the Director, Pan American Sanitary Bureau, Regional Office of the World Health Organization.* Official Document No. 124, Table 32. Washington: PAHO, 1973.
World Health Organization. *World Health Statistics Report,* 26(11), Tables 3 and 5. Geneva: WHO, 1973.

inconsistencies in the definition of "reasonable access" to water supply and "adequate disposal" of excreta. Nevertheless, even from these approximate data, it is evident that rural populations in the poorer developing countries have access to almost no sewage disposal facilities. In urban areas, there is considerable reliance on buckets, pit privies and septic tanks which are not connected to a public sewer system. Facilities connected with the city sewer systems are not widespread, except in the higher-income developing countries.

---

[16]See World Bank. "Water Supply and Sewerage." World Bank Operations: Sectoral Programs and Policies, pp. 239-254. Washington: World Bank, 1972.
[17]World Health Organization. World Health Statistics Report 26(11):720-783, 1973.

In most countries, only a small proportion of the rural population has access to modern water systems. In the urban areas of countries with per capita incomes below $150, roughly a third of the population depends on public standposts, and only the middle- and higher-income groups use more sophisticated facilities. A substantial part of the population—rural and urban—relies on polluted river water, or similar sources.

For both water supply and sanitation facilities, the proportion of the population which is well-served rises with the level of socioeconomic development. Rural and shanty-town populations, however, still have access to no, or only the most rudimentary, facilities.

The link between sanitary conditions and health is illustrated by studies that report on health improvement resulting from better water supply and sewage facilities. Studies in several developing countries document a reduction in diarrheal diseases brought about by better water supply and sanitation facilities.[18] Privy construction in Costa Rica helped halve the death rate from diarrhea and enteritis between 1942 and 1954.[19] In a Philippines case study, improved water supply and toilet facilities cut cholera incidence by about 70%.[20] In nineteenth-century Britain, cholera was brought under effective control several decades before the causative agent, *cholera vibrio*, was discovered. Studies in California and Kentucky indicate that the incidence of dysentery in children varies dramatically, depending on the water and sewerage standards of dwellings.[21] The incidence among children living in dwellings with inside water supply, but outside privies, was twice as great as for children in dwellings with inside water and flush toilets. The rates of incidence doubled again for children in dwellings using both outside water supplies and outside privies.

Not all studies, however, show that better water supply systems and sanitation facilities result in improvements in health. Several studies have concluded that the source of water supply for a family matters less than might be expected; "the bacteriological purity of water as

[18]Van Zijl, W. J. "Studies on Diarrheal Disease in Seven Countries." Bulletin of the World Health Organization 35:249-261, 1966.

[19]Schliessman, D. J. "Diarrheal Disease and the Environment." Bulletin of the World Health Organization 21(3):381-386, 1959.

[20]Philippines Cholera Committee. "Field Evaluation of Environmental Sanitation Measures against Cholera." World Health Organization, Strategy of Cholera Control, BD/CHOLERA/71.5:31, Table 5. Geneva: WHO, 1971.

[21] For a review, see Schliessman, D.J. "Diarrheal Disease and the Environment." Op. cit., pp. 381-386. Many studies of the impact of environmental factors on health have failed to control for the effects of correlated variables—most notably, the level of socioeconomic development and of nutrition. Thus, they overestimate the importance of environmental measures. Several studies have sought to resolve this problem; e.g., Hollister, Arthur C., Beck, M. Dorothy, Gittelsohn, Alan, and Hemphill, Emmarie C. "Influence of Water Availability on Shigella Prevalence in Children of Farm Labor Families." American Journal of Public Health 45(3):354-362, 1955.

measured by type, city or well, did not influence infection rates."[22] The answer to this paradox may possibly be found in the cultural practices of the populations studied. For example, drinking water is often stored in cooling jars, which are nearly always contaminated. Or families may continue to drink well or river water because of greater convenience, better taste, social patterns or its supposed special qualities.

Cases can also be found where privies had little effect on the prevalence of disease,[23] or even had a negative effect.[24] Here, too, cultural habits may offer an explanation. A poorly maintained privy may be worse than none at all. Alternatively, even where public acceptance of privy campaigns in areas of Latin America has been good, the privies have frequently been used as chicken coops or grain silos.[25] Obviously, the health benefits will be limited in such cases. The ambiguous findings do not cast doubt on the link between sanitary conditions and disease. Rather, they point to the difficulties encountered in trying to change traditional patterns of behavior.

Relatively simple techniques of waste and water treatment are available which, if applied, would greatly diminish the risks of catching fecally-transmitted disease. Sanitary storage of human excreta accomplishes a great deal; within two weeks, many of the harmful bacteria die because they cannot survive for long outside the human host. Viruses are also delicate organisms and can be expected to die quickly. Helminths can remain a hazard for a longer period of time, particularly in the form of resistant cysts; eventually the cysts also die. Another technique of waste disposal is sedimentation or filtration. In both cases, the solid particles to which bacteria cling are separated out and retained till harmless. In addition, two decomposition processes, which occur naturally, render sewage harmless: oxidation (using oxygen from air or water) and anaerobic fermentation. Which of the two processes occurs depends upon the availability of oxygen for oxidation. Many "modern" processes, such as trickling filters and aeration, are simply intended to speed the natural process. Most decomposition processes rely on successive biological cycles which involve different algae. During the course of these cycles, organisms that are harmful to man are destroyed. Even helminths may be killed by the heat generated by a composting system of anaerobic fermentation. If at all pos-

[22]Stewart, William H., McCabe, Jr., Leland J., Hemphill, Emmarie C., and DeCapito, Thelma. "The Relationship of Certain Environmental Factors to the Prevalence of Shigella Infection." American Journal of Tropical Medicine and Hygiene 4:718–724, 1955 (July).

[23]Scrimshaw, N. S., Taylor, C. E., and Gordon, J. E. Interactions of Nutrition and Infection. Op. cit., pp. 248-249.

[24]Van Zijl, W. J. "Studies on Diarrheal Disease in Seven Countries." Op. cit., p. 252.

[25]Wagner, E. G., and Lanoix, J. N. Excreta Disposal for Rural Areas and Small Communities. World Health Organization Monograph Series No. 39, p. 22. Geneva: WHO, 1958.

sible, a biologically pure source of water should be chosen. If not, processes such as storage and sedimentation-filtration should be employed. Chemical treatment by chlorination of water is also highly effective in destroying a wide variety of disease agents.

In addition to poor sanitation and water supplies, very sizable proportions of the total population of cities in developing countries live in substandard dwellings lacking in space, ventilation and sunlight. Such conditions tend to increase the incidence of air-borne diseases. It is probable that overcrowding is the main reason why children in low-income countries contract air-borne diseases at an earlier age than in developed countries. In addition, the extended family system brings the child into regular contact with many other children at a very early age, thus increasing his exposure to disease. Among children whose immune response is not yet fully developed, the risk of serious multiple infections is very high. In developed countries, the risk does not arise until the child enters school.

Causes of Improved Health

To recapitulate, the *core health problems* throughout the developing world, except among middle- and upper-income urban groups, are fecally-transmitted diseases, air-borne diseases and malnutrition. These three elements interact cumulatively and synergistically. This is particularly true of those below the age of five, but also applies to the older age groups. Improved water supply and sanitation check the fecally-related disease cycles. More spacious, well-ventilated living conditions cut down the transmission of air-borne and fecally-transmitted diseases. Better nutrition reduces susceptibility to infection, and greatly diminishes the severity as well as the duration of illness; it is of special importance for infants and young children.

Few worthwhile studies have been conducted concerning the effects of health services on health status, and those that exist are difficult to evaluate. In some cases, concurrent improvements in water supply, sanitation or housing have not always been fully taken into account, or nutrition may have improved, but its effect has not been identified.

Sophisticated health approaches are inappropriate unless backed up by outreach and preventive services. Modern drugs, in some instances, bring immediate relief, or even eventual cure, but may have no lasting effect on the health of a person who must return to a disease-ridden environment. Treatment for parasitic infection may mitigate the clinical symptoms, but is not likely to keep a person from becoming reinfected. A medical school program for hospital care of premature infants in Colombia achieved survival rates comparable to those in North America, but 70% of the infants discharged from the premature nursery were dead within three months.[26]

Three research projects—in Guatemala, Nigeria and the United States—have demonstrated that primary health care and increased nutrition could have a substantial impact on mortality among both infants and children in the one-to-four age group (see Table 7). The studies also show that such health care could be effective even if delivered by auxiliaries, with only limited referrals to physicians[27] or hospitals.[28] However, the relative importance of nutrition *vis-à-vis* primary health care is very difficult to determine. In addition, infant mortality in an environment of poverty is likely to remain greatly in excess of that in a developed country. Child morbidity is likely to remain at a high level too.

In general, better water supply, sanitation and housing alter the *incidence* of disease, and in this way affect morbidity and mortality. Nutrition alters both the *incidence* and the effects of clinical disease. Even under very favorable circumstances, curative health care can do little to alter the incidence of disease,[29] although it can reduce its harmful effects. Curative health care systems will, therefore, benefit the population principally by lessened *effects* rather than lessened *incidence* of disease, unless there is a strong emphasis on preventive health in the services offered.[30]

[26]J. D. Wray, *personal communication, cited in Bryant, John.* Health and the Developing World, *p. 240. Ithaca: Cornell University Press, 1969.*

[27]*In the cases covered by the Guatemalan study, 99% of all visits were handled by primary care personnel and only 1% were referred to a physician. Even if no such referral had been possible, and all those referred would otherwise have died, the fall in mortality would have been considerable due to care by auxiliaries. See Habicht, Jean-Pierre. "Delivery of Primary Care by Medical Auxiliaries: Techniques of Use and Analysis of Benefits Achieved in Some Rural Villages in Guatemala." Pan American* Health Organization, Medical Auxiliaries. *Scientific Publication No. 278, pp. 24-37. Washington:* PAHO, 1973.

[28]*During a year, according to the study at Imesi, Nigeria, roughly 30 children per 1,000 were referred to a hospital. Even if no such referral possibility had existed and all these children had died, the fall in child mortality would have been impressive due to care by auxiliaries. See Morley, David.* Paediatric Priorities in the Developing World, *pp. 146 and 318. London: Butterworths, 1973.*

[29]*In the United States study, the Navajo Many Farms scheme, very intensive and expensive curative health care, with considerable efforts at preventive health, achieved significant reduction in the incidence of tuberculosis and ear infection; this might well have been more difficult to achieve in a less scattered community. Incidence of active trachoma, and of the pneumonia-diarrhea disease complex, was not affected. Presumably in both cases the reservoir of infection and ease of transmission remained too great. See McDermott, Walsh, Deuschle, Kurt W., and Barnett, Clifford R. "Health Care Experiment at Many Farms." Science 175: 4-5, 1972 (January 7).*

[30]*It is likely that health care in the areas covered by the Nigerian study was so effective because of the strong emphasis on preventive health services, including family planning. The desired family size was down sharply compared to a control village, although still very large (see Morley, David, Paediatric Priorities in the Developing World, op. cit., Table 50), and children attended clinics an average of 20 times per year in the one-to-four age group (Morley, ibid., Table 20). In this context of overall concern for community health, it was possible to achieve a cut in the malaria parasite rate (Morley, ibid., pp. 124-147). How much was due to curative health care is unclear. Certainly, health care that is so intensive is rarely available in developing or developed countries.*

Table 7

**Experimental Impact of Health and Nutrition
Improvements on Mortality[1]**

Project Area	Infant mortality rate per 1,000 live births		Mortality rate per 1,000 children among children one to four years old	
	Before	After	Before	After
Navajo Many Farms study	150	70	N.A.	88
Nigerian study	295	72[2]	69	28[3]
Guatemalan study	139[4]	55	28	6
United Kingdom (1966)	19		0.8	

Notes:

[1]All these programs involved costs such that they would be difficult to replicate on a national scale in a developing country. For instance, health care costs were about $5 to $8 per year per child in the Nigerian and Guatemalan projects, although this figure may exclude some overhead costs. Indirect health care costs, such as nutrition, were not specified.

[2]After an additional year, the infant mortality rate was 48.

[3]After an additional year, the child mortality rate was 19.

[4]This figure is based on recall by mothers and can be compared with the national official statistic at that time of 89.

Sources: Navajo Many Farms study: McDermott, Walsh, Deuschle, Kurt W., and Barnett, Clifford R. "Health Care Experiment at Many Farms." *Science* 175:23-31, 1972 (January 7) (especially Table 2). Experiment provided nutrition; university-supported, physician-staffed primary care; and excellent hospital referral. Staff included two field physicians, two nurses, one Navajo teacher and four Navajo auxiliary health workers for each 1,000 population. Consultants were often available onsite from the parent university. Facilities included several automobiles with two-way radio-telephones for visits to the homes, and in daylight with favorable weather, the availability of a light airplane to remove critically injured persons.

Nigerian study: Morley, David. *Paediatric Priorities in the Developing World*, pp. 316-340, especially Table 52. London: Butterworths , 1973. Experiment provided some nutrition, physician-staffed primary care, and some hospital referral.

Guatemalan study: Habicht, Jean-Pierre. "Delivery of Primary Care by Medical Auxiliaries: Techniques of Use and Analysis of Benefits Achieved in Some Rural Villages in Guatemala." *Medical Auxiliaries*. Scientific Publication No. 278, pp. 24-37, especially Table 10. Washington PAHO, 1973. Experiment provided nutrition, auxiliary staffed primary care, and some referral to physicians and hospitals.

Chapter 3: APPROACHES TO HEALTH POLICY

Programs to improve health can be viewed both as "consumption," which is the final aim of economic development, and as productive investment. A systematic description of both aspects is necessary in considering present and future policy in this field. In principle, the benefits and costs of health schemes should be assessed to determine the order of priorities; in practice, the calculations often turn out to be far too difficult and unreliable. Where benefit-cost analysis is not feasible, cost-effectiveness analyses may provide information which is useful in improving resource allocation within the sector.

A Social Goal

It is obvious that health contributes directly to human well-being and may, in fact, be regarded as one measure of welfare. Good health permits participation in personal, family, social and political activities.

Health care has an important human support function in comforting the afflicted and counseling the anxious. Whether or not illness can be cured or even mitigated, health care satisfies a felt human need— one to which people have been prepared to devote substantial manpower and financial resources in nearly all societies at all times.

A Productive Investment

The impact of health on the productive capacity of society is somewhat easier to measure than its direct consumption value. Ill health is thought to impose economic costs by: (1) reducing the availability of labor; (2) impairing the productivity of employed workers and capital goods; (3) wasting current resources, particularly nutrients; and (4) impeding the development of natural resources, animal wealth and tourism potential. Each of these costs is elaborated in the following discussion.

Reducing Availability of Labor

Both premature death and absenteeism due to illness reduce the availability of labor. However, the sizable unemployment and underemployment in developing countries implies that premature mortality may not impose an economic cost in itself. If ill health results in replacement at no cost, of deceased workers by the able-bodied unemployed, there may be no reduction in output.

Morbidity in the labor force leading to absenteeism may have a greater economic impact. Absenteeism usually disrupts the production process; even under conditions of high unemployment, the temporary replacement of absent workers is likely to result in loss of output. Only a few surveys provide data on the effects of diseases on absenteeism and, therefore, on output. A careful study of tuberculosis control in the Republic of Korea concluded that an optimal disease program resulting in increased work life and decreased absenteeism would yield a return of $150 for each dollar spent.[1] Additional examples of disease control programs that have substantially reduced absenteeism include antimalaria programs in the Philippines and southern Africa, and yaws control programs in Haiti.[2] Various efforts have been made to estimate the cost of absenteeism due to disease, by valuing days lost at current wages. The resulting estimates are often very large, although they are misleading under conditions of high unemployment.

[1] *Feldstein, Martin A., Piot, M. A., and Sunderesan, T. K.* Resource Allocation Model for Public Health Planning: A Case Study of Tuberculosis Control. *Supplement to Volume 48 of the* Bulletin of the World Health Organization, *p. 95. Geneva: WHO, 1973.*
[2] *Winslow, C. E. A. The Cost of Sickness and the Price of Health. WHO Monograph Series No. 7, pp. 22, 25, and 30. Geneva: WHO, 1973.*

Impairing Productivity of Labor

Ill health affects the productivity of workers since their strength, stamina and ability to concentrate suffer. The statistical evidence on this is limited. A recent Bank study of construction and rubber plantation workers in Indonesia showed that the effects can be very important. The prevalence of hookworm infestation was 85%, and 45% of the victims suffered from a resulting iron deficiency anemia. Treatment of the anemic workers with elemental iron for 60 days, at a total cost of 13 U.S. cents per laborer, resulted in an increase in productivity of approximately 19%.[3] This implies a benefit-cost ratio of 280 to 1. However, one of the most careful studies undertaken on the effects of disease on labor productivity in a developing country found the effects of schistosomiasis and certain other diseases in St. Lucia to be slight.[4] These findings are qualified by the fact that the economic effects of many helminthic infections, including schistosomiasis, depend upon the intensity of infection, and the St. Lucia form of schistosomiasis is not very severe.

A conceptually distinct effect of ill health on productivity derives from its impact on education and training. Ability to learn is impaired by sickness and malnutrition.[5] Absences from school because of disease may reduce cognitive achievements. Early mortality and disability will reduce the period of time over which the pay-off from an investment in human capital can be expected, and thus diminish the productivity of training.

Wasting Current Resources

Many helminthic diseases waste resources because nutrients are consumed by the helminths themselves. A waste of calories occurs in the case of fevers, because of the extra metabolic demands made on the body. In enteric diseases, intestinal absorption of nutrients is impaired. One study in Panama reports, for example, that the value of excess food consumed in cases of enteric infections amounted to about $10 per person per year.[6]

Disease also leads to expenditures on treatment. Coverage by modern health services is limited in many developing countries, but often

---

[3]Basta, S. S., and Churchill, A. "Iron Deficiency Anemia and the Productivity of Adult Males in Indonesia." World Bank Staff Working Paper No. 175, pp. 6-8. Washington: World Bank, April 1974.

[4]Weisbrod, Burton A., Andreano, Ralph L., Baldwin, Robert E., Epstein, Erwin H., Kelley, Allen C., and Helminiak, Thomas W. Disease and Economic Development, pp. 72-80. Madison: University of Wisconsin Press, 1973.

[5]Selowsky, Marcelo, and Taylor, Lance. "The Economics of Malnourished Children: An Example of Disinvestment in Human Capital." Economic Development and Cultural Change 2(1):18-19, 1973.

[6]United States Office of International Health, Department of Health, Education and Welfare. Syncrisis: The Dynamics of Health, Vol. I: Panama, p. 44. Washington: Government Printing Office, 1972.

money is spent in other ways on treating diseases: self-medication with local or modern drugs, or payments to injection men, traditional healers or spirit doctors. Whether or not modern or traditional medicine is effective, the costs of treating illness are a burden on the community.

Impeding Development of Resources

An enormous waste of resource occurs when poor health conditions restrict settlement in areas with fertile land or other natural resources. The presence of onchocerciasis has restricted access to land and resources in Western Africa. Studies of Nepal, Sri Lanka and parts of Mexico show instances where malaria eradication has induced a movement of labor and capital into resource-rich districts from less well-endowed areas, with a net increase in the total output.[7] A similarly successful settlement scheme was carried out in the Anchau Corridor in Nigeria after the control of sleeping sickness.[8]

Some human diseases also infect animals in certain areas,[9] and programs can improve human and animal health simultaneously, thereby facilitating exploitation of animals as food or as draught animals. The possibilities of fostering livestock development while benefiting human health are not limited to disease-control programs only. For example, providing water in arid areas not only permits the development of livestock and crops, but can also help improve the health of human beings. It may cut time spent in carrying water back and forth, which can be a considerable saving.[10]

The tourism potential of a country can be undermined if the likelihood of contracting serious diseases is unusually high. One example is sleeping sickness in game parks. Sudden epidemics of disease can have a particularly dramatic effect on tourism; they may even affect commodity exports because of controls imposed by importing countries.

Better Health for Socioeconomic Development

Health is at the heart of a complex set of interrelationships. As shown in previous chapters, the entire disease pattern in a particular area is intimately related to levels of fertility, standards of living and cultural habits. Poverty, ill health, high fertility, high mortality, fatalism

---

[7] Taylor, Carl E., and Hall, Marie-Françoise. "Health, Population and Economic Development." Science 157:651-654, 1967 (August 11).

[8] McKelvey, Jr., John J. Man Against Tsetse, pp. 156-173. Ithaca: Cornell University Press, 1973.

[9] The pork and beef tapeworm, trypanosomiasis, brucellosis, anthrax, hydatid disease, and sometimes schistosomiasis in the S. Japonicum form.

[10] Wagner, E. G., and Lanoix, J. N. Water Supply for Rural Areas and Small Communities. WHO Monograph Series No. 42, p. 19. Geneva: WHO, 1957.

and short time horizons constitute a possible low-level social equilibrium. In practice, this equilibrium has already been disturbed in most developing countries by a fall in the death rate, and in some countries by the start of a fall in birth rates. Better health is one way human beings achieve more positive control of their environment, and that, in turn, increases their desire and ability to plan their future. Within this framework are many linkages. Economic and educational development may encourage family planning[11]; family planning improves nutrition; nutrition improves health; health can improve attitudes to family planning, reduce absenteeism, increase labor availability and productivity, and facilitate exploitation of natural resources. The net impact of these factors on economic development, however, is ambiguous, and will depend critically on the time lags involved and the magnitude of each response.

Paradoxically, health improvements may pose a threat to well-being if the net effect is to increase the rate of population growth significantly. Changes in health status affect population growth in a number of ways. Firstly, any generalized improvement in health in a developing country will lower mortality among the very young; this, by itself, will tend to increase population growth. Secondly, by reducing the many diseases that interfere with completion of pregnancy, better health and nutrition tend to increase fecundity. Thirdly, lower maternal mortality will also increase the number of surviving women who can bear children. For example, venereal diseases reduce fecundity; infectious hepatitis, tuberculosis and malaria interfere with completion of pregnancy; malnutrition contributes to maternal mortality, fetal loss, shorter fertile time-spans and absence of menstrual periods. Thus, better health and nutrition may well increase the *ability* to produce healthy babies and their chance of survival. The effects of better health on the will to reproduce, however, is less clear.

If parents aim for a target number of surviving children, a decline in mortality among young children could lead to a reduction in fertility. There is some evidence that parents respond to a child's death by a desire to replace it, suggesting that a fall in child mortality would tend to be partly compensated by a fall in fertility.[12] Some empirical evidence on the relationship between a fall in infant mortality and a fall in fertility is shown above in Table 5.

---

[11]*Especially education for women. See U.N. Secretariat. "Women's Rights and Fertility."* U.N. World Population Conference, Bucharest, Romania, August 1974, Conference Background Paper, *E/CONF. 60/CBP/5, pp. 3-9. New York: United Nations, 1974. Many of the factors affecting fertility have been discussed in World Bank,* Population Policies and Economic Development, *Appendices A and B, pp. 141-163. Baltimore and London: The Johns Hopkins University Press, 1974.*

[12]*World Bank.* Population Policies and Economic Development, *pp. 52-53.*

The data suggest that a decline in the birth rate is related to a fall in the infant mortality rate, but that the birth rate is less than perfectly responsive. Studies of sharp changes in mortality, such as those conducted in Sri Lanka and Mauritius, suggest that the birth rate falls less sharply than the death rate.[13] There are also cases, such as Jamaica, where death rates fell steadily but birth rates did not decline significantly for a long time. While death rates and birth rates have tended to move together, it is impossible to determine which is the causative factor; it does seem, however, that a fall in mortality is frequently accompanied by a less pronounced fall in fertility. The speed and the extent of the response may perhaps be increased by the delivery of effective family planning services.[14]

When satisfactorily integrated with other socioeconomic advances, health improvements are a vital part of the development process. But if promoted in isolation, improved health could have unbalancing effects, because the adverse effects of more rapid population growth may undermine health gains. A constructive health policy will aim at maintaining the delicate balance between better health and overall economic development.

Role of Government

The private market cannot be expected to allocate to health either the amount or the composition of resources that is best from a social perspective. The most critical failure of the market derives from the inability of consumers of health services to choose rationally. This inability is in part a consequence of the extraordinary complexity of medical problems and the consumer's lack of experience as a patient. Market failure also results from the presence of externalities. For example, procedures which halt the spread of communicable disease yield benefits to entire communities and, therefore, cannot be chosen properly by individuals acting in their own interest. The health care system possesses many of the characteristics of public utilities. Often the unit producing services (health station, clinic or hospital) must be large relative to the local service area so that effective competition is not possible. For these and other reasons, governments have found it necessary to intervene in the health sector.

The role of governments in the health sector can be illustrated by reference to three distinct situations. The first relates to health for a special group of workers or in a small zone of critical economic importance. Often the private market mechanism will direct resources to

---

[13]Frederiksen, Harald. "Feedbacks in Economic and Demographic Transition." Science 166(3907): 837-847, 1967 (November 14).

[14]World Bank. Population Policies and Economic Development, pp. 133-140.

those health expenditures which have an attractive financial payoff. Private corporations frequently undertake disease control before opening up new land for commercial plantation or mineral exploitation. Private industry provides nutritional supplements or subsidized dispensary facilities for workers if this causes profits to rise as a result of reduced absenteeism and increased labor productivity. Financially rewarding opportunities for health investment do exist, but the market mechanism breaks down all too frequently due to ignorance, the riskiness of health technology, and the presence of indivisibilities, and of external economies and diseconomies.

In principle, public investment need not be circumscribed by imperfections of cost-price signals and many outlays on health can be justified if planners are sensitive to the health dimension of production or infrastructure projects. Lack of such sensitivity in the past has caused considerable damage to the health status of populations residing in the areas in which government projects are located. The neglect of the health aspect has been most unfortunate in projects connected with the use of water: hydroelectric dams, irrigation and drainage schemes. They may have contributed to the spread of water-related diseases, such as malaria, onchocerciasis and schistosomiasis. These adverse consequences can be mitigated by giving explicit attention to the health aspect at the project design stage and by introducing health components, if necessary. Wherever the extra cost of the health component is more than offset by additional benefits, the overall economic return on the investment will rise. Economic benefits of health outlays can usually be identified, but there will be many instances in which they defy precise measurement. Accordingly, it is easier to specify the critical minimum size of the health component that should be introduced in a project than to determine its optimum level.

Secondly, it is necessary to consider programs to control specific diseases on a nationwide basis. In this case, indivisibilities and external economies are such that the market mechanism is most unlikely to function. The application of cost-benefit analysis may, however, help to identify a sizable volume of government expenditure on health which can be justified as "investment." Alternatively, cost-effectiveness analysis may provide suggestive evidence. However, even at this level, the possible importance of demographic effects may make a standard economic approach to project analysis hazardous.

Thirdly, there are programs to improve the general health of the bulk of the population. In this case, the private market mechanism undeniably operates but the distortions are very serious. Maldistribution of incomes in countries where average incomes are also very low means that the health needs of the poor are not translated into effective

372

demand. While the distortion caused by income inequality applies to all sectors, the consequences for health are particularly tragic. Because of the emotional appeal of health issues, it may be politically attractive to redistribute welfare through government provision of health care.

Affluent groups in developing countries have the economic capacity to pay at market prices for most of the health services they require. Public subsidy to them is difficult to justify by any standard. However, it would appear appropriate for governments to encourage the development of insurance schemes and prepayment mechanisms for the relatively affluent. While such a program might be expected to enroll only a small part of the population, it would nonetheless foster the private alternative in health care and relieve the public sector health budget. It is important that any private scheme be devised in such a way that it does not claim a disproportionate share of health resources or encourage their misallocation.

To achieve the best results from available resources, government health programs should be designed on the basis of cost-effectiveness studies. This is a subject which has not been explored adequately, so there are many unanswered questions. It is possible, however, to illustrate the technique by comparing the cost-effectiveness of immunization and sanitation measures in the case of cholera. Vaccination gives only about 50% protection from cholera for four to six months. The per capita cost of such immunization is 15 cents. Under admittedly favorable conditions in the Philippines, rudimentary privies were built at a cost of under $1 per privy, excluding self-help labor. This is equivalent to a per capita cost of about 15 cents. Such privies, if properly maintained, cut cholera rates by about 60%. Even after allowing for maintenance and replacement costs, privy construction is clearly more cost-effective than immunization. Even when the costs of privies is three times that of immunization, the privy program will be cheaper after the sixth year.[15]

In comparing privy construction with merely treating those who fall ill, the rate of incidence of fecally-related diseases is an important factor to be taken into account. Viewed as a way to cut down on the incidence of cholera alone, privy construction would tend to be slightly the more expensive alternative—even in a cholera endemic area—because clinical cholera occurs in only a small proportion of those infected and, in any case, is a relatively rare disease even in endemic areas. However, privy construction can also reduce the incidence of a whole range of other killing or disabling diseases. Epidemiological

[15]Cvjetanovic, B. "Sanitation versus Vaccination in Cholera Control: Cost-Effect and Cost-Benefit Aspects." World Health Organization, Strategy of Cholera Control, BD/CHOLERA/71.5, p. 36. Geneva: WHO, 1971.

models which represent biomedical realities adequately are extremely difficult to construct, so that rigorous cost-effectiveness analysis is difficult to conduct.[16] Nevertheless, the diseases whose incidence can be reduced through improved water supply or improved sanitation are many, and account for a very large part of the total disease pattern. The fact implies that privy facilities which are properly used and maintained would be far more economical than personal curative care.

Chapter 4: PRESENT POLICIES OF DEVELOPING COUNTRIES

Few governments in developing countries have tried to select health policies after rational consideration of the questions discussed in the previous chapter. The objectives of health expenditures in terms of consumption and investment have rarely been articulated. The administrative framework for making decisions is usually fragmented, the data base is deficient, and specific measures are seldom evaluated for cost-effectiveness.

Expenditures on Health

Government expenditures on health in low-income countries seldom exceed 2% of GNP. The small sum spent per capita is one reason for the narrow coverage provided by public health services. Annex 3 presents data on government health expenditures per capita and as a percentage of the national budget. Of the 65 developing countries for which data are available, in 17 countries governments make health outlays that are less than $1 per capita, and the average outlay for the very poor countries with a per capita income of under $100 is only 87 cents. The average rises to $1.42 for countries with per capita incomes between $101 and $200, and to $2.85 for countries with per capita incomes between $201 and $300. The pattern of government health outlays per capita is summarized in Table 8.

Public health services cover only a small proportion of the population in developing countries because heavy emphasis is placed on high-cost, individual, curative medicine, as opposed to environmental

---

[16]A very sophisticated attempt is made by Cvjetanovic, B., Grab, B., and Uemura K., in "Epidemiological Model of Typhoid Fever and Its Use in the Planning and Evaluation of Antityphoid Immunization and Sanitation Programmes." Bulletin of the World Health Organization 45:53-75, 1971.

Table 8

Per Capita Government Health Expenditures in Developing Countries

(Figures are for recent years)

		Government health expenditures per capita					
Per capita GNP	Total number of countries	Less than $1.00	$1.01 to $2.00	$2.01 to $3.00	$3.01 to $5.00	$5.01 to $10.00	Above $10.01
		(Number of countries)					
Less than $100	12	9	2	0	1	0	0
$101–200	15	7	3	4	1	0	0
$201–300	16	0	4	5	5	1	1
$301–600	14	1	1	3	4	4	1
$601–1000	8	0	0	2	1	0	5
Totals	65	17	10	14	12	5	7

Source: Based on Annex 3.

and preventive measures. The bulk of the limited government outlays for health go toward maintaining expensive, well-equipped hospitals manned by highly trained medical personnel. For various reasons discussed later in this chapter, large numbers of people living in the countryside or city slums are allowed to remain beyond the reach of the modern medical sector. Thus, present health policies are not only inefficient but also inequitable in most developing countries. The limited data available on private expenditures for health suggest that private health spending is often considerably larger than government spending, and the ratio between the two types of expenditures varies widely.

Most private and public expenditures on health services in both poor and rich countries are devoted to episodic curative care. Individuals have a tendency to neglect preventive measures and early diagnosis, choosing instead to call on professional care only during health crises. Governments have ratified the practice by supporting the construction and staffing of curative care facilities. Quantitative evidence on the extent of the bias is not available, in part because a standard of cost-effective preventive health care has not been established. The fragmentary data that are available on the extent to which people rely on curative care in developing countries are shown in Annex 4.

Resources for Medical Care

A large part of government funds are spent on hospitals, particularly on inpatient services manned by highly and expensively trained doctors and nurses. These modern medical facilities are concentrated in urban centers. In Ghana, for example, 62% of physicians in 1969 were in urban areas, where 15% of the total population lived.[1] Similarly, the Greater Accra Metropolitan Area in the same period had 23% of the nation's hospital beds, but only 9% of the total population. Figures for physician availability reinforce the impression that the geographical distribution of their services is very uneven in developing countries (see Annexes 8 and 9).

Physicians usually settle in urban centers rather than respond to the critical needs of rural areas. In addition, many physicians from developing countries migrate to the developed world for specialty training not available at home. As a result, some developed countries have large, circulating pools of physicians from developing countries: the United States has about 12,000; the United Kingdom, 5,000; and Canada, 1,300. Most of these physicians return home after about three years. However, about 1,500 physicians a year from developing countries establish permanent residence in the United States; several hundred per year do so in the United Kingdom.[2] There are similar flows to other developed countries. Annex 13 provides additional data on the emigration of physicians from developing countries. The countries of emigration are India, Pakistan, Philippines, Thailand, the Republic of Korea, Argentina and Colombia. While the highest rate of migration shown, 67%, is for Thailand, only an estimated 4% of Thai emigrant physicians practice abroad permanently. On the other hand, 17% of the 22% of Turkish physicians who emigrate do not return to their native land.

The education of physicians is extremely expensive—often costing more than $25,000 per physician at 1974 prices, but occasionally exceeding $80,000. These estimates are for recurrent costs alone and exclude the capital costs of medical schools. They also do not include the exceptional costs of providing the elaborate teaching hospitals that are often attached to medical schools.

A considerable proportion of international assistance has been given to developing countries for the training of medical personnel. Often the emphasis has been on sophisticated clinical treatment of acute illness in individuals rather than on improving the health level of a whole community on a continuing basis. The training abroad of clinical specialists has often served to increase the status of sophisticated hospital services, and has almost certainly helped to divert both funds

---

[1]Sharpston, M. J. "Uneven Geographical Distribution of Medical Care: A Ghanaian Case Study." Journal of Development Studies 8(2):210, 1972 (January).

[2]The Committee on the International Migration of Talent. International Migration of High-Level Manpower, pp. 695-696. New York: Praeger Publishers, Inc., 1970.

and manpower from an extension of the coverage provided by health services.[3]

Coverage of Official Health Services

Although the evidence is fragmentary, it appears that public health services cover only a small part of the population in many developing countries. In some cases, the proportion covered is so small that the influence of the services on the nation's health can at best be negligible.

Most patients visiting health facilities come from the immediate vicinity. In Kenya, 40% of the outpatients attending a health center lived within five miles; 30% lived five to ten miles away; and only 30% lived more than 10 miles away.[4] An Indian study showed that the proportion of a community attending a dispensary decreased by 50% for every additional half-mile between the community and the facility.[5] In another Indian study, over 60% of the patients came from within one mile of the primary health center.[6] To a large extent, the area of influence of an outpatient health facility is limited by the distance patients are prepared to walk.[7]

The decline in inpatient use of health facilities is somewhat less rapid, but still rather dramatic. In Uganda, the use of inpatient facilities halved for every three miles; outpatient attendances halved every two miles. In Ghana, 80% of the inpatients at the five major hospitals came from the urban district in which the hospital was located.[8] From these facts (often known as the patient care "gradient") it is possible to calculate the proportion of a country's population without access to government health coverage, although the calculation may err on the op-

---

[3]*Equipment may even be bought specifically to satisfy the "need" of a physician who has received specialized overseas training, without reference to the priority health requirements of the relevant population: see Sharpston, M. J. "Uneven Geographical Distribution of Medical Care: A Ghanaian Case Study," op. cit., p. 215. On the general issue, see Weller, Thomas H. "Tropical Medicine: Obligations and Responsibilities." Presidential Address,* American Journal of Tropical Medicine and Hygiene *14(2): 184-185, 1965 (March).*

[4]*Fendall, N. R. E. "Medical Planning and the Training of Personnel in Kenya." Journal of Tropical Medicine and Hygiene 68:12, 1965.*

[5]*Frederiksen, H.* Maintenance of Malaria Eradication. Duplicated Report WHO/Mal/429, p. 2 and p. 6, Table 1. *Geneva: WHO, February 1964.*

[6]*India, Rural Health Training Centre, Najafgarh.* The Services from a Primary Centre (1964). *Cited in Roemer, Milton I. Evaluation of Community Health Centres, p. 25. Geneva: WHO, 1972.*

[7]*For a review of this subject, see Jolly, Richard, and King, Maurice. "The Organization of Health Services." Medical Care in Developing Countries, Maurice King, (ed.), pp. 2.6-2.7. Nairobi: Oxford University Press, 1966. For additional supporting evidence for Tanzania, see Gish, Oscar. "Resource Allocation, Equality of Access and Health." World Development 1(12):38-39, 1973 (December).*

[8]*Study by Saakwa-Mante, cited in Sharpston, M. J. "Uneven Geographic Distribution of Medical Care: A Ghanaian Case Study." Op. cit., pp. 211-212.*

timistic side because it assumes that coverage within a stated geographical radius of a health facility is adequate.[9] In Ghana, only about half of the population was covered on this basis. In Thailand only 32% of the total districts have physicians who have authority to diagnose disease and treat patients.[10]

Given the poor transport typical of rural areas in the developing world, distance is a serious impediment to obtaining health care. Dirt roads often become impassable in the rainy season and, in any case, travel on foot or by draught animal may be the only form of transport available to the inhabitant of a rural area, particularly in an emergency. Yet speed can be essential to effective treatment.

For infants with acute diarrheal disease, timely oral rehydration by a medical auxiliary close by is likely to be more effective than belated but sophisticated parenteral rehydration at a distant hospital. To some extent, the same applies for adult patients. It is estimated that cholera patients who arrive at a hospital within three hours of the onset of symptoms run no risk of death; that those who arrive after three to six hours have a 10% fatality rate; and that after six hours, the fatality rate is 30%.[11] There is a similar need for speed in the case of some deliveries.[12] For chronic conditions, a long trek to a distant health facility may not seem worthwhile until a long period of increasing debility has been suffered. By then, however, irreversible damage may have occurred. Perhaps more importantly, distance is an overwhelming obstacle to use of the health care system when no crisis exists, and prevention is thus neglected.

It has become declared policy in most developing countries to pro-vide a "pyramid of health care"—starting with health centers or health posts, through district hospitals, up to a national referral-teaching hos-pital. Yet in all but the most advanced and geographically small devel-oping countries that have exceptional transport and communications facilities, the problems of long-distance use of health facilities seem almost insurmountable. In Ghana, the Central Hospital absorbed 149 of the 298 physicians available to the official health services, yet only about 1% of the patients in this hospital had been officially referred by

[9]Sharpston, M. J. Op. cit., pp.211-213. It was assumed that health care within the urban district (or similar size area) containing a health facility was "adequate."

[10]Muangman, Debhanon. "Rural Health Care in Thailand." Paper presented at Quaker International Seminar, Philippines-Indonesia, July-August 1973 (unpublished), p. 5.

[11]Mathen, K. K., Barua, D., Cvjetanovic, B., and Uemura, K. "Costs of Treatment and Prevention and Economic Losses due to Cholera." World Health Organization, Strategy of Cholera Control, BD/CHOLERA/71.5, p. 14. Geneva: WHO, 1971.

[12]In theory, it would be both possible and desirable to screen high-risk pregnancies in advance, so that the need for possible special treatment was already organized as the woman went into labor. In fact, however, few such systems actually exist.

medical personnel outside the hospital. Another 7% had referred themselves, coming into the Accra region from outside for treatment.[13]

A wide cultural gap may exist between the personnel at a modern health facility and the tradition-bound people it is designed to serve. Even a relatively unsophisticated facility can encounter resistance. In Ghana, health posts were equipped with maternity beds, although rural Ghanaian women apparently preferred delivery at home. As a result, the maternity facilities were underutilized.[14] A study of rural Thailand found the health service underutilized because people apparently preferred such alternatives as herbalists, priests, spirit doctors, pharmacists, "quack" doctors or injectionists, traditional midwives, and friends and relatives.[15] A survey in a peri-urban area of Cali, Colombia, found that 40% of the population used a well-staffed health center, 28% knew of its existence but did not use it, and 32% did not know about the center at all.[16] Even in a developed country, hospitals are frightening places to many people, only to be visited in times of extreme need. A villager is even more likely to react with anxiety to the sophisticated clinical facilities of an urban hospital. In addition, the cultural gap between physician and patient, even if the physician is a fellow-national, may be so great that discussion of symptoms can be very difficult.

The combined impact of geographical, administrative and cultural factors seriously limits effective health coverage in many developing countries. In 1970, a countrywide health survey undertaken in Thailand[17] found that, on the average, sickness occurred twice per year per person[18] but that only 17% of the surveyed population utilized public health facilities during a year. Even in the metropolitan area of Bangkok, 45% of the people treated themselves with the aid of a pharmacy; in the rural areas this figure rose to 61%. Private clinics were important sources of health care in Bangkok, serving 31% of the people, and traditional doctors or priests were quite important in the rural areas of Thai-

[13]Study by Saakwa-Mante, cited in Sharpston, M. J. "Uneven Geographical Distribution of Medical Care: A Ghanaian Case Study." Op. cit., pp. 209-211.

[14]Sharpston, M. J. "Health and Development." Journal of Development Studies 9(3):455–456, 1973 (April).

[15]Cunningham, Clark E. "Some Social Aspects of Rural Medicine in North-Central Thailand: A Preliminary Data Paper." Cited in Bryant, John. Health and the Developing World. Ithaca: Cornell University Press, 1969.

[16]Llanos, Guillermo, personal communication (1967), cited in Bryant, John. Health and the Developing World, p. 88.

[17]Ministry of Public Health and the Faculty of Public Health, Mahidol University, Bangkok, Thailand (1970), cited in Muangman, Debhanom. "Rural Health Care in Thailand." Op. cit., p. 5.

[18]This low figure implies a severe interpretation of "sickness." In the United States or the United Kingdom, in an average month, one person in four consults a doctor, and disease incidence is certainly far lower. See White, K. L., Williams, T. F., and Greenberg, B. G. "The Ecology of Medical Care." New England Journal of Medicine 265:885–892, 1961. Cited in Fendall, N. R. E. "Primary Medical Care in Developing Countries." International Journal of Health Services 2(1):301, 1972.

land, serving 12% of the people.[19] In Cali, Colombia, where the physician-population ratio is 1:910, 17% of the children who die are not seen by a physician, and another 19% have no medical attention during the 48 hours preceding death.[20] A study in rural Punjab, India, found that for every 100 of the population, there were 89 yearly contacts with health personnel in the public sector, against 221 with registered indigenous medicine practitioners.[21] A recent study in a village close to New Delhi showed that only 7% of illness came to the attention of the medical services.[22] In another study of Punjab, 8,000 episodes of illness were reviewed: 36%, or 3,000, did not require health services. Of the remaining 5,000, 10% were dealt with by the public sector, 29% by private practitioners (mostly indigenous), and 61% received no care at all. "In Egypt, which has a more widely distributed health service than India, one study showed that only 20–25% of families made use of National Child Health Centers and up to 80% of mothers were dependent on traditional midwives for delivery."[23]

Effectiveness of Official Health Services

Despite their obvious limitations, official health services have achieved some measure of success. A striking example is ·the use of residual insecticides for malaria eradication, where very significant results were obtained with large-scale international assistance. Other diseases have also been controlled by environmental measures. Trypanosomiasis has been controlled in much of Africa by cutting down undergrowth which forms a suitable habitat for the tsetse fly. Smallpox has been successfully controlled by immunization throughout much of the developing world. If sufficient coverage can be achieved,

---

[19]A Colombian study showed that only 23% of those who fell sick sought medical advice; of those, 28% consulted pharmacists, nurses, traditional healers and others (rather than a physician). However, nearly 40% became sick in a two-week period, which suggests that mild ailments were included, for which self-treatment would be normal even in a developed country. See Ministry of Public Health, Colombia, and Colombian Association of Medical Schools. Health Manpower and Medical Education in Colombia—Vol. II: Preliminary Findings, pp. 25–30. Washington: Pan American Health Organization, 1967.

[20]Personal communication from Guillermos Llanos, cited in Bryant, John. Health and the Developing World, pp. 52–53.

[21]Kakar, D. N., Srinivas Murthy, S. K., and Parker, R. L. "People's Perception of Illness and their Use of Medical Care Services in Punjab." Paper presented at Seminar on Behavioral Research in Health and Medical Care sponsored by the Indian Council of Medical Research, New Delhi, March 1972 (unpublished mimeo), cited by Morley, David. Paediatric Priorities in the Developing World, p. 57. London: Butterworths. 1973.

[22]Personal communication from Ghai, O. P. (1971), cited in Morley, David. Paediatric Priorities in the Developing World, p. 57.

[23]Hamman, M., Allah, A. F. A., Hammouda, A. M., and Shaurawz, A. E. A. "Field Training in Family Health Care for Medical Students in Assuit University." Paper presented at the Conference on the Teaching and Practice of Family Health, Benghazi, 1973, cited in Morley, David. Op. cit., p. 59.

measles may soon be similarly contained by immunization.[24] Yaws has also been contained throughout much of the world, an achievement possible only since the discovery of penicillin. Cholera control has reduced deaths in India from 800,000 per year during the epidemics at the turn of the century, to the current rate of 3,000 a year.[25]

The extent to which personal health services have helped reduce the effects of disease probably varies widely according to the level of official health coverage. For example, in Sri Lanka and Cuba, the impact has probably been considerable, because of the excellent coverage and availability of doctors, even in the rural areas. In Sri Lanka, the provision of cheap or free rice has probably improved general nutrition and, therefore, health levels as well.

Recently several countries have initiated health service programs that rely on very low levels of technology, and focus broadly on community activities rather than exclusively on personal services. These programs have recruited indigenous service providers, systematically building on public trust and social discipline to implement impressive programs of vector control, sanitation, health education and public health. The most notable of the programs has been developed in the People's Republic of China. Although the information available is limited, it is useful to summarize what is known about this program.

In the 1950s, the People's Republic of China placed considerable emphasis on providing new urban hospital beds.[26] Probably in response to Russian influence, "middle medical schools" were set up where students, who had reached the intermediate level in secondary school, attended a three-year course to become "assistant doctors." At the time of the "great leap forward" in 1958, an increased effort was made to provide health care to rural areas, and to promote cooperation between practitoners of traditional and Western medicine. Interest in rural health services may have diminished somewhat in the period that followed. However, the "cultural revolution" brought major changes. "In medical and health work, put the stress on the rural areas," stated a directive of June 26, 1965. Commune members with only primary education were selected to receive three months of training, periodically augmented by refresher courses, thus becoming "barefoot doctors." They were trained to give first aid, supervise immunizations, oversee refuse and excreta disposal, and promote public health campaigns. Some divided their time between agricultural and health work, according to the commune's decision. By now,

---

[24] A very efficient vaccine now exists. See, for example, Morley, David. Op. cit., pp. 226–230.

[25] Mathen, K. K., Barua, D., Cvjetanovic, B., and Uemura, K. "Costs of Treatment and Prevention and Economic Losses due to Cholera." Op. cit., pp. 20–21.

[26] Horn, Joshua S. Away with All Pests, p. 60. New York and London: Monthly Review Press, 1969.

about one million "barefoot doctors" have been trained, or roughly one per 800 people.

The high level of participation in the socioeconomic development of the People's Republic of China greatly facilitated the implementation of public health measures. Because of widespread environmental and preventive measures, health problems have greatly diminished, despite the fact that water and sanitation facilities are much poorer than in developed countries. Typhoid still exists and the pneumonia-diarrhea complex of early childhood is still a major problem. Syphilis may well have been brought under control. Schistosomiasis continues, although control efforts probably have greatly improved the situation. In southern China, malaria has been brought under reasonable control by the use of DDT. Hookworm still exists, but its serious clinical effects are not in evidence. Tuberculosis has been greatly diminished, although it is still found on a larger scale than is typical in a developed country.[27] The same is true of trachoma.[28] "Barefoot doctors" have probably performed a useful first aid function, not least in terms of providing human support. They may have done little to supervise intensive nursing of sick infants, but by use of modern drugs, including those normally prescribed only by a physician in the West, have had some impact on disease and suffering in older age-groups. Although no national data are available, informed observers believe that health levels are remarkably high, considering the stage of development reached by the People's Republic of China.

Chapter 5: A HEALTH POLICY FOR THE FUTURE

Per capita health budgets and the availability of trained manpower vary greatly among developing countries. The potential for extending the coverage of official health services, therefore, is very different at different levels of development, as are the health reforms that might be implemented. It may be feasible for some countries to think in terms of developing a network of health services staffed mainly by well-trained paramedicals who refer complex cases to physicians and district hospitals, but at the moment such a possibility seems remote for the poorest countries. However, even very poor countries can extend some sort of health services on a nationwide basis. How rapidly

---

[27]Sidel, Victor W., and Sidel, Ruth. "The Delivery of Medical Care in China." Scientific American 230 (4):21, 23 and 26, 1974 (April).

[28]McDermott, W., and Stead, Jr., Eugene A. Pattern of Disease (unpublished paper, 1974), pp. 58-64.

the target can be reached and what standard of service can be provided will vary from country to country. In the final analysis, the allocation of public funds for this purpose remains a matter of value judgment and political feasibility. As argued earlier, public health expenditures to improve the quality of life of the poor can be justified on moral and economic grounds, although the complex and dynamic interaction of demographic, social and cultural forces affected by health makes it difficult to say, on economic grounds, how large such expenditures should be.

Substantial savings can be secured by nationalizing existing hospitals, curtailing hospital construction, and overhauling policies on the pricing of health services. Reforms of the health system for expanding coverage of village communities and the urban poor should emphasize environmental and preventive measures aimed at controlling the incidence of disease, combined with the use of standard drugs and simple procedures for treating illness. Implementation of such a scheme would require a new approach to training health personnel and organizing delivery systems. Essentially, the aim would be to promote health from *within* the community on a continuing basis, rather than from without on an episodic, crisis basis.

Financing Extended Coverage

Restricting the use of government funds for construction of new urban hospitals or expansion of existing ones is the easiest method of freeing resources for expansion of coverage. Furthermore, if hospital services in developing countries were subjected to a thorough cost-effectiveness analysis, substantial savings could be secured. This is because, firstly, too much is spent on inpatient services compared with outpatient services. The former are extremely expensive. In Kenya, in the mid-1960s, an average inpatient stay cost about $12 at a district hospital, $24 at a regional hospital and $52 at a national hospital.[1] These estimates exclude sizable capital costs. A large part of recurring inpatient costs are essentially "hotel" costs—laundry, catering, heating, airconditioning—which have a remote relation to treatment or cure. There is reason to believe that the bulk of serious illness typical of developing countries—diarrheal diseases, malnutrition conditions, leprosy, tuberculosis—can be treated effectively on an outpatient basis.

Secondly, the stay of an inpatient can be shortened in various ways. For example, the duration of a cholera patient's stay in a hos-

---

[1]Jolly, Richard, and King, Maurice. "The Organization of Health Services." Medical Care in Developing Countries, Maurice King (ed.), Chapter 2. Nairobi: Oxford University Press, 1966.

pital can be reduced dramatically by the use of antibiotics.[2] Thirdly, many savings can be realized through administrative and cost-control measures that include avoiding wastage through time-expiration of drugs, pilferage and bad maintenance of buildings and equipment.

The system of pricing government health services is critically important, not only for mobilizing funds but also for resource allocation in the health sector. It is important to devise methods for discouraging malingerers and those inclined to use sophisticated medical facilities irrespective of need. A policy of full-cost pricing of health services would create substantial financial incentives for people to avoid hospitals (particularly inpatient services), and to rely instead on less expensive visits to outpatient facilities and local health posts. Such a scheme would also mobilize some funds for the government to finance activities for which it cannot charge users. It is tempting to introduce different charges for the rich and the poor, if at all administratively feasible, but care should be taken that this does not encourage the expansion of higher revenue-earning services for the rich rather than services for the poor.

The Reformed Health Service

The main conclusion of the last chapter was that the official system of health care at present is top-heavy; too much is being spent on doctors and hospitals in urban areas, while coverage in the countryside is extremely limited. Future policy should correct this bias by (1) extending the coverage of the primary health care system; (2) increasing the responsiveness of existing health posts and district hospitals to the needs of the primary health worker; and (3) planning the extension of primary care with the aim of supplementing the role played by traditional healers in village society.[3]

To be effective, the health care system must be very close—both geographically and culturally—to the community it serves, and it must enjoy the full confidence of the community. By identifying health problems close to their onset, and by motivating, supervising and educating individuals and families to avoid infection and to seek appropriate treatment, the local primary health worker would be in a better position to exploit the potential of environmental health measures and modern medical science than his counterpart in the conventional official systems of health care. Generally, the latter

---

[2]Mathen, K. K., Barua, D., Cvjetanovic, B., and Uemura, K. "Costs of Treatment and Prevention and Economic Losses due to Cholera." World Health Organization, Strategy of Cholera Control, BD/CHOLERA/71.5, p. 13. Geneva: WHO, 1971.

[3]Mahler, H., Director-General of the World Health Organization. "Address to the World Health Assembly," 27th World Health Assembly. Geneva: World Health Organization, May 1974.

lacks the capacity to penetrate the community, is not familiar with local life styles, and tends to emphasize curative medicine.

The community health worker, under the reformed system, should reside in the community he serves and should command the respect of the community. He should be integrated into the local society so that he can identify disease without patient-initiated contacts at the health post. Routine periodic house visits may sometimes be required to make such assessments; in other instances, local political, social or religious institutions may offer opportunities for ongoing surveillance of community health conditions.

The health worker can be male or female, an old traditional healer or birth attendant, or a young primary school graduate. The choice should reflect cultural attitudes, and literacy would not be an essential qualification. There would be community involvement in selecting the worker who, in many cases, would also hold other employment. He would receive brief training in treating some of the most common diseases. Training in clinical skills would be very limited; complicated cases would have to be referred to health centers, district hospitals or possibly traditional healers. The limitation on the curative skills of the health worker would be desirable to ensure adequate time for environmental and preventive work. The worker would be taught the fundamentals of maternal and child care, of delivery, and of monitoring the growth of young children, particularly for nutritional problems. The worker would organize mothercraft sessions for feeding malnourished children and the nutrition education of mothers, provide immunizations, and be responsible for encouraging family planning.

The worker would also be responsible for organizing community efforts in environmental health, water supply and sanitation. A large range of simple technologies is available for excreta disposal, and pit latrines can be easily constructed with local labor and materials and only a minimum of technical assistance.[4] Provision of water at low cost with only limited outside technical assistance is often much more difficult. It is not always feasible to provide bacteriologically safe water at a price which can be afforded, and with equipment which can be maintained. Planning for maximum water quality standards may, in effect, condemn much of the population to completely unimproved water supplies for an indefinite period. In such cases, there might be a trade-off between water quality and quantity, especially since for health purposes simple dilution of the disease agent is very important.

[4]For a review of this subject, see Wagner, E. G., and Lanoix, J. N. Excreta Disposal for Rural Areas and Small Communities, pp. 17-24 and 159-164. Geneva: WHO, 1958.

Community-based health workers would probably best receive their training in stages: perhaps one day every two weeks for six months if travel distances are short; or a continuous training period of two weeks, followed by an interval of several months, and then possible further training. The curriculum should be carefully designed so that it is easy to understand and is of practical use in terms of the exact disease and cultural patterns of the local population. Although continuous refresher training with the same material would always be required, the teaching of progressively more advanced curative skills should be related to successful performance of community workers in the basic fields of preventive and environmental health. Indicators of success could be such measures as contraception acceptors, immunizations performed, latrines built, and the state of the village water supply. The traditional health care system will probably continue to be important for a long while.

Such health workers would be much better suited, technologically and socially, to cope with the disease pattern of poor communities than the clinical physician. The health worker's great virtue would be his socioeconomic and cultural origin—the same as that of the people he is servicing—and thus his capacity to interact with them in a style and idiom they understand. However, it should be recognized that his socioeconomic origin is also the source of his weakness; he can easily be exploited by dominant groups in the village, and his relatively brief training can be swamped by a lifetime of tradition or custom. To be effective, the health worker must be monitored, supervised and supported by other ranks in the hierarchy of the health delivery system.

The immediate supervision of these community health workers would be provided by auxiliaries. Such auxiliaries would be full-time community health promotion workers, with perhaps 18 months to two years of health training in addition to primary or, if possible, middle school education. A substantial part of their training would be spent on water supply and sanitation technology, elementary medical sociology and traditional medicine. Some clinical skills would also be taught, but it would be important to ensure that adequate emphasis is given to promotion of community health rather than to care of disease on an individual basis.

Two alternatives exist for higher management of this service. Under one system, the supervisory auxiliary would, in turn, report to a "primary-care managerial physician." Compared with a typical clinical doctor, such a physician would have training that is less clinical and has a different emphasis: much less attention would be given to the degenerative diseases and more to the treatment of infectious diseases common in developing countries. A primary-care managerial physician would be trained to perform emergency surgery with limited equipment. He would be better trained than the typical clinical doctor in epidemiology—the science of the causes of diseases in their social setting. More generally, he would receive education in community health promotion on a continuing basis rather than in episodic curative health care provided on an individual basis. All this would involve a study of local customs and an acquaintance with methods of traditional healers. He would need to have an elementary familiarity with agronomy, the nutritional value of crops and the place of livestock in rural life. He should be able to participate in general efforts at rural development and to discuss health-related improvements with community leaders.

The great majority of medical schools in the developing world are not capable of producing primary-care managerial physicians. However, efforts to reorient training and education programs are now being made in Mexico, Colombia, Israel and Cameroon. Experiments are under way in Mexico to move medical teaching away from lavishly equipped special hospitals to provincial hospitals and health centers under conditions which approximate normal situations in the field. In Israel, attempts are being made to associate training with community health by giving medical schools some responsibility for providing health services in a district.

An alternative approach to managing the supervisory auxiliaries is to entrust the management of the reformed health service to people who have a broad background in rural development, community work and administration, but who are not physicians. In this case, the managers would obtain technical support in medical care and public health from others, although it would also be necessary for these managers to receive some public health training.

The curriculum proposed for the primary-care managerial physician is exacting. Once in the field, such persons might feel—with some reason—that their advanced medical training is somewhat wasted. In addition, the natural human urge to do clinical work, and to save lives which perhaps only the physician can save, could tend to distract the managerial physician from his assigned tasks of community health promotion, supervision and, particularly, administration. The second alternative of putting individuals who are not physicians in charge of such programs would free managers from these pressures. If they are familiar with community work, they would have an attitude appropriate to community health promotion.

The reformed health service proposed here would be expected to provide greater access to health care, greater penetration into the community and lower unit costs. To operate economically, the system needs procedures and drugs that are as simple and inexpensive as possible. The sophisticated diagnostic work-ups of advanced Western medicine would not be possible. The basis for choice of procedures or drugs would be that, even if administered casually, they would generally improve the health of the community. If community support is to be preserved, it is also important to guard against excessive risk of what the community views as untoward side effects. Failure to observe these principles would probably undermine the effectiveness of the health care system.

The economies obtainable under the reformed system will be offset to some extent by salaries for a much larger number of primary health workers. Not to pay attractive salaries to all personnel would be a false economy and would injure the entire package. On balance, however, the reformed system is likely to be less expensive to operate per capita than the existing traditional system.

Increasing Effectiveness of Official Health Services

Financing extended coverage through measures that improve the cost-effectiveness of hospitals has already been considered in this chapter. The underlying premise of the reformed health service is the need to change the emphasis from expensive treatment of illness in individuals on an intermittent curative basis only, to the promotion of health on a *continuous* basis at the *community* level. This requires a change in the ecological and cultural situation in which disease thrives. It will not be easy to achieve for it requires a systematic and sustained approach aimed at changing living habits and attitudes, as well as household and community action to improve water supply and sanitation practices. The aim is not to ignore the demand for curative care but to bring about a balance between measures that treat disease and measures that control its incidence. Attempts to provide health education or environmental health will encounter resistance if they are divorced from curative care. The problem is to make certain that curative care does not preempt all other approaches.

The proposed mix of training and activity for community health workers, auxiliaries and managers is designed to address this problem. The reformed health service will provide limited curative care based on standard drugs and simple procedures which can be administered in the field by workers who have had brief training. These activities will be combined with a strong emphasis on measures to improve nutrition, water supply, sanitation and health education. To maintain this balance over time will require repeated reinforcement through

monitoring and evaluation procedures aimed at preventing the dislocation of preventive and environmental measures in favor of curative services, for which there is a ready demand. In turn, the monitoring and evaluation should be linked directly to criteria for giving
salary increases and promotions to community workers within the
health service.

The case studies which have already been cited, and the experiences of the People's Republic of China, Tanzania and several Latin
American countries, indicate that community-based health promotion
services can be highly effective. However, in practice, various factors may combine to lower the effectiveness of such services in improving the health of the general population. At a technical level,
insufficient emphasis on preventive and environmental health supervision, and health and nutrition education, may greatly diminish the
impact on morbidity and mortality. At a sociopolitical level, inegali-
tarian distribution of power within a community may limit access by
some of the population to such services, and confer excessive benefits on certain groups. Furthermore, the degree of effectiveness of
community-based health promotion services, will inevitably depend
upon the degree of social cohesion and sense of social responsibility
of a community. Nevertheless—and provided there is adequate commitment on the part of the government—such services offer perhaps the
best hope of achieving a major improvement in the health levels of
the larger part of the population of developing countries.

Chapter 6: WORLD BANK LENDING FOR HEALTH-RELATED PROJECTS

The health sector in developing countries has not been the object
of the World Bank's lending activities, but the Bank has financed a wide
range of activities that influence health conditions. The proportion of
Bank-supported projects containing health components has been
growing; the growth reflects the attempt over the last five years to
broaden the Bank's lending in ways which directly attack problems
of poverty. Since 1970, lending activities have also reflected the Bank's
concern with environmental issues. Though the figures are not all-
inclusive, Tables 9 and 10 identify a number of health-related projects
receiving Bank assistance. These grew from five projects in fiscal 1969
to 20 in fiscal 1973. Excluding the grant for the onchocerciasis program

Table 9

World Bank/IDA Lending for Health-related Projects: Population, Nutrition and Water Supply and Sewerage, FY1962-78

	FY 1962-68	FY 1969	FY 1970	FY 1971	FY 1972	FY 1973	FY 1974	FY 1975	FY 1976[1]	FY 1977[1]	FY 1978[1]
Population											
Number of projects	–	–	1	2	2	2	2	3	3	5	6
Amount of loans and credits	–	–	2.0	7.8	34.4	21.5	17	43	54	69	89
Nutrition											
Number of projects	–	–	–	–	–	–	–	0	1	1	1
Amount of loans and credits	–	–	–	–	–	–	–	0	20	25	20
Water supply and sewerage											
Number of projects	14	5	3	9	4	11	8	14	13	15	17
Number of projects with sewerage component[2]	(3)	(1)	(2)	(4)	(2)	(5)	(3)	(7)	(5)	(7)	(8)
Amount of loans and credits	138.1	34.6	32.5	224.7	78.7	299.0	173.7	305.0	320.0	357.0	423.0

[1] Proposed lending.
[2] Figures for FY1976 are based on an average of 40-45% per year.

in Western Africa, the total for such loans and credits in 1973 was $487 million; of this amount, $299 million was for water supply and sewerage. The total of loans and credits for population projects was $22 million. Loans and credits for the health components of projects in the fields of education, rural development, irrigation and drainage, and sites and services for low-income housing totaled about $19 million.

Only in the population and education projects, however, is there evidence that health considerations have had any significant effect on the basic design of projects. In the case of water supply and sewerage, little systematic analysis of health benefits has been made, although it is assumed that these projects generated such benefits. A health component has been attached to some of the irrigation, drainage, land settlement and rural development projects, but aspects other than health have rarely, if ever, been modified significantly by health considerations. In general, health components have been a small proportion of total project costs. Population projects differ somewhat; their health components have typically been very large.

The Bank's activities in the field of population have led it into a

Table 10

World Bank/IDA Lending for Health and Projects with Health Components: Education, Rural Development, Irrigation and Drainage, and Sites and Services, 1970-73[1]

(US $ millions)

	1970	1971	1972	1973
Education				
Number of projects with health components	1[a]	1[b]	—	2[c]
Amount of loans and credits	13.8	7.3	—	43.3
Health component of projects	n.a.	0.3[2]	—	7.75
Health component as percentage				
of total project costs	n.a.	5.6%[2]	—	19.5%
Rural development				
Number of projects with health components	1[d]	2[e]	2[f]	3[g]
Amount of loans and credits	21.5	14.7	8.9	32.8
Health component of projects	n.a.	0.4	0.8	3.3
Health component as percentage				
of total project costs	n.a.	1.4%	6.4%	6.2%
Irrigation and drainage				
Number of projects with health components	—	—	—	1[h]
Amount of loans and credits	—	—	—	36.0
Health component of projects	—	—	—	8.1
Health component as percentage				
of total project costs	—	—	—	6.5%
Sites and services				
Number of projects with health components	—	—	1[i]	—
Amount of loans and credits	—	—	8.0	—
Health component of projects	—	—	0.4	—
Health component as percentage				
of total project costs	—	—	3.8%	—
Health				
Number of projects with health components	—	—	—	1[j]
Amount of loans and credits	—	—	—	n.a.[3]
Total cost of projects	—	—	—	54.0

[1] By calendar year of appraisal report.

[2] Capital cost only.

[3] 0.75 as first grant.

[a] Greece
[b] Uganda II
[c] Tanzania IV, Zambia III
[d] Jengka II (Malaysia)
[e] Karonga (Malawi), Caqueta (Colombia)
[f] Upper Volta, Alto Turi (Brazil)
[g] Jengka III (Malaysia), Rwanda, Mauritius
[h] Upper Egypt Drainage
[i] Senegal
[j] Western Africa: Control of River Blindness

much more direct concern with health than has been the case in other fields. Financing health facilities used for the delivery of family planning services (health centers, maternity hospitals, vehicles and training institutions) have taken up the bulk of the loans and credits. The total cost of the nine population projects for which Bank/IDA assistance of approximately $81 million was approved through fiscal 1974 is about $154 million. Of this amount, $94 million, or 62%, has gone to health facilities; another $59 million, or 38%, consists of funding health manpower training costs and operating costs.

The Bank has been active in population projects only since 1970. The first four years of operations have seen the initial approach to providing family planning services evolve from the concept of a service-delivery system somewhat independent of general health considerations, toward a much closer integration with general health-delivery systems. The early projects show a relatively heavy emphasis on the construction of urban maternity hospitals and on postpartum programs as major channels of acceptor recruitment. Recent projects in Indonesia, India, Malaysia, Iran and Egypt reflect increasing emphasis on rural health delivery systems, on the training of nursing and lower-level health auxiliaries, and on the integration of family planning and general health services—particularly maternal and child health services.

In most cases, identification of population projects to be supported by the Bank has been preceded by sector surveys which have increasingly included fairly extensive reviews of the potential borrowers' health delivery systems. These reviews are not designed to cover the entire health sector and they generally omit a number of important aspects. The Bank's work has brought it into increasingly close relations with WHO and, to a lesser extent, with the United Nations Children's Fund (UNICEF). A Memorandum of Understanding was signed by WHO and the Bank in November 1973, outlining the interests of each institution in population questions.

The Bank's activities in the water supply and sewerage sector started in 1961. Because of the state of operations in many countries, considerable emphasis was initially put upon administrative competence and financial viability. From the start, cross-subsidization has been accepted, and this is now being actively encouraged. Since the establishment of the Bank-WHO Cooperative Program in 1970, extensive sector surveys have been undertaken as a background to project identification.

Progress toward quantifying the impact on health of water supply and sewerage projects is illustrated by the Sao Paulo water supply and pollution control project (1971) and the Minas Gerais water supply and sewerage project (1973) in Brazil, and by the Addis Ababa project (1972) in Ethiopia. In the appraisal of the Sao Paulo project, the health benefits were not quantified; they were explicitly stated in the report to justify expenditure on sewerage mains which, on other grounds, showed an economic return of only 5%. The Minas Gerais project followed from a Bank-WHO Cooperative Program Sector Survey which reviewed the Brazilian National Sanitation Plan and covered the entire state of Minas Gerais. It was innovative in several respects, including the lending technique, the extent of cross-subsidization and the degree of emphasis on rural areas. Health questions did influence the technical design of the project in some respects (for example, avoiding intermittent water supply), but not in others (for example, choosing between standpipe and water piped to houses). By seeking to reach lower-income groups, health benefits were expected to be increased. The appraisal of the Addis Ababa project attempted to measure the social cost of water-borne diseases, attributed to the project the potential elimination of these diseases among a small proportion of the population, and thus arrived at an estimate of the health benefits in quantitative terms.

The first Bank-supported project to finance sites and services for housing was in Dakar, Senegal, in 1972. It included construction and equipment of five health centers at a cost of about $400,000, or roughly 4% of total expenditure on the project. The number of health centers was derived from the concept that one per 100 hectares was needed, but no particular justification was given for this figure, and no estimate was made of the health impact of either the project or the priority of the health center component. Similar components are included in other sites and services projects now being prepared, and it is hoped that future housing projects will include a more sophisticated analysis of the health component.

Early Bank-assisted projects in education concentrated on "hardware"—mainly constructing and equipping school buildings. In the late 1960s, increasing emphasis was placed on both technical assistance and such software as curriculum reform and educational planning. At the same time, there was a move away from general secondary education to various kinds of teacher training and technical education. This has led to the training of health personnel in a few projects, all since 1970. No definite trends have emerged in the Bank's policy for health manpower training. The first project, in Greece (1970), financed health manpower training mainly for such hospital staff as administrators, laboratory technicians, physical therapists and X-ray technicians. In contrast, the second education project, in Uganda (1971), supported the training of paramedical personnel for rural preventive services. The fourth education project, in Tanzania (1973), provided for the training of doctors who will supervise the health care given by paramedical personnel in the rural areas. In addition to paramedical training, the third education project, in Zambia (1973), included a Health Services Training School at Ndola which will use a new 650-bed hospital to train hospital staff. Thus, although there is greater awareness today of the need to emphasize rural health needs and train paramedical staff, Bank-supported projects continue to put considerable emphasis on hospital manpower.

In all cases, health manpower training has been only one component of larger projects. In the Tanzania and Zambia projects, for example, this component accounted for about 20% of the total project cost, less contingencies. In assessing the need for health manpower, the tendency has been to rely largely on national statements of manpower requirements—for instance, in the project identification work done under the Bank's Cooperative Program with the United Nations Educational, Scientific and Cultural Organization (Unesco), and in the work done by Bank consultants. The requirements have typically been based upon norms derived from the WHO targets for the first U.N. Development Decade. But the target ratios of health manpower-to-population are merely arbitrary global goals, and do not recognize differences in disease patterns or resource availability in different countries. However, in a recent development, both the Tanzania and Zambia projects included some analysis of health sector priorities as they relate to local conditions.

Studies of health manpower training have been conducted as part of education sector surveys. The Bank, however, has not yet been actively involved in curriculum development for health manpower. There is some feeling in the Bank that traditional urban-based medical schools are undesirable, and that training in a rural setting is preferable.

The increasing tendency to include a health component in agricultural projects is clearly related to the Bank's growing social concerns. Virtually all Bank-assisted agricultural projects that have health components date from 1970. During this period, the emphasis in agricultural lending has shifted from building large-scale irrigation infrastructure to providing assistance to the small farmer. Some of the recent projects involve irrigation and drainage, but they are no longer single-sector projects; rather, they are multisectoral in that they combine a number of activities, including marketing, agricultural extension and community development.

In some land settlement schemes, health facilities have been provided as part of the "minimum package" necessary to make the settlement viable. From the outset, in the Caqueta land colonization project in Colombia (1971), availability of health services was considered an important factor in influencing a settler's decision to settle permanently in a remote area with a history of high disease prevalence. In other settlement schemes—as in the Alto Turi land settlement project in Brazil (1972), or the Jengka triangle project in Malaysia (1970 and 1973)—health was conceived of as a social service to be provided at increasingly sophisticated levels as the settlement became established and financial resources permitted. In these cases, health facilities were considered important if settlers were to remain in the area.

A few rural development schemes have had health components, either to guard against the possibly harmful side effects of the project (for example, the use of schistosomiasis control measures against the effects of irrigation in the Karonga rural development project in Malawi) or as part of an attempt to integrate social and economic development (for example, the rural development project in Mauritius). Sometimes health components have been added after the first phase of a project (for example, in the Shire Valley and Lilongwe agricultural development projects in Malawi). Previous phases of the Malawi projects had not included a health component; the construction of health centers generated active self-help efforts among the rural people, who then helped build some health posts.

At least one rural development project—the rural development fund project in Upper Volta—also provided for a water supply facility, in the hope that this would benefit health. In some cases, human health has benefited incidentally from an agricultural project. For example, the successful eradication of the tsetse fly under the agricultural development project in Rwanda will benefit human as well as animal health, since the trypanosomiasis carried by the tsetse fly affects both human beings and cattle.

A typical health component of a land settlement or rural development project is the provision of health posts, clinics or centers—in theory at least for both curative and preventive health work. However, hospitals have also been included in two projects—(the Alto Turi land settlement project in Brazil, and the Caqueta land colonization project in Colombia). Environmental health measures against specific diseases have been a common element in many projects—for example, mollusciciding in Karonga for schistosomiasis, dispensing malaria prophylactics and helminthicides in the Caqueta project, and spraying houses for malaria in the Alto Turi project. A second phase of the Caqueta project may have nutrition and health education components. Already rural health promoters, selected from settlers' families and trained locally, provide first aid, vaccinations, and aid at childbirth;

dispense malaria and helminthiasis drugs; and distribute birth control materials. A typical health component entails only a very small addition to project costs—less than 1% in the Caqueta and Alto Turi projects, 4% in Kenya and 6.5% in Mauritius.

The health components that have been added to land settlement and rural development projects have not always been systematically designed. Once it has been decided to include a health component in a project, a consultant is hired to formulate the design of the component in the light of any existing health plan or development plan. Considerable enterprise has been shown in the ways in which health components have been added to agricultural projects, but no attempt has been made at a cost-effectiveness analysis of varying mixes of disease control measures—that is, vector control, water supply, and sanitation, vaccination, curative measures and health education. Nor has the technical design of nonhealth project components significantly reflected health considerations.

There are times when irrigation and drainage projects may adversely affect the health of the people unless precautions are taken. Early projects, including the Nile delta drainage project in Egypt, launched in 1969, contained no health component. In the next phase of Bank policy—illustrated by the Semry rice project in Cameroon launched in 1971—a public health consultant was employed to consider the health aspects after the basic project had been formulated. He concluded that the project would have both good and bad effects; it would reduce malaria by draining and leveling swamps, but would increase schistosomiasis in an area where the disease was already endemic. A number of control measures were considered, but were rejected on technical and financial grounds. A study of disease prevalence and of the snail population was initiated, which might lead eventually to selective mollusciciding.

In the latest phase of Bank policy, represented by the Upper Egypt drainage project launched in 1973, a consultant was employed to consider the health aspects of the project. As a result, a health component was included. The Bank is financing the foreign exchange costs of both preventive and curative measures for schistosomiasis control. One engineering design feature of the basic project—the use of closed rather than open field drains—may have been influenced by health considerations, but would probably have been chosen anyway because it saved land and required less maintenance. However, the specification of the schistosomiasis control area certainly did reflect technical vector control requirements; the control area was larger than the project area.

No attempt was made either in the Upper Egypt project, or elsewhere, to quantify the economic benefits of disease control. Furthermore, there was no cost-effectiveness analysis of alternative measures of disease control. In addition, with the one possible exception of the Upper Egypt project, the basic engineering design of projects apparently has not been affected by health considerations; and although schistosomiasis control measures have been incorporated, measures to control other water-borne diseases—for example, malaria, which can also be affected by irrigation and drainage projects—have not yet been undertaken.

The onchocerciasis project in Western Africa is a new departure for the Bank. The purpose of the project is to control onchocerciasis in a wide belt of savannah. It is estimated that one million people in the region are at present affected by the disease; a large proportion suffers from varying degrees of blindness, and about 50,000 or more are totally blind. Effective drugs for mass chemotherapy to treat the disease have not yet been developed, though some funds have been allocated for research into possible methods of mass chemotherapy. The project is essentially based on vector control by aerial spraying. The cost of the first six-year phase of this 20-year program is estimated to be $54 million.

Small-scale onchocerciasis control projects in the region have been going on for some years, and various aid organizations have been involved, notably WHO, the U.S. Agency for International Development (USAID), the Fonds d'Aide et de Coopération, the European Development Fund, and the Organisation de Coordination et de Coopération pour la Lutte contre les Grandes Endémies. However, the Bank was a central force in organizing the new, large-scale operation. There is now a Steering Committee made up of the Bank, FAO, the United Nations Development Programme and WHO; WHO is the executing agency and the Bank is the financial coordinator. Several donors—including Canada, France, the United States, the Netherlands, the United Kingdom, the Bank, and the participating aid agencies—subscribed to the Onchocerciasis Fund Agreement in March 1974, and indicated their willingness to support the program on a continuing basis. Subsequently, the Federal Republic of Germany joined the donor group; and recently Iraq and Belgium have indicated their intention to participate. Additional countries may subscribe in the future. Prospects are good that more than three-quarters of the financing required for the first six-year phase can be obtained from these donors and the African Development Bank. The World Bank itself has made a total grant of $750,000.

The program is expected to reduce debility, and also the economic burden of blindness. However, it is envisaged that the principal economic benefit will be that the program will help reclaim for human settlement the fertile river valleys that now lie deserted because of the disease. Resettlement will involve investment in infrastructure, and simultaneously provide opportunities to raise agricultural productivity.

Chapter 7: POLICY ALTERNATIVES FOR THE BANK

The Bank's earlier position, that it generally did not finance health activities, has in practice been substantially modified in recent years. There has thus already been an evolution in operational policy. Looking ahead, one policy option, which may be called Option One, is for the Bank to allow these trends to continue, to strengthen them and thereby to increase the effectiveness of its activities in the field of health. Under this option, health benefits from Bank-assisted projects would continue to increase, but the broad patterns of lending would remain basically unchanged. The health benefits would be viewed as important supplementary benefits of projects, rather than as constituting the main objective of lending.

A second policy option, Option Two, is for the Bank to add lending for basic health services to its current activities. This would increase the range of instruments it has for dealing with health problems.

The distinction between the two options is especially marked if seen in operational terms. Option Two may well seem to be the logical conclusion of the Bank's concern with all major aspects of socioeconomic development. The basic policy choice might be posed as to whether the present is the appropriate time for the Bank to move into the financing of basic health services. Both options imply increasing its expertise and experience in the health sector; the choice of Option One at this time does not preclude the adoption of Option Two later. The implications of each option are explained below.

Option One: Continue Progress in Increasing Health Benefits within Present Patterns of Lending.

The continuation of present trends in lending, within the existing lending patterns, would be likely to involve some increase in the amount of Bank lending for health-related activities. Whatever the size of the increase, the case is strong for the Bank's modifying its present approach to health questions. Until now, health factors have not always been fully considered in the basic design of a project. For example, different cropping patterns in an agricultural development scheme may have different nutritional implications, and different agricultural technologies can involve very different health risks. Thus, one might avoid increasing the prevalence of a water-borne disease by relying on intermittent application of irrigation water, rather than ponding, in growing rice. Excavation in connection with construction projects might be undertaken in a way that avoids creation of mosquito-breeding ponds. At the engineering design stage of a hydroelectric, irrigation or drainage project, one might minimize the number of sites which can harbor snails (schistosomiasis vectors) or breed simulium flies (onchocerciasis vectors).

At present, "health components" are often added at a late stage of project preparation and do not receive the consideration necessary for exploiting available opportunities and achieving cost-effectiveness. The installation of health posts or health centers in projects for rural development, or sites and services, may not amount to much unless the basic approaches are examined thoroughly. The proper balance between environmental, preventive and curative aspects of health care, the orientation and training of health personnel and the relation of health workers to the community are fundamental issues. It may not be appropriate to raise questions of far-reaching importance for health policy when health is a rather small component of a project which does not have the improvement of health as its main objective. However, it may be possible in such cases to persuade some project authorities to conduct field experiments on a small scale, along the lines discussed above. Although it might not be possible to build a complete prototype of the reformed health service under the rubric of, say, a rural development project, it should be possible to introduce selected elements on a pilot basis and evaluate the results. Such experimentation would, of course, be much easier in countries where there is a congenial climate for health reform.

In the future, health considerations will become more important in selected projects. The proportion of project finance for health-related activities may become larger, though projects would still largely be justified in terms of objectives other than health improvements per se. For example, in a "water and health" project, the Bank would identify the most important local diseases whose prevalence could be reduced. It would investigate existing patterns of behavior related to water use, and modify the design of the project to ensure proper utilization. This information would also assist in designing a health education program for the community.

Another new step might be to support specific disease-control projects in areas where the diseases primarily affect the working-age

399

population, and also limit the use of fertile land. The Bank is already coordinating the financing of the onchocerciasis project in Western Africa, and will be providing a portion of the finance. It is playing a critical role in mobilizing other financial resources; similar opportunities may arise in the future. The Bank's participation does not necessarily have to be on a grant basis. Where investment in health would permit major new exploitation of natural resources, the normal lending criteria can be applied. In such cases, it would be logical to link disease-control operations closely to programs for land settlement and rural development.

Such projects could be accommodated readily within the present pattern of lending. At this point, the number of viable disease-control projects is unknown, but is not likely to be very large. Control of sleeping sickness in parts of Africa is an obvious possibility, particularly in view of the scope for agricultural settlement and livestock development. Joint work on this possibility is already being done by WHO and FAO.[1]

For onchocerciasis, there is at present no suitable drug for mass chemotherapy, so that the project in which the Bank is currently participating is based solely on vector control. Diseases requiring a mixture of environmental measures, individual treatment and community health promotion cannot be handled under Option One. The uncertainties involved in specific disease campaigns based on vector control are considerable. Estimates of costs can only be tentative, and unforeseen epidemiological factors may make control much more difficult. Pilot projects and careful research on the cost-effectiveness of alternative control measures may be essential preliminary steps. Research may also be necessary on the economic and demographic impact of the programs. It should be recognized that the time-lag between initiation of disease-control measures and successful land settlement will often reduce the rate of return from disease control—if viewed solely as an investment.[2]

Criteria would need to be formulated for appraising the nature and size of health components, and also for deciding the extent to which

---

[1] For an example of work already completed, see Agency Terminal Report Kenya: Operational Research on Human and Animal Trypanosomiasis Eradication in Nyanza and Western Provinces, PD/71.1, KEN 14/KENYA 2301-ex 0041, PD/71. Geneva: World Health Organization, July 1971.

[2] There are cases in which development of key pesticides, for example molluscicides, and drugs needed for control programs is inhibited by the fact that the market for them is very small. At present, such chemicals and drugs are available, if at all, only at very high cost. Thus a possible advantage of the Bank's involvement in major disease control programs is that its influence—direct or indirect—may promote research and development and a reduction in drug costs, thereby making control programs more attractive. It is not easy to estimate the general strength of this argument, but it apparently holds for both onchocerciasis and schistosomiasis, and on this basis alone, is not to be ignored.

basic project design should be modified on health grounds. Where possible, an attempt should be made to calculate an economic rate of return for the health component or the rise in the cost of the basic project due to the design being altered for health reasons. The benefits would take the form of reduced costs of poor health conditions to the country. Often the imponderables would make it impossible to quantify project benefits within tolerable margins of error. Judgments would then need to be made, to the extent feasible, on the basis of cost-effectiveness. The Bank currently uses methods of evaluation other than the economic rate of return for its education and population projects.

Option One would require at least a brief analysis of the health sector as a whole, if projects are to be designed with consideration for health priorities. The depth of the sector analysis required would depend on the degree of experimentation envisaged and the extent of the Bank's involvement with health in each project. For example, take an education project with a component for training health manpower; it may need only a general guideline, supported by a review of the country's health sector to establish that there is a need for, say, rural auxiliaries or rural health workers, but not for clinical specialists. Far more complex are the population projects in which the Bank would significantly strengthen the network of primary health services. In these cases, a more thorough investigation of the whole health promotion system, at least below the regional hospital level, would be virtually indispensable. To assist in health sector analysis, it would be possible to make increasing use of WHO country health "profiles," as well as other sources such as the USAID "syncrisis" studies.

Option One mainly implies that it should be possible to make substantial improvements in health benefits from Bank-supported projects, without a major change in the pattern of lending.

Option Two: Bank Lending for Basic Health Services.

The Bank's population projects have large components for health facilities and for training health manpower; and they involve discussions with governments of cost-effectiveness in major parts of the health sector. However, these operations have relatively little impact on overall planning in the health sector. If the Bank were to begin financing projects that explicitly support basic health services, it would have a wider mandate to discuss general health issues with health ministries and would tend to have greater influence on health services, particularly if the Bank and WHO reinforce each other in their advisory roles.

401

If Option Two is chosen, the Bank would be committed to careful country-specific sector analysis, with the collaboration of WHO and other aid agencies operating in the health field. It is not likely that the Bank would want to support the existing health care systems in their present form in most developing countries. Despite declarations in planning documents, effective political commitment to health care for the bulk of the population poses considerable problems for many governments. Under such circumstances, the case is strong for not starting World Bank operations in a country where health priorities are inconsistent with equitable health programming approaches, and where the government is not willing to consider significant reforms. In such circumstances, and on such a fundamental social and political issue, it would appear likely that the Bank's influence, even in conjunction with WHO, would be limited.

Furthermore, some countries which now borrow for population projects may do so largely to finance health facilities. To avoid a possible shift of emphasis away from family planning, it would be important to ensure that all Bank-supported health operations keep population goals in mind.

Drawing up a lending program for basic health services would not be an easy task, even in countries that are judged to be eligible for Bank assistance because they accept the general idea of health reform and are willing to pursue family planning objectives alongside health programs. The Bank can rely on little experience with defining concrete goals for health promotion in developing countries; a great deal would have to be learned from experience. To train health personnel of the kind required for staffing a viable health care system, the Bank would have to stimulate the process of curriculum development. Current thinking on this topic is still very much at an experimental stage.

To exercise this Option Two, the Bank would have to take the following steps:

1. Substantially build up staff and consultants. The budgetary implications of Option Two would depend on the scale on which the Bank wishes to finance basic health services. However, even if the aim were to enter the field primarily to learn through experimental projects, it would be essential to create a critical mass of staff and other resources.

2. Establish a structural unit to identify, formulate, appraise and evaluate health projects. This unit would be responsible for implementing the Bank's lending program in the health area.

3. Undertake field research into the cost-effectiveness of different health promotion systems.

Conclusions

Before evaluating these two options, it is useful to recall the Bank's objectives and its limitations in view of certain characteristics of the health sector. The sector is one which has many characteristics similar to those of the education sector. Projects in both sectors generate benefits of "human value" as well as economic returns similar to those from infrastructure investment—for example, irrigation or roads. In the education sector, the Bank's policy has been to support projects which have a strong productive element. Without abandoning this orientation toward productive expenditures, the Bank's approach to education has been widening in recent years, and recognition has been given to the potential for welfare redistribution through education projects aimed specifically at lower-income groups. Similarly, in the area of nutrition, the Bank has emphasized activities which have both a redistributive impact, because they are directed toward the poor, and an investment orientation, since their economic returns, though difficult to measure, may well make the projects attractive on those grounds alone.

Whichever option is adopted, the approach in the health area should generally be similar to that in education; projects should be sought that combine promotion of economic development with redistribution of welfare.

The Bank makes three types of contributions to the development of its borrowers. Firstly, it transfers financial resources from richer countries to developing countries. Secondly, it encourages the more effective use of the borrower's own resources in the sector in which it is making a loan. Thirdly, it conveys the insights gained from experience in one developing country to other developing countries. The potential importance of these types of contributions differs in different sectors of lending.

The transfer of resources would not seem in itself an important reason for the Bank's involvement in the health field. This aspect is usually most significant to the recipient where projects require large-scale imports, and large and lumpy outlays. This is not likely to be the case in the health field, except in urban water supply where the Bank is already active, and in the construction of hospitals (which usually does not have high priority). To have health projects of the scale customary for Bank loans in small countries, the Bank would have to finance a very large share of the growth of total national government expenditure on health. There does not seem to be any special justification for this. At present, it is not possible to say what the appropriate national total for health expenditures should be. The Bank's action in the health field cannot be justified on grounds that the sector as a whole receives too few resources, and that these resources ought to be supplemented by the Bank.

However, the evidence is ample that, in most developing countries where cost-effectiveness and equitable welfare distribution are regarded as important national goals, health expenditures are misallocated. The Bank might be able to achieve some limited beneficial effect by bringing to the attention of member governments the changes needed in current patterns of resource allocation for health. Of course, the larger the Bank's involvement in the health sector, the greater its possible influence. The amount of influence the Bank can exert over national policies also depends on the confidence that governments place in the Bank's expertise and, therefore, on its ability to carry out its third role—that of transferring relevant international experience. The general direction in which health policies should be changed is clear, but determining what will prove best for any individual country within this framework still requires careful study. Faced with similar uncertainties in other areas of human resource development, the Bank has chosen to encourage borrowers to carry out carefully monitored projects with experimental components. This has been the case with the population projects in India, and basic education projects in Western Africa.

A final general consideration concerns the role of the Bank in relation to other donors. Health programs have attracted financial and technical assistance from multilateral and bilateral sources (see Annex 1) although, in contrast to aid for family planning, the assistance has made up only a small part of national expenditures. Therefore, the need for the Bank to expand in the health field is not, *prima facie*, proven. However, two large donors in the health field have invited greater Bank involvement. One national agency has recently suggested joint operations with the Bank to finance low-cost health delivery services combined with family planning. The Director-General of WHO has proposed collaboration between his organization and the Bank, particularly in improving the allocation of national resources devoted to health. The types of assistance that WHO and the Bank provide and the services they have available are complementary. WHO does not finance large capital expenditures. It has much technical expertise, but limited strength in conducting economic analysis. The Bank's position is the reverse. Thus, substantial scope exists for collaboration with WHO and other agencies—as has already taken place with WHO in the Western Africa onchocerciasis project.

In the light of the Bank's objectives and limitations as outlined above, it is intended that Option One will be adopted as the Bank's policy—namely, to continue progress in increasing health benefits within the present patterns of lending. Although this implies less Bank involvement with health than Option Two, the scope and potential of Option One should not be underestimated. A policy based on Option One would allow the Bank to:

1. Minimize the adverse side effects on health of its lending operations in other sectors (projects involving water use, land settlement, etc.).

2. Make a number of key interventions necessary for improving the health status of low-income groups (for example, projects involving water supply, sewerage, nutrition, family planning, sites and services for low-cost housing and training of health personnel).

3. Conduct field experiments to test selected elements of reformed health promotion systems within projects concerned with rural development, population, nutrition and sites and services.

The Bank's policy on health, as in other fields, will require periodic reexamination. In the interim, Option One would enable the Bank to improve substantially its assistance in the health area and to gain experience which would enable it to assess whether it can effectively assist in the development of health systems that are appropriate to developing countries. This option would also enable the Bank to participate, under appropriate circumstances, in major disease-control projects and programs, such as the one relating to onchocerciasis in Western Africa.

HEALTH
ANNEXES

INTERNATIONAL ASSISTANCE FOR HEALTH PROGRAMS

International assistance for health programs began over a century ago with efforts to control communicable diseases.[1] As commercial relations expanded across national frontiers, the spread of great epidemics of smallpox, malaria, typhus, cholera, plague and yellow fever required international action. The International Sanitary Bureau—the parent of the Pan American Health Organization (PAHO)—was founded in 1902, and began to replace quarantine with preventive sanitation measures throughout the Americas. The Rockefeller Foundation started its activities in 1913 with heavy emphasis on endemic disease control. In its early years after World War II, WHO concentrated on the control and eradication of communicable diseases.

Later, multilateral and bilateral health assistance expanded support of research, development of health delivery systems and training of health manpower for developing countries, both locally and abroad. In recent years, following experience with family planning, many donor countries have placed growing emphasis on low-cost health delivery systems that can reach the poor. In many cases family planning and health activities are so interwoven that it is difficult to distinguish between aid expenditures on population and aid expenditures on health.

As shown in Table 1:1, the health sector receives a significant amount of assistance from a variety of donors. However, the assistance represents only a small proportion of public-sector health spending in recipient countries. The bulk of external aid has gone to training and technical assistance rather than to the financing of capital costs. Donor efforts are only now beginning to assist countries in improving their resource allocation and in increasing the effectiveness of health projects through comprehensive health sector planning.

WHO ranked first in health assistance in 1972, providing $115 million. The United States, working through the Agency for International Development (USAID) was in second place, although health constituted only 2.5% of its foreign aid commitments. Germany was third with $42 million. UNICEF spent $36 million—about 30% of its total age-specific program expenditures—on health. Through the Swedish International Development Authority (SIDA), Sweden spent 13.5% of

---

[1] This annex provides a general picture of international health assistance. An exhaustive description is not possible because comprehensive data on health activities in various agencies frequently are not assembled and definitions are not always consistent among countries.

International Assistance for Health Programs from
Major Donors Other than the Bank
(US$ thousands)

Donor	1969	1972	Description
WHO	77,736	115,274	Includes family planning activities. Figures include funds from UNDP and U.N. Fund for Population Activities (UNFPA).
PAHO	16,649	25,512	Excludes funds from WHO Regional Office. Includes family planning activities.
UNICEF	27,950	35,780	Includes family planning activities. Figures include UNDP and UNFPA funds.
Denmark	4,200	7,100	
France	n.a.	3,400	1973 figure. Excludes outlays of Office de la Recherche Scientifique et Technique d'Outre-Mer.
Germany, Federal Republic of	n.a.	42,000	Approximate average annual disbursement 1971-73. Total disbursements through 1970 amounted to $171 million.
Japan	—	9,000	
Sweden	6,897	12,685	Includes family planning activities.
United Kingdom	n.a.	8,000	Average annual disbursement in 1967-72. Excludes technical assistance.
United States	55,375	41,881	

its 1972 assistance on health and population planning; the sum was devoted to carefully focused and executed programs which sought primarily to reach the poor. The British, French, German and Finnish aid programs also contained allocations for health. The health programs of some private foundations, such as the Rockefeller Foundation, while highly innovative, have involved relatively small outlays.

Table 1:2 shows the distribution of expenditures, by region, for WHO and USAID. The WHO assistance is fairly widely distributed: Asia accounts for about 40%, Africa 21%, Latin America 13% and Europe 7%. Another 19% was spent by WHO on interregional activities in which the regional distribution cannot be identified. The bulk of USAID health expenditures, or about 72%, was devoted to interregional and supporting assistance, including medical schools in the United States and hospitals abroad. Other USAID efforts were concentrated in Latin America where 19% of its health expenditures were disbursed. Africa accounted for 7% and Asia for less than 2%. UNICEF's regional allocation pattern, which follows criteria of per

Regional Distribution of Health Assistance by Major Donors, 1972

	Africa	America	Asia	Europe	Interregional activities supporting assistance	Total
WHO	16,186	10,625	30,455	5,702	14,280	76,887[1]
USAID	2,953	7,947	709	—	30,182	41,881

[1]Excluding nonproject outlays.
Sources: Annual and Financial Reports of WHO and USAID.

Table 1:3

WHO Project Costs by Area of Activity
(As percentage of total project costs)

	1969	1972
Public health services[1]	20.6	23.9
Environmental health	13.0	13.9
Education and training	12.3	13.8
Malaria	15.0	8.0
Family health	2.3	7.2
Smallpox	6.2	4.9
Nursing	5.4	4.8
Communicable diseases—general activities	2.5	3.3
Vital and health statistics	1.7	2.3
Nutrition	2.7	1.9
Tuberculosis	3.3	1.9
Other activities	15.0	14.1
	100.0	100.0

[1]Including WHO and zone representatives.
Source: WHO Financial Reports.

capita GNP and child population, strongly emphasized Asia. SIDA's bilateral health assistance is concentrated in a limited number of countries, mainly in Africa and Asia.

Table 1:3 gives the distribution of WHO's project costs by area of activity. Control of communicable diseases is still the organization's top priority. Funds allocated to malaria campaigns dropped in relative importance between 1969 and 1972. Public health services, environmental health, education and training, and family health rank high in project costs, and their relative importance has been growing in recent years. Similar changes in the "mix" of the program took place at USAID, as shown in Table 1:4.

411

USAID Health Expenditures by Area of Activity
(As percentage of total health expenditures)

	1969	1972
Health services	56.8	69.4
Malaria eradication	15.2	11.8
Environmental health	15.4	7.4
Health manpower	4.0	6.5
Measles, smallpox	7.4	2.7
Other disease control	1.2	2.2
	100.0	100.0

Source: USAID. Reports on Health, Population and Nutrition Activities.

UNICEF is increasingly moving away from specialized campaigns (for example, milk feeding or vaccination) and small, isolated projects toward more integrated health programs with well-defined priorities (for example, primary level education in rural areas). Less emphasis is now placed on narrow, child-oriented programs. Instead, there are more programs with a broader focus (such as rural water supply or eradication of slum conditions) and with a cross-sectoral approach (such as health education in schools and nutrition training in agricultural extension).

The Rockefeller Foundation's health activities in more recent years have been in three major areas: (1) development of medical schools as part of its university development programs, with special emphasis on curriculum design (for example, in Colombia and Thailand); (2) planning of health care delivery (in Colombia and the Philippines); and (3) schistosomiasis control (in St. Lucia).

In 1973, French aid for health was distributed as follows: 40% for preventive health services, 58% for curative health services and 2% for research. Aid for preventive health went mainly to the Service des Grandes Endémies. As of March 1, 1974, 1,025 technical assistance personnel for health were posted; 403 were fulfilling their military service in this way. Although the French aid policy is to concentrate on preventive health, aid for curative health was the largest category of expenditure. French aid has also supported the establishment of full university-level medical schools in several Francophone countries. Another important component of French aid for health is research conducted under the auspices of the Office de la Recherche Scientifique et Technique d'Outre-Mer, which undertakes studies in many areas of special relevance to tropical countries.[2]

---

[2]This research is not included in the assistance figures in Table 1.1.

In the five years, 1967–72, the U.K. Ministry of Overseas Development disbursed bilateral grants for health totaling $12.7 million, and loans of $7 million, making an annual average disbursement close to $4 million. In addition, on June 30, 1972, 798 health personnel, plus 193 volunteers financed by U.K. bilateral aid, were working abroad. At the same time, 697 nationals from developing countries were receiving health training financed by Britain. A major feature of British aid is research into tropical medical problems; the U.K. spends an additional $4 million per year on this effort, some of it financed by the Medical Research Council. In the past, the U.K. has financed teaching hospitals, but interest is now growing in providing rural health services.

German aid for health comes under the two main heads of "Kapital Hilfe" and "Technische Hilfe." In recent years, the former has been just under $30 million per year, while the latter has fluctuated between $12 million and $15 million annually. A substantial part of this aid is channeled through church organizations. In addition, the Deutsche Entwicklungsdienst provides significant aid for the health sector in the form of personnel. In the past, a large proportion of the total aid has been for isolated hospital projects, partly in response to the perceived priorities of aid recipients. More recently, the policy has decisively shifted toward integrated basic health services for an entire region, although some of the hospital projects are still under way. Considerable emphasis is projected on the training of paramedical personnel.

During the period 1970–74, Finland sponsored a number of projects for health improvement in Tanzania, and organized health-related training programs. Over the period, approximately $1.4 million was provided to Tanzania for the construction of Rural Medical Aid Schools, assistance to the Kilimanjaro Christian Medical Centre and the Red Cross Society of Tanzania, and large water development projects in the provinces of Mtwara and Lindi. Finland has also contributed funds to such diverse health-related projects as construction of a milk-processing plant (India) and maternity units (Cuba), and to programs including pediatric field training, child feeding and vaccine supply.

Sweden's bilateral health assistance program is concentrated in a relatively small number of countries in order to achieve impact with limited financial resources. Bangladesh, Botswana, Chile, Cuba, Ethiopia, India, Kenya, North Viet-Nam, Pakistan, Tanzania, Tunisia and Zambia are currently "program countries" under this policy. SIDA sponsors children's hospitals and health centers, and rural and maternal-and-child health programs; it also assists in health sector planning.

Measures of Health Status by Level of Per Capita
Gross National Product (GNP) in Selected Countries

Country	Per[1] capita GNP	Crude[2] birth rate	Crude[2] death rate	Infant[3] mortality	Life[2] expectancy
Burundi	60	41.8	24.9	150[4]	39.0
Upper Volta	70	48.5	24.9	180	39.0
Ethiopia	80	49.5	23.8	162	40.0
Indonesia	80	44.8	18.9	125[4]	45.4
Yemen Arab Republic	90	49.5	20.0	160	45.5
Malawi	90	47.7	23.7	148[4]	41.0
Guinea	90	46.6	22.8	240[5]	41.0
Sri Lanka	100	28.6	6.3	50	67.8
Dahomey	100	49.9	23.0	110[4]	41.0
Tanzania	110	50.1	23.4	122[5]*	44.5
India	110	41.1	16.3	139	49.2
Sudan	120	47.8	18.5	130	47.2
Yemen, People's Democratic Republic of	120	50.0	22.7	160	45.3
Uganda	130	46.9	15.7	160[4]	50.0
Pakistan	130	47.6	16.8	130	49.4
Nigeria	140	49.3	22.7	150-175[6]	41.0
Central African Republic	150	43.2	22.5	190	41.0
Mauritania	170	48.8	23.4	187[5]	41.0
Bolivia	190	43.7	18.0	60	46.7
Liberia	210	50.7	22.3	159	43.5
Sierra Leone	210	41.9	20.2	197[5]	43.5
Thailand	210	43.7	10.4	23	58.6
Egypt, Arab Republic of	220	37.8	15.0	120	50.7
Viet-Nam, Republic of	230	41.8	23.6	100	40.5
Philippines	240	43.6	10.5	62	58.4
Senegal	250	47.3	22.2	93[4]	42.0
Ghana	250	48.8	21.9	156[4]	43.5
Congo	270	45.1	20.8	180	43.5
Paraguay	280	42.2	8.6	39	61.5
Syrian Arab Republic	290	46.9	14.4	24[4]	53.8
Honduras	300	49.3	14.6	37[4]	53.5
Ecuador	310	41.8	9.5	87[6]	59.6
Tunisia	320	41.0	13.9	76	54.1
El Salvador	320	42.2	11.1	58	57.8
Ivory Coast	330	45.6	20.6	138[4]	43.5
Turkey	340	39.4	12.7	153	56.4
Algeria	360	49.4	16.6	86[4]	51.5
Iraq	370	49.2	14.8	26	52.6
Colombia	370	40.6	8.8	81	60.9
Zambia	380	51.5	20.3	259[4]	44.5

Measures of Health Status by Level of Per Capita
Gross National Product (GNP) in Selected Countries (continued)

Country	Per[1] capita GNP	Crude[2] birth rate	Crude[2] death rate	Infant[3] mortality	Life[2] Expectancy
Guatemala	390	42.8	13.7	83	52.9
Malaysia	400	39.0	9.8	38	59.4
Dominican Republic	430	45.8	11.0	49	57.8
China, Republic of	430	26.7	10.2	18[7]	61.6
Iran	450	45.3	15.6	160[6]	51.0
Nicaragua	450	48.3	13.9	45[6]	52.9
Brazil	460	37.1	8.8	110[6]	61.4
Peru	480	41.0	11.9	67	55.7
Albania	480	33.4	6.5	87[4]†	68.6
Cuba	510	28.9	5.9	28	72.3
Costa Rica	590	33.4	5.9	56	68.2
Mexico	700	42.0	8.6	63	63.2
Jamaica	720	33.2	7.1	27	69.5
Portugal	730	18.4	10.1	50	68.0
Yugoslavia	730	18.2	9.2	44	67.5
Romania	740	19.3	10.3	40	67.2
Chile	760	25.9	8.1	71	64.3
Panama	820	36.2	7.1	34	66.5
Bulgaria	820	16.2	9.1	26	71.8
Hong Kong	900	19.4	5.5	17	70.0
Trinidad and Tobago	940	25.3	5.9	35[4]	69.5
Venezuela	1,060	36.1	7.0	52	64.7
Singapore	1,200	21.2	5.1	19	69.5
U.S.S.R.	1,400	17.8	7.9	23	70.4
Japan	2,130	19.2	6.6	12[4]	73.3
Israel	2,190	26.2	6.7	24	70.5
United States	5,160	16.2	9.4	19	71.3

Symbols: * for 1968
† for 1965

Note:
Crude birth rates and death rates are births and deaths per 1,000 population per year. Infant mortality rate is number of deaths of children under one year of age per 1,000 live births per year. Life expectancy is expected length of life in years at birth.

Sources:
[1] World Bank. *World Bank Atlas,* 1973: "Population, Per Capita Product and Growth Rates," pp. 6-14. Washington: World Bank, 1973.
[2] United Nations projections, 1973. Unpublished data: averages for 1970-75.
[3] World Health Organization. *The Fifth Report on the World Health Situation, 1969-72—Part II: Review by Country and Territory,* "Population and Other Statistics," by country, except where other sources are indicated. Unless otherwise noted, figures are for 1970-72. Geneva: WHO, 1974.
[4] United Nations. *Statistical Yearbook 1972,* Table 21, latest available year. New York: United Nations, 1973.
[5] World Health Organization. *Malaria Control in Countries Where Time-limited Eradication is Impracticable at Present.* Report of a WHO Interregional Conference. WHO Technical Report Series No. 537, Annex 2, Table 2; figures are for 1971. Geneva: WHO, 1974.
[6] World Bank estimates, latest available year.
[7] United Nations. *Demographic Yearbook 1970,* Table 16; figure is for 1969. New York: United Nations, 1971.

Health Expenditures in Developing Countries

Country	Source	Health budget as percentage of national budget	Health budget as percentage of GNP	Government health expenditures per capita (US$)
Rwanda	a	8.7	0.8	0.45
Upper Volta[1]	b	4.8	0.7	0.56
Somalia	c	6.7	2.0*	1.40
Ethiopia	a	6.9	0.8	0.67
Burma	a	6.2	1.1	0.85
Malawi	a	6.1	0.8*	0.50
Sri Lanka	b	8.1	3.6*	3.76
Tanzania	c	6.3	1.5*	1.68
India	c	4.9	0.9	0.91
Haiti	c	13.7	0.7*	0.78
Uganda	c	9.6	1.7*	2.24
Togo	c	6.5	1.0*	1.51
Central African Republic	b	8.4	1.9*	2.81
Kenya	a	6.4	1.7	0.14
Bolivia	b	3.6	2.0*	3.74
Cameroon	c	7.8	1.0*	2.02
Liberia	c	7.4	1.4*	2.90
Sierra Leone	c	6.2	0.9*	1.95
Thailand	b	6.0	1.2	2.45
Egypt, Arab Republic of	c	8.4	1.8*	3.91
Viet-Nam, Republic of	b	2.3	0.4*	1.00
Philippines	a	5.4	0.5	1.06
Senegal	b	9.1	1.4*	3.49
Ghana	a	7.3	1.3	3.76
Jordan	b	9.5	2.8	10.10
Congo	b	6.1	1.8*	4.82
Paraguay	b	26.4	2.4	6.77
Mozambique	c	4.9	0.9*	2.47
Korea, Republic of	a	1.4	0.5	1.33
Syrian Arab Republic	a	2.6	0.7	2.03

Health Expenditures in Developing Countries (continued)

Country	Source	Health budget as percentage of national budget	Health budget as percentage of GNP	Government health expenditures per capita (US$)
Honduras	a	7.6	1.3	3.33
Ecuador	c	2.8	0.3	1.04
El Salvador	b	12.6	1.5	4.40
Turkey	b	21.4	2.6	8.21
Algeria	a	5.3	1.4	4.53
Colombia	a	10.4	0.6*	2.04
Angola	c	5.1	1.1*	3.95
Malaysia	b	6.7	2.5	7.18
Dominican Republic	b	8.6	1.4	7.71
Iran	c	2.5	0.6*	2.60
Brazil	c	1.4	0.2*	0.80
Lebanon	c	3.5	0.6*	3.80
Mexico	c	5.9	0.4*	2.64
Jamaica	c	10.0	2.7*	19.54
Yugoslavia	a	38.2	10.1*	73.75
Romania	a	5.7	2.5	18.56
South Africa	c	1.8	0.3*	2.61
Panama	b	16.7	2.2	16.70
Trinidad and Tobago	a	7.8	1.8	14.27
Venezuela	b	18.4	4.1*	43.18
U.S.S.R.	c	5.8	3.4*	47.04
Libyan Arab Republic	c	5.8	2.4*	35.00
Japan	c	1.9	0.3*	5.45
United Kingdom	c	9.5	4.3*	105.16

*Calculated by dividing "per capita expenditure" figure in last column by estimates of per capita GNP for 1971, as published in *World Bank Atlas,* 1973.
(1)GNP extrapolated from 1968.

a = World Bank estimates.
b = World Health Organization. *The Fifth Report on the World Health Situation, 1969-72.* Geneva: WHO, 1974.
c = World Health Organization. *World Health Statistics Report,* Vol. 26, No. 11, Table 2. Geneva: WHO, 1973.

Analysis of Government Health Expenditures
in Selected Countries

Country	Year	Total public expenditures ($ millions)	Percentage for public health or prevention	Percentage for curative care	Percentage for training and research
Sri Lanka	1957–58	34.3	23.3	74.4	2.3
Tanzania	1970–71	19.5	4.9	80.3	4.4
India	1965–66	236.0	37.0	55.5	7.5
Laos[1]	1971–72	2.3	14.3[2]	19.9[3]	44.8
Kenya	1971	27.8	5.2	83.8	11.0
Thailand[1]	1971–72	83.6	28.1[4]	46.6[3]	19.1
Paraguay[1]	1972	10.0	10.5[5]	84.6[3]	—
Tunisia[1]	1971	15.8	—	86.3[3]	—
El Salvador[1]	1971	30.4	3.3[6]	52.9[3]	1.1
Turkey[1]	1972	303.7	16.3[7]	—	13.5
Colombia	1970	203.0	18.7	79.3	2.0
Mongolia[1]	1972	—	—	—	7.2
Chile	1959	63.8	18.3	77.0	4.0
Panama	1967	28.4	30.0	- - - -(70%)- - - -	
Venezuela	1962	—	18.0	76.5	5.5
Israel[1]	1959–60	82.7	4.9	80.3	4.4

[1]Classification of residual categories of expenditure is unknown.
[2]Expenditure for "environmental health services."
[3]Expenditure for government hospitals only.
[4]Expenditure for "control of communicable diseases, laboratory services, environmental health services and occupational health services."
[5]Expenditure for "campaigns against communicable diseases, maternal and child health and vaccinations and laboratory services."
[6]Expenditure for "immunization and vaccination activities, laboratory services and environmental health services."
[7]Expenditure for "mass campaigns against communicable diseases, immunization and vaccination activities, laboratory services and environmental health services."

Sources: Sri Lanka, Chile, Venezuela and Israel: Abel-Smith, Brian. *Paying for Health Services.* WHO Public Health Paper 17, Table 13. Geneva: WHO, 1963. Abel-Smith, Brian. *An International Study of Health Expenditures.* WHO Public Health Paper 32, Tables 12-14. Geneva: WHO, 1967.

India: Government of India. *Health Statistics of India.* Delhi: Publications Division, 1965.

Colombia: World Bank, Dragoslav Avramovic and associates. *Economic Growth of Colombia: Problems and Prospects.* Report of a Bank mission to Colombia in 1970. Baltimore and London: The Johns Hopkins University Press, 1972.

Kenya: Ministry of Health. *Recurrent and Development Budget, 1971-72.* Nairobi: Ministry of Health, 1972.

Panama: U.S. Office of International Health, Department of Health, Education and Welfare. *Syncrisis: The Dynamics of Health. Vol. I, Panama,* Table 45 and pp. 55-65. Washington: U.S. Government Printing Office, 1972.

Tanzania: Segall, Malcolm. "The Politics of Health in Tanzania." *Development and Change,* IV(1), (1972): Table 1.

Laos, Thailand, Paraguay, Tunisia, El Salvador, Turkey and Mongolia: World Health Organization. *The Fifth Report on the World Health Situation, 1969-72 — Part II: Review by Country and Territory.* Geneva: WHO, 1974. "Government Health Expenditure," by country.

Percentage Distribution of Health Expenditures
in Selected Countries, 1961
(By focus of service)

Country	Personal medical services		Public health services (%)	Teaching and research (%)
	Inpatient (%)	Outpatient (%)		
Kenya	- - - - 89 - - - -		8	3
Sri Lanka	50	44	5	2
Tanzania	45	50	4	1
Yugoslavia	43	50	4	3
Czechoslovakia	48	44	2	6
United Kingdom	52	44	2	2
France	41	56	2	2
Sweden	53	42	1	4
United States	38	57	1	5

Source: Winkelstein, Jr., Warren. "Epidemiological Considerations Underlying the Allocation of Health and Disease Care Resources." *International Journal of Epidemiology,* 1(1), (1972): Table 1. London: Oxford University Press. (Data from the Epidemiology Program, School of Public Health, University of California, Berkeley.)

Health Resources in Developing Countries

Country	Population per hospital bed	Percentage of government hospitals in total number of hospitals	Population per physician	Percentage of government-employed physicians in total number of physicians	Population per non-physician primary health workers	Support personnel per physician
Rwanda	769	64	58,000	99	4,910	7.3
Burundi	787	—	59,066	—	11,770	7.5
Mali	1,389	—	41,471	100	43,630	15.9
Upper Volta	1,667	—	92,828	—	88,260	27.7
Bangladesh	8,333	—	8,932	—	87,250	0.1
Somalia	571	—	21,424	—	16,440	7.5
Afghanistan	6,667	94	17,698	100	19,670	1.0
Ethiopia	3,030	67	73,289	—	24,800	10.5
Indonesia	1,724	83	26,367	49	10,230	7.0
Burma	1,190	—	8,976	86	3,940	1.6
Chad	775	92	61,695	—	30,330	13.5
Nepal	6,667	—	50,045	—	11,830	0.8
Malawi	637	50	75,254	47	5,170	4.8
Zaire	318	50	26,184	—	10,460	13.1
Guinea	813	—	51,688	—	4,570	25.4
Niger	2,222	94	58,261	100	68,140	8.5
Sri Lanka	311	—	3,860	—	2,480	1.5
Dahomey	862	—	29,118	81	14,100	10.0
Tanzania	699	53	20,702	53	8,360	4.1
India	1,612	—	4,805	—	11,500	0.6
Haiti	1,369	71	13,481	—	20,200	4.1
Sudan	1,041	—	15,934	86	4,180	8.2
Laos	1,190	61	16,547	6	7,350	3.8
Khmer Republic	917	73	17,529	87	5,280	6.9
Uganda	641	69	9,215	33	5,410	0.9
Pakistan	1,667	—	4,329	—	10,200	0.3
Nigeria	1,851	81	20,525	32	3,830	4.9
Malagasy Republic	352	90	31,645	75	6,310	9.2
Togo	820	—	27,943	100	8,930	7.0
Central African Republic	465	—	36,952	—	3,910	27.8
Kenya	775	58	7,829	—	3,360	5.3
Mauritania	2,778	—	17,206	92	6,000	4.3
Bolivia	490	86	2,301	—	58,010	0.9
Cameroon	480	67	25,938	60	59,550	10.7
Liberia	526	51	13,818	—	5,020	4.8
Sierra Leone	1,041	69	17,148	67	1,630	6.7
Thailand	847	94	8,397	61	1,700	1.6
Egypt, Arab Republic of	463	87	1,913	—	2,130	1.2
Viet-Nam, Republic of	478	74	9,203	—	2,630	2.8
Philippines	855	45	9,097	—	7,880	1.9

Health Resources in Developing Countries (continued)

Country	Population per hospital bed	Percentage of government hospitals in total number of hospitals	Population per physician	Percentage of government-employed physicians in total number of physicians	Population per non-physician primary health workers	Support personnel per physician
Senegal	730	—	14,715	—	12,990	9.0
Ghana	758	67	12,954	59	2,840	12.8
Jordan	962	68	3,805	34	3,870	2.9
Morocco	690	—	13,244	—	—	—
Congo	171	94	57,368	—	181,670	15.9
Paraguay	625	—	2,326	—	9,950	1.4
Mozambique	636	89	15,520	—	26,740	3.1
Korea, Republic of	1,923	—	2,207	8	3,370	1.4
Syrian Arab Republic	1,010	81	3,757	—	6,700	0.9
Honduras	568	76	3,621	—	21,720	3.6
Ecuador	434	—	2,929	—	58,030	1.9
Rhodesia	395	62	6,375	—	1,580	6.0
Tunisia	410	—	5,874	—	25,000	8.2
Papua New Guinea	152	47	11,635	—	5,280	6.6
El Salvador	526	94	4,039	—	—	4.5
Ivory Coast	676	—	13,918	81	26,140	4.9
Turkey	490	66	2,222	53	3,110	1.2
Algeria	341	—	8,439	—	21,290	3.1
Iraq	775	98	3,348	80	3,430	1.8
Colombia	446	77	2,285	—	2,500	2.1
Angola	362	42	8,463	—	26,070	4.9
Mongolia	108	—	—	—	510	2.3
Zambia	314	55	13,472	—	2,130	5.0
Guatemala	457	91	3,617	—	—	3.1
Malaysia	380	—	4,347	—	1,730	3.7
Dominican Republic	348	64	2,102	41	32,540	0.5
China, Republic of	2,941	—.	3,224	—	7,430	0.3
Iran	775	56	3,297	90	7,820	1.5
Nicaragua	410	89	2,065	—	—	2.9
Brazil	262	—	1,963	—	46,570	0.6
Peru	474	84	1,978	—	13,670	2.6
Albania	167	—	1,875	—	1,330	3.5
Cuba	213	—	1,199	—	—	1.7
Saudi Arabia	1,136	—	9,558	—	10,950	2.2
Costa Rica	254	96	1,619	—	—	14.5
Lebanon	260	15	1,435	—	5,940	1.2
Mexico	935	—	1,491	—	—	0.9
Jamaica	244	92	2,659	—	21,950	1.7
Portugal	164	47	1,181	—	6,050	1.1
Yugoslavia	179	—	1,008	—	4,200	3.0

Sources: Derived from World Health Organization. *World Health Statistics Annual – Vol. III: Health Personnel and Hospital Establishments,* Table 1. Geneva: WHO, 1974. World Health Organization. *World Health Statistics Report,* 26(3), Table 2. Geneva: WHO, 1973.

Indices of Hospital Utilization

Country	Year	Beds	Discharges	Patient days	Average days of stay	Occupancy rate (%)
General Hospitals						
Malawi	1965	1,025	24,528	293,817	12.0	78.5
Morocco*	1965	12,157	267,835	3,469,668	13.0	78.2
Senegal*	1967	2,424	33,944	813,237	24.0	91.9
Tunisia*	1967	6,655	222,813	2,059,619	9.2	84.8
Colombia	1967	34,399	871,911	7,226,563	8.3	57.6
Honduras	1967	3,408	78,488	980,737	12.5	78.8
Jamaica*	1967	3,034	82,565	914,679	12.5	78.8
Jordan	1967	1,980	43,087	293,618	6.8	40.6
Thailand	1967	20,161	790,338	4,606,036	5.8	62.6
Turkey	1967	32,686	895,912	7,235,542	8.1	60.6
Local and Rural Hospitals						
Dahomey*	1965	250	2,143	44,196	20.6	48.4
Malawi	1965	3,620	153,335	1,592,593	10.4	120.5
Morocco*	1965	1,639	30,826	288,255	9.4	48.2
Senegal	1967	591	14,327	132,575	9.3	61.5
Tunisia*	1967	2,317	86,364	602,640	7.0	71.3
Chile	1967	1,500	38,788	329,757	8.5	60.2
Costa Rica	1967	204	6,286	14,862	2.4	20.0
Surinam	1966	225	4,109	31,413	7.6	38.3
Cyprus*	1967	94	610	2,997	4.9	8.7
Laos*	1967	267	3,764	33,630	8.9	34.5

(*)Government hospitals only.
Source: World Health Organization. *World Health Statistics Annual, 1967 — Vol. III: Health Personnel and Hospital Establishments,* Tables 4 and 5.2. Geneva: WHO, 1970.

Population per Medical Doctor
in Urban and Rural Areas in Selected Countries

Country	Year	Population /medical doctor		
		Nationwide	Urban	Rural
Pakistan	1970	7,400	3,700	24,200
Kenya	1969	12,140	800	50,000
Philippines	1971	3,900	1,500	10,000
Honduras	1968	3,860	1,190	7,140
Colombia	1970	2,160	1,000	6,400
Iran	1967–70	3,752	2,275	10,000
Panama	1969	1,790	930	3,000

Sources: Panama, Honduras, Philippines: United States Office of International Health, Department of Health, Education and Welfare. *Syncrisis: The Dynamics of Health. Vol. I, Panama,* p. 59, Tables 6 and 37a; *Vol. II, Honduras,* p. 11, Tables 1 and 27; *Vol. IV, The Philippines,* pp. 37, 52-53, Tables 14 and 45. Washington: Government Printing Office, 1972.

Pakistan, Iran: Bowers, John Z., and Rosenheim, Lord. *Migration of Medical Manpower,* pp. 26, 91, 96. New York: Josiah Macy Foundation, 1971.

Colombia: World Bank, Dragoslav Avramovic and associates. *Economic Growth of Colombia: Problems and Prospects.* Report of a Bank mission to Colombia in 1970. Baltimore and London: The Johns Hopkins University Press, 1972.

Kenya: Wheeler, Mark. "Medical Manpower in Kenya." *East African Medical Journal,* 46(2), (1969):93-101.

Distribution of Medical Doctors between the Capital
and the Remainder of the Country in Selected Countries, 1968

Country	Population/medical doctors		
	Nationwide	Capital city	Remainder of country
Haiti	14,700	1,350	33,300
Kenya	10,999	672	25,600
Thailand	7,000	800	25,000
Senegal	19,100	4,270	44,300
Ghana[1]	18,000	4,340	41,360
Tunisia	6,486	2,912	10,056
Colombia[1]	2,220	1,000	6,400
Guatemala	4,860	875	22,600
Iran	3,750	906	6,220
Lebanon	1,470	650	3,000
Jamaica	2,280	840	5,510
Panama	1,850	760	4,400

[1]Major urban centers instead of capital city.

Sources: Panama, Colombia, Guatemala, Haiti: Pan American Health Organization. *Health Conditions in the Americas 1965-1968.* Scientific Publication No. 207, Table 58. Washington, D.C.: PAHO/WHO, 1970.

Jamaica, Senegal, Thailand, Iran: Bryant, John. *Health and the Developing World,* Table 14. Ithaca, New York: Cornell University Press, 1969.

Ghana: Sharpston, M. J. "Uneven Distribution of Medical Care: A Ghanaian Case Study." *Journal of Development Studies,* 8(2), (1972):206-213 and Tables IV-VI.

Tunisia: Le Ministère de la Santé Publique, unpublished data.

Kenya: Wheeler, Mark. "Medical Manpower in Kenya." *East African Medical Journal,* 46(2), (1969):93-101.

Lebanon: Zahlan, A. B. "Migration Patterns of the Graduates of the American University of Beirut." The Committee on the International Migration of Talent, *The International Migration of High-Level Manpower,* p. 293. New York: Praeger Publishers, Inc., 1970.

Comparative Costs of Medical Education
in Selected Countries, 1965
(US$)

Country	Per medical doctor graduated[1]	Per medical assistant	Per nurse graduated	Per auxiliary nurse	Per health assistant	Per auxiliary sanitarian
Senegal	84,000	—	835	—	—	—
Jamaica	24,000	—	1,385	—	—	—
Guatemala	19,200	—	2,700	—	—	—
Thailand	6,600	—	1,200	—	700	350
Kenya	22–28,000	2,890	3,380	2,167	787	1,680
Pakistan	12,600	—	2,960	—	—	—
Colombia	29,000	—	3,000	1,000	—	—
United States	19,630	—	—	—	—	—

[1]Obtained by dividing total recurrent costs as assignable to medical education by number of students graduating.

Sources: Bryant, John. *Health and the Developing World,* Tables 27 and 43. Ithaca, New York: Cornell University Press, 1969. Fendall, N. R. E. "The Medical Assistant in Africa." *Journal of Tropical Medicine and Hygiene,* 71(4), (April 1968):90.

Percentage of Deliveries Attended by a
Physician or by a Qualified Midwife in Selected Countries

Country	Year	In hospital	At home	In hospital or at home
Sri Lanka	1972	75.0[1]	20.0[1]	95.0[1]
Sudan	1971	–	–	10.0[2]
Malagasy Republic	1971	–	–	71.1[1]
Bolivia	1971	5.5[3]	12.8[3]	18.3[3]
Thailand	1971	19.2[3]	–	–
Viet-Nam, Republic of	1972	80.3[1]	0.7[1]	81.0[1]
Paraguay	1972	–	–	55.4[1]
El Salvador	1972	26.0[1]	–	–
Iraq	1971	6.5[3]	21.7[3]	28.2[3]
Guatemala	1970	–	–	25.0[2]
Dominican Republic	1972	40.2[3]	–	–
Peru	1971	15.2[3]	–	–
Panama	1972	–	–	69.2[1]
Venezuela	1972	61.5[2]	0.0[4]	61.5[2]
Singapore	1972	80.0[1]	8.2[1]	88.2[1]
Poland	1972	–	–	99.9[1]
Libyan Arab Republic	1972	48.8[2]	3.7[2]	52.5[1]
Israel	1972	–	–	98.3[1]
France	1971	97.0[1]	3.0[1]	100.0[1]

Note: Percentage figures which have been calculated from the total number of live births may overestimate the actual percentage by one or two points.

[1] Percentage figure given in the source.
[2] Percentage figure calculated by dividing number of deliveries by total number of live births.
[3] Percentage figure calculated by dividing number of deliveries given in the source by World Bank estimates of total number of live births.
[4] Only 141 deliveries out of 412,435 live births.

Source: World Health Organization. *The Fifth Report on the World Health Situation, 1969-1972—Part II: Review by Country and Territory,* "Population and Other Statistics" and "Specialized Units," by country. Geneva: WHO, 1974.

Utilization of Official Health Services
in Selected Countries, 1962

Country	Population (millions)	Hospital admissions	Outpatient attendances at hospitals, health centers and dispensaries (millions)	Average visits per person per year
Jamaica	1.8	68,828	1.1	0.6
Guatemala	3.8	136,154	0.9	0.2
Senegal	3.1	65,673	7.8	2.5
Thailand	28.0	541,000	17.5	0.6
Kenya	9.3	146,740	5.2	0.5
Tanzania	10.0	231,598	26.0	2.6
Uganda	7.2	172,279	9.6	1.4

Source: Fendall, N.R.E. "Primary Medical Care in Developing Countries," *International Journal of Health Services,* Vol. 2(2), (1972): Table 4.

Emigration of Medical Doctors to the Developed World

Country	Years	Medical doctors emigrating each year (as percentage of total graduates)	Permanent loss each year (as percentage of total medical doctors)
India	1961–64	18	7
Thailand	1968	67	4
Philippines	1962-67	20	13
Turkey	1964	22	17
Latin America,[1]	1965–68	5	—
comprising:			
Haiti		20	—
Colombia		14	—
Guatemala		8	—
Dominican Republic		16	—
Nicaragua		18	—
Brazil		1	—
Peru		2	—
Mexico		5	—
Jamaica		—	—
Chile		10	—
Argentina		3	—

[1]Some 80% of all Latin American medical doctors are produced by six countries—Argentina, Brazil, Colombia, Cuba, Mexico and Venezuela—and 67% are produced by Argentina, Brazil and Mexico alone.

Source: The Committee on the International Migration of Talent. *The International Migration of High-Level Manpower.* New York: Praeger Publishers, Inc., 1970.

India: Loc. cit. Domrese, Robert J. "The Migration of Talent from India," Table 9.1.

Thailand: Loc. cit. Ruth, Heather Low. "Thailand," p. 111.

Philippines: Loc. cit. Idem. "The Philippines," p. 63.

Turkey: Loc. cit. Franck, Peter Goswyn. "Brain Drain from Turkey," p. 305.

Latin America: Loc. cit. Kidd, Charles V. "Migration of Highly Trained Professionals from Latin America to the United States," Table 16.8.